Microeconomics Principles, Applications, and Policy Implications

Microeconomics Principles, Applications, and Policy Implications

1st Edition

Nurul Samiul Aman

University of Massachusetts - Boston

SAN DIEGO

Bassim Hamadeh, CEO and Publisher
John Remington, Executive Editor
Gem Rabanera, Senior Project Editor
Christian Berk, Production Editor
Jess Estrella, Senior Graphic Designer
Trey Soto, Licensing Coordinator
Natalie Piccotti, Director of Marketing
Kassie Graves, Vice President of Editorial
Jamie Giganti, Director of Academic Publishing

Cover image copyright © 2011 Depositphotos/rabbit75_dep.

Printed in the United States of America.

3970 Sorrento Valley Blvd., Ste. 500, San Diego, CA 92121

To my wonderful wife, Nilufar Aman, and our son, Samuel Mahmud Aman

ACTIVE LEARNING

This book has interactive activities available to complement your reading.

Your instructor may have customized the selection of activities available for your unique course. Please check with your professor to verify whether your class will access this content through the Cognella Active Learning portal (http://active.cognella.com) or through your home learning management system.

Brief Contents

Detailed Contents

Acknowledgments

In the long process of writing this introductory microeconomics textbook, I am greatly honored to have received valuable ideas and generous support from my dear friends and distinguished colleagues Jennifer Clifford, University of Massachusetts Boston; Adugna Lemi, University of Massachusetts Boston; Sid Abdullah, Central Connecticut State University; Khalilur Rahman, World Trade Organization; John Remington, Cognella Publishing; Gem Rabanera, Cognella Publishing; Danielle Menard, Cognella Publishing; Jess Estrella, Cognella Publishing; Jess Wright, Cognella Publishing; and, Chelsey Schmid, Cognella Publishing. I am very grateful for their tremendous support and encouragement throughout the journey of writing this text.

Gratitude to My Distinguished Reviewers

It has been a great honor and privilege to have the tremendous support of my distinguished colleagues who have generously given their precious time in reviewing my preliminary textbook. Without their valuable inputs and suggestions, it would not have been possible to produce this first edition of this textbook. I sincerely extend my thanks and gratitude to the following honorable colleagues and friends for their valuable suggestions in revising some of the content.

Abu Abdullah, Duke University
Siddiq Abdullah, Central Connecticut State University
Kenneth Ardon, Salem State University
Jennifer Clifford, University of Massachusetts Boston
Ellen Frank, University of Massachusetts Boston
Farida Khan, University of Colorado Colorado Springs
Ahmed Mushfiq Mobarak, Yale University
Joanne Spitz, University of Massachusetts Boston

My Indebtedness to My Family

My final note of thanks and sincere indebtedness goes to my beloved wife, Nilufar Aman, and our only son, Samuel Mahmud Aman, for their continuous support and encouragement during the entire journey leading to the final production of this text. Their moral support and understanding have been a big contribution to this effort.

Preface

B ack in early 1972, my country, Bangladesh, became a sovereign nation after struggling for independence and experiencing 25 years of economic and religious suppression by the military rule of Pakistan. As I was about to attend my college freshman year in a newly independent country with no resources for the people and government to move forward, widespread famine broke out which cost millions of innocent lives in the newly independent nation. Witnessing that horrific human tragedy while getting ready for my college education motivated me to concentrate my higher education on understanding the sources of poverty and starvation and investigating how to eliminate these centuries-old struggles encountered in so many countries. That motivation pulled me into choosing economics as my major.

Going forward, I studied economics with a great deal of passion. That passion and a keen observation of real-world economics helped me land a job after graduation as a junior economist at the Industrial Bank of Bangladesh. But my eyes and mind were focused on higher studies in economics at an institution in Boston, Massachusetts. I eventually made my vision a reality by getting admitted to graduate school at Northeastern University in 1982. From there I moved on to corporate jobs and a teaching career in Boston. However, I had never thought of writing an economics textbook at this late stage of my career. But writing this microeconomics textbook (and macroeconomics a year earlier) did not come from my own list of wishes. In February 2013, I received an email from John Remington, the executive editor of Cognella Publishing, inviting me to consider writing an economics textbook. I was hesitant to accept this invitation right away for two practical reasons: first, my teaching commitment and family responsibilities required plenty of time; second, writing a successful textbook in economics would require a deeper understanding from the point of view of resources constraints and existing market conditions. I heard from John Remington again in 2016 with the same invitation. That is when I accepted this daunting task to write the preliminary editions of both the macroeconomics and microeconomics textbooks, published in December 2018 and December 2019, respectively. I must convey my sincere gratitude to John Remington for not giving up on me in pursuing this project.

After going through two years of extensive peer review from my distinguished colleagues and valuable feedback from my dedicated students, I am delighted to present this first edition of *Microeconomics Principles, Applications, and Policy Implications.* In this very first edition, I have introduced the basic principles of economics and their links to our everyday lives in a constantly changing business and social environment and in a world of high-tech innovation with a digital economy powered by the Internet Revolution.

The focus of this textbook was reorganizing the basic foundations of economics knowledge, which has already been developed and published by so many distinguished philosophers and the greatest thinkers in social sciences over the last few centuries—the first economic philosophy book *The Wealth of Nations* was written and published by Adam Smith in 1776. Since this textbook is specifically written for undergraduate students in an introductory economics course, I have made the best effort to simplify the concepts of economics terminologies and to connect these concepts to real-world applications in business and society. With that in mind, I have introduced the application of demand-and-supply models of economics in the areas of sports, music entertainment, the housing market, the bond market, the stock market, the loanable funds market, and other related financial markets. In **Chapters 1 through 5** students are expected to process theoretical concepts into applications and will relate basic theories to our real world of business and economics.

Chapter 1 begins with the concept of scarcity of economic resources and the rationale for studying economics to efficiently use limited resources and thus fulfill our economic and social desires. In this context, I explain and discuss the importance of understanding the concept of **opportunity cost** and its application in making decisions (e.g., accepting a job after high school or going to college for higher education). This chapter also distinguishes the structural differences between the factory-based **old economy** of the twentieth century and the knowledge-based **new economy** of the twenty-first century.

Similarly, I have introduced the concept of the basic demand-and-supply model in **Chapter 2**, where I explain its working mechanism with theoretical foundation. Then I relate the model structure to the economics of the housing market in **Boston** with its policy implications. I have also extended the demand-and-supply concept further into sports economics and music entertainment with an emphasis on the power of competition in market behavior to determine the right price and quantity.

Chapter 3 explains the criteria to measure market efficiency and its applications with real-world examples. I also explain the rationale for government policy intervention in case of market failure to maximize the economic efficiency and welfare for society as a whole. **Chapter 4** extends the application of the demand-and-supply model in the area of healthcare and its micro and macroeconomics policy implications in the context of the US economy. This chapter is particularly important for learning about healthcare economics, the fastest growing industry in the United States, and its important contribution to the GDP and to an increasingly aging population. **Chapter 5** is an extension of the demand-and-supply model, applying the concepts in the **bond market, stock market, and financial markets.** This Wall Street approach of market dynamics is also related to both micro and macroeconomics with their important policy implications.

Chapter 6 introduces the key concepts of price elasticity of demand-and-supply behavior and how to measure them conceptually and numerically by using actual data along with their real-word applications in business and marketing strategies and government policy perspectives.

Chapter 7 introduces the concept of consumer behavioral economics and its applications in utility maximization with a given price of goods and services with budget constraints. Several applications of the theory of utility maximization of consumers are provided in this chapter for students to have different perspectives on allocating our limited resources efficiently.

Chapter 8 introduces the basic principles of cost and production functions as the foundation for measuring the profit maximization and cost minimization for a typical business firm both in the short run and long run. The relevant types of cost functions in a typical firm's production process are defined and compared with their relationship as a typical cost and production structure.

Chapter 9 introduces four market structures on the supply side of production based on the degree of competition among firms within the same industry. The four market structures are perfect competition, monopoly, monopolistic competition, and oligopoly. The profit maximization rule and the determination of profit maximizing output and prices under perfect competition are analyzed in this chapter with their real-world applications and policy implications both in the short run and the long run.

Chapter 10 analyzes the profit maximization rule of the monopoly market structure and explains how to determine price and output at the point of equilibrium. The efficiency of production, pricing, and cost of production are also discussed here under monopoly profit maximization with its pros and cons from economic efficiency perspectives. A comparison between monopoly and perfect competition is also explained in terms of efficiency in pricing and resource allocation for production and distribution. The price discrimination techniques under monopoly are also explained here with real-world business applications and policy implications.

Chapter 11 introduces the conditions of market structures under monopolistic competition and the process of profit maximization in both the short run and long run. Special focus is made on terms of product differentiation by brand names and their applications in pricing strategy and non-price advertising strategy.

Chapter 12 introduces conditions under which oligopoly market structure operates, which are distinctly different from the other three market structures discussed in Chapters 9 through 11. The condition of interdependence among a few firms in determination of maximizing profits is explained. The state of interdependence among competing firms makes a list of alternative solution for equilibrium price and quantity under oligopoly. Those alternatives are called cartel, collusion, price leadership, kinked demand model, game theory, and the

Nash equilibrium of game theory. The applications of all these categories of oligopoly are discussed along with their policy implications for antitrust laws in the United States.

Chapter 13 introduces the efficiency criterion of production and distribution under perfect competition and their comparison with production and distribution under the imperfect competition of monopoly, monopolistic competition, and oligopoly discussed in the previous four chapters. The policy implications of government regulations and their effect on improving efficiency are critically discussed in this chapter, with special reference to the regulatory aspects of US antitrust laws.

Chapter 14 introduces the concept of public good and its distinct characteristics compared with private goods and common pool resources. This chapter also explains the case for government provision of public goods and its role in dealing with common pool resources to preserve the environment and natural resources from potential overuse, called the tragedy of the commons. The economic model for price and output determination of public goods is also discussed in this chapter along with its policy implications.

Chapter 15 introduces the basic concept of positive and negative externalities and their relevance in education funding and pollution control. The economic models for internalization of externalities are also analyzed and explained with their policy implications for alternative legislative measures for pollution control.

Chapter 16 introduces the basic principles of factor market behavior of production process, with special focus on labor market equilibrium. The derivation of labor market demand-and-supply curves from production function and labor force characteristics are discussed in more detail here with their policy implications. The economic models of wage determination under perfect and imperfect market conditions are also introduced and explained. Wage discrimination and unfair labor practices are discussed as well, with efficiency of government legislation to mitigate wage discrimination.

Chapter 17, the last chapter of the book, introduces the basic concepts of income inequality and poverty with a special focus on existing structures of income distribution and poverty in the US economy. Both structures of wealth gap and income disparity are discussed here with specific data analysis for the US economy. The structure of poverty and the sources of poverty are also critically discussed here in the context of the US economy. Policy recommendations are also made with reference to sources of poverty, along with the scope and limitations of legislative actions to fight against poverty and income distribution.

Suggested Notes to Students

It is my great pleasure to introduce my first edition of this microeconomics textbook to the students. In order to learn the key concepts of economics effectively, I suggest that you read the key objectives in the beginning of each chapter. The key learning objectives will guide you through the contents in subsequent sections of each chapter.

As you keep reading the sections in each chapter, there are three important things to keep in mind for understanding the concepts and applications. First, read the concepts and try to relate them to real-world examples. Second, connect the concept to the diagram provided in that section. Third, relate the concept and diagram(s) to the data, if given, and analyze for practical use and policy implications. These three important steps will assist you in grasping the concepts and their applications effectively.

Also read the summary of the chapter contents at the end of each chapter to further review key terms and concepts in each of the sections. Reviewing those key areas will help you learn effectively. I have also provided some basic questions at the end of each chapter under **Application Activities**. Those questions are intended to be part of your homework and are based on the contents of the chapter. The questions are also directly related to real-world applications of the theoretical concepts introduced in the chapter sections.

Supplementary materials such as PowerPoint presentations, test banks, and digital materials will be available as needed.

Chapter 1

Key Concepts of Economics and Its Application in the Financial Well-Being of Society

Learning Objectives

As they read the chapter, students will learn the following:

▶ The Core Concepts of Economics and the Opportunity Cost of Making Alternative Decisions in Allocating Time and Resources

▶ The Concept of Opportunity Cost and Real-World Applications

▶ Examples of Economics in Everyday Life and Entertainment

▶ Economics, Technology, and Society: A New Perspective on Economics in the Digital Age of Information Science

▶ Understanding Economics with Graphs, Equations, and Data

Introduction

We live in a world with a great deal of interdependence not only among individuals and institutions, but also between human society and other living species and natural resources. The continuous interdependence among resources, human and non-human, creates an environment with unlimited wants of human being with limited resources to meet unlimited desires. The scarcity of those resources creates enormous obstacles to fulfill their unlimited wants and desires to achieve better economic and social wellbeing. The challenges every human being faces to overcome those obstacles do actually force everyone to make the best value out of the limited resource used. The process of the best practice of using resources for better achievement is called efficient allocation of resources. This efficiency we see in the performance of manufacturing goods and services, sports and music entertainment, in the Wall Street business activities, and communication and transportation. This introductory chapter focuses on the importance of economics study as a distinct discipline as the primary objective explaining how to allocate limited resources to produce goods and services efficiently. The chapter starts with the core concept of economics and its outlook to figure out how the production and distribution of goods and services ought to be made efficiently by interacting among three major economic agents: Producers in private sector, individual consumers and the government institutions. Therefore, the chapter explains the concept of opportunity cost in making tradeoff between choosing of different goods and services in exchange for giving up others. This chapter also provides examples of opportunity cost in our everyday lives by interacting with business, technology and society. At the end, the chapter will also introduce the basic understanding of economics and analyze it with the model structure of equations, graphs and data – the three major steps in understanding the core of economics.

1.1 The Core Concept of Economics and the Opportunity Cost of Making Alternative Decisions in Allocating Time and Resources

The core concept of economics comes from the answer to the question asked in all economics textbooks: "Why study economics?" Although there is no simple answer to this broad question, economics is a branch of social science that deals with the unlimited desires/wants of human beings and the limited resources available to fulfill them. Unlimited wants are the natural behavior of human beings for good reasons: they are a thriving force to keep everyone moving to accomplish their infinite desires. However, the constraints resulting from limited resources make it a challenge to fulfill everyone's unlimited desires. The study of economics as a discipline addresses this challenge by finding ways to allocate limited resources efficiently and thus to maximize unlimited wants and desires. The best practice of economics is to use alternative models to integrate limited human and material resources so as to maximize the material well-being of society. More specifically, economics tries to answer three questions. The following questions relate to the efficient allocation of limited resources to satisfy unlimited wants.

Q1. What products should be produced? This question focuses on offering the right selection of products to satisfy the needs and wants of individuals.

Q2. How should the products be produced? This question deals with the technology of production.

Q3. Who are the products produced for? This question focuses on distributional tasks.

To answer these three core questions, there are numerous theories, models, paradigms that have been developed by economists, philosophers, and historians over the last few hundred years. The fundamental model developed by those philosophers came from the structure of the theory of demand and supply originally developed by Adam Smith in his famous book *The Wealth of Nations* (1776). The core concept of demand and supply is still the basic tool to use to respond to the three questions and apply their answers to every aspect of human society. The next few sections of this chapter will analyze the dimensions of demand and supply in greater detail so that students will gain a better understanding of demand and supply.

1.2 The Concept of Opportunity Cost and Real-World Applications

Opportunity cost means the next best or the most desired goods and services are forgone (given up) to obtain the alternative choice. It means that given the scarcity of resources, including time, money, knowledge, skills, and other related capabilities, every individual has to make trade-offs in their decisions every single day. In making those decisions, they must trade-off between the available options to achieve the best possible results. For example, every individual has only 24 hours a day and 7 days a week to do several things, depending on what type of mission or tasks each individual has. A college student, for example, has to allocate time and other resources between classes and extracurricular activities every day. The opportunity cost of taking one class could be giving up another class at the same time of day. Choosing a major in college as an alternative to other desirable majors is a common dilemma for many college students. From a broader perspective, the opportunity cost of going to college can be looked at from several considerations, depending on individual preferences and ambitions, which vary widely from person to person. The following example of taking a job with a high school diploma or going to college is a common measure of opportunity cost when making a rational choice.

Choosing either a job after high school or pursuing a college degree can explain the importance of understanding the real-world application of opportunity cost. Suppose the average wage structure for taking a job with a high school diploma has modestly declined over the years.[1] Given this trend, the following question arises: Will the opportunity cost for pursuing a college degree decrease (regardless of the rising dollar cost of college tuition) or not? In this scenario, the hidden cost of not going to college in favor of declining wages with a high school degree is a part of opportunity cost. This part of opportunity cost could be much higher than current dollar expenses for college tuition. In this case, the dollar cost (explicit cost) for college tuition is not the only opportunity cost because the wages forgone from the job in favor of going to college, in a true sense, could be much less than the higher wages and career advancement in a specialized job after gaining a college degree. If real-world statistics reveal the case for the latter, then the opportunity cost for going to college is definitely lower than the potential benefit from the college degree in the long run.

---

1 Jillian Berman, "A High-School Diploma Is Pretty Much Useless These Days," *HuffPost*, last modified December 6, 2017, https://www.huffingtonpost.com/2014/05/27/value-college-degree_n_5399573.html.

1.2.1 Opportunity Cost Application in Sports Economics

Just as the concept of opportunity cost is important when considering a college education as a point for making a rational choice, the same concept is commonly used in the world of sports economics, such as professional football (National Football League [NFL]) and professional basketball (National Basketball Association), every year. For example, on December 31, 2017, Penn State running back Saquon Barkley announced that he would participate in the 2018 NFL Draft by giving up his mission to pursue his college degree at Penn State. This is a good example of Mr. Barkley making a rational decision because there was nothing left for him at Penn State other than the golden opportunity to be drafted for an NFL career. Many other college football athletes made similar decisions in the past, such as the quarterbacks Andrew Luck of the Indiana Colts and Cam Newton of the Carolina Panthers. Famous entrepreneurs and tech moguls, such as Bill Gates of Microsoft, Steve Jobs of Apple, Mark Zuckerberg of Facebook, and Larry Ellison of Oracle, dropped out of college because they saw high opportunity costs for staying in school compared to pursuing the much greater business ventures they envisioned and ultimately achieved.

The same logic of opportunity cost applies in international trade between countries deciding what to produce domestically and what to import from other countries. This is called the theory of comparative advantage.

1.3 Examples of Economics in Everyday Life and Entertainment

Assuming that people in general do in fact behave rationally, they will make decisions to allocate their limited time and resources in ways that maximize the benefits they desire to obtain. Given that assumption, it has been observed that people as both buyers and sellers in the market do respond to incentives. Without incentives, the outcome from market interaction may not be efficient enough to maximize the level of individuals' to fulfill their desires. That is where the concept of market behavior comes into play: demand and supply behavior in the marketplace reflects the pattern of incentives for buyers and sellers to respond rationally. The behavior of demand and supply interaction, then, determines the price of all goods and services as a signal to clear the market, usually called the equilibrium price. The details of the demand and supply model structure will be explained in Chapter 2. At this point, it is important to realize the power of market forces to signal the right price for the efficient allocation of resources. This process of market forces is explained next in the analysis of the marginal value concept.

1.3.1 Real-World Examples of Marginal Value and Applications

In the context of measuring the efficiency of allocating limited resources, the rational choice theory suggests that people think at the margin when making optimal decisions in everyday activities. Although it may be true that individuals and firms do not necessarily make the best choices during their decision-making process, it is fair to assume that economic agents put together all available information in the best possible ways to buy and sell goods and services to achieve optimal levels of satisfaction. The benefits of the cost of selling and the expense of buying must satisfy individuals' desires during each transaction. For example, Apple Inc. priced its highest-end iPhone X smartphone at around $1,000 in the US market when it was released in the fall of 2017. The first release of the iPhone X at this price sold out very quickly, and the demand continued to rise, resulting in backorders for weeks and months to follow. Now, it may be possible that the marketing management at Apple might have underestimated the demand side of the market and could have raised the price over $1,000 per unit to make more profit for the company. However, rational choice theory assumes that given the best possible information Apple management had, the decision to set the price of the first release at $1,000 was the best decision they could have made to reach their target volume of revenue and profit. They could adjust the price and quantity with the new information gathered afterward.

Another real-world example is the economics of Super Bowl tickets that are purchased every year after the championship games between the American Football Conference and the National Football Conference (NFC). The winning teams face off at the Super Bowl matchup on the first Sunday in February. For 2018, the starting price of Super Bowl tickets in the secondary market was between $5,000 and $50,000 per ticket, depending on the position of the seats in the U.S. Bank Stadium in Minneapolis, Minnesota. Given the fixed seats of 73,000 in the stadium, these price ranges were driven by the changes in demand for tickets from the buyers' desire to purchase them. There are a number of factors that determined the price ranges, such as ability to pay, tastes of the fans who were willing to buy at certain prices, and availability of the limited tickets against the number of fans looking to buy them. Since the number of fans willing to purchase the tickets was much higher than the 73,000 seats, the prices for all the seats continued to rise until all the tickets were sold out. The highest bidders of the tickets, whether sold in the regular secondary market or via scalping, reflected the true market price. This is clearly a real-world example of the maximum willingness to pay for tickets as a rational choice made by the fans who wanted to watch the biggest game of the year. The value the buyers placed on each of the tickets purchased had to be higher than the dollar amount they paid for the tickets in order for them to enjoy the seating in the stadium. The same concept of rational choice applies to purchasing decisions for concert tickets to see performances by superstars in pop and rock genres in the music industry.

Another example is the increase in ticket prices for the Red Sox games against the New York Yankees during the baseball season every year in Fenway Park in Boston. Since the traditional rivalry between these two teams is quite popular among Red Sox fans, the willingness to pay for the tickets during the Red Sox versus Yankees's matches keeps rising, thus increasing the demand for tickets given the fixed supply of total seats in Fenway Park. The response by Red Sox fans of paying much more than the ticketed price is a reflection of the rational choice to see the real value of watching the game as much higher than the dollar price they pay for the tickets. The same concept of rational choice theory applies to the number of college applicants for freshman year far exceeding the number of admission slots available at top-rated colleges in the United States. In those cases, the smaller increase in tuition and boarding costs doesn't matter that much because the potential benefit from receiving a higher education tends to outweigh the rising cost of education charged by the universities.

1.4 Economics, Technology, and Society: A New Perspective of Economics in the Digital Age of Information Science

Amid the emergence of the internet revolution in the 1990s, the technological advancements for providing goods and services have rapidly expanded in the global economy. The rise in productivity of both labor and capital in the digital era of the twenty-first century has transformed the structure of the US economy, as well as the world economy, which has changed from factory-based to a new information-age economy. In this new information-based economy, the integration of economics, technology, and society has resulted in new ways of thinking and market behavior during the first two decades of this new century. The emergence of e-commerce enterprises, such as Amazon, Alibaba, eBay, YouTube, Pinterest, Facebook, Snapchat, Twitter, Instagram, Spotify, WhatsApp, Google, Uber, Lyft, and Airbnb, has been the key driving force in the new economy, with online technology transforming the society and guiding it toward a different path. The characteristics of these newly emerged digital enterprises are driven by rapid globalization, information science, and faster rates of credit flow. Given the new environment of the knowledge-based economy, the productivity of labor and capital (both human capital and physical capital) has increased significantly in recent years. The high productivity of factors of production raised the income level of workers across the world by increasing wages and living standards. The technological advancements in a digitally charged work environment have also changed the structure of labor market behavior. Under the new structure, members of the labor force make different choices at their workplaces as compared to the workers in the old economy. The workers in this new economy do not tend to rely on traditional desk jobs with fixed 8–5 work schedules. The speedy growth of specialization in high technology industries has opened up new opportunities for young workers and structurally displaced aging workers to create their own jobs in the form of self-employment, individual contracting, and freelancing. This new trend in the labor market structure in the so-called gig economy is expected to reshape the rational choice and preference patterns of the skilled labor force in the coming decades.

It is also argued that the productivity for knowledge-based skilled workers and their incomes may have increased at the expense of low-skilled workers of the old economy in the manufacturing sector. This mismatch between the capital-intensive new economy and labor-intensive old economy might have caused the rise in unemployment in low-skilled workers. This mismatch of the factor intensity of the production process might have contributed to the increase of income inequality at an alarming rate. This ongoing problem of imbalance between the rapid growth of technology and income inequality and unemployment for unskilled workers has resulted in a new wave of challenges in making rational choices for the labor and capital combination. The rising level of global warming further complicated these new challenges with related environmental degradation, which is attributed to rapid industrialization from the massive use of fossil fuel energy. The utopian economic theories of the market system do not seem to have adequately addressed these challenges. The market-based concept of economic efficiency actually ignores the problem of externalities caused by increasing levels of market power and environmental degradation. To address these challenges, the economy must increase the role of public policy and regulations that certainly contradict traditional laissez-faire economics (leave the market alone). This issue of contradiction and conflicting theories of economics and social science seems to call for a new way of thinking to transform the current education system, social structure, and technology so that they are compatible with the sustainable economic reality of the society. In doing so, human capital and educational reforms in relation to innovative public policies are needed. This book will discuss these issues in greater detail in later chapters.

1.5 Understanding Economics with Graphs, Equations, and Data

In the study of economics principles, the use of simple mathematical concepts in explaining the connection among basic economic theories and the use of real-world data to fit the theoretical models is absolutely necessary. For example, the use of demand and supply equations, their real-world data collection, and illustration in graphs for interpretation of the theories are the basic foundations of economics. Therefore, the introductory levels of algebra, calculus, and geometry are important to review as basic tools for this course of economics. The following tools are useful for reading the contents of the demand and supply model in the next chapter.

1.5.1 The Slope of an Equation: Linear and Nonlinear Equations

The slope of an equation of two variables is the ratio of changes between the variables. This ratio indicates the behavior or pattern of the relationship between those two variables as the values change. Consider the following equation of two variables X and Y.

$Y = f(X)$, where Y is a dependent variable, and X is an independent variable, meaning that if the value of X changes, it will change the value of Y. The slope of the equation can be expressed by taking the derivative of this general expression as follows:

dY/dX = the slope (the ratio of change between Y and X). More specifically, the earlier general expression of the equation can be stated with real-world values:

$$Y = a + bX \qquad\qquad \text{Eqn (1.1),}$$

where a is a constant value of Y independent of X or when X = zero, and

b is the slope of Eqn (1.1), thus explaining the pattern of the relationship between X and Y when the value X increases.

The slope would be as shown in Figure 1.1 by taking the derivative of this equation:

$dY/dX = b$, and the derivative of a constant value "a" in the equation is zero.

Since the value of b stays the same as the value of X changes, this is a linear equation of Y for X. If the value of b were changing as X changed, it would be a nonlinear function (not shown here). With real-world data to fit this equation, the relevant graph is illustrated in Figure 1.1.

Figure 1.1 A Graph of a Linear Equation

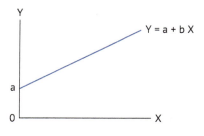

In Figure 1.1, the hypothetical linear curve indicates the specific relationship between independent variable X and dependent variable Y such that the point "a" on the vertical y-axis is called the intercept or the fixed value of variable Y when the value of X is zero. However, as the value of X starts increasing from zero, the value of Y will also increase at the rate of value "b" (dY/dX), which is called the slope of the equation of Y for X. More specifically, the straight-line equation Y = a + bX, shown in Figure 1.1, indicates that the constant slope "b" is the rate at which the value of variable Y will increase in response to a given increase in the value of X.

1.5.2 The Data and Equation to Draw the Graph

The previous linear equation can be applied in real-world examples with a set of hypothetical data on a typical consumer's income and spending. Suppose an individual spends his or her after-tax weekly income (economists call it disposable income after taxes are paid), shown in Table 1.1 with different combinations of income and spending, with the assumption of *ceteris paribus* (other things staying the same). The *ceteris paribus* assumption is important to make here because there are other factors than just income that influence the spending behavior of all individuals. In this simple example of a linear equation, only changes in income are considered, keeping other factors unchanged. The other factors could be lifestyle, tax policy of the government, changes in family composition or size, and other similar factors related to the spending of individuals and households.

Table 1.1: Data Estimation of a Linear Equation

Income (X) in $s	Spending (Y) in $s	Slope of Income and Spending Equation ΔY/ΔX	Saving (S)	Slope of Income and Saving Equation
0	50	–	−50	–
100	130	80/100 = 0.80	−30	20/100 = 0.20
200	210	80/100 = 0.80	−10	20/100 = 0.20
300	290	80/100 = 0.80	+10	20/100 = 0.20
400	370	80/100 = 0.80	+30	20/100 = 0.20
500	450	80/100 = 0.80	+50	20/100 = 0.20

Table 1.1 represents a hypothetical data set for an individual, indicating the relationship between income (net of taxes paid) and spending behavior, where Y is spending that varies at a constant rate as income (X) increases by the same amount of $100. As we see in the data, when income is zero, there is still some spending of $50 for fulfilling basic necessities, such as food and other daily expenses. However, as income rises at an equal increment of $100 per week, the spending also increases by a constant amount of $80. The slope of this spending behavior is calculated in Column 3 as ΔY/ΔX shown as a constant rate of 0.80. Since the individual in this example did not spend all of his or her income, the third and fourth columns show the estimation of the corresponding savings equation S = (X − Y), and its slope is shown as 0.20 in the last column on the right-hand side. The numerical value of this estimation is plotted in a linear equation (Eqn (1.2)).

$$Y = 50 + 0.8X, \qquad \text{Eqn (1.2)}$$

where 50 is the intercept and 0.8 is the slope of the equation.

The estimated linear Eqn (1.2) indicates that an individual spends at an increasing constant rate of 0.8 cents of every dollar increase in income for his or her successive increase in income by the same amount. By the same token, the savings pattern of this individual in Columns 4 and 5 in the table shows that the corresponding savings rate is also constant at 0.2, as the slope of the savings equation (Eqn (1.3)) shows next.

$$S = X − Y = X − (a + b\,X) = X − a − bX = −a + (1 − b)\,X, \qquad \text{Eqn (1.3)}$$

where S = savings equation and 1 − b is the slope of the savings equation.

Plugging in the values of intercept and slope of savings estimated in Table 1.1, the estimated savings (Eqn (1.4)) is

$$S = −50 + 0.2\,X. \qquad \text{Eqn (1.4)}$$

The graphical representation of these two linear equations (Eqn (1.2) and Eqn (1.4)) of spending and saving, respectively, are illustrated in Figure 1.2.

Figure 1.2   Graph of Linear Equations for Spending and Saving

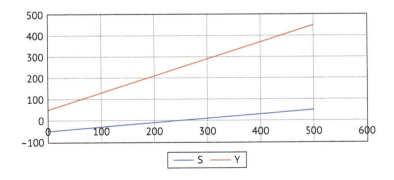

Figure 1.2, the numerical values of the spending and saving equations are plotted in a single diagram to illustrate how a linear equation demonstrates the constant slope of the changes in two variables. In this example, students may notice that the slope of spending, the Y curve against income (X), is 0.80, and the slope of saving, the S curve against the same increase in income is 0.20. The spending and saving values are plotted on the vertical axis against corresponding increases in income (X) on the horizontal axis. Students may also practice the same model using different income and spending combinations by creating a table and doing the graphs in an Excel spreadsheet. It is also important to note that these two linear curves are based on the *ceteris paribus* assumption. However, if the *ceteris paribus* assumption is not considered in a situation when changes in other factors, such as tax policy, consumer confidence, or household status, take place, then the curves in Figure 1.2 will shift either to the right or to the left depending on the course of change that occurs. We will come back to this simple technique of measuring many other economic variables in different contexts throughout this textbook. For now, we end this introductory chapter by highlighting the basic reasoning for studying economics and its importance in our daily activities to maximize our goals for gaining material interests. As students continue to read the subsequent chapters of this textbook, they will use the basic understanding of the **opportunity cost** concept and its related application by learning many other related models and their relevant applications in the real world, along with the importance of government policy implications.

Chapter Summary

Section 1.1 of this chapter started with the concept of *economics* as a study of a distinct discipline for understanding the importance of efficiency in allocating our limited resources to maximize economic well-being for everyone. Since the resources are limited, learning the efficiency techniques in allocating our scarce resources is the primary objective of studying economics. In the process of learning the core concept of efficiency in allocating resources, economics study helps answer three core questions:

> **Q1. What products should be produced? This question focuses on offering the right selection of products to satisfy the needs and wants of individuals.**

> **Q2. How should the products be produced? This question deals with the technology of production.**

> **Q3. Who are the products produced for? This question focuses on distributional tasks.**

In answering these core questions, the subsequent chapters of this textbook will demonstrate numerous theories and model structures to go deeper into the process of various aspects of economics and its policy implications for the constant improvement of the economic well-being of the society.

Section 1.2 introduced the concept of *opportunity cost* as a trade-off in allocating our limited time and resources for an alternative choice of activities. Opportunity cost means the most desired goods and services are forgone to obtain something else. This concept is useful for making rational choices in our daily decision-making process. The real-world examples of the opportunity cost concept included whether to attend a four-year college or get a job with a high school diploma. The importance of cost-benefit analysis for making alternative decisions is primarily attributed to rational choice theory, powered by the effective use of opportunity cost. Numerous examples are given in this section in the context of sports economics, college education, and similar choices people have to make every day.

Section 1.3 introduced the concept of *marginal value* as an important principle for measuring efficiency in allocating limited resources. The rational choice theory of efficiency in the allocation of resources is based on the marginal value from each of our everyday activities. Although individuals do not necessarily make their best choices during the decision-making process, it is reasonable to say that buyers and sellers are rational enough on average to gather the best possible information to maximize their satisfaction from each transaction they make. To fulfill that objective, economic agents must think at the margins, the basic criteria to achieve efficiency. Examples are given in this section in the context of the smartphone market, sports economics, and related market behavior of consumers and producers' decision-making processes.

Section 1.4 discussed the effect of the digital technology revolution on society, economics, and business in this new century of information economics. The emergence of e-commerce enterprises, such as Amazon, Alibaba, eBay, YouTube, Pinterest, Facebook, Snapchat, Twitter, Instagram, Spotify, WhatsApp, Google, Uber, Lyft, and Airbnb, is the key driving force in the new economy. The newly emerged digital enterprises are driven by rapid globalization, information science, and faster rates of credit flow. The digital economy of the twenty-first century is the knowledge-based economy with high productivity of labor and capital (both human capital and physical capital), which thus raised the income level and standard of living for skilled workers globally. The labor market structure has also changed in the digital economy under which the labor force does not tend to rely on traditional desk jobs with a fixed 8–5 work schedule. The speedy growth of specialization in high technology industries has opened up new opportunities for young workers and structurally displaced aging workers to create their own jobs in the form of self-employment, individual contracting, and freelancing. This new trend of labor market structure in the so-called gig economy is expected to reshape the rational choice and preference patterns of the skilled labor force in the coming decades. The challenge of this new trend in the labor market is to cope up with the growing income inequality and the remaining massive poverty in the majority of the nations in the world. The study of economics in understanding these challenges is rewarding for students.

Section 1.5 introduced the technical aspects of graphs, equations, and data to integrate the economic variables and their relationships in an effort to measure economic efficiency. The main focus was on the two-variable case, with the example of linear equations used to understand the numerical values for estimations. Eqns (1.1) through (1.4) were useful for understanding the technical concept of measuring the relationship between two variables. Table 1.1 showed the hypothetical data on spending and income to fit Eqn (1.4). This section also demonstrated the technique for integrating the theoretical concept with the data and graphing the result as the basic foundation for analyzing the economics model with real-world data. Students are encouraged to practice the examples given in this section and to answer the practice questions under the "Application Activities" section.

Application Activities

Q1. Why is the study of economics an important part of social science? Give an example from the real world.

Q2. If the real wage rate (adjusted for inflation) declines for the jobs for high school graduates, would the true opportunity cost of attending college or spending on higher education decline? Give an example.

Q3. How do you measure the efficiency of resource allocation? Give an example from a real-world application of measuring the efficiency of resource allocation.

Q4. Use the following table to measure the opportunity cost of two jobs performed by two different workers in a factory and then answer the questions that follow.

   a. Which of the two workers has the lowest opportunity cost in doing Job 1?

   b. Which of the workers has the comparative advantage in doing Job 1?

Workers	Job 1: Hours to Finish	Job 2: Hours to Finish	Opportunity Cost
Worker 1	3	6	?
Worker 2	4	16	?

Q5. Use the table to answer the questions that follow.

Spending and Income Data

Income (Y)	Consumption (C)	Slope of Consumption	Saving (S)	Slope of Saving
0	100			
100	175			
200	250			
300	325			
400	400			
500	475			

   a. Fill out the rest of the columns from the information given in Columns 1 and 2 for a typical household with income as Y after taxes and consumption as C given in Column 2.

   b. Interpret the slopes for C and S functions in economic terms, as explained in Section 1.5 earlier.

   c. Graph the data for Y, C, and S in a single diagram to illustrate your answer in 5.a and 5.b and explain in your own words.

Chapter 2

Market Systems and Their Determination of Price

Demand and Supply Interactions with Real-World Examples

Learning Objectives

As they read the chapter, students will learn the following:

▶ Market Behavior and Efficient Allocation of Resources: The Foundation of Demand and Supply Behavior and Applications

▶ Applications of Demand and Supply Models in Sports Economics

▶ Applications of Demand and Supply Models in the Music Industry

▶ Applications of Demand and Supply Models in College Education

Introduction

Chapter 1 has introduced the basic objectives of studying of economics as a distinct discipline to allocate the limited resources to fulfill the unlimited desires of human being with its challenges and opportunities. Chapter 2 introduces the economic models and techniques to analyze the behavior of market system to allocate the resources efficiently. While studying economics as beginners, the learners must ask the key question- how to allocate limited resources efficiently. The best to way answer to this fundamental question in economics is to understand the theory and application of demand and supply behavior. The interaction between demand and supply functions for all goods and services help determine the best possible pricing scheme for both consumers and producers. The principles of demand and supply and their scope and limitations to determine the efficient price and quantity are the basic foundations of economics. This chapter explains the various aspects of demand and supply models and their real-world applications in sports and music industries as well as college education. Extended analyses of demand and supply models are further discussed in chapters 3, chapter 4 and chapter 5 with more applications and policy implications in other fields of business and economics.

2.1 Market Behavior and Efficient Allocation of Resources: The Foundation of Demand and Supply Behavior and Applications

The fundamental tool for allocating limited resources is the basic demand and supply model of the market system. In both microeconomics and macroeconomics, the two broad areas of the science of economics, there is demand and supply, which determine equilibrium and effect in price changes, inflation trends, unemployment and full employment, and implications for government policies on taxes, regulations, environmental protection, social welfare, universal health care, and national defense. Therefore, the concept of the free market system versus the impact of government intervention in the free market system has been a subject of great debate since the Great Depression of the 1930s, when the market system of free enterprise failed to keep the economy moving with a state of full employment. Although the role of government has significantly increased the fine-tuning of the economy and maximizes the economic well-being of the society in general, the power of demand and supply under the free market system still prevails as a major tool for the efficient allocation of resources. Analysis of this ongoing debate will be discussed in Chapter 3. Before then, the key focus in this chapter is to understand the basic concept of demand and supply interactions to determine the price and quantity of goods and services under the assumption of both the free market and government intervention.

The analysis of the free market system dates back to 1776, when Adam Smith explained the concept of the invisible hand through the free flow of demand and supply behavior. Smith's support for the policy of laissez-faire was attributed to his explanations of the efficient allocation of resources for both producers (to maximize their profits) and consumers (to maximize their satisfaction). His support for the philosophy of the laissez-faire policy is still valid in today's market behavior in regard to housing scarcity in urban areas, interest rates in capital markets, regulated markets for health insurance, and utilities, medicines, sports, and transportation industries. However, the role of legislative actions via price control or quantity control with taxes and subsidies has also been a common case in practice in those industries. Despite the good intentions of the government to distribute the economic pie more fairly, the effects of legislation may not necessarily make the resource allocations efficient in most cases. The detailed analysis of demand and supply models in the next section will help us to better understand the real economics behind this debate by observing the pros and cons of the free market system versus the rationale for government intervention in the free market system.

2.1.1 Law of Demand

The law of demand states if the price of any goods and services rises, say rent for housing for college students in a college town like Boston, then the quantity demanded for rental housing will decline and vice versa, *ceteris paribus*. The *ceteris paribus* assumption means all other possible factors affecting the same demand behavior stay the same for the time being. The other factors are income, location in terms of proximity to public transportation or the college campus, rent in alternative areas, size and number of rooms, and other related facilities. The possible general equation for this demand behavior is expressed next:

D for rent = f (rent, income, college tuition, alternative to rent, distance from public transportation or campus, on-campus housing)

In the previous general equation, "f" is the symbol for "function of" the variables mentioned in parentheses. All right-hand side variables in parentheses are independent variables that determine or affect the values of quantity demanded on the left-hand-side variable "D for rent." In other words, D for rent in the left-hand-side variable is the dependent variable and the right-hand side variables are all independent variables.

The *ceteris paribus* assumption made earlier implies that for any given short period of time, we change the key variable of the D function (such as rent only) and see how that change (the price of housing) affects the changes in quantity demanded for housing in the college town of Boston. After detailed analysis of the changes in rent and the quantity of housing, we extend the topic in a situation where the assumption of *ceteris paribus* is no longer valid. Given the law of demand stated from the general equation, it will be easier to use a demand schedule with different hypothetical values of rent and quantity demanded in Table 2.1.

Table 2.1: The Demand Schedule with *Ceteris Paribus* Assumption

Rent for Housing ($ in thousands)	Quantity Demanded for Housing (in thousands)
0	900
1	700
2	500
3	300
4	100
5	0

The previous demand schedule indicates the consistency of the law of demand as an inverse relationship between quantity demanded and the rent for housing, assuming other things (factors) stay the same. The graphical representation of the aforementioned demand schedule is presented in Figure 2.1 as a demand curve for a visual presentation. We will use more graphs in subsequent sections and chapters.

Figure 2.1 The Demand Curve

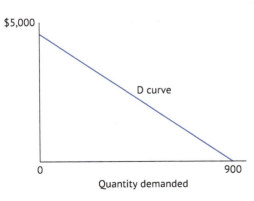

The downward-sloping demand curve in Figure 2.1 illustrates the rent and quantity combinations in the table for a demand schedule with a quantity of 900,000 housing (apartments) units on the horizontal axis against $0 of rent and zero demand for apartment rentals against $5,000 per unit of housing. The other combinations of rent and number of apartments will sit in between the two extreme points to reflect the entire schedule along the demand curve. Given this demand curve, we have accomplished three basic flows to understand the concept of demand behavior for any goods and services, including the market for housing in Boston. First, we stated the law of demand as the theoretical concept. Second, we have made a hypothetical table of data presenting quantity demanded against different prices/rents of housing as the demand schedule. Third, we have combined the first and second parts of the demand theory to illustrate in the downward-sloping demand curve in the previous graph to complete the whole structure of the demand curve under the *ceteris paribus* assumption. These three steps represent a common process of understanding and analyzing economic models to determine the efficiency of the allocation of limited resources. The next step in this demand theory is to find out what happens when the *ceteris paribus* assumption is not valid, a situation we call *changes in demand curve instead of changes in quantity demanded.* In other words, changes in quantity demanded happen because of changes in price per unit—a situation in which the price and quantity combinations move along the same demand curve. On the other hand, changes in demand happen because of changes in factors other than price changes—a situation that occurs when the whole demand function changes or the whole demand curve shifts either to the right or to the left depending on the effect on the demand function. The explanation of changes in demand with graphical illustration is provided next.

2.1.2 Changes in the Demand Curve (the Shifts of the Demand Curve)

The restrictive assumption of *ceteris paribus* previously made in the context of the downward-sloping demand curve implies that the changes in the price/rent of housing will move all combinations of price and quantity along the same demand curve. However, when the assumption of *ceteris paribus* is not the case, meaning that other factors (determinants) of demand do change, then the entire demand curve will shift inward to the left or outward to the right. This situation is called changes in demand. For example, suppose the enrollment for college students admitted to all Boston area colleges has significantly increased given the information about the demand schedule and the demand curve illustrated in Table 2.1 and Figure 2.1, respectively. This new increase in the enrollment of students will shift the demand curve for housing given the current rental structure in Table 2.1. Suppose the overall rental demand has increased by 50 percent with the current rental structure based on the supply of housing (availability). This 50 percent increase in demand for housing is shown in Table 2.2.

Table 2.2: The Demand Schedule without *Ceteris Paribus* Assumption

Rent for Housing ($ in thousands)	Quantity Demanded for Housing (in thousands)
0	1,350
1	1,050
2	750
3	450
4	150
5	0

With the new demand schedule attributed to the increase in college enrollment shown in Table 2.2, the corresponding shift in the demand curve from Figure 2.1. is illustrated in Figure 2.2.

As indicated by the arrow in Figure 2.2, the demand curve has shifted outward to the right because of the increase in enrollment. Using the same concept of the factors that change the demand for hous-

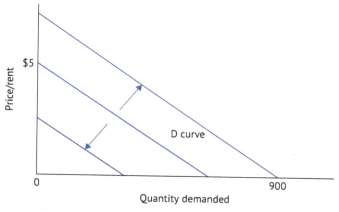

Figure 2.2   The Shift of the Demand Curve

ing, suppose the education funding by the State of Massachusetts and the US Department of Education has been significantly reduced because of the new policy tightening of government budget expenses. The new changes in policy will definitely have a negative effect on the enrollment of college students in Boston and elsewhere in the country. In other words, the reduction of the government's education funding at both state and federal levels will have a negative effect on the demand for college admission and thus will reduce the demand for housing in the city. This effect is illustrated in Figure 2.1 by shifting the demand curve inward to the left. It is important to note here that the positive effect of such changes in the determinants will usually shift the demand curve outward to the right, and the negative effect of changes in the same determinants will usually shift the demand curve inward to the left. In general, the most common determinants of the demand curve that shift the demand are summarized in Table 2.3.

Table 2.3: Common Determinants (Factors) That Shift the Demand Curve

Determinants of Demand	Explanation of the Effects on Demand Shifts
Consumer tastes and preferences	Changes in consumer tastes and preferences, regardless of price per unit of goods and services, will shift the demand rightward or leftward depending on the positive or negative preference patterns of individual consumers. In the previous example of college enrollment, changes in the preference patterns of admitting students would shift the demand for housing because college attendance and demand for housing go together.
Changes in the ability to pay (income)	The ability to pay is an important factor in terms of changes in the demand curve. Given tastes or preferences, changes in income do alter the demand. Also, changes in income may sometimes affect changes in tastes or preferences as well.

Market size of consumers	The market size of the consumer is an important factor that affects the demand curve. As the number of consumers increases, the demand curve shifts to the right, and vice versa.
Expectations of consumers	The change in expectations is a powerful factor in changes in the demand behavior of consumers. Future expectations regarding variables related to the demand curve of any good or service do directly affect the demand curve.
Substitution and complementary goods and services	The changes in the price of substitute and complementary goods and services changes the demand. For example, housing facilities near universities do affect changes in demand for the off-campus housing market.
Government policies	Changes in government policies, such as tax policy and environmental regulations on the use of goods and services, will affect changes in demand for those goods.

2.1.3 Law of Supply

The law of supply states that if the price of any goods or services, for example, rent for housing for college students in a college town like Boston, increases, then the quantity supplied will also increase and vice versa, *ceteris paribus*. The *ceteris paribus* assumption means that all other factors affecting the same supply behavior stay the same for the time being. The other possible factors are location in terms of proximity to public transportation or college campus, rent offered by other apartment owners or size and number of rooms and other related facilities, on-campus housing offered by universities, city government policy in giving permits for building new apartments, zoning and environmental policies in city housing construction, and rent control policies of the state or federal housing subsidies. The general equation for this supply behavior is expressed next:

> S for rent = g (rents of similar apartments, alternative transportation to college, alternative to rent, rent for other types of apartments, government policy on housing construction, on-campus availability of housing for enrolled students, cost of construction of new housing, and compliance with environmental requirements)

In the previous equation, "g" is the symbol for the "function of" the variables mentioned in parentheses. All right-hand side variables in parentheses are independent variables that determine or affect the values of quantity supplied from the left-hand-side variable "S for rent." In other words, the variable S for rent on the left-hand side is the dependent variable and the right-hand side variables are all independent variables.

The *ceteris paribus* assumption made earlier implies that for any given short period of time, we change only the key variable of the S function (such as rent only) and see how that change in rent (the price of housing) affects the changes in quantity supplied for housing in Boston. After detailed analysis of the change in rent and the quantity of housing supplied, we extend the topic to a situation in which the assumption of *ceteris paribus* is no longer valid.

Given the law of supply stated from the general equation, such as the demand analysis, it will also be easier to use a supply schedule with different hypothetical values of rent and quantity supplied in Table 2.4.

Table 2.4: The Supply Schedule

Rent for Housing ($ in thousands)	Quantity Supplied for Housing (in thousands)
0	0
1	100
2	200
3	300
4	400
5	500

The aforementioned supply schedule indicates the consistency of the law of supply as a direct relationship between quantity supplied and the rent for housing, assuming other factors remain the same *(ceteris paribus)*. The graphical representation of the aforementioned supply schedule is illustrated in Figure 2.3 as a supply curve for a visual presentation and for use in more graphs in subsequent sections and chapters.

Figure 2.3   The Supply Curve

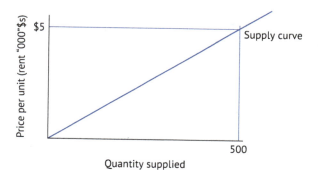

The upward-sloping supply curve in Figure 2.3 illustrates the price/rent and quantity combinations in the table for the supply schedule with a quantity of 500,000 apartment units on the horizontal axis against $5,000 per rental fee and zero supply for apartment rentals at $0 per unit of housing. The other combinations of rent and number of apartments are plotted in between the two extreme points to reflect the entire schedule along the supply curve. Given this supply curve, we have accomplished three basic flows for understanding the concept of supply behavior (just like the demand curve in Section 2.1.2) for any goods and services, including this market for housing in the city. First, we stated the law of supply as the theoretical concept. Second, we have made a hypothetical table of data on the quantity supplied against different prices/rents of housing as the supply schedule. Third, we have combined the first and second parts of the supply theory to illustrate in the upward-sloping supply curve in the previous graph to complete the whole supply model structure under *ceteris paribus*.

The next step of this supply theory is to find out what happens when the *ceteris paribus* assumption is not valid—a situation we call *changes in the supply curve instead of changes in quantity supplied*. In other words, changes in quantity supplied happen because of changes in price/rent per unit—a situation in which the price and quantity combinations move along the same supply curve. On the other hand, changes in supply can happen because of changes in factors other than its own price changes—a situation in which the whole supply function changes or the whole supply curve shifts either to the right or to the left depending on the effect on the supply function. The explanation of changes in supply with graphical illustration is shown next.

2.1.4 Changes in the Supply Curve (the Shifts of the Supply Curve)

Again, the restrictive assumption of *ceteris paribus* previously made in the form of an upward-sloping supply curve implies that the changes in price/rent for housing will move all combinations of price/rent and quantity supplied along the same supply curve. However, when the assumption of *ceteris paribus* is not the case, meaning there are other determinants of the change in supply, then it will actually change the entire supply curve by shifting inward to the left or outward to the right. This situation is called changes in supply. For example, suppose the city authority of Boston has significantly increased the number of permits given to developers for the construction of new apartments in the vacant areas near college campuses. This change in the housing policy by the City of Boston will increase the availability of apartments under the same rental fees given in Table 2.4 and Figure 2.3, respectively. Suppose the overall supply of new apartments has increased by 20 percent with the current rental structure. This 20 percent increase in the supply of rental apartments is shown in Table 2.5:

Table 2.5: The Supply Schedule

Rent for Housing ($ in thousands)	Quantity Supplied for Housing (in thousand)
0	0
1	120
2	240
3	360
4	480
5	600

With the new supply schedule resulting from an increase in the number of newly constructed apartments shown in Table 2.5, the corresponding shift in the supply curve from Figure 2.3 is illustrated in Figure 2.4.

As illustrated by S' in Figure 2.4, the S curve has shifted outward to the right because of an increase in the availability of new apartments. Using the concept of factors changing the supply of housing, suppose that instead of the city authority giving new permits for housing construction to developers, the conservation department in Boston and the Environmental Protection Agency impose strict regulations on building new houses in the same area. The new environmental restrictions will probably increase the cost of regulatory compliance for the developers building new houses or apartments. As a consequence, the supply of available apartments for rent will be reduced. In other words, the legislative restrictions will have a negative effect on changes in the supply of housing by shifting the entire supply curve inward to the left. This possible effect is illustrated in Figure 2.4. As mentioned earlier in the demand curve model, it is also important to note that the positive effect of such changes in the determinants will usually shift the supply curve outward to the right and the negative effect of changes of the same determinants will usually shift the supply curve inward to the left. In general, the most common determinants of the supply curve that shift the supply are summarized in Table 2.6.

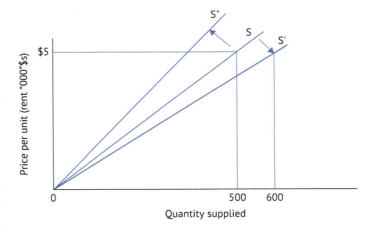

Figure 2.4   The Shift of the Supply Curve

Table 2.6: Common Determinants (Factors) That Shift the Supply Curve

Determinants of Supply	Explanation of the Effects on Supply Shifts
Legislative policy of the government	An increase in government restrictions on housing construction reduces the supply of housing and vice versa.
Changes in policies on tax and subsidies	An increase in taxes on gasoline consumption reduces the supply of goods and services produced by using the gasoline as inputs.
Change in the technology of production	Technological improvement in production, such as software industries, reduces the cost of production and increases the productivity of labor and thus shifts the supply curve rightward.
Change in labor cost and labor productivity	An increase in wages bargained by a labor union and hiring unskilled workers increases the cost of production in factories and service industries and thus shifts the supply to the left and vice versa.
Change in the cost of other inputs and capital	A decrease in cost capital, such as interest rate and other costs of raw materials, will lower the cost of making durable goods, such as cars and household appliances, and thus shifts the supply curve toward the right.
Change in the expected profit or state of the economy or government policy	An increase in expected profit in goods and services, such as smartphone sales, will increase the supply of smartphones. If the economy is expected to do better and the government policy is favorable for a company's growth and profit, the supply will shift rightward. The opposite will happen with negative expectations.

Changes in the number of competitive suppliers	An increase in the number of suppliers of the same products will shift the market supply curve rightward. For example, the rise in e-commerce companies has increased the supply of products available for purchase online.
Changes in the competitive prices of other goods and services	If the price of substitutes increases for, say, the price of Starbucks coffee and drinks, then the supply of Dunkin Donuts coffee and drinks may increase in response to the demand for alternative coffee and drinks by more customers.

2.1.5 Demand and Supply Interaction and Determination of Market Equilibrium

To analyze the efficiency of allocating the limited resources in the market, it is necessary to bring the market demand (the consumers or buyers) and market supply (the producers or suppliers) together to clear the market. Since desires for consumers/buyers and producers/sellers are just opposite in their act of exchanging goods and services, under normal circumstances, the demand curve is downward sloping and the supply curve is upward sloping. In the free market environment, the demand and supply curves moving in opposite directions must interact at the point of the intersection of the demand and supply curves to determine the equilibrium point where the buyers and sellers shake hands, which is called the market-clearing point. To explain the process of this equilibrium point, Table 2.7 combines the data from Table 2.1 (the demand schedule) and Table 2.4 (the supply schedule).

Table 2.7: Equilibrium of Rent and Quantity of Housing in the Free Market Environment

Rent ($ in thousands)	Quantity Demanded (in thousands)	Quantity Supplied (in thousands)	Shortage/ Surplus	Change in Price (Increase/ Decrease)
0	900	0	shortage	increase
1	700	100	shortage	increase
2	500	200	shortage	increase
3	300	300	equilibrium	equilibrium
4	100	400	surplus	decrease
5	0	500	surplus	decrease

Table 2.7 indicates the process of demand and supply interactions in the housing market for rent with six combinations of prices (rent) and quantity of apartments displaying responses from both demand (tenants) and supply (owners), with equilibrium price and quantity demanded equal to supply at $3,000 and 300,000 units, respectively. This is the only price and quantity combination to clear the market (the handshake point of intersection). The data in the table is illustrated in Figure 2.5.

Figure 2.5 illustrates the equilibrium position at the intersection between the demand and supply curves at $3,000 per unit apartment with the quantity demanded equal to the quantity supplied of 300,000 units. It is also clear that any other rental price above this equilibrium price of $3,000 per unit, the quantity demanded would be less than the quantity supplied, creating a surplus (see Table 2.7 and Figure 2.5). Assuming that other things stay the same *(ceteris paribus)*, the surplus at prices above the equilibrium price will pull the price down to $3,000 per unit to clear the market.

Figure 2.5 Market Equilibrium

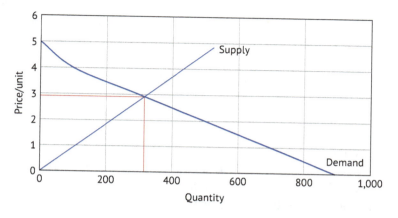

Conversely, with the same *ceteris paribus* assumption, any rental prices below $3,000 per unit will push the price up until it reaches equilibrium at $3,000 per unit, which clears the market. This process of equilibrium price and quantity combination is the point where buyers and sellers shake hands to clear the market. In other words, the equilibrium price is a signal that clears the market without any misallocation or distortion of limited resources in the form of surpluses (inventory accumulation) or shortages (inventory diminution). However, this mechanism of market equilibrium price and quantity demanded equal to quantity supplied is not static in the sense that the *ceteris paribus* assumption is a restrictive assumption for a short period of transactions. There are several factors mentioned previously that do actually change the direction of demand and supply behavior in the free market. Those factors constantly change over time and so does the *ceteris paribus* assumption. This phenomenon is called the process of shifting demand and supply functions and their curves because of changes other than price. These changes in demand and supply do eventually alter the equilibrium point of market interaction. Such changes in equilibrium price and quantity are explained in Section 2.1.6.

2.1.6 Changes in Equilibrium Price and Quantity because of a Shift in Demand and Supply

As previously explained, with some outside factors that may shift the demand and supply curves to the right or to the left, the equilibrium price and quantity demanded and supplied will end up with a new position in the market to clear the market. For example, the new data on demand for housing depicted in Table 2.2 and the same for the supply of housing shown in Table 2.5 were attributed to changes in two outside factors. The increase in college enrollment of students shifted the demand for housing to the

Figure 2.6 New Equilibrium of the Housing Market

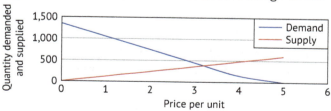

right by 50 percent given the same list of rental prices. At the same time, the supply of newly constructed apartments has also increased by 20 percent with the increased permit initiative by the city authority. Given those new demand and supply increases with the same set of rental prices, the new equilibrium of the housing market is illustrated in Figure 2.6. The new equilibrium price is close to $3,500, and the quantity demanded and supplied is about 400,000 units. This is consistent with the concept of demand and supply analyzed so far.

2.1.7 The Scope and Limitations of Demand and Supply Models under Imperfect Competition

In Section 2.1.6, the determination of the market equilibrium price and quantity was based on the assumption of perfect competition without any outside forces that may disrupt the process of the free market system. Those forces are very common in the economics of the real world when the market system of laissez-faire is disrupted by outside factors, such as natural calamities, war, geopolitical trade wars, government legislation, price support, tariffs, subsidies, rent control, minimum wage law, and taxes. These factors are so common in business and economics that the free market assumption does not hold true most of the time. As a consequence, the demand and supply behavior constantly changes (by shifting) in response to those outside factors that obviously influence the outcome of market equilibrium.

For example, when making changes in legislative action to protect consumers' health and safety, the legislative agencies of the government may increase restrictions on food, medicine, transportation, construction, automobiles, cigarettes, and other health-related products. In compliance with those legislative laws, the cost of production would increase. As a result, the effect of the increasing cost of production in those goods and services would shift the supply curve to the left. Given that the demand curve is unchanged, the new equilibrium price would increase and the quantity demanded and supplied at the new equilibrium point would be lower. In general, the increase in the cost of production is a negative shock on the supply side and thus shifts the supply curve to the left. Conversely, technological advancement with an increase in the efficiency of production and labor productivity will have a positive shock on the supply side and thus would shift the supply curve to the right. For example, the increase in tariffs proposed by Donald Trump in January 2017 on fruits and vegetables imported from Mexico to pay for the border wall would definitely shift the supply curve to the left, and American consumers would end up paying for the wall at a higher equilibrium price with a lower quantity of imported goods from Mexico. Similarly, the price support and subsidies from the government to dairy and fruit/vegetable industries would induce the supply curve to shift rightward for those affected products in response to the support program. As a result, the price would decrease and quantity in equilibrium would increase.

The changes in the demand side of the market are also influenced by several outside factors. In general, a negative shock on the demand side because of changes in outside factors would shift the demand curve to the left, and given that the supply curve is unchanged, the new equilibrium price and quantity would decline. For example, a decrease in government subsidies for higher education would decrease the demand for college admission and thus would shift the demand curve inward to the left. Given the supply curve for college admission capacity, tuition will decrease with an overall decrease in enrollment. On the other hand, a positive shock because of changes in outside factors, such as an increase in subsidies for higher education would increase the demand for admission and, therefore, increase the equilibrium quantity of enrollment and tuition. Based on this general concept of demand and supply changes, students may think about many other real-world examples of economic goods and services and their constant changes in price and quantity with their implications for the welfare of both consumers and suppliers. The effects of government policies on the welfare of both buyers and sellers come from minimum wage law (price floor legislation); rent control (price ceiling legislation); agriculture and manufacturing

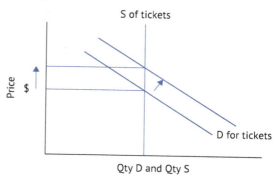

Figure 2.7 The Market Equilibrium for a Baseball Match

subsidies, tariffs on imported goods, such as aluminum and steel; and taxes on cigarettes, alcohol, and petroleum oil. In the next three sections of this chapter, applications and policy implications for changes in demand and supply behavior are discussed in the context of the economics of sports, music, and higher education.

2.2 Applications of the Demand and Supply Model in Sports Economics

Figure 2.7 illustrates that changes in ticket prices will not affect the movement of the quantity of seats, which is fixed in supply, as drawn as a vertical supply curve in the figure. Given the downward-sloping demand curve, the equilibrium price and quantity for each category of seats will be determined at the point of intersection between the vertical supply curve and the demand curve. The process of this market interaction has nothing to do with the price on the actual tickets the baseball fans purchase. This is because the ticketed prices are predetermined long before the season starts every year. Now when the number of fans willing to purchase more tickets than the total tickets available for each category of seats increases (with different pricing schemes on the tickets), the demand curve will shift rightward. As a result, it will increase the equilibrium price with no change in the quantity of seats bought and sold. In other words, it is fair to conclude that the price of the baseball

Super Bowl 52 Ticket Prices: Minnesota Flooded with Eagles Fans as Demand Soars

If you have a digital edition of this book, please click on the link that follows to access the report by CBS Sports about the price increase for 2018 Super Bowl tickets.

https://www.cbssports.com/nfl/news/super-bowl-52-ticket-prices-minnesota-flooded-with-eagles-fans-as-demand-soars/

If you have a print edition of this book, please use your cell phone to scan the QR code that follows to access the article:

tickets may not necessarily reflect their true market price because it is predetermined. That is why the actual market price is the scalping price for tickets purchased in the secondary market. The shifting of demand to the right goes up even at higher rates during the playoffs, not only for baseball games but also football, basketball, hockey, and soccer. A real-world example of such a rightward shift of the demand curve for the Super Bowl in 2018 is illustrated in the following article published by CBS Sports on February 4, 2018.

On February 4, 2018, various sports journals reported that the Super Bowl LII ticket price for the February 6 NFL championship game was increasing at a much faster rate than it was a year before for Super Bowl LI.

Figure 2.8 Market Trends in the Music Industry

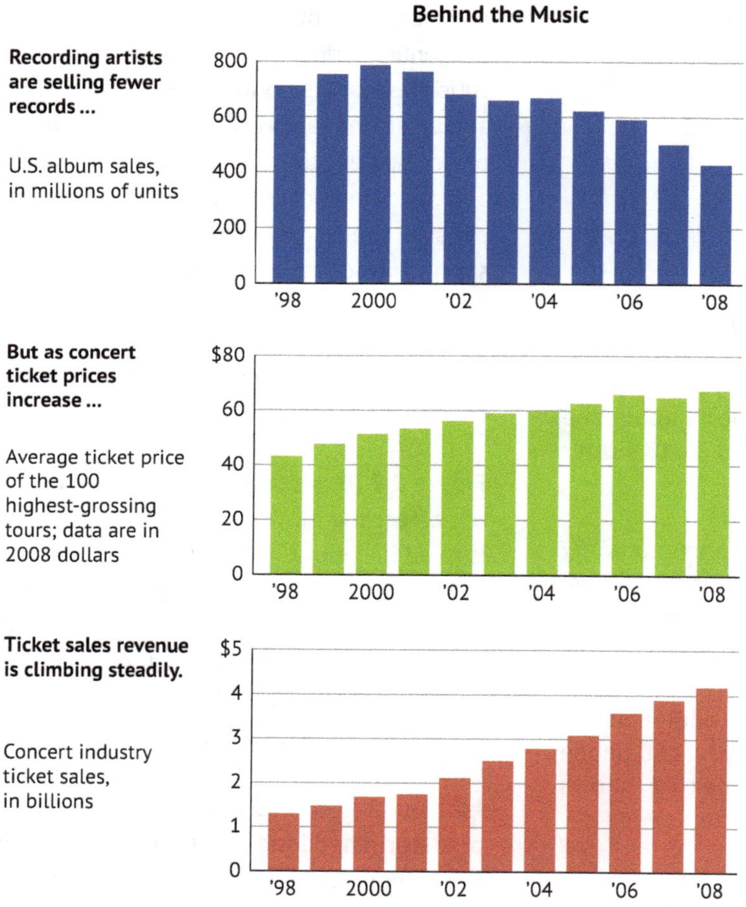
Behind the Music
Recording artists are selling fewer records ...
U.S. album sales, in millions of units
800
600
400
200
0
'98
2000
'02
'04
'06
'08
But as concert ticket prices increase ...
Average ticket price of the 100 highest-grossing tours; data are in 2008 dollars
$80
60
40
20
0
'98
2000
'02
'04
'06
'08
Ticket sales revenue is climbing steadily.
Concert industry ticket sales, in billions
$5
4
3
2
1
0
'98
2000
'02
'04
'06
'08

Source: Ethan Smith, "Can He Save Rock 'n' Roll? Irving Azoff Wants to Concentrate Power in the Music World Like Never Before; Bruce Springsteen Objects," *Wall Street Journal, February 21,* 2009.

Based on the price information presented earlier and its relevance to the application of the theories of demand and supply behavior in sports economics, the following three conclusions can be drawn, among others.

1. **The rise of the market price was caused by the limited supply of tickets for sale.**
2. **The increase of the market price across the board was due to the Eagles winning than NFC Championship against the Minnesota Vikings.**
3. **The increase of the market price caused by the rise in demand for tickets in the secondary market was also because of the covered dome of the U.S. Bank Stadium in Minneapolis, Minnesota, in the bitter cold of February.**

With similar concepts of market behavior, the next section will analyze the demand and supply model in the music industry.

2.3 Applications of the Demand and Supply Model in the Music Industry

Like the market interaction in sports events, music entertainment events, such as concerts and Broadway musicals, have a limited number of seats for each show. Depending on the popularity of a particular event, the demand curve will keep shifting to the right until the prices ended up at the highest bidding equilibrium point at the point of intersection between the vertical supply curve and the downward-sloping demand curve—the same model structure illustrated in the case about NFL games in Section 2.2. Figure 2.8 presents data on the market for music concerts in 2008 in the United States that was published by *Pollstar* magazine.

From the previous chart, it can be observed that between 1998 and 2008, sales of recording albums in the United States were down almost 50 percent from their 2000 peak. But over that same period, concert ticket revenues more than doubled to 4.2 billion in 2008 despite significant increases in average concert ticket prices. The data in the chart clearly indicate that the rise in ticket prices has been over 50 percent in response to an almost 100 percent increase in ticket sales because of the continuous shift of the demand curve to the right with limited increases in seats at the events (except the number of concerts have been increased). The simultaneous increase in price and tickets sold are mainly attributed to a faster increase in demand for concert-going fans. On the other hand, the decline in sales revenue for rock albums may be attributed to two factors. First, the increasing number of concertgoers might have reduced the purchase of rock albums in those years. Second, the advancement of digital technology to download music and music videos via YouTube, iTunes, Amazon Music, Spotify, and other competitors lowered the price of selling rock albums. However, it does not necessarily mean that the demand to purchase audio music has declined at the same time. What might have happened is that the per-unit cost of digital music sales has declined significantly to reflect the decline in sales revenue for rock albums. The next section of this chapter will explain the demand and supply behavior of higher education and its effects on the costs and benefits of higher education.

2.4 Applications of the Demand and Supply Model in Higher Education

In Section 1.2 of this chapter, an explanation was given about the concept of opportunity cost in the context of making the decision to go to college. In that discussion, the long-term benefits of going to college apparently outweighed the short-term opportunity costs of attending college. As an extension of that discussion, the statistics show that college enrollment has significantly increased in recent years, not only in the United States but also globally, where the trend is even higher. According to the report published (May 2017) by the National Center for Education Statistics (www.NCES.ed.gov), college enrollment increased by 30 percent in the United States between 2000 and 2015 (from 13.2 million to 17 million). The same report projected enrollment would increase to 19.3 million by 2026 (an increase of 13.5 percent). Another report published by Inside Higher Ed (www.insidehighered.com) in September 2017 projected a 15 percent increase in college enrollment by 2025. These statistics clearly indicate that the demand curve for college admission will continue to shift rightward given very limited growth in available seats in college to accommodate the rising trend of students seeking higher education. The result of these demand and supply forces in college education help the students of economics to expect a steady rise in college tuition in the years to come. The rising trend of international students seeking admission in both undergraduate and graduate schools in the United States is an expected rightward shift of the demand curve, even faster than the statistics for US students seeking college admission. To learn more details about the statistics of demand for higher education, students may also visit the US Department of Education website (www.ed.gov).

In Chapter 3, more applications of the demand and supply model will explain the context of efficiency and equity under perfect competition. The rationale for government intervention when the free market fails to allocate resources efficiently will be discussed as well.

Chapter Summary

Section 2.1 introduced the basic theoretical foundation of the market system in terms of market demand and supply models with their scope and limitations for allocating resources efficiently. After introducing the concept of the demand and supply paradigm, the power of demand and supply was explained, with special reference to Adam Smith's theory of laissez-faire (*The Wealth of Nations*) in achieving efficiency in production and distribution. The law of demand and its application in real-world economics were discussed by integrating hypothetical data and related graphs with the theory of demand for housing in the City of Boston. Similarly, the law of supply was discussed with the hypothetical data on the supply side of the housing market in Boston. The equilibrium condition for demand and supply interactions was also explained in detail with the *ceteris paribus* assumption by changing the price per unit of housing. The changes in equilibrium condition were further explained by relaxing the assumption of *ceteris paribus*. The other factors, such as income, tastes, and government policies on the housing market, were allowed to change with the absence of *ceteris paribus* assumption. The changes in those variables do affect the changes in equilibrium by shifting demand and/or supply curves to arrive at a new equilibrium. The policy implications for changes in market equilibrium price and quantity were also discussed at the end of this section.

Section 2.2 presented the application of the demand and supply models in sports economics. Specific examples were provided, such as ticket prices and seats allocated in the stadiums for baseball and football games. Students are encouraged to read the theories of demand and supply first and then to relate to the real-world application of sports economics in major games, such as football, hockey, baseball, basketball, and soccer.

Section 2.3 dealt with the application of the demand and supply models in the music industry. This section explained how the cost and pricing for live music concerts versus digital downloads have significantly changed with the emergence of the digital economy and, thus, have brought a major change to the market behavior of the music industry. The digital download system has revolutionized the cost and price structure of music CDs and application-based music marketing and sales. Examples of live rock concerts and their sharp contrast to digital music downloading were discussed at the end of the section.

Section 2.4 discussed the application of the demand and supply models in higher education. The concepts of demand and supply were applied to determine the market efficiency concerning the cost and benefit of going to college. Students are also encouraged to extend these three applications of demand and supply to other industries.

Application Activities

Q1. Define and describe the concept of opportunity cost with an example. What would be your opportunity cost for taking online classes to get a degree at the University of Massachusetts Boston (UMB) compared to taking traditional face-to-face classes at UMB or elsewhere? Provide examples in your answers.

Q2. Draw a supply–demand diagram of the market for rental apartments in Boston in the neighborhoods surrounding UMB. Illustrate the effect on monthly rents of increased public funding from the State of Massachusetts and a simultaneous increase in enrollment capacity for freshman year admission by the university with no increase in tuition and fees. Explain your diagram in your own words.

Q3. Suppose the geopolitical tension in the Arab states in the Middle East and Persian Gulf region has severely disrupted oil exports to the United States. Illustrate and explain the effect on the price of natural gas and the quantity demanded equal to quantity supplied in the US market because of this decline in the supply of petroleum (fossil fuel) from the Middle East and the Persian Gulf. Hint: Please assume that petroleum and natural gas are substitutes.

Q4. Suppose the state government decided to impose a tax on cigarette purchases to discourage smoking and thus prevent health-related issues for the general public. By drawing a graph of the demand and supply curves, illustrate and explain briefly the effect that a

$2-per-pack cigarette tax will have on the equilibrium price and the quantity of cigarettes in the market. In other words, illustrate the increase or decrease of the equilibrium price and quantities after the imposition of a tax of $2 per pack. Briefly explain whether the price change of cigarettes would rise by more than, less than, or exactly $2. Hint: You start with an initial equilibrium price and quantity with demand and supply of the cigarette market followed by changing the demand or supply curves in response to tax imposed by the government.

Q5. Suppose the government passed new legislation for stricter safety and fuel efficiency conditions in the manufacture of new automobiles. Draw a demand and supply diagram and then illustrate and briefly explain the effect of such legislation on the equilibrium price and the quantity of newly manufactured vehicles vis-à-vis the market for used vehicles.

Q6. Suppose the ticket prices for next year's Super Bowl were announced a year ahead at a range from $1,000 to $25,000, with rates in between for all categories of seats for the stadium. Without any prior information regarding what teams will play, briefly explain why these price ranges do not reflect the true market price of Super Bowl tickets. Do you expect to see the actual market prices go much higher, lower, or remain the same? Why?

Q7. Ed Sheeran, a British pop and rock singer, is scheduled to perform a concert on September 14, 2018, at 7 p.m. in the Gillette Stadium in Foxborough, Massachusetts. The ticket price ranges are from $62 to $8,668. Based on your knowledge of the demand and supply models for the music entertainment market, briefly explain whether these price ranges truly reflect the market prices. Why or why not?

Chapter 3

Measures of Market Efficiency versus the Economics of Government Intervention in the Free Market Mechanism

Learning Objectives

As they read the chapter, students will learn the following:

▶ Criteria for Measuring Market Efficiency and Equity

▶ The Foundation of the Free Market System: The Case for Laissez-Faire

▶ The Sources of Free Market Failure and Their Effects on Society

▶ The Case for and against Government Intervention in a Free Market System and Its Effects on Society

▶ Pros and Cons of Government Intervention in the Market System

Introduction

This chapter is an extension of Chapter 2 where the basic techniques of allocating resources efficiently was introduced through demand and supply behavior. The core objective of this chapter is to introduce the concept of efficiency as the value at the margin and to analyze the criteria of measuring efficiency in production, consumption and distribution of limited resources. The criterion of measuring efficiency is the fundamental principle of economics, which help understand the techniques and policy prescriptions to maximize the economic and financial wellbeing of individuals and institutions. In delivering the efficiency criteria, the importance of free market mechanism called *laissez faire* is introduced with its pros and cons from real world perspectives. This chapter has also discussed the sources of market failure under free market system. The limitations of free market system require the government intervention to bring the market efficiency back to work. However, the government policy intervention itself may not necessarily solve all the problems in free market systems. The learners are expected to learn these basic foundations of economics in this chapter with further applications of demand and supply models in the field of healthcare industries introduced in Chapter 4, and more applications in the field of economics of the Wall Street in Chapter 5.

3.1 Criteria for Measuring Market Efficiency and Equity

As mentioned in Chapter 1, the key purpose of studying economics is to learn how to allocate limited resources efficiently. It is also important to extend basic understanding to the distributional pattern of the economic pie so that the disparity between rich and poor can be fairly minimized. This section discusses the economic principles and applications involved in measuring efficiency and equity for better use of resources in both the production process and distribution of goods and services produced.

3.1.1 What Is Economic Efficiency?

In general, economic efficiency comes from two sides of the original model of demand and supply in the market for goods and services. Demand-side efficiency represents the welfare of consumers, called distributional efficiency. Supply-side efficiency represents the welfare of producers. In other words, efficiency in economics looks at two types of efficiency:

1. **Efficiency in distribution for consumers**
2. **Efficiency in production for producers**

The original theory of the two types of efficiency was developed by Italian economist Vilfredo Pareto in the nineteenth century, and it is called Pareto efficiency in distribution and production (Pareto, 1909). Pareto efficiency is said to be a state of production and distribution of goods and services aimed at attaining a maximum point of efficiency. A reallocation of resources from that point will either make someone better off or worse off. This concept was developed by Pareto in the context of the microeconomics of production and distribution. However, in the field of macroeconomics, the Pareto efficiency theory may have different implications from what Pareto applied in the field of microeconomics.

Conditions for Pareto efficiency in microeconomics: If resources were allocated to the point of equilibrium, they must fulfill the following criteria of Pareto efficiency.

1. *Efficiency in allocative distribution:* Price per unit (P)t = Marginal utility (MU) = Marginal cost (MC)
2. *Efficiency in allocative production:* Price per unit (P) = Marginal revenue (MR) = Minimum average total cost (ATC)

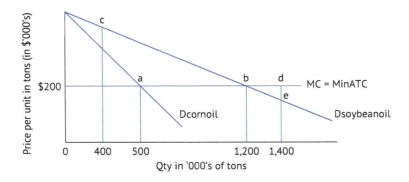

Figure 3.1 Pareto Efficiency

Combining both the demand and supply-side of the two criteria, the complete Pareto condition can be rewritten with the following equation:

P = MU= MC = MR = Minimum ATC.

Basic assumptions for the efficiency criteria for validity are as follows:

- Perfect information about the goods and services to both consumers and producers
- Technology of production is the most efficient to produce at minimum ATC
- No external cost involved

For example, consider the production and distribution of soybean oil and corn oil in the United States. The hypothetical demand curves for both markets are illustrated in the same diagram (Figure 3.1), with the assumption of an identical cost structure in both production and technology. It is also assumed that MC = Minimum ATC at $200,000 per ton and the MR for simplicity is ignored.

In Figure 3.1, the Pareto efficiency points for soybean oil production and distribution are at 500 and at 1,200 for corn oil, with their corresponding price and minimum ATC at points "a" and "b," respectively. If some resources are taken away from soybean oil production to produce more corn oil, then the utility lost by soybean consumers at a higher price above $200 cannot be compensated by the lower price paid by corn oil consumers at below $200. Of course, this simplification of the model structure is based on the three assumptions mentioned earlier. Those assumptions are based on the perfectly competitive market structure called *laissez-faire*. However, under the conditions of imperfect market competition, such as monopoly or oligopoly market power, Pareto efficiency conditions are lost because monopoly and oligopoly markets charge higher prices than MC and MU. Even under conditions of perfect competition, it is not necessarily guaranteed that Pareto efficiency will be attained for two reasons:

1. The distribution of wealth and income may not be equitable.

2. The economics of externality (negative and positive externalities) may affect the third parties in the society who were not invited to the party of demand and supply equilibrium.

The first reason is quite common in every society; income distribution is not equitable. For example, if the government imposes high tax rates on higher income and wealthy individuals and corporations and the extra tax revenue is spent on national defense and low-income welfare recipients, then the demand and cost structure illustrated in Figure 3.1 will shift to different positions. Under that scenario, Pareto efficiency may not be possible to attain. Other examples could be the unrestricted or unregulated logging industry or fishing industry, which may cause negative externalities through deforestation and harming marine biology, respectively. In these examples, the social MC of externality would be much higher than the conditions of the Pareto efficiency criteria because the prices the industries charge do not necessarily reflect the true social scarcity of resources or costs to the society. Industrial pollution is a classic example of such negative externality. To internalize these externalities, government regulations are needed so that the marginal social benefit (MSB) is equally distributed to match with the marginal social cost (MSC). The benefit of government intervention to internalize the externality is discussed in Section 3.4. Students will learn more technical detail with real-world examples of this logic in the discussion of microeconomics.

3.2 The Foundation of the Free Market System: The Case for Laissez-Faire

The concept of the free market system dates back to the classical theory of demand and supply originally developed by Adam Smith in his famous book *The Wealth of Nations* published in 1776. The core principle of the free market system is known as laissez-faire, which means "leave the market alone." This principle implies that the equilibrium price and quantity determined by an uninterrupted demand and supply foundation of free market behavior may be the most efficient point of resource allocation. This point of efficiency is supposed to provide the highest possible value. As discussed in Section 3.1, the efficiency conditions of Pareto optimality as MC = Price = MR = MU = Minimum ATC are the basic case for the laissez-faire principle. The advocacy of Smith (1776) and subsequent classical economists for the free market system without government intervention is known as the theory of capitalism or the economic system of capitalism. The capitalist system of market behavior is also known as industrial capitalism; the system originally emerged from the Industrial Revolution in the United Kingdom during the second half of the eighteenth century.

The Industrial Revolution of the United Kingdom was primarily attributed to the invention of the spinning jenny, spinning mule, and innovation of power looms in the textile industry during the 1760s. These technological breakthroughs transformed the social structure of Britain from a predominantly agrarian economy to an industrial-based economy with an increase in labor productivity and thus improved living standards. This development was further enhanced by the invention of steam engine technology by English inventor Thomas Newcomen in 1712 and further developed by Scottish inventor James Watt (1770s). The use of steam engine technology was an integral part of the Industrial Revolution in the late eighteenth century in England, and its spillover affected the rapid growth of industrial capitalism in neighboring Western European nations, such as France, Belgium, and Germany. This spillover effect also eventually exported to the northeastern region of the United States at the beginning of the twentieth century. The Second Industrial Revolution in the United States made America the world leader of industrial capitalism. The power of free market enterprise became the key driving force toward rapid economic growth and prosperity with improving living standards for workers and owners involved in industrial capitalism on both sides of the Atlantic.

The economic boom and rise of living standards in Europe and the United States continued to flourish at a rapid rate during the first three decades of the twentieth century. However, rapid industrialization without the US government's legislative control caused an economic boom and bust cycle in the late 1920s. The continued boom of the economy in the 1920s brought skyrocketing stock prices and enormous profits for financial and industrial corporations. In response to this rapid rate of industrial and manufacturing growth, consumers and savers invested in stocks and bonds issued by corporations. As a result, the stock prices far exceeded their intrinsic value (the actual value as opposed to market value). The resulting speculative bubble on Wall Street eventually burst and resulted in the stock market crash on October 29, 1929. The stock market crash was mainly attributed to the massive sale of stocks because of a loss of confidence in equity values plus inventory pileup of manufactured goods and appliances. The stock market crash was followed by massive unemployment and the closure of thousands of banks and financial institutions across the United States. This was the beginning of the Great Depression of the 1930s, which lasted until 1939. It ended with the breakout of World War II in Europe.

Despite the increase of the unemployment rate to more than 25 percent, along with a significant decline in industrial production and massive bank failure between 1929 and 1931, the president, Herbert Hoover, still believed in free market capitalism and did not intervene in the market to deal with the crisis. However, by the end of 1932, the US economy faced the worst economic depression in its history. Given the severity of the social and economic crisis, then Democratic presidential candidate Franklin D. Roosevelt (known as FDR) came up with his campaign promise that stated the government would take an active role in ending the Great Depression if he got elected. After winning the election, President Roosevelt declared his economic reform, the New Deal, with the promise of full government intervention to end the economic crisis. The declaration of his New Deal was historically known as the birth of Keynesian economics, named after English economist John Maynard Keynes. Keynes actually pioneered the development of modern macroeconomics by calling for the direct involvement of government fiscal and monetary policy prescriptions to save the economy during the Great Depression. The theories and applications of Keynesian economics were written in his book *The General Theory of Employment, Interest and Money* published in 1936. The recommendations made in his book were a major departure from the classical economic principle of *laissez-faire*. The case for government intervention is discussed in more detail in Section 3.3.

3.3 The Sources of Free Market Failure and Their Effects on Society

It is evident from the discussion in Section 3.2 that the efficiency of the free market system measured by Pareto efficiency conditions is based on three restrictive assumptions: (1) perfect knowledge and information about the technology of products and the type of product quality and utility for both producers and consumers, (2) absence of the external cost of production and distribution, and (3) distribution of income to labor and capital are equitable, if not equal. However, we also discussed that, in reality, those restrictive assumptions may not be valid most of the time. Therefore, the Pareto efficiency criteria do fail even under the free market system. The economic crisis of the Great Depression was an example of a massive market failure. The key reasons for market failure include the following:

- The emergence of market power, such as monopoly and oligopoly
- The rise of externalities, such as loss of consumer confidence, loss of profit
- Inventory accumulation of manufactured goods
- Information asymmetry and its effect on moral hazard

Given the factors for market failure, the economy loses its market efficiency. The loss of efficiency in production and distribution of income is expected to have negative effects on the economic well-being of the entire society. Examples of some of those negative effects would include an increase in unemployment, decline in living standards, unequal distribution of income, social and political unrest, rise in crime, and uncertainty of future. The foundation of modern macroeconomics developed by Keynes in the 1930s was the theory of economic policy in which government plays an active role in fine-tuning market failure. The case for a government role in the market is explained in Section 3.4.

3.4 The Case for and against Government Intervention in a Free Market System and Its Effects on Society

3.4.1 Government Legislation: The Case for Price Control and a Price Ceiling

As the debate continues about whether the doctrine of *laissez-faire* guarantees market efficiency to maximize production and distribution, the case for an invisible hand (the metaphor of the laissez-faire) has been challenged by government legislators since the beginning of the market system. Government legislators believe that the price and quantity combination determined by the invisible hand under the free market system does not necessarily serve the best interest of consumers. They argue that in many cases, in market transactions, prices charged are either too high or too low when compared to what should be a fair price for consumers. Although the concept of a fair price is difficult to determine (if not impossible), government agencies impose price and quantity restrictions to maximize the well-being of consumers. In this section, such government restrictions on prices are called **price ceiling** and **price floor**, and their economic implications are discussed with real-world examples.

Price Ceiling and Its Economic Effects

A price ceiling is a maximum limit on price imposed by government legislation; the supplier or producer of a product cannot legally charge buyers above that ceiling price. Examples of such legislation of the price ceiling include essential foods, housing in cities, essential but nongeneric drugs and medicines, tickets for concerts and sporting events, and other similar basic necessities. The way the price ceiling affects the equilibrium price and quantity is shown in Figure 3.2 in the case of rent control in the city of Cambridge, Massachusetts. Rent control legislation was imposed in Cambridge in 1970, and it ended in 1995 by a referendum of the general election.

It can be observed from the graph in Figure 3.2 that the market equilibrium price at $P_0 = \$1,600$ for property rental was much higher than imposed rent control at a rent of $P_1 = \$1,000$. Although the government had good intentions to make housing affordable for low-income city dwellers, the economic consequence of a rental ceiling did not seem to serve the government's purpose of providing affordable housing opportunities for low- or middle-income residents. Here is how the economics of rent control had more negative effects than intended. It immediately created a housing shortage because of the gap between q_1 and q_2, as indicated in Figure 3.2 at the rent-controlled price of $1,000. The other consequences are disincentives for property owners to renovate and develop their existing properties, decline of rental properties not under rent control, absence of new construction of apartments, increase in new applicants waiting for a limited supply of rent-controlled units, illegal activities that include bribing rental agents to get a contract at a higher than legal ceiling, false reporting of income, low maintenance of properties, and, most of all, decline in investment in housing development in both rent-controlled and uncontrolled areas of the city. In addition, the subsidy was paid by the government to the affected property owners to compensate for the loss of rent from the rental ceiling. The evidence of the negative impact was reported in a research study published by the National Bureau of Economic Research in 2012. The report showed that right after the rent control legislation was abolished, the spillover effect of property values in terms of rent and related market prices went up to $1.8 billion between 1994 and 2004.*

Figure 3.2 Rent Control Scenario in Cambridge Housing Market

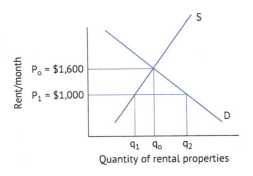

Price Floor and Its Economic Effects

A price floor is a legislative measure that is imposed as a legal minimum price below which it would be illegal to charge or offer a product or service. Two real-world examples are price support in agricultural farms and minimum wage law set by the federal government. The economic impact of minimum wage law is illustrated in Figure 3.3 (a–b).

In Figure 3.3 panel (a), the minimum wage is imposed at $12 per hour. But the equilibrium market wage rate is already $15 per hour. In this labor market condition, minimum wage is not a binding constraint because the demand and supply forces indicate the actual market

Figure 3.3   Minimum Wage Scenario in the Labor Market

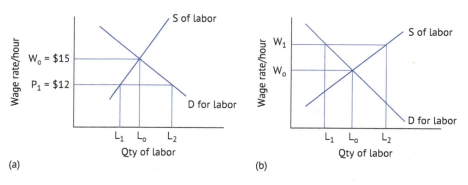

(a)

(b)

wage rate of $15 per hour, which is much higher than the legal minimum of $12. If that is the case, then what is the argument for a minimum wage? The rationale behind the minimum wage is still strong in the sense that it protects the employees with low bargaining power and fewer skills to maintain their minimum standard of living. It also protects laborers from employers' potential exploitation and discrimination in the absence of minimum wage legislation. On the other hand, in panel (b) of Figure 3.3, the minimum wage at W_1 is at a higher level than the market equilibrium wage rate at W_0. In this case, there is a binding constraint by the employers to at least the legal minimum wage at W_1 if they hire someone. This binding constraint will have mixed economic effects on employees and consumers in the form of creating unemployment from the gap between L_1 and L_2. How does that unemployment happen with the minimum wage legislation? Here is how: The demand curve for labor is the willingness to hire more or less labor as the wage rate goes up or down. So with a higher legal minimum wage at W_1 than at W_0, the employers will be willing to hire L_1 number of workers instead of L_0 number of workers to minimize the increasing labor cost associated with complying with minimum wage legislation. On the supply-side, the labor supply curve indicates the quantity of labor offered by employees at different wage rates. So with the legal minimum wage rate at W_1, the number of workers will increase to L_2 from L_0. Therefore, the gap between L_1 and L_2 is the result of unemployment caused by the minimum wage legislation when the market wage rate is below the minimum wage rate. The other related economic costs from the scenario of panel (b) in Figure 3.3 are increases in the prices of goods and services charged by suppliers to cover the rise in labor costs from minimum wage laws and the increases in subsidies paid to small businesses by the federal government to minimize the job loss or profit loss affected by the legislation. It is also important to note that the difference between panel (a) and panel (b) is common in different states and cities across the United States. Panel (a) could be a case in a place like Boston where there is a severe labor shortage in both skilled and unskilled workers. Panel (b) could be a scenario common in the South and some parts in the Midwest where surplus labor has less bargaining power in the labor market and limited job opportunities.[1]

---

1   Jay Fitzgerald, "The End of Rent Control in Cambridge," National Bureau of Economic Research, n.d., https://www.nber.org/digest/oct12/w18125.html.

3.4.2 The Great Depression of the 1930s and the Economic Policy of FDR's New Deal

Keynes, the founder of modern macroeconomics, explained that the Great Depression of the 1930s was not caused by the failure of capitalism but because of the deficiency in aggregate demand in the free market system. To increase the aggregate demand, Keynes suggested that the government get involved in public-sector spending and thus create jobs. The details of the Keynesian macro model are discussed in Chapter 6. For now, it is important to mention that the active role of government intervention in Keynesian economics was first adopted by President Roosevelt in his economic policy reform called the New Deal, established in 1932. The New Deal was the first experiment of using government fiscal policy to combat the Great Depression. Thus the Keynesian economy was born. The key policy prescription of the New Deal was to invest heavily in physical infrastructure, such as roads and highways, hydraulic power plants, railways and other transportation infrastructure, airports and railway stations, and dams and bridges.

In addition, new financial legislation was enacted to protect the depositors' money in banks by creating the Federal Deposit Insurance Corporation (FDIC) and separating investment banks from commercial banks so that personal savings could not be used in volatile and risky equity markets.

3.4.3 The Market Power and Antitrust Act

As discussed earlier, the existence of the monopoly and oligopoly power of corporations seems to have negative effects on efficiency in the form of charging higher prices for consumer products, paying unfair wages, producing less, or using resources inefficiently, and making abnormal profits. To minimize these problems of market power, the government played a significant role by enacting antitrust legislation. The Sherman Antitrust Act of 1890, with several modifications in subsequent decades, has significantly reduced the externalities caused by market powers in the US economy.

3.4.4 Externalities and Government Legislation

Economists define externalities as the external cost or external benefit to a party caused by a system of production and distribution by making that party either better off or worse off without being paid or compensated for the loss or gain for the party. This externality concept is also known as the spillover effect. The gain of the spillover effect is called *positive externality*, and loss to the party is called *negative externality*. The classic example of negative externality is air pollution caused by the industrial use of fossil fuels, such as oil, coal, natural gas, and petroleum. Since the increasing air

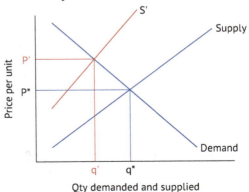

Figure 3.4 Internalization of the Externality of Pollution

pollution from emitting carbon dioxide into the air is blamed for part of global warming, the Clean Air Act, amended in the 1990s, was a major government initiative to internalize the level of externalities caused by rapid industrialization. Figure 3.4 is an example of the process of internalizing the externalities of pollution as a result of the government taking different legislative measures.

In Figure 3.4, suppose the supply curve and demand curve for a hypothetical market for good X produces a quantity of q* with its equilibrium price at P*. The possible pollution caused by this equilibrium position of the market would be an example of negative externality in the form of emitting carbon dioxide into the air. Since air pollution causes health hazards to the entire society in the area affected, the equilibrium price and quantity combination at q* and P* do not reflect the true cost to the society at that marginal value. Assuming that the demand side is equal to social MU or marginal benefit, but the MC of production on the supply-side is less than the external cost to the society, then government legislation is needed to minimize the social MC paid by both buyers and sellers in the market. By imposing government legislation through the restriction of the amount of pollution produced, the supply curve can be shifted to the left until a new equilibrium is reached at the combination of P* and q*, where MSB = MSC. This outcome from government intervention is called the internalization of externality.

There are a number of ways that the government internalizes the externality of pollution or water contamination caused by rapid industrialization. Some of those actions include the imposition of a pollution tax, pollution quota, marketable permits, and penalties. Although all of these legislative measures are not equally effective or efficient, it is imperative to implement these important measures to minimize the market failure caused by externalities and thus maximize the social marginal benefit from the Clean Air Act legislation. Another example of negative externalities is overfishing in common-pool resources, such as in oceans, lakes, rivers, and ponds, which can cause harm to marine biology with severe environmental degradation to marine lives. The other examples of negative externalities are extracts of contaminated sludge and related by-products caused by steel mills, textile mills, oil refineries, chemical factories, fertilizer industries, nuclear waste, motor vehicles, and electricity grids—just to name of a few.

The example of *positive externality* is the benefit society gets at a higher value than the individual or the economic action a person or institution generates for society. Investing in science and education is a great example of generating positive externality. Educated individuals and new scientific invention and innovation generate much more economic benefits to society when compared to the benefits individuals receive from increased income and institutions from increased profits. Internalization of positive externality is a little bit different and opposite to what is illustrated for the case of negative externality in Figure 3.2. In the case of positive externality, the demand curve needs to be shifted to the right so that MSB = MSC, where the quantity produced would increase at a higher social price. If positive externality comes from the cost side of competing corporations, then the supply curve has to shift to the right with MSC = MSB at a lower social price and higher quantity of production. By the same token, if negative externality occurs on the demand side, then the demand curve has to be shifted to the left with a lower social price and less quantity of output produced. To summarize the process of internalization of externality by regulatory measures of the government, the following four possible graphical illustrations can be made.

1. *Negative externality in production:* Shift the supply curve to the left
2. *Negative externality in consumption:* Shift the demand curve to the left
3. *Positive externality in production:* Shift the supply curve to the right
4. *Positive externality in consumption:* Shift the demand curve to the right

The last section of this chapter points out the arguments for and against government intervention in the free market system.

3.5. Pros and Cons of Government Intervention in the Market System

From the discussion in the previous four sections of this chapter, students are expected to become familiar with the theoretical foundation on the concept of the free market system called *market capitalism*. However, the theory of market capitalism is based on certain restrictive assumptions that may not be the case in real-world economics when the market fails to accomplish the objectives of economic outcomes under the utopian model of demand and supply behavior. The students have also learned how to measure the efficiency of the production and distribution of output under those assumptions of the market system. However, those efficiencies cannot be achieved in the case of market failure.

Therefore, when the market fails because of the existence of the market power and externalities discussed earlier, government intervention is recommended. However, the role of the government in the case of market failure is not to eliminate the market but to stimulate market activities by bringing consumer and investor confidence to market activities. That is the core foundation of modern macroeconomics developed by Keynes (1936) to deal with the Great Depression of the 1930s. Despite the continued success of the Keynesian economic policy adopted in most of the countries since then, the debate over the role of the government and its effectiveness is still very much active in both academia and political spectrums on both sides of the Atlantic. The brief highlights of the debate are summarized next as the pros and cons of policy intervention in Table 3.1.

Table 3.1: Pros and Cons of Government Intervention in the Free Market

Cases for Government Intervention	Cases Against Government Intervention
1. Assumptions of perfect competition are not realistic.	1. Market failure is temporary, and the market will correct itself in the long run without government intervention.
2. Market power makes allocation inefficient and distorts resource allocation.	2. Market power is capable of maximizing efficiency in the production and allocation of resources in the long run.

(continued)

3. Externalities must be internalized by government regulations to maximize social marginal benefit and minimize social MC.	3. Government regulations make production costs increase and cause cost inefficiency; they reduce production and employment.
4. Government policy helps distributional equity.	4. The use of interventions such as high taxes to pay for welfare reduces the incentive to work and invest.
5. Government intervention restores consumer and investor confidence.	5. Loss of confidence is temporary, and it restores in the long run.
6. The government helps the poor and low-income workers with welfare benefits as a social responsibility.	6. Self-interest is the guiding principle for reducing poverty and increasing productivity.
7. The government controls inflation and recession.	7. Government intervention destabilizes the conditions of inflation and unemployment crises.
8. Keynes argued that without government intervention during an economic crisis, all would be dead in the long run.	8. Wage and price flexibility would restore full employment in a short period of time.

The debate over the earlier arguments for and against government policy intervention in the free market mechanism has been going on and on since the publication of *The Wealth of Nations* in 1776. The advocacy of Smith for laissez-faire economics remains popular in the United States and some parts of Europe. As a matter of fact, this debate over philosophical difference has divided the political culture in both Europe and North America into two major ideological factions: The conservatives versus the liberals. The conservatives advocate for less and less government intervention for growth and production efficiency. On the other hand, the liberals argue for more government involvement for combating inflation and recession, providing for the safety of consumers, decreasing poverty, reducing income inequality, diminishing discrimination based on ethnic and national origins. This ongoing debate is still very active with no signs of slowing down anytime soon. In the United States, the whole society is caught up in the middle of this political divide by which the real economic agenda is overshadowed. Nevertheless, the role of government policy is not going to decline in the near future. Instead, it is expected to strengthen in the decades to come to support the rapid rise of the new technology and knowledge-based economy to compete with the emerging economies in Asia and the Pacific regions. Further details of this aspect of the debate will be highlighted in the study materials in the remaining chapters of this textbook.

Chapter Summary

Section 3.1 introduces the criteria to measure the efficiency of allocating resources and the connection to equity. Efficiency in general is also categorized into two segments: Efficiency in production and efficiency in distribution. The criteria for measuring these two types of efficiency are as follows:

1. **Efficiency in allocative distribution: Price per unit (P) = MU = MC**

2. Efficiency in allocative production: Price per unit (P) = MR = Minimum ATC

Combining both the demand and supply-side of the two criteria, the complete Pareto condition can be rewritten with the following equation:

P = MU = MC = MR = Minimum ATC

Basic assumptions for the efficiency criteria for validity are as follows:

- Perfect information about the goods and services to both consumers and producers
- Technology of production is the most efficient way to produce at minimum ATC
- No external costs are involved

The real-world example of measuring these criteria is illustrated in Figure 3.1 in the context of soybean oil and corn oil production and distribution in the US market. However, it is also mentioned that even the state of perfect competition may not necessarily satisfy these criteria of measuring efficiency because of the existence of income and wealth inequality and externality of production and consumption.

Section 3.2 focused on explaining the theoretical foundation of the free market system, known as laissez-faire or capitalism. A bit of history on the concept of laissez-faire was introduced in this section in reference to Adam Smith's theory of capitalism, written in his book *The Wealth of Nations* published in 1776. The theory of Smith's free market system also seems to be consistent with the efficiency criteria of P = MU = MC = MR = Minimum ATC discussed in Section 3.1. Historically speaking, the free market system of capitalism without government intervention actually emerged during the Industrial Revolution of England in the late eighteenth century. The spillover effect of England's Industrial Revolution paved the way in the twentieth century for the Second Industrial Revolution in the United States, with the continuous expansion of economic growth and prosperity in most of the nations in Western Europe and North America until the Great Depression of the 1930s.

The Great Depression was primarily caused by excessive inventory, loss of inventory and consumer confidence, information asymmetry of the market value of equity and financial assets, and the subsequent stock market crash in 1929. To cope with the Great Depression and unemployment rate of 25 percent, the then President Roosevelt adopted the Keynesian model of macroeconomics with active government intervention in the economic recovery. The economic policy undertaken and implemented by FDR was dubbed "the New Deal," and the birth of Keynesian economics led to an alternative to the complete laissez-faire doctrine of classical economics. This was the beginning of the modern macroeconomics institution that is still very much active today. Keynes explained the rationale for active government intervention in fine-tuning the economic depression not because of the failure of capitalism but because of the demand deficiency in the market system. His advocacy intended to boost the aggregate demand side through the active fiscal policy of increasing government spending to create jobs for unemployed workers and thus rebound the economy.

Section 3.3 explained the sources of market failure that caused the Great Depression. The criteria of market efficiency described in Section 3.2 seemed to fail during the 1920s economic boom and bust cycle, as attributed to the factors listed next.

- The emergence of a market power, such as a monopoly or oligopoly
- The rise of externalities, such as the loss of consumer confidence or loss of profit
- Inventory accumulation of manufactured goods
- Information asymmetry and its effect on moral hazard

The foundation of modern macroeconomics developed by Keynes is the fiscal policy framework used to fine-tune the market failure caused by the reasons listed previously.

Section 3.4 explained Keynesian arguments for the government to expand spending to boost market demand. The Keynesian argument for expansionary fiscal policy in the form of massive government spending to create jobs highly dominated the economic policy framework under "the New Deal" established by President Roosevelt in 1933. The New Deal is still the dominant blueprint of economic policy today, not only for the US economic policy institution but also for most of the countries in the world. The other legislative actions undertaken as a part of the New Deal in the 1930s were antitrust acts against monopoly and oligopoly powers of corporations, creation of the FDIC to insure bank deposits by the public, environmental measures to internalize the externality caused by pollution, and other related measures for economic growth and stability. The process of internalization of such externalities caused by market power was explained and illustrated in Figure 3.2.

Section 3.5 explained the pros and cons of government intervention under the New Deal and afterward. Since the debate on the extent of government intervention in handling the business cycle fluctuations of market failure is far greater than ever, the arguments for and against the government policy intervention were listed in Table 3.1. Students are encouraged to read those pros and cons effectively to realize the complexity of government intervention in a free market system of private enterprises in a market system like the one in the United States.

Application Activities

Q1. While defining the concept of market efficiency, briefly describe the theoretical basis of measuring efficiency under a perfectly competitive market.

Q2. What are the assumptions made in answering Q1? What happens if those assumptions are not valid?

Q3. What are the sources of market failure? Provide a real-world example.

Q4. What is the rationale for government intervention in economic and market activities?

Q5. Briefly describe the causes of the Great Depression of the 1930s.

Q6. What is Keynesian economics? How did it combat the Great Depression of the 1930s?

Hint: It is not necessary to mention any technical aspects of the model.

Q7. In your own words, provide at least two pros and two cons of government intervention in a free market system with examples.

Chapter 4

Application of Demand and Supply to Measure the Economics of Retirement and the Health-Care Industry with Case Studies in the US Economy

Learning Objectives

As they read the chapter, students will learn the following:

▶ Demand and Supply Model in Microeconomics and Macroeconomics

▶ Application of Demand and Supply of Health Care and Pensions for the Aging Population and Their Policy Implications

▶ Examples of the General Economics of the Health-Care Industry and Society

▶ The Health-Care Industry in the Context of Macroeconomics

Introduction

From understanding the pros and cons of free market mechanism in Chapter 3 and the role of the economic policy of the government when market fails, this chapter provides the applications of demand and supply principles in the healthcare industries. Since the healthcare industry and its related institutions in both public and private sectors is the largest business and economic agent in the US economy (with 18% of GDP contribution in 2019), understanding the process of demand and supply behavior and the pricing scheme is an important part of healthcare economics. This branch of economics and business is the fastest growing industry as a distinct branch of business and economics, which has significant policy implications in terms of both micro and macroeconomics. This chapter starts with understanding the distinction between demand and supply model in Microeconomics vis-à-vis in Macroeconomics. The remaining sections of this chapter introduced the complex nature of healthcare industry and its rising cost of healthcare coverage provided by both government and private sector institutions. A particular focus is made on the economic issues of healthcare expenses for aging population and low-income households. The chapter concluded its discussion with theories of general economic issues of healthcare economics with its policy implications for both micro and macroeconomics perspectives.

4.1. Demand and Supply Model in Microeconomics and Macroeconomics

4.1.1 Demand and Supply Model in Microeconomics

As explained in Chapter 2 with the example of the housing market in the City of Boston, the demand and supply behavior in microeconomics focuses on individual goods and services bought and sold in the market. Those goods and services have their price per unit determined by the interaction between market demand and market supply. In general, the demand and supply functions not only depend on the price of goods or services but also many other factors that indirectly or directly affect the demand and supply. The functional relationship between quantity demanded for a commodity, say X, and the quantity supplied of the same commodity X is given next.

Suppose you have a commodity X, and its price/unit is Px to determine the market equilibrium price and quantity based on the basic principle of economics: the law of demand and the law of supply.

> Demand function Dx = f (Px Py Pz income, taste, social and political status, war, etc.), where Px is its own price, Py = price of y, and Pz is the price of z, as y and z could be substitutes and/or complementary goods of x.

Note: Dx = f(...) means demand for commodity X is a function of ... as a general expression demand function.

> Supply function Sx = g (Px, Py, Pz, cost of production, weather condition, war, income growth of consumers, technological advancement, expected profits, etc.)

Note: Sx = g(...) means supply for commodity x is a function of ... as a general expression of the supply function.

The law of demand states that if Px increases, quantity demanded will decrease and vice versa *ceteris paribus* (other variables like Py, Pz, ... stay with the same values). It means the demand curve is downward sloping and price changes will change the quantity demanded in the opposite direction, thus moving along the same demand curve.

The law of supply states that if Px increases, the quantity supplied will increase and vice versa *ceteris paribus* (other variables like Py, Pz, ... stay with the same values). It means the supply curve is upward sloping and price changes would change the quantity supplied in the same direction and thus moving along the same supply curve.

However, changes in demand and supply curves (not quantity demanded and quantity supplied) occur by shifting the demand or supply curve (not moving along the same curve) when *ceteris paribus* assumption does not hold. It means the shift of the demand and supply curves happens not by changes in price but by changes in other factors, such as Py, Pz, and income, for the demand curve shift and changes in the cost of production, expected profits, tax policy, etc., for the supply curve shift.

For example, if X and Y are tea and coffee, respectively, then a change in Px will change the quantity demanded (if we consider Dx) for tea, and it will move along the same demand curve for tea. But if the Py (price of coffee) changes, then Dx will shift depending on which direction the change in the price of coffee shifts. In this case, X and Y are substitutes.

A supply-side example would look like this: if the price of oranges changes, then the quantity of oranges will move along the same supply curve. But if inclement weather adversely affects the production of oranges, then the supply curve of oranges will shift to the left.

In either case, the equilibrium price and quantity will change because of the shift in demand and/or supply curve and end up with a new point of intersection between demand and supply.

Another real-world example would be the changes in equilibrium prices of Starbucks (SB) coffee and Dunkin Donuts (DD) coffee in the New England coffee market, where these two top brands are close competitors. On June 7, 2018, several news media announced that SB raised the price of its coffee drinks across the United States by 10 to 20 cents based on the different sizes of cups. The company's reason for the price hike was due to the rise in operating costs. Given the explanations of demand and supply behavior, it is easy to expect that the price of DD coffee will increase as well. The economic explanation for this prediction is simple. Although most of SB's customers will not be persuaded to go to DD, there will a considerable number of SB customers who will move to DD to keep up with their limited budgets. That means the demand curve for DD coffee is expected to shift out to the right given the company's supply curve. As a result, the new equilibrium price and quantity would be at a higher point of intersection then the new demand shift along the same supply curve.

The last point: Only the equilibrium point between supply and demand will clear the market. Every other point will either create a surplus or a shortage, and the movement of the prices will continue until the equilibrium point is reached. During the shifting of the curve, the equilibrium point itself will move from one point to another.

4.1.2 Aggregate Demand and Aggregate Supply Curve Model in Macroeconomics

Unlike the demand and supply structure defined and explained in microeconomics, demand and supply in macroeconomics are structured and analyzed differently. In macroeconomics, the demand and supply functions represent all goods and services produced and consumed in aggregates. That is why instead of using the terms "demand" and "supply," economists use "aggregate demand" (AD) and "aggregate supply" (AS) so that the model structure includes the transactions of all goods and services for the entire economy. To help students understand this distinction between the micro and macro models, the hypothetical equations for AD and AS are stated next:

$$AD = C + I + G + EX - IM,$$

where C = consumption expenditure,

    I = investment expenditure,

    G = government expenditure,

    EX = exports expenditure demanded by buyers abroad,

    IM = imports expenditure demanded by domestic buyers' imports from abroad, and

    AS = gross domestic product (GDP) = $P_1Q_1 + P_2Q_2 + P_3Q_3 + ... + PnQn = \Sigma PiQi$;
    i = 1 to n number of goods and services.

The AS equation indicates the adding of all final goods and services by their respective per unit prices for a particular calendar year. Adding them all together provides the total market value of the final goods and services produced. The prices for each of those final goods and services are considered to be the current market prices. However, the price level used in AD-AS model structure does not come from those individual prices. To make the model structure easier to understand, economists use a different pricing technique called the price index or price level. The price level is an estimated index price derived by using a ratio of nominal GDP (calculated by the previous AS equation at the current price) to real GDP (RGDP; calculated by using base-year prices). The base year prices are selected by economists who consider a year in the most recent past when the price was normal without an inflation increase.

For example, suppose in the year 2017 the nominal GDP estimated by the previous AS equation is about $19,390,600,000. And the real GDP estimated by using the base year of 2009 as $\Sigma(P2009 \times Q2017)$ is $17,096,200,000. Then the price index that is also called the GDP deflator (GDPD) would be estimated as follows:

GDPD for 2017 = (nominal GDP/real GDP) × 100 = (19,390,600/17,096,200) × 100

Or GDPD for 2017 = 1.13420 × 100 = 113.42

The index price is used as the price level indicator for the entire economy in the AD-AS model. If that index increases beyond a considerable level of the economy, then it is in a state of inflationary trend. If the index starts declining, then the economy is in a state of deflation. More detailed discussion about measuring inflation and deflation appears in the macroeconomics textbook. For now, Figure 4.1 illustrates the AD-AS model of macroeconomics.

Figure 4.1 illustrates the basic structural model of macroeconomics where the vertical axis displays the price level with 2009 as the base year price with the price index = 100 because nominal GDP and real GDP are identical for the base year. For the year 2017, the RGDP was $17,096,200,000 at the equilibrium point E_1 and in 2009, it was $14,418,700,000 at the equilibrium point E_2. Figure 4.1 also helps explain how equilibrium RGDP can be increased by shifting the AD to the rightward direction by increasing any of the components of AD, such as C, I, G, or EX-IM, thus creating employment opportunities (increase in RGDP always creates more job opportunities and helps

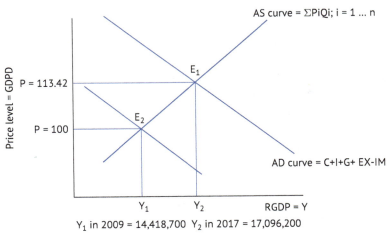

Figure 4.1   AD-AS Model

AS curve = $\Sigma PiQi; i = 1 \dots n$

E_1

Price level = GDPD

$P = 113.42$

$P = 100$

E_2

AD curve = C+I+G+ EX-IM

Y_1 Y_2 RGDP = Y

Y_1 in 2009 = 14,418,700 Y_2 in 2017 = 17,096,200

lower the unemployment rate). This expansion of the AD curve by sifting to the right is called Keynesian demand-side economic expansion by fiscal or monetary policy actions. It is also possible to shift the AS curve to the right, which is called supply-side economics, to increase RGDP and thus create more jobs.

It is also worth noting that the approximate GDP contributions by each of the components of AD for the US economy are as follows:

C = 67 percent

I = 18 percent

G = 23 percent

EX-IM = net export = −8 percent

From the relative contributions to GDP by each of the components of the AD for the more than $20 trillion economy in 2020, some implications can be made. First, US consumers contribute to more than two-thirds of the economy (67 percent of GDP). Second, the private investment and business contributions are much less than the government-sector contribution (18 percent vs. 23 percent). Therefore, the US government plays a significant role in raising GDP. It also shows that more than 108 percent of economic activities come from domestic sources, thus implying that the US economic structure is predominantly domestic based, with relatively low dependence on foreign trade. The −8 percent net export balance indicates that the US economy imports much more than it exports to other countries in the world. The economics of this Keynesian macro model and the role of the US fiscal budget expenses and tax policies are the topics of macroeconomics and thus beyond the scope of this chapter.

The next section focuses on the economics of the health-care industry as an important part of both micro and macroeconomics for its significant increases in health-care expenditures as a percentage of GDP (18 percent of GDP in 2015) in the last few decades (National Health Expenditure [NHE], www.cms.gov).

4.2 Application of Demand and Supply of Health Care and Pensions for the Aging Population and Their Policy Implications

This section focuses on one of the fastest-growing sectors in the economy not only in the United States but also in almost every industrialized country in the world. The importance of health-care services has become one of the top economic, social, and political agenda items in improving the status of human capital in newly emerged economies, such as China and India. The services under health care are multidimensional, as they include doctors' visits, surgical and preventive treatments, prescription drugs, cancer and cardiovascular treatments, vaccinations, and other epidemic diseases. These services are vital for the maintenance of good health for the sustained social and economic well-being of citizens. The maintenance of good health is also essential for improving the quality of education and productivity for the labor force for faster economic growth and prosperity. For the United States, the total expenditures for the health-care industry were estimated as more than 17 percent of GDP in 2016 (Center for Medicare and Medicaid Services, www.cms.gov). Table 4.1 indicates the rise of health-care expenses in the US economy since 1960.

Table 4.1: US Health-Care Expenditure Data since the 1960s

	1960	1980	2000	2016
NHE in billions of $	27.2	255.3	1,369.1	3,337.2
Population in million	186	230	282	322
GDP in billion	543.3	2862.5	10,284.8	18,624.5
Annual % change in NHE	7.1 (between 1960 and 1961)	15.3	7.2	4.3
Per capita NHE	146	1,108	4,855	10,348
NHE as % of GDP	5.0	8.9	13.3	17.9

Source: www.cms.gov
https://www.cms.gov/Research-Statistics-Data-and-Systems/Statistics-Trends-and-Reports/NationalHealthExpendData/NationalHealthAccountsHistorical.html

The data in Table 4.1 indicate a significant rise in health-care expenditures, along with their rising contribution to total GDP between 1960 and 2016. For example, health care expenditures went from $27 billion in 1960 to $3.337 trillion in 2016, which accounts for an increase of 12,169 percent over 65 years. The annual percentage increase of NHE also shows a rate increase that has grown faster than the long-term GDP growth rate of 3 percent. The per capita increase of NHE between the same period shows expenditures from $146 in 1960 to $10,348 in 2016, an increase of 6,988 percent. The data documenting the skyrocketing rise in health-care costs also reflect the percentage share of GDP from 5 percent in 1960 to 17.9 percent in 2016 with almost $3.5 trillion of a $19 trillion economy. Despite this significant share of GDP, the health-care system in the United States was not available to everyone until the passage of landmark legislation in 2010: the Patient Protection and Affordable Care Act (ACA), which is also known as "Obamacare" because the initiative was undertaken by then president Barack Obama under intense opposition from the Republican legislators in the US Congress.

Before the ACA legislation was signed into law by Obama in March 2010, there were more than 45 million Americans without health insurance coverage and more than 80 percent of them were elderly citizens. Research indicates the reason such a vast portion of the population went without health insurance coverage was the high cost of insurance premiums required of private individuals. Since the implementation of the ACA with its mandatory provision to purchase health insurance and government subsidies, more than 30 million Americans have purchased health insurance during the last nine years (2010–2019). Given the controversy and political rhetoric against the ACA, the debate is still very much active in the US legislative body about whether to repeal the ACA by replacing it with an alternative or allow its expansion to include more uninsured Americans to guarantee health care coverage. The two key points surrounding the controversy are the rising cost to the federal and state governments to subsidize the coverage and the mandatory sign up with a provision of penalty of about $700 per individual or 2.5 percent of their income, whichever is greater, for refusal to secure coverage. Given the controversial issue concerning the universal health-care provision of the ACA, it is important to look at the current structure of health-care coverage and its payment systems to understand the significant role of both federal and state governments in covering the rising costs of health-care services.

After the implementation of the ACA in 2010, the payment system for health-care coverage in the United States was expanded by four main categories: employer-provided, health-care coverage (34 percent); Medicare (for those age 65 years and above, 20 percent); Medicaid (for low-income individuals and families, 17 percent); and individual private coverage (11 percent). The sponsoring agencies for these four categories of coverage are the federal government and individuals (28 percent), private business enterprises (20 percent), and state and local governments (17 percent). The reasons for the continuous rise in health-care costs at a faster rate than any other service in the US economy are given next.

- **The rise of an aging population:** According to data published by the Center for Medicare and Medicaid Services (www.cms.giv), more than 55 million Americans were enrolled in Medicare in 2016. Because of the use of special medical technology and equipment for the treatment of elderly patients health-care costs are estimated to be about six times higher for older people than for younger generations. With the baby boomer generation (born between 1946 and 1964) retiring (beginning in 2010), Medicare expenses are expected to increase at a high rate in the coming decades.
- **Improved health conditions and life expectancy at birth:** With an increase in life expectancy at birth and a significant reduction of infant mortality over the last 100 years,

Americans' life expectancy has increased to more than 80 years in 2016 as compared to 51 years in 1900 (www.ssa.gov). Life expectancy for individuals with good health who are over 65 is 85 years for males and over 90 years for females. The statistics clearly indicate a further rise in the cost of medical expenses for elderly populations in the decades to come.

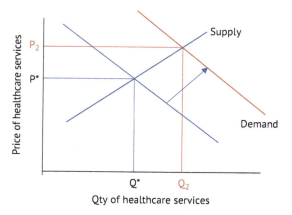

Figure 4.2 Demand and Supply Behavior of Third-Party Payment System

- **Decrease in out-of-pocket, health-care expenses:** The third-party payment system through health insurance companies for hospital care, doctors' visits, preventive care, and prescription drugs are considered to be the key reasons for the rising cost of health-care coverage. For example, employers in most of the cases usually pay 80 percent of the total premium for their employees to purchase insurance coverage. The other 20 percent is paid by the employees with tax deducted for the entire amount of premium. Under Medicare, Medicaid, and ACA, the cost is covered almost 100 percent by government agencies. This third-party payment process has significantly decreased out-of-pocket expenses from a 50 percent share in 1965 to only 11 percent in 2016 (www.cms.gov). The demand and supply behavior illustrated in Figure 4.2 helps explain how the rising cost of health-care services is partly attributed to the process of the third-party payment system.

Figure 4.2 illustrates that with the full percentage of the out-of-pocket price at P*, individuals would receive Q* level of health-care services. However, with a third-party payment of almost 100 percent of costs covered by insurance companies, the demand for health-care services would shift to the right to settle at a higher equilibrium price and quantity of health-care services, say at P_2 and Q_2, respectively. The way insurance companies make a profit is by pooling hundreds and thousands of customers covered under the same plan to minimize the risk of reimbursing every individual because only a small fraction of the insured in the pool will use health-care services.

4.2.1 Policy Implications for the Rising Cost of Health Care

The previous explanations for the trend of rapidly increasing health-care costs since the 1960s help students of economics and business realize the importance of the health-care industry in the context of both microeconomics and macroeconomics. According to recent data from the Bureau of Labor Statistics (www.bls.gov), the health-care industry and its related affiliations have become the largest employers in many states in the country. With the rapid increase in industries related to service and entertainment, knowledge-based research, and development and biotech industries and the simultaneous decline in the manufacturing industry, the growth of health-care services is expected to occur at a much faster rate than any other industries in the coming decades. With the rising trend of an aging population in relatively good health, the cost burden of providing health care for the elderly is expected to increase more than the tax revenue received from the contributions made by the working population for Social Security, Medicare, and Medicaid funds. The Congressional Budget Office (CBO) (www.cbo.gov) of the US Congress has predicted that much of the growing cost of Medicare and Social Security payments would be attributed to the baby boom generation retiring. The CBO has also predicted that the federal deficit may go up by 150 percent of GDP by 2047 if the health-care pension cost plus debt service payment (interest payment on government debt) continues to rise at its current rate. This means the Social Security and Medicare funds are expected to run out by 2047.[1] Therefore, the macroeconomic policy implications are important for stabilizing health-care spending and pension funds before it is too late. More details of different aspects of policy strategy are discussed in later chapters. In the context of the general economics of health care, Section 4.3 will focus on the positive and negative externalities of existing health-care markets in the United States.

4.3 Examples of the General Economics of the Health-Care Industry and Society

Since the health-care industry and its affiliated organizations contributed almost 18 percent of the $19 trillion GDP in 2019, the market system of health-care services is far from perfect. Given the enormous size of the industry, along with highly regulated and government-sponsored programs, such as Medicare, Medicaid, and the ACA, the US health-care industry is much more complicated than the health-care industry in any other industrialized countries in the world. For example, Canada has a single-payer system that is paid by the government to all privately held health-care providers with very high taxes. On the other hand, the health-care system in the United Kingdom is fully socialized and provided directly by the government via a high rate of tax on the labor force. In Japan, the health-care system is called universal health care and includes a mandate for everyone sponsored by both government and private institutions. The health-care system in Japan is similar to the current US system. The only difference is individuals in Japan pay a much higher premium rate. Given the complexity of US health-care economics, the following insights are worth explaining under the theory of positive and negative externalities discussed in Chapter 3.

4.3.1 Issues with Data Sharing and Information Asymmetry

Given the enormous health-care costs in the United States, there is a growing demand and expectation from both sides of the political aisle and health-care consumers of better quality services at a lower cost. In economics, it is called *measurable cost-effectiveness*. Given the nature of the complex health-care system and the strict privacy legislation in the United States, data sharing and data availability are the biggest challenges in health care. For

---

1   "The 2017 Long-Term Budget Outlook," Congressional Budget Office, March 30, 2017, https://www.cbo.gov/publication/52480.

example, information on the sources of difficult diseases, such as cancer, cardiovascular issues, and deadly virus attacks on infants and the elderly are not easy to collect in advance. Also, information regarding life expectancy at birth, infant mortality rates, occupational hazards, genetic diseases, substance abuse issues, and women's health are not necessarily accurate in most cases. The equipment and professional staff and doctors are not equally distributed and placed based on patients' needs. The level of information availability and the sharing process also vary from region to region in the country. These ongoing problems with information gaps and accuracy are called *information asymmetry*. The term was developed by George Akerlof in 1970 in the context of markets for lemons (used car market), where the information gap between buyers and sellers of used cars drives the price lower, leaving only lemons behind.

The concept of information asymmetry is very much applicable in the health-care industry because the beneficiaries of health-care services know more about their health conditions than the health insurance companies do. This information asymmetry causes a problem for health-care providers and insurance companies. Depending on the level of information asymmetry, the expected payoff by insurance companies can be determined after paying the insurance claims. The larger the information gap, the greater the degree of uncertainty insurance companies usually face in predicting their expected payoff (revenue from premiums minus cost of claims). Unlike fire insurance for houses and auto insurance for cars (which are easy to predict with a low probability of loss), information asymmetry in health-care insurance is much higher. The two most common consequences of information asymmetry are *adverse selection* and *moral hazard*. These two consequences are the key factors for financial collapse on Wall Street and the rise of insurance costs in the health-care industry. They are briefly explained with examples next.

Adverse Selection in the Health-Care Industry

Since health-care service recipients are more knowledgeable about their health conditions than the insurance companies are, the *adverse selection* of insured customers with more illness is highly likely. In that case, insurance companies may end up paying more medical claims than payments they receive from all premiums. If the premium is increased to cover the rising costs, it could cause more problems because customers with good health will forego the purchase of insurance. As a result, adverse selection may cause more financial drain for insurance companies. To avoid this problem, mandatory purchase of insurance by all individuals through legislation is a common practice in many states, especially in the auto insurance industry. A similar mandate was included in the ACA. But the individual mandate has caused huge controversy nationwide, leading the issue to be taken all the way to the Supreme Court.

Moral Hazard in the Health-Care Industry

Moral hazard is the negative outcome of a financial condition caused by the excessive adverse selections explained earlier. In the financial industry, including banks and holding companies, the rise in adverse selections from information asymmetry may cause financial collapse—an example of moral hazard. Similar events can happen in the health-care industry as a result of too many adverse selections. For example, mandatory health insurance coverage under the ACA brought more than 30 million Americans who did not have health insurance coverage before the law into the health-care industry in 2010. But after the law was enacted, many of the insured individuals changed their behavior by making frequent visits to doctors, which they would not do have done without ACA coverage. There is also a likelihood of these individuals getting more people ill because they are more careless with their health maintenance than they would have been without insurance. These changes in behavior raise the cost of health care significantly for both insurance companies and government agencies. The ACA's moral hazard problem was never intended. But it happened because of adverse selection, which was unavoidable under the mandatory purchase of insurance provision in the ACA. One way to deal with this problem is to increase the copayments and deductibles, which is common these days.

Similar incidents might happen as a result of an increase in the number of auto accidents following the passage of a mandatory law requiring people to use a seat belt while driving. Although the mandatory seat belt law did not intend to promote the behavior of careless driving, the implementation of the law changes the behavior of drivers, and they become less careful because of the perceived protection from wearing a seat belt. The increase in the number of car accidents in this case is an example of moral hazard.

4.3.2 Positive and Negative Externalities in Health-Care Services

In addition to information asymmetry and its consequences of adverse selection and moral hazard, explained in the previous section, there is the issue of distortion of resources discussed here by using the demand and supply behavior of health-care services. The market imperfection in the health-care industry causes some forms of externalities. Students may recall the concept of externalities and their examples discussed in Section 3.4 of Chapter 3; similar examples of externalities are found in health-care market. The sources of market imperfection in health care are the results of information asymmetry, cost inefficiency, service inefficiency, third-party payments, and government subsidies. Since health-care services do not meet the qualifications of a public good—nonexclusiveness and nonrivalry—there is a policy debate over whether the government should own and operate the entire health-care system like the governments of Canada and the United Kingdom do. The answer to this question can be understood better by explaining the external cost or gain incurred by the existing health-care system in the United States.

Figure 4.3 Internalization of Positive Externality

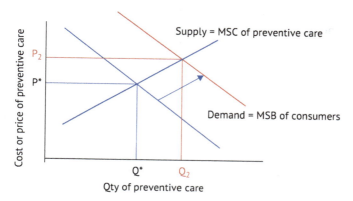

Positive Externalities of US Health-Care Programs

There are certain programs at the Centers for Disease Control and Prevention that are called programs for preventive diseases. Vaccination to prevent seasonal flu and other viruses is a good example of such programs creating positive externality. Private hospitals collaborating with health insurance companies do provide routine annual or semiannual check-ups for the prevention of unpredictable diseases, such as cancers, cardiovascular problems, and high blood pressure. Both of these programs are popular with health-care consumers in the sense that the MSB of these programs far exceeds the actual MC of these programs. Government-owned programs and routine checkups provided by private hospitals are very important for generating additional economic and social benefits to society to maintain high productivity with better health and happiness while minimizing the cost to individuals for preventive care. Government plays a significant role in internalizing this positive externality by expanding services through government funding. Figure 4.3 illustrates the internalization of positive externality.

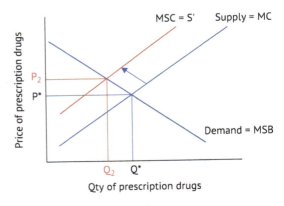

Figure 4.4 Internalization of Negative Externality

Negative Externalities in the Health-Care Industry

Similar to positive externality shown earlier, examples of negative externalities are also common in the health-care industry. For example, there may be many side effects of prescription drugs, which are supplied by a firm in the pharmaceutical industry with no competitors. Selling the medicine to individuals with no alternatives may lead to negative health hazards. To internalize this externality, government legislation on pharmaceutical firms and related biotechnology firms must shift the supply curve to the left where MSC = MSB. This process of internationalization of negative externality is illustrated in Figure 4.4.

From the previous two examples of the problem of externalities and the importance of government legislation to internalize the externality, we can see that the role of the government is vital despite the fact that health-care services are not pure public goods. Government legislation, subsidies, and direct coverage, such as Medicare and Medicaid, will certainly improve the MSB and safety of health-care recipients while keeping the cost down for maximizing health-care services to society as a whole. In addition, given the basic necessity of prescription drugs and surgical needs for fixed-income and low-income consumers, government intervention is necessary to the internalization of externality caused by overpricing or safety issues. This legislation is important, even if the majority of voters prefer market-based, health-care services.

4.4 The Health-Care Industry in the Context of Macroeconomics

As noted in previous sections of this chapter, the four components of AD function of the macroeconomic model are (1) consumption (C), (2) government expenditure (G), (3) investment expenditure (I), and (4) net export (EX-IM). The share of health-care expenditure at 18 percent of total GDP goes into all four components of GDP contribution. Therefore, the implications for the health-care policy of the government involve the working mechanism of the AD-AS model of macroeconomics. More detailed discussions on this topic can be found in Chapters 6 and 9. In this last section, readers need to be aware that the health-care policy implications of the government at both the federal and state levels are integral parts of the macroeconomic model and its application to the aging population in this century.

Chapter Summary

Section 4.1 has provided a distinction between the demand and supply behavior in microeconomics vis-à-vis the AD and AS model in macroeconomics. The demand and supply mechanism in the context of microeconomics was explained as an extension from its theoretical foundation introduced in Chapter 2. The example of price and quantity allocation of the housing market in the City of Boston was further explained in Section 4.1.1.

Section 4.1.2 introduced the macroeconomic model as AD = C + I + G + (EX-IM), where

1. C = consumption expenditure,
2. I = investment expenditure,
3. G = government expenditure,
4. EX = exports expenditure demanded by buyers abroad,
5. IM = Imports expenditure demanded by domestic buyers, and
6. AS = Gross Domestic Product (GDP) = $P_1Q_1 + P_2Q_2 + P_3Q_3 + ... + P_nQ_n = \Sigma P_iQ_i$,

where i = 1 to n, number of goods and services. The estimation technique of GDP and the average price level (GDPD) was explained clearly in this section. Students are strongly encouraged to practice the numerical examples of indexing the price level provided in this section and review the illustration depicted in Figure 4.1.

Section 4.2 focused on the economics of the health-care industry in the United States as one of the fastest-growing sectors in the economy and the growing importance that it be compatible with improvements in the status of human capital. The discussion in this section was mainly based on the key importance of improving the health economics of the labor force and children as an integral part of good health, education, and labor productivity for sustainable economic growth. The total expenditures for the health-care industry were estimated at more than 17 percent of GDP in 2016 (Center for Medicare and Medicaid Services). Table 4.1 summarizes the rise of health-care expenses in the US economy since 1960. The reasons for the continuous rise in health-care costs at a higher rate than any other service in the US economy are explained by the three key sources, among others, that follow:

1. The rise of an aging population
2. Improved health conditions and life expectancy at birth
3. Decrease in out-of-pocket, health-care expenses because of a third-party payment system

Figure 4.2 in this section illustrated the demand and supply behavior in the health-care industry and explained how the rising cost of health-care services is partly attributed to the third-party payment system.

Section 4.3 provided several examples of the general economics of the health-care industry that include its contribution of 18 percent to the US GDP. In addition to private-sector, health-care funding, the key role of the government in providing the funds for Medicare, Medicaid, and ACA was discussed in more detail. Similar, but a little different, health-care systems in Canada, Japan, and the United Kingdom were also compared to the system in the United States. The issues with data sharing and patents' privacy were also introduced in this section with the related problems of information asymmetry (the information gap between health-care providers, health insurance companies, and patients). The effect of information asymmetry in the form of adverse selection and moral hazard was explained with examples in the context of the US health-care system. The application of positive and negative externalities was also explained with examples in health-care economics. The process of the internalization of positive and negative externalities of health-care expenses was discussed in detail with graphical illustrations in Figures 4.3 and 4.4. Students are strongly recommended to review this part of the section with its important policy implications.

Section 4.4 briefly introduced the important consideration of health-care economics integrated into the macroeconomics framework so that health-care economics becomes an important part of the macroeconomic policy of the government at both the federal and state levels.

Application Activities

1. Based on the concept of the law of demand and law of supply in microeconomics, explain the difference between changes in quantity demanded (and/or changes in quantity supplied) and changes in demand and/or changes in supply. Give a real-world example with a graph and explain the graph. No specific data is required for drawing the graph.

2. Based on your explanation in Q1, draw a graph of demand and supply for consumer goods in the US market. From the concept of demand and supply behavior in the marketplace, show and explain the effect of Donald Trump's imposition of tariffs on imported consumer goods from Canada, China, Mexico, and European Union countries. Specifically, show and explain who would actually end up paying for the tariffs with the effects on changes in equilibrium price and quantities of imported goods and services in the US consumer market.

3. How do you distinguish between the concepts of demand and supply functions in microeconomics and the concepts of AD and AS functions in macroeconomics? Why are they different?

4. Briefly explain how the problem with information asymmetry can cause financial collapse on Wall Street and financial trouble in the health-care industry. Give examples for each of these cases.

5. From your own real-life experience, provide an example of adverse selection and its possible moral hazard. How can you avoid or at least minimize the problems of adverse selection and moral hazard?

6. Make a list of pros and cons of the individual mandate in the ACA.

Chapter 5

Economics of the Stock Market, Bond Market, and Loanable Fund Market

The Wall Street Approach to Microeconomics and Macroeconomics

Learning Objectives

As they read the chapter, students will learn the following:

▶ Understanding the Bond Market, Stock Market, Loanable Fund Market, and Currency Market

▶ Application of the Demand and Supply Model to Government Bond Markets and Corporate Bond Markets

▶ Application of the Demand and Supply Model to the Stock Market

▶ Application of the Demand and Supply Model to the LF Market and Currency Market

Introduction

With further extension of application and policy implications of demand and supply behavior discussed in Chapter 4 for healthcare industries, this chapter introduces the importance of understanding mechanism of demand and supply theories applied in the economics of the Wall Street. The wall street activities with economic models help learners understand the basic concept of investment portfolio and its trickledown economic impact on the main street. The areas of investments in the wall street are mainly bond market, stock market, future commodity market, mutual fund market, currency market and loanable fund market, among others. The bond market has two broad distinct markets: corporate bond market and Government Bond market. This chapter starts with introducing the concept of types of investment in these markets and their distinction in terms of risk and return on investment. The subsequent sections of the chapter are focused on applications of demand and supply principles in bond market, stock market, loanable fund market and currency exchange market. Students are expected to learn a very broad perspective of Wall Street Economics and the relevant tools to analyze how the investment market process works. The learning curve from chapter 1 to Chapter 5 is expected to provide the students the basic foundation to move forward to get hands on practice in subsequent chapters for both microeconomics textbook and macroeconomics textbook.

5.1 Understanding the Bond Market, Stock Market, Loanable Fund Market, and Currency Market

Before we get to the complete model of macroeconomics in Chapter 6, it will be useful to understand the concept of these financial markets separately as basic learning tools of Wall Street. The activities in the financial markets are closely related to the theories and applications in macroeconomics and their policy implications. First, we start with bond market activities.

5.1.1 Bond Market: Corporate Bonds and Government Bonds

Corporate bonds are issued by major corporations to finance their operations by borrowing from public investors. These bonds are debt securities issued with a guaranteed fixed interest rate (called yield to maturity) with a stated face value (FV) on the bond with its expiration at a future date. The law mandates that the issuer of the bond pay its principal and interest under the terms and conditions of the bonds issued by corporations. On the other hand, the US government also issues its own Treasury securities to public investors and foreign governments to borrow money to finance budget deficits and other government spending, which are not covered by the tax revenue collected from individuals, businesses, and corporations. US Treasury securities are composed of three broad categories based on their terms of maturity. The short-term securities issued with maturity from 90 days to less than a year are called Treasury bills (TBs). The medium-term securities issued with maturity between one year and ten years are called Treasury notes (TNs), and the long-term securities with maturity over ten years are called Treasury bonds. The volume of bond market transactions in both the corporate bonds and Treasury securities markets are much larger than the stock market and loanable fund (LF) market traded on weekdays on Wall Street in New York City. The total volume of bonds outstanding in the US market is about $40 trillion, and the volume of the global bond market is more than $100 trillion. On the other hand, the volume of total stocks outstanding in the US domestic market is less than $20 trillion, with the volume of the global market at about $64 trillion.[1] The daily trading volume in the secondary market of bonds in the United States is estimated to be on average of $700 billion, as compared to that of the stock market at $200 billion.

---

1   Motley Fool Staff, "5 Bond Market Facts You Need to Know," Motley Fool, last modified December 23, 2016, https://www.fool.com/knowledge-center/5-bond-market-facts-you-need-to-know.aspx.

Because of the uncertainty during economic crises caused by business cycle fluctuations (state of recession and inflation), the corporate bond market is not immune to the risks of investment. The common risk factors of financial investments are default risk, liquidity risk, tax implications, and inflation risks. Since corporations can suffer from bankruptcy during economic downturns, corporate bonds pass these four common risks on to bond investors, causing volatile patterns of price changes. On the other hand, government bonds issued by the US Treasury do not have those risks, except the inflation risks for long-term bonds. The reason for the risk-free bonds from the US Treasury is the zero-default risk, zero liquidity risk (bondholders can cash in their bonds any time before expiration), and very low taxes on interest earned. The general perception is that the US government can never default because it has no history of defaults and a long record of full employment and economic stability since 1945. This level of confidence makes investing in US government bonds a haven.

5.1.2 Stock Market

Unlike the bond market, the stock market is an equity market with no expiration or limit to terms of maturity. The stock market is created by initial public offerings (IPO) of common stocks by publicly limited corporations to raise funds for operating expansions. Investment bankers usually purchase IPO stocks from the issuing corporations and sell them to the secondary markets for trading. The shareholders of corporate stocks own a stake in the company's equity as a percentage of the share of the stock holdings. If the company's expected profit goes up, so does the price of the stocks—the rise in stock market price. On the other hand, when the corporations perform poorly with expected decline in profits, the stock price falls and the stockholders lose their equity value. The process of these changes in demand and stock prices are seen in the daily news on the Dow Jones Industrial Average Price Index of 30 blue-chip companies, S&P Index of Fortune 500 companies, and NASDAQ Composite Index. Since the total shares of stocks traded in these secondary stock markets are fixed in supply, the supply curve is vertical. The change in equilibrium price happens as a result of changes in the demand side only. The application of this stock market behavior is discussed in Section 5.2.

5.1.3 LF Market

The LF market refers to the capital investment market in which all financial intermediaries provide loans to business investors and individual consumers. They use the capital funds received from savers and other sources of surplus funds. These surplus capital funds are given as loans to firms and individual borrowers in exchange for the interest rates charged. There are many types of loans, such as small business loans, car loans, construction loans, mortgage loans, credit card loans, vacation loans, personal loans, and student education loans, and just to name a few. Therefore, the LF market has various segments with their own demand and supply behavior with varying rates of interest. These interest rates are actually the price of LFs. The difference in interest rates for each of the segments is attributed to the difference in risk, volume, terms of maturity, and credit ratings of borrowers. The application of this market is explained in Section 5.4.2.

5.1.4 Currency Market

Unlike the bond market, stock market, and LF market, the concept of the currency market is a bit different because this market is focused on demand and supply of domestic legal tender currency issued by a country's central bank against the currencies of other countries. For example, the trading of US goods and services against the goods and services of China creates demand and supply of both countries' currencies (renminbi against the US dollar) to exchange for exports and imports. The demand and supply for these currencies are influenced by the demand for capital investments in both countries. If Chinese investors want to invest in US bonds, stocks, and real estate, they will need to purchase US dollars against their own currency. Given the supply of US dollars, the increase in demand for the US dollar will raise the value of the dollar against the renminbi. This is called the increase in the exchange rate. Similarly, if American investors want to invest in China and buy more Chinese products, the demand for the renminbi will increase and so will its value against the US dollar. The same process of the exchange system in the currency market can be explained in the case of trade relations between the United States and other countries. In Section 5.4.2, a specific model structure of the currency market is discussed.

5.2 Application of the Demand and Supply Model in Government Bond Markets and Corporate Bond Markets

Since the market behavior of both corporate bonds and government bonds works in the same pattern, except the difference in risk factors, this section focuses on US Treasury securities only for simplicity. There are two kinds of bonds issued by the US Treasury: coupon bonds and discount bonds. The way coupon bonds work against the FV of a bond at a fixed rate of interest is a little complicated equation, and it is beyond the scope of this textbook. Therefore, the relationship between a bond and its yield for US Treasury securities with the maturity of a one-year discount bond (called TNs) is illustrated by Eqn (5.1). This example is a typical discount bond issued by the US Treasury, for it uses TBs and TNs to finance the government budget deficits.

$$\text{Yield} = [(FVb - Pb)/Pb] \times 100, \qquad\qquad \text{Eqn (5.1)}$$

where FV is the value stated on the face of a bond, like a promissory note with terms of maturity.

Pb is the discounted price of the bond initially issued at the auction desk.

Suppose a promissory note of one-year TN is sold to an investor at the auction desk conducted by the Federal Reserve Bank's Open Market Committee at a discounted price of $940 with a FV of $1,000. The yield to maturity is estimated next by plugging this information into the previous equation to get its yield.

$$\text{Yield} = (1{,}000 - 940)/940 \times 100 = 60/940 \times 100 = 6.38\% \text{ approximately}$$

If the same note were issued at a higher price, say at $960 against its FV of $1,000, then the estimated yield would be

Table 5.1: Bond Price and Yield US Treasury Bonds

Bonds, Rates, and Credit Markets Overview
5:05 p.m. EDT 06/08/18 Treasury

	Price Chg	Yield (%)
1-Month Bill*	−0/32	1.771
3-Month Bill*	0/32	1.933
6-Month Bill*	0/32	2.118
1-Year Note*	−0/32	2.289
2-Year Note*	−1/32	2.500
3-Year Note*	−2/32	2.636
5-Year Note*	−3/32	2.784
7-Year Note*	−5/32	2.897
10-Year Note*	−7/32	2.949
30-Year Bond*	−14/32	3.090
* at close		

See full daily closing prices

Source: "Bonds & Rates," Wall Street Journal, *last modified May 15, 2020, http://www.wsj.com/mdc/public/page/ mdc_bonds.html?mod=mdc_topnav_2_3050.*

Yield = (1,000-960)/960 × 100 = 40/960 × 100 = 4.17% approximately.

From the examples of two different prices of the same FV TN, it is clear that the bond price and yield always move in opposite directions. In other words, when the price of a TN increases, its yield decreases and vice versa. Table 5.1 shows typical Treasury bonds trading in the secondary market with an inverse relationship between bond prices and bond yields. The data in Columns 2 and 3 show that as the price falls with different terms of maturity, the prices of the bonds and their yields move in opposite directions.

It is also worth noting that the market volatility in the secondary market of bonds traded on the New York Stock Exchange and other exchange markets is only influenced by changes in demand for bonds with a fixed supply of total bonds outstanding. The supply of bond holdings typically stays unchanged in secondary market trading. It is the demand side that fluctuates based on changes in several external and internal factors of business and economic expectations. The changes in factors influence the demand to shift to the left (because of negative expectations) or to the right (because of positive expectations). For example, suppose a rise in inflation in the near future is in the economic forecast because of the state of a booming economy in 2018 with an unemployment rate at an 18-year low of 3.8 percent in May 2018. This rise in expected inflation would make the purchase of bonds less attractive to investors because the real value of interest rates after being adjusted will decline. This phenomenon is the real expected interest rate versus the nominal interest rate depicted in the following equation called the Fisher equation, developed by American economist Irving Fisher in the early twentieth century.

Real Expected Interest Rate = Nominal Interest Rate − Expected Inflation Rate   Eqn (5.2)

Eqn (5.2) clearly indicates that with a zero expected inflation rate, the real expected interest is the same as the nominal interest rate. Since the interest rate charged under the LF market is the nominal interest rate, changes in future or current inflation rates would change the value of the real interest rate, which is the real purchasing power of interest earned. Based on this insight from the Fisher equation, investors find it useful to consider expected inflation when figuring the real worth of interest when bonds are purchased at a fixed rate of return for future interest income. An example of this concept is demonstrated in the bond market model next. The resulting change in equilibrium price and quantity of bonds in the secondary market would be at a lower price and quantity, as illustrated in Figure 5.1. Because of a leftward shift of the demand curve for bonds, equilibrium has declined from $960 per $1,000 FV bond to $940. As a result of this downward shift of the demand curve, the bond yield will increase because bond price and yield always move in opposite directions (from Eqn (5.1) and Table 5.1).

Figure 5.1   Bond Market Behavior and Changes in Price and Yield

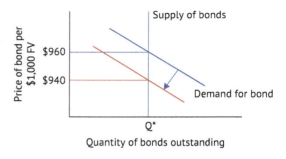

5.3 Application of the Demand and Supply Model to the Stock Market

As mentioned earlier, the stock market is an equity market without expiration or maturity, and stocks are actively traded in secondary markets on Wall Street in everyday financial transactions. Stock market fluctuations are closely watched by all investors, policy makers, economists, business leaders, and professionals in investment industries. This is because the rise and fall of the stock market price index has its economic and business implications on expectations of employment, inflation, corporate profits, GDP growth, and investment returns. As explained earlier, massive stock market crashes cause panic to all economic agents, resulting in increasing uncertainty about the health and stability of the economy. Historically, many of the economic recession cycles, including the Great Depression of the 1930s, were followed by stock market crashes. The application of the stock market to macroeconomics is developed by its connection between changes in macroeconomic variables, such as corporate earnings; corporate profits; unemployment rates; inflation rates; interest rates; expected inflation rates; inventories of durable goods, cars, and real estate; and factory orders. Changes in these important macroeconomic variables are considered the key indicators of economic forecast trends in the near future. Therefore, changes in these variables do have immediate effects on trading moods by shifting the

Figure 5.2 Stock Market Behavior and Changes in Stock Price

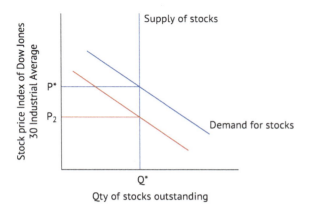

Qty of stocks outstanding

demand curve to the right (if changes are positive indicators) or to the left (if changes are negative indicators).

Using the same example of inflation expectations in the bond market earlier, suppose inflation is expected to increase at a higher rate than projected or targeted by the Federal Reserve policy-making body called the Federal Open Market Committee. This higher expected rate of inflation may have a negative effect on real income and consumer expectations about future economic trends. That means investors may perceive a downward trend in consumer spending habits on goods and services produced by corporations with their large stock holding in the stock market. If this downward expectation also causes expected loss of corporate profits and earnings, then the demand for stocks will decline. This decline in demand will shift the demand curve to the left and thus lower the equilibrium price of stocks and equity value of the stocks. This process of real-world stock market behavior is depicted in Figure 5.2.

In Figure 5.2, the hypothetical diagram for the stock exchanges in Dow Jones 30 Industrial Average Index, the equilibrium price before changes in profit expectations caused by a rise in inflation expectations is shown at the combination of P* and Q*. As explained earlier, the supply curve here is vertical because the total stock of common shares outstanding in secondary market is unchanged. It is like an eBay market transaction of used products traded in the market. The downward shift of the demand curve to the left lowered the equilibrium price to P_2. Students may use this model structure by looking at the changes in the other macroeconomic variables, such as consumer confidence, interest rates, and trade wars based on changes in government policies on tariffs on imported goods to figure out which direction the demand curve will shift and thus to easily determine the changes in equilibrium prices. The stock market volatility on both the Dow Jones and S&P 500 indexes in the first half of 2018 was primarily attributed to the imposition of high tariffs by the Trump administration on imported goods from China and European Union countries.

5.4 Application of the Demand and Supply Model to the LF Market and Currency Market

Unlike the vertical supply curve in the bond and stock markets explained in Sections 5.2 and 5.3, the supply curve in the LF market is a standard upward-sloping curve because the quantity supplied in the former markets responds directly to changes in price. More specifically, if the interest rate (the price of the LF) increases the quantity supplied of the LF will also increase and vice versa, *ceteris paribus.* The same principle of supply function applies to the currency market, as an increase in the exchange rate will increase the quantity of currency supplied and vice versa, *ceteris paribus.* On the demand side, the shape of the demand curve is downward sloping because of the inverse relationship between prices and quantity demanded in both markets, *ceteris paribus.* Real-world applications of these two markets are illustrated and explained in the following subsections.

Figure 5.3 Interest Rate and Quantity of the LF Market

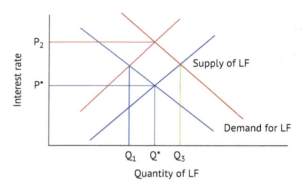

5.4.1 Demand and Supply Interaction in the LF Market

Based on the principle of the downward-sloping demand curve and the upward-sloping supply curve, the equilibrium interest rate and quantity demanded equal to the quantity supplied is illustrated in Figure 5.3. This hypothetical model is an abstract form of a theoretical example representing the overall picture of the complex nature of LF markets. In reality, several financial products and assets, such as business loans, personal loans, credit card loans, car loans, and mortgage loans, to mention just a few, are traded between financial institutions and borrowers. However, the way the segmented LF market works is no different than the illustration shown in Figure 5.3.

Figure 5.3 indicates the interaction between the demand and supply curves of the LF market with the changes in external factors, such as the expected inflation rate. The demand curve represents the borrowers and the supply curve represents the lenders with the initial equilibrium interest rate and quantity at the point of intersection with P* and Q* combination. An increase in expected inflation, the Fisher equation Eqn (5.2) explained earlier in Section 5.2, predicts that real interest is expected to decline. The decrease in real interest is expected to negatively affect the expected real return from lending so that the supply curve will shift to the left. On the other hand, a decrease in the real interest rate will attract more borrowers to the LF market, which will then shift the demand curve to the right. This process continuously shifts demand and supply curves in opposite directions, as shown by the curves in the figure. It also indicates that because of the shift of these two curves in opposite directions, the new equilibrium interest rate will definitely increase. However, it is not clear whether the quantity in the LF market will increase or decrease or remain unchanged depending on the net effect of the movement of the demand and supply curves. If the demand curve shifts at a higher magnitude than that of the supply curve, then the quantity of LFs will increase and vice versa. If the net effect is zero, meaning if the magnitude of shifts cancels each other out, then the quantity will remain unchanged. With this analysis, students may practice the same process by using other related macroeconomic variables to shift the curve(s) in the appropriate

Figure 5.4 Currency Exchange Market Equilibrium

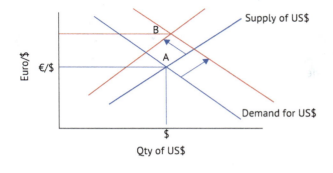

Qty of US$

direction. The practice will help determine the changes in equilibrium interest and the quantity of the LF.

5.4.2. Application of the Demand and Supply Model to the Currency Market

As explained in Section 5.1.4, the currency of any country is just like any other commodity to exchange for the currency of another country to trade goods and services between them. The currency exchange rate is also determined by the free flow of the demand and supply mechanism in the foreign exchange currency market traded through international banking divisions of major banks in every country. For example, the value of the US dollar against the euro or British pound, or the Japanese yen, or the Chinese renminbi is determined by changes in the demand and supply shifting around the clock. This process of exchange-rate determination is administered by foreign exchange market specialists called foreign exchange dealers who operate in a computer-generated demand and supply software. The way the transactions are carried out is exactly the same technique used by dealers to determine stock prices in demand and supply operations for the NASDAQ Composite Index for high technology company stocks. Figure 5.4 illustrates an example of the currency exchange market between the US dollar and the euro under the free market system of demand and supply.

In Figure 5.4, the euro/per US dollar is the price of the dollar against the euro. The equilibrium exchange rate at point A, the point of intersection between demand for and supply of the US dollar against the euro, determines the currency exchange of the euro per unit of the US dollar. Since the demand and supply of the currency market are constantly changing because of trading activities and capital inflow and outflow by investors in the global market, the equilibrium exchange rate also changes every minute. As indicated by shifting the demand curve to the right and the supply curve to the left for the US currency market against the euro, the new equilibrium is arrived at by point B. Capital inflow by foreign investors to the US economy would shift the demand for the US dollar to the right. Keeping everything else constant, the exchange rate of the US dollar will increase. On the other hand, if foreign investors and domestic corporations take the US dollar out of the US market and invest in European Union countries, then the demand for the euro will increase and the exchange rate of the US dollar will decrease. Changes in currency exchange rates have several trade and policy implications for macroeconomic stability and trade balance. More detail on the exchange rate controlled by legislation from the government versus flexible exchange rates will be discussed in Chapters 14 and 15. At this point, it is important to know that increases in the exchange rate of the US dollar make exported US-produced goods and services more expensive for foreigners to import. At the same time, imports of goods and services from other countries to the US become cheaper. As a result, net export causes trade imbalances for the US against other countries under consideration. The opposite happens to other trading partners. The direction of the trade balance reverses when the currency exchange rate of the US dollar decreases against its trading partners. Again, the external factors that affect the fluctuation of exchange fluctuation will be discussed in more detail in Chapters 14 and 15. In Chapter 6, we will begin with the discussion of the complete Keynesian macroeconomics model developed in the 1930s.

Chapter Summary

Section 5.1 introduced the conceptual differences in four types of financial markets. They are the bond market, stock market (also called equity market), loanable fund market, and currency market. The bond market is debt security with its expiration date in the future and a promised return of fixed interest rate payments until maturity. Bonds are issued by both corporations in the private sector and in the government sector. For the US government, the general term for government securities is Treasury securities, which are of three types based on the length of maturity. Short-term securities are called Treasury bills. Medium-term securities are called Treasury notes, and long-term securities are called Treasury bonds. The stock market is the equity market with no expiration issued by corporations to the investors for a stake in corporations' equity value. The equilibrium price of stocks fluctuates based on changes in the demand for stocks with a given supply of stocks in the secondary market. Changes in demand are influenced by several factors that directly or indirectly affect the shareholders' equity value. Both bonds (corporate and government) and stocks are traded daily on Wall Street in New York City. The interest rate differentials among different bonds are primarily attributed to the degree of risk factors, such as default risk, liquidity risk, tax consideration, and inflation risk. Details about those risks and the reason for very low risks for government bonds and thus very low yield were discussed with examples.

The loanable fund market is the market for financial lending and borrowing between banks and borrowers. The price of a loanable fund is the interest rate, which is determined by demand and supply interactions in the financial market. The currency market is the market for exchange rate determination of domestic currency against the foreign currency it trades with. The exchange rate is determined by the demand and supply interactions between the two countries' currencies.

Section 5.2 explained the theoretical foundation of the bond market for both corporate bonds and US Treasury bonds with the example of how the bond price and its interest rate (called the yield) are determined in the bond market transaction. A specific example of the inverse relationship between bond price and yield was given in Eqn (5.1) and illustrated the changes in price and yield in Figure 5.1.

Section 5.3 explained the theories and applications of stock market behavior with a real-world example of price determination on the Dow Jones Industrial Average Index traded daily on Wall Street. The changes in the equilibrium price index of the stock market composite index is influenced by the shift of the demand curve with the given total supply of common stocks outstanding. The process of changes in the equilibrium price by external and internal factors was explained with examples and illustrated in Figure 5.3.

Sections 5.4.1 and 5.4.2 explained the demand and supply behavior of the loanable fund market and currency market, respectively. In the loanable fund market, the interaction between demand and supply determines the equilibrium interest rates. The changes in the equilibrium interest rate are influenced by other economic and financial factors that relate to the demand and supply of loanable funds. Demand for loanable funds represents the borrowers and the supply for loanable funds represents the lenders. Detailed explanations of the changes in equilibrium interest and quantity were given in this section and illustrated in Figure 5.3. Currency market behavior was also introduced in this section and how the exchange rates fluctuate with domestic currency value against foreign currencies was explained. The changes in the equilibrium exchange rate because of the changes in demand and supply of currency were illustrated in Figure 5.4. It is recommended that students make their own examples of currency market behavior and sources of constant change by identifying the relevant economic variables.

Application Activities

Q1. Briefly describe the difference in bond markets and stock markets in the context of investment and return. Why is corporate bond investment usually riskier than investing in US Treasury securities?

Q2. During a recession, the yield for corporate bonds tends to increase, and the yield for US Treasury securities tends to decrease. Briefly explain why. Give a real-world example as part of your reasoning.

Q3. Estimate the rate of return (yield to maturity) if you as an investor purchase a one-year US Treasury note at the market price of $955 with a face value of $1,000. Make sure you show your work in when making the numerical estimation by using the yield equation.

Q4. Draw a hypothetical demand and supply curve for S&P 500 stocks and explain briefly the effects of unexpected inflation caused by a sudden rise in energy prices.

Q5. Draw a demand and supply curve of the loanable fund market and explain the effects on equilibrium prices and quantities of loanable funds in response to the same situation described in Q4.

Q6. Suppose the increase in tariffs on goods and services from China and European Union countries caused a capital flight of currency from the United States. Show the effects on US exports, imports, and trade balances from this capital flight by foreign investors.

Chapter 6

Theories of Price Elasticity of the Demand and Supply Models and Their Applications in Analyzing Corporate and Government Revenue

Learning Objectives

As they read the chapter, students will learn the following:

► Concept of Price Elasticity of Demand and Types of Price Elasticity Demand

► Application of Price Elasticity of Demand in Measuring Sales Revenue

► Determinants Affecting the Values of Price Elasticity Demand

► Price Elasticity of Supply and Its Applications

► Price Elasticity of Demand/Supply and Implications for Government Tax and Tariff Policy

Introduction

As a continuation of theories of demand and supply models and their applications in business and economics, this chapter focuses on analyzing the changes in behavior of consumers and producers in response to changes in prices, income and other related variables in the market transactions. The terminologies used for understanding the degree of sensitivity of consumers and producers are price elasticity of demand, price elasticity of supply, cross-price elasticity of demand and supply for substitute and complimentary products and services, and income elasticity of demand function. This chapter involves the use of simple concepts of algebra, calculus and geometry for graphs through estimation of elasticity values

71

and illustrate the effect of changes in prices and income on the behavior of consumers and producers. The chapter begins with basic concepts and relevant equations for estimating price elasticity of demand and supply and their applications on consumers benefit and loss; sales revenue of producers and their impact on profit and loss. The external factors that affect the values of price elasticity are explained in detail. The last section of the chapter provides the policy implications for the role of the government to understand the concept of price elasticity to evaluate the ramifications on changing and imposing taxes and tariffs on various goods and services.

6.1 Concept of Price Elasticity of Demand and Types of Price Elasticity Demand

From the theories of demand and supply functions and their applications in previous chapters, the students have learned that the slope of a demand curve is usually downward, implying that changes in price per unit and demanded for goods and services move in opposite directions (inversely related), *ceteris paribus* (assuming all other factors remain the same). This section of this chapter introduces the elasticity of the demand curve, explaining the different possible shapes of the demand curve depending on the degree of responsiveness by consumers in response to changes in prices. Depending on the degree of responsiveness, the steepness of the demand curve will vary widely from vertical to downward sloping to even a horizontal shape of the demand curve. These different shapes of the demand curve reflect the degree of necessity of goods services available for purchase by consumers as prices change, given that their income and other factors are unchanged at the time of consideration. Understanding this important part of consumer reaction to price changes has several implications for government policies on taxes, legislation on pricing, quality and safety controls, marketing strategies for corporate product pricing, health-care services, medicine and drug policies, transportation fees, and many other related products and services.

For example, if the government increases the cigarette tax by 20 percent to reduce smoking habits, the measure of price elasticity of the demand curve for those targeted smokers would help us understand how much smoking would be reduced by imposing a 20 percent tax on each pack of cigarettes. If the demand curve for cigarette smoking is relatively steep, then the reaction to the imposition of the 20 percent tax will have less impact on reducing the smoking habit than with a relatively flatter demand curve for cigarette smoking. In other words, with a downward-sloping demand curve for smoking cigarettes, the level of imposition from new taxes will reduce the quantity of cigarette smoking. However, the amount of reduction in smoking will depend on the degree of responsiveness to reflect the exact shape of the demand curve. The technical definition of price elasticity is given in Eqn (6.1).

6.1.1 Price Elasticity of Demand
The price elasticity of demand is defined by

E_d = (% change in quantity demanded)/(% change in price per unit), algebraically expressed as

$$Ed = (\Delta Q/Q)/(\Delta P/P), \qquad\qquad \text{Eqn (6.1)}$$

where Δ is the change (delta) divided by original quantity and prices per unit.

To be more precise, suppose that the tax increase on cigarettes per pack has raised the market equilibrium price of cigarettes from $5 to $6 per pack.[1] Also, assume that because of the increase in price is affected by the tax increase, the quantity of cigarettes demanded by a consumer has decreased from eight packs to seven packs per week. Plugging this information into Eqn (6.1), the numerical value of elasticity is estimated next.

$$Ed = [(7 - 8)/8)]/[(6 - 5)/5] = (-1/8)/(1/5) = -0.125/0.2 = -0.625 \qquad \text{Eqn (6.2)}$$

The numerical value of elasticity measured in Eqn (6.2) indicates that a 20 percent increase in price per pack of cigarettes from taxes has reduced cigarette consumption by 12.5 percent, resulting in the price elasticity of demand for cigarettes at -0.625. In other words, an increase in taxes by $1 per pack of cigarettes would result in the reduction of cigarette smoking by 0.625 of each increase of $1. This implies that Ed is less than 1. Ed = 0.625 < 1 is called *inelastic demand*.

It is important to note here that the negative sign in this value of elasticity is due to the downward-sloping demand curve as part of the negative slope. The negative sign has no bearing on the elasticity itself. Students can consider the value of elasticity as absolute by ignoring the negative sign.

Now, if a change in the quantity of cigarette consumption decreases from 8 to 6 instead, given the same increase in price from $5 to $6, the elasticity measured in Eqn (6.2) would change to

$$Ed = [(6 - 8)/8)]/[(6 - 5)/5] = (-2/8)/(1/5) = -0.25/0.2 = -1.25. \qquad \text{Eqn (6.3)}$$

Eqn (6.3) indicates that an increase in taxes by $1 per pack would result in the reduction of cigarette smoking by 25 percent of each increase of $1 (20 percent). In other words, Ed of 1.25 > 1 is called *elastic demand*.

Taking another example, if a change in the quantity of cigarette consumption reduced from 8 to 6.4 with the same increase of $1 in tax, Eqn (6.3) would change as shown in Eqn (6.4).

$$Ed = [(6.4 - 8)/8)]/[(6 - 5)/5] = (-1.6/8)/(1/5) = -0.2/0.2 = -1 \qquad \text{Eqn (6.4)}$$

Eqn (6.4) indicates an increase in taxes by $1 per pack, resulting in a reduction in cigarette smoking by the same 20 percent, for an increase of $1—a case of unit elasticity. So, Ed = −1 is called *unit elasticity of demand*.

Similarly, if there is no change in quantity demanded on the numerator in the previous equation, then the elasticity of demand Ed = 0 is a case of zero elasticity.

---

1   The price of a cigarette does not necessarily increase by the same proportion of tax increase because of the downward-sloping demand curve of the cigarette market to intersect with the upward-sloping supply curve.

$$Ed = (0\% \text{ change in quantity})/(\% \text{ change price}) = 0 \qquad \text{Eqn (6.5)}$$

The other extreme situation would be a 0 percent change in price in the denominator divided by any change in quantity in the numerator. This measure is called *infinite elasticity*.

$$Ed = (\% \text{ change in qty demanded})/(\text{zero \% change in price}) = \infty \qquad \text{Eqn (6.6)}$$

6.1.2 Types of Price Elasticity of Demand

The five different types of elasticity shown earlier in Eqns (6.2) to (6.6), based on the general elasticity in Eqn (6.1), are summarized next, followed by a graphical illustration.

Ed < 1 called inelastic demand curve

Ed > 1 called Ed curve

Ed = 1 called unit Ed curve

Ed = 0, called zero Ed curve or perfectly inelastic demand curve

Ed = ∞ called infinite Ed curve or perfectly Ed curve

6.1.3 Graphical Representation of Types of Price Elasticity of Demand

The graphical representation of five different possible types of price elasticity of demand explained in Section 6.1.2 is illustrated in Figure 6.1 from panel (a) to panel (e).

In Figure 6.1, the five possible shapes of the demand curve indicate different types of elasticities visualizing of each of the demand curves. Students may observe that the relative steepness of the demand curve indicates a specific type of elasticity that was explained numerically in the previous section. The steeper the demand curve, the lower the value of elasticity and, conversely, the flatter the demand curve the higher the value of the elasticity. For example, panel (a) indicates a very steep demand curve with Ed less than one and its extreme scenario is in panel (d) with the vertical demand curve and the perfectly inelastic demand curve with Ed = zero. Panel (b), on the other hand, has a flatter demand curve with Ed>1 and its extreme scenario is shown in panel (e) as a perfectly Ed curve with Ed = infinity (∞). Panel (c) is the exceptional case with its elasticity is equal to 1 at all points of the Demand curve called a rectangular hyperbola. The economic interpretation of these five different shapes of the demand curve with five different values of elasticities is summarized next.

Ed curve reflects the degree of responsiveness by consumers to changes as more than proportionate changes in price. For example, panel (b) in Figure 6.1. implies that in response to a 20 percent increase of price, consumers intend to purchase more than 20 percent of the same goods and services. Panel (a) implies that in response to a 20 percent increase, consumers intend to purchase less than 20 percent of the quantity of the same goods. Panel (c) with its unit elasticity implies that a 20 percent change in price (increase or decrease), consumers will intend to purchase more (less) at the same proportion of price changes. Panel (d) implies that with zero elasticity, the consumers have no choice but to buy a minimum

Figure 6.1   The Shapes of the Demand Curve with Different Price Elasticities

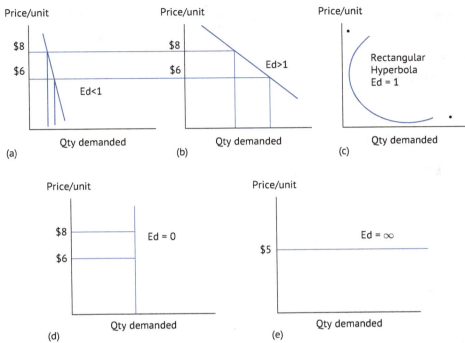

quantity of necessary goods and services regardless of the price changes. Panel (e) is just opposite panel (d), which implies that at a given fixed price, consumers may feel free to purchase as much as they'd like.

In understanding the degree of sensitivity of price changes to affect the demanded for goods and services, it is clear that basic food items, clothing, shelter, medicine, utilities and transportation, energy sources, and related services have low price elasticity of demand at less than one. The goods and services that are considered luxury items only purchased by high-income consumers will fall under the category of Ed market. All other goods and services may fall in between, depending on the actual nature and degree of necessity and price structure of the products. For example, high-end fashion products, jewelry, luxury cars, furniture, and houses have a high elasticity of demand. Some real-world examples of goods and services that fall under the categories of different demand elasticity are listed in Table 6.1.

Table 6.1: List of Some Estimated Price Elasticities of Demand[2]

Inelastic Ed<1 (approx.)	Elastic Ed>1 (approx.)	Unit Elastic Ed = 1 (approx.)
Cigarette 0.75	Transportation 2.55	College education 1.15
Gasoline 0.25	Furniture 1.75	Movies in theater 0.95
Heating oil and electricity 0.9	Seafood 2.35	Used motor vehicle. 1.1
Newspaper by institution 0.1	Restaurants meal 2.45	New tires. 1.0
Newspaper by individual 0.8	Plane tickets 2.35	Household appliances 1.2
Medical and prescription drugs 0.5	Motor vehicles (new) 1.30	
Basic food and beverages 0.6	Sailboats 2.55	

In the next section, another explanation is made with a different scenario of a demand curve, where price elasticity of demand is different at different segments of the same demand curve.

6.1.4 Shape of a Demand Curve with Different Elasticities

The price elasticity of demand calculation explained in Section 6.1.3 is based on the basic Eqn (6.1) found at the outset of this chapter. However, depending on the different shapes of the straight-line, downward-sloping demand curve (a linear demand) with a constant slope, it is possible to see different values of elasticity at different points on the same demand curve. To calculate elasticity at different points, it is important to introduce two more concepts of elasticity measures called point elasticity and arc elasticity.

Point elasticity is the elasticity at a single point on a demand curve, as denoted by the following equation.

$$Ed = (\% \text{ change in quantity demanded})/(\% \text{ change in price})$$

$$= (\Delta Q/Q)/(\Delta P/P) = (\Delta Q/\Delta P) \times (P/Q) \qquad \text{Eqn (6.7)}$$

In Eqn (6.7), $(\Delta Q/\Delta P)$ is the reciprocal of the slope of the demand curve and P/Q is the ratio of price to corresponding quantity demanded at a single point on the demand curve. Now, Eqn (6.7) can be rewritten as Eqn (6.8).

$$Ed = (\Delta Q/\Delta P) \times (P/Q) = 1/\text{slope} \times P/Q = 1/(\Delta P/\Delta Q) \times (P/Q), \qquad \text{Eqn (6.8)}$$

where $1/(\Delta P/\Delta Q)$ is a constant value of slope for a straight-line demand curve.

Arc elasticity, on the other hand, is the elasticity measured between two different points on the same demand curve by using two alternative methods of calculation, as given next:

---

2 *Source: The data on elasticities of theses selected goods and services were compiled from various sources of studies published by different publications. Since there is no single source data for all items listed earlier, the compilation of data is approximately the average values estimated from different sources. The actual data also vary from one location to another and from region to region in the continental United States.*

Ed = (ΔQ/Q)/(ΔP/P) by using the original price and quantity as denominators.

Or alternatively,

Ed = [ΔQ/(Q1 + Q2)/2] ÷ [ΔP/(P1 + P2)/2] by using the midpoint average of both price and quantity changes in denominators.

Both methods of elasticity measures have their own advantages. Using the original price and quantity method is close to the same as the point elasticity method. However, the disadvantage is getting different values of elasticity depending on which direction the changes in price and quantity demanded move on the same demand curve. A specific example will illustrate that difference. The midpoint average method, on the other hand, provides more accurate elasticity when measured between two points and thus helps to minimize the bias toward the original price and quantity.

To illustrate the difference between point elasticity and arc elasticity measures, Figure 6.2 represents a hypothetical demand curve for a coffee market, say SB coffee.

Figure 6.2 Demand Elasticity of the SB Coffee Market

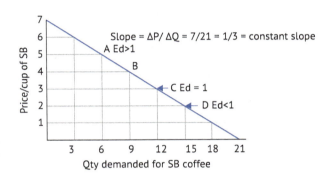

From the previous hypothetical demand curve for SB coffee, point elasticity at different points on the demand curve is measured as follows:

At point A, Ed = 1/slope × P/Q = 1/(1/3) × (5/6) = 15/6 = 2.5>1 = Elastic

At point C, Ed = 1/slope × P/Q = 1/(1/3) × (3/9) = 9/9 = 1 = Unit elastic

At point D, Ed = 1/slope × P/Q = 1/(1/3) × 2/15 = 6/15 = 0.12<1 = Inelastic

The point elasticities measured from the previous demand curve for coffee indicate that at different points on the demand curve, the elasticities vary, with the elasticities to the left of C greater than one and the elasticities on points to the right of point C less than one, and at point C, Ed = 1. This scenario implies that despite the constant slope of a downward-sloping demand curve, depending on the price/unit (high or low), the degree of responsiveness from coffee drinkers may vary, as reflected in the different values of the elasticities at different points on the same demand curve.

The arc elasticities, a similar concept to the midpoint average method of measuring elasticity, of the previous demand curve are calculated next:

Ed from point A to B = Ed = [ΔQ/(Q1 + Q2)/2] ÷ [ΔP/(P1 + P2)/2]

= [(6 − 9)/(6 + 9)/2] ÷ [(5 − 4)/(5 + 4)/2] = 3/7.5 ÷ 1/4.5 = 3/7.5 × 4.5 = 1.8.

Students are encouraged to calculate elasticities at other points on the previous demand curve.

6.2 Application of Price Elasticity of Demand in Measuring Sales Revenue

Understanding the concept of elasticities is important for analyzing the effect of price changes on firms' sales revenue. Although the law of the downward-sloping demand curve indicates that lowering the price will increase the goods and services sold, the values of own price elasticity of demand will determine whether the total sales revenue will increase or decrease or stay the same when prices decrease or increase. This important relationship between sales revenue and own price elasticity is explained under different scenarios in the examples in the following subsections.

6.2.1 Sales Revenue and Price Changes

Total Revenue (TR) = P × Q, where P = Price per Unit and Q = Quantity Sold

Now, with a downward-sloping demand curve, as shown in Figure 6.2, a decrease in price will increase the quantity sold. So the change in sales revenue is expressed as

ΔTR = ΔP × ΔQ.

Since the ΔP and ΔQ move in opposite directions, the net effect of ΔTR will be determined by the value of the price elasticity of demand. Knowing the price elasticity of demand, a firm can make a clear prediction about changes in its sale revenue when the price is increased or decreased. Since the primary goal of firms is to maximize sales revenue to maximize profits (Profit = TR − Total Cost), using the price elasticity of demand is an important part of the pricing strategy for every business and government tax policy and regulation. It is important to keep in mind that maximizing profit is not the same as maximizing revenue. Profit maximization theories and applications will be covered in Chapters 9 through 11. The focus here is to analyze the changes in sales revenue due to changes in prices for given price elasticities of demand.

Using the price elasticity of demand, the effect of changes in prices on changes in sales revenue will depend on whether the elasticity is greater than one, less than one, or equal to one, as outlined in Table 6.2.

Table 6.2: Elasticity, Price, and Sales Revenue

Elasticity Value	Price Change	Change in TR
Ed<1	Increase Price	Increase TR
Ed>1	Increase Price	Decrease TR
ED<1	Decrease Price	Decrease TR
Ed>1	Decrease Price	Increase TR
Ed = 1	Increase or Decrease Price	No Change in TR

Table 6.2 indicates Ed and its influence to determine the outcome of TR because of changes in prices with many implications for revenue-maximizing strategies, government policies on price control and pricing legislations, and market competition. It is also clear from the chart that a firm's TR is maximized when Ed = 1. This is because at Ed<1, a price increase will increase revenue. And with Ed>1, a price decrease will increase revenue. Therefore, TR must be maximum when Ed = 1. Students are encouraged to check Figure 6.2 in the SB coffee example that at Price = $3/cup of coffee, the TR is the maximum at 36 because Ed at point C is = 1.

6.2.2. Other Concepts of Elasticity than Own Price Elasticity of Demand

In addition to the own price elasticity of demand explained in theories and applications in Section 6.1, there are two other important concepts of elasticities of demand called *cross-price elasticity of demand* and *income elasticity of demand*. Cross-price elasticity of demand represents consumers' behavior in response to changes in relative prices of substitutes or complementary goods and services. Income elasticity of demand represents the changes in quantity demanded in response to changes in income. They are discussed in detail in this section.

Cross-price elasticity of demand: The cross-price elasticity of demand, say Edxy, represents changes in quantity demanded by consumers in response to changes in the prices of other goods and services, which are either substitutes or complementary. The equation for this concept of elasticity of demand is stated next.

$$\mathbf{Ed}_{xy} = (\% \textit{ change in quantity demanded for x}) \div (\textit{change in price of y})$$

The equation indicates that changes in quantity demanded for good x because of changes in the price of good y provides the degree of responsiveness by consumers in making decisions in the quantity to buy. For example, SB and DD coffee are close substitutes in the coffee market in general. Any changes in the price of SB coffee tend to change the quantity demanded by DD coffee drinkers. If the price of SB coffee increases, obviously some SB coffee drinkers are expected to switch to DD coffee given the other factors of demand, such as income, tastes, and preferences. If the price of SB coffee decreases, then the opposite reaction is expected by some DD coffee drinkers. Other common examples of the substitutability nature of cross-price elasticity of demand are mobile phone services and equipment, athletic gear, sports gear, cable services, motor vehicles, and so many food and drink products. Depending on the value of elasticity, the degree of substitutability is determined between x and y.

If Edxy is >0, that means they are substitutes. The higher the positive value, the closer the degree of substitutability, and vice versa. It implies that a small change in price makes consumers switch to substitute goods promptly or vice versa. In this context, the antitrust legislation of the government intends to prevent mergers and acquisitions of many big corporations that produce similar goods and services. If the value of Edxy is high with positive value, then the merger and acquisition may not have that much power to raise prices on consumers after the market share of the merged firms increases. If Edxy = 0, then the goods x and y are not substitutes at all.

On the other hand, if Edxy<0, the goods x and y are complementary goods, such as coffee and cream, shoes and socks, plus other sports gear, winter gear for skiers and mountaineers, cooking ingredients, and many other household appliances. Again, the higher the negative value of Edxy, the higher the degree of complementarity between goods x and y, and vice versa. It implies that a little change in price will make consumers buy more of both goods, and vice versa. Again, if Edxy is zero, they are neither substitute nor complementary.

Income elasticity of demand: Income elasticity of demand, say **Edi**, represents the changes in quantity demanded by consumers for goods and services in response to changes in their income levels. The mathematical expression for this concept of elasticity is stated next.

Edi = *% change in quantity demanded ÷ change in income*

Unlike the cross-price elasticity of demand, the behavior of Edi is a little bit more complicated in the sense that change in income also changes the preference pattern of consumers, whether a typical consumer tends to buy the same goods or something different. Depending on that preference pattern, the nature of a good is classified as a *normal good*, *inferior good*, or *luxury good*. For a normal good, the value of Edi is expected to be greater than zero but less than one. For an inferior good, Edi is less than zero (a negative value), and for a luxury good, Edi is supposed to be greater than 1. The economic interpretations with real-world examples are given next.

For a normal good, the value range is between 0<Edi<1, a positive value but less than one, which means when income rises (or falls), the quantity demands for normal goods and services do increase (or decrease) as well but not at the same proportion of income change. In other words, if income increases by 20 percent, the change in quantity demand for normal goods and services is expected to increase by less than 20 percent but more than 0 percent. The real-world examples are new cars, houses, condos, restaurant meals, travel, clothes, basic food items, and related consumer goods purchased daily.

For an inferior good, the value is Edi < 0, a negative value, which means as income rises (or falls), the quantity demand for inferior goods and services does actually decrease (or increase) at any given level of the price of those goods and services. In other words, if income rises by 20 percent, the demand for that inferior good will decline more than 20 percent of its current level of quantity consumed by a typical consumer, and vice versa. The real-world examples are used cars, less preferred food items considered to be relatively unhealthy or lower quality, low-cost housing and lodging, and used clothes. The point is that the relative nature of the products consumers buy widely varies among individuals as income changes given their tastes and preference patterns. The classic example of this kind of income elasticity for inferior goods goes back to the Irish Famine in the 1840s when the demand for potatos significantly increased at the outbreak of the famine, causing massive migration to the United States.

For a luxury good, the value is Edi>1, which means as income rises (or falls), the quantity demand for luxury goods is expected to increase (or decrease) greater than proportionate increases in income at any given price level. For example, if income increases by 20 percent, the demand for luxury goods tends to increase by more than 20 percent, and vice versa. Some real-world examples of luxury goods are luxury motor vehicles, high-end restaurant meals, luxury boats, private jets, high-end houses and summer houses, personal services and spas, high-end brands of fashion clothes and designer products, and other related expensive items for conspicuous consumption.

Another application of the three concepts of elasticity of demand explained earlier is relevant to the marketing and product price strategy of diversification by firms given in different states of the economy. As discussed in Section 6.2.1 concerning the relationship between Ed and TR, the concept of cross-price and income elasticity can be applied to maximize the sales revenue of a firm by understanding these concepts of elasticity of demand and, therefore, making the appropriate adjustment of switching their resources between different high-end and low-end products depending on changes in income and the state of the economy. For example, during an economic boom, firms can move more resources to luxury goods and relatively high-end products to maximize their revenue by taking advantage of the increase in income for a majority of consumers. The opposite strategy can be undertaken during an economic recession. Another related elasticity concept to use by business firms is called price elasticity of supply. The theories and applications of price elasticity of supply are explained in Section 6.4 of this chapter.

6.3 Determinants Affecting the Values of Price Elasticity of Demand

The factors affecting the actual value of price elasticity of demand are not only the own price of goods and services but also other important variables of the demand function. Those variables are relative prices of substitute goods and complementary goods, income levels and percentage of income spent on particular goods, nature of goods and services (goods of luxury or necessity), time length of products out in the market, and social and economic status of different groups of consumers. Some important highlights of those factors are explained here in regard to how they affect the elasticity of demand significantly.

Proportion of income spent on specific goods and services: In regard to different values of price elasticity of demand discussed in previous sections, statistical data over the decades has revealed that the lower the proportion of income spent on some goods and services, the lower the price elasticity of demand. For example, on average, American consumers spend about 7 to 9 percent of their household income on gasoline consumption for driving. The price elasticity is 0.25 (listed in Table 6.1) with a little more percentage of income spent on heating and electricity (Ed = 0.9). An increased percentage in the prices of goods of necessity does not change the quantity demanded significantly. On the other hand, the proportion of income spent on cars, house/rent, and furniture is much higher with more Ed (>1). It means a small percentage change in Ed for goods and services has more than a proportionate change in the increase or decrease in quantity demanded.

Degree of substitutability and complementarity: As explained in Section 6.2.2, the cross-price elasticity of demand depends on the degree of substitutability and complementarity of goods and services. If there are more substitute goods to switch from one good to another without much of a loss of consumer satisfaction, then the higher the elasticity. Several food items, electronic products, clothing, cosmetics and beauty products, sports gear, and fashion products have a higher price elasticity of demand. On the other hand, the necessity of goods and services such as transportation, utilities, and medical services have low substitutes with a low price elasticity of demand. Similarly, if the goods are highly complementary, then the price elasticity of demand for those goods is greater than for those with no or less complementarity.

Necessities versus luxury goods and elasticity: The nature of goods and services, whether they are necessary or luxury, affects the relative values of elasticity. Goods of necessity are usually characterized by a price elasticity of demand less than one. As explained previously, the price elasticity of demand for basic foods, housing rental, gasoline fuel and electricity, medical and public transportation, and clothes has low elasticity. On the other hand, luxury items such as high-end clothes, vehicles, furniture, sailboats, seafood, and transportation have an elasticity greater than 1. Those items are listed with their respective elasticities in Table 6.2.

Time length of product in the market: Goods and services that are out in the market for a long time usually have a relatively lower price elasticity (with some exceptions). When new products come out in the market, the consumers are usually slow in adding the new product to their market basket of consumption habits. For example, back in the 1980s, computers and mobile phones were newly emerging products. The price elasticity of demand was elastic (>1). But by the year 2000, those two products and other related hardware and software products and services had become goods of necessity, along with the internet revolution in the late 1990s. The price elasticity of a laptop, mobile phone, tablet, Wi-Fi, and cable TV is now much lower than during the 1990s. The price elasticity of some goods of necessity also changes from low elasticity to high elasticity over time depending on the availability of more substitutes produced by new firms over time.

Share of input cost of production by the producers: Price elasticity is higher on goods and services in which the proportion of input cost is larger. Similarly, the higher the proportion of income spent on a good, the higher the price elasticity of demand. For example, luxury cars, high-end houses, and expensive jewelry have a higher price elasticity of demand with a large percentage of income spent on those purchases.

Category of consumers: Price elasticity of demand widely varies in travel and entertainment industries depending on the type of consumers receiving the same services. For example, for airfare and hotel rates in major tourist and business destinations, the service providers usually charge different prices for different types of consumers. Business travelers are charged higher rates for hotel, air, and car rental rates than those who are not business travelers, such as students and excursionists. The difference in rates for the same services is

Figure 6.3   Shapes of Price Elasticity of Supply

mainly attributed to the difference in price elasticity of demand, with lower elasticity for business travelers than pleasure trippers.

6.4 Price Elasticity of Supply and Its Applications

In the previous section, the analysis was focused on three different types of elasticity of demand: (1) own price elasticity of demand, (2) cross-price elasticity of demand, and (3) income elasticity of demand. This section is focused on the price elasticity of supply in the market. The price elasticity of supply is expressed by the Eqn (6.8). Depending on the actual shape of the supply curve in the market for various goods and services, the price elasticity of supply is different.

$$\text{Price Elasticity of Supply} = Es = (\Delta Qs/Qs) \div (\Delta P/P) \qquad \text{Eqn (6.8)}$$

Eqn (6.8) is expressed as the percent of change in quantity supplied because of a certain percentage change in its own prices. Es measures the degree of responses from producers/suppliers to changes in prices of the same goods and services. From the concept of the law of supply learned in previous chapters, the normal shape of the supply curve is upward sloping (if price increases, quantity supplied also increases, and vice versa, *ceteris paribus*). Therefore, the price elasticity of supply for the upward-sloping supply curve is always positive regardless of whether Es is greater than or less than one or equal to one. The rule of thumb for figuring out the relative value of Es for the upward-sloping supply curve is expressed as the flatter the supply curve, the higher the elasticity, and the steeper the supply curve, the lower the elasticity. Figure 6.3 illustrates the three different shapes of an upward-sloping supply curve with Es >1 for S_1, Es <1 for curve S_2, and Es = 1 for curve S_3.

It is also important to note that there are many circumstances in the market for goods and services, especially in the travel and entertainment industries, medicine and agricultural products, and sports and music events where price elasticity of supply is equal to either zero or infinity. If the supply curve is perfectly vertical, then elasticity is zero, and if it is perfectly horizontal, then elasticity is infinite. These two extreme shapes of supply curves are illustrated in Figure 6.4.

Figure 6.4   Zero and Perfectly Elastic Supply Curves

As shown in panel (a) of Figure 6.4, the elasticity of a perfectly vertical supply curve is zero, meaning that price changes up and down would not have any effect on the quantity supplied of this product or service. The most common examples of this type of elasticity are stadium seats for

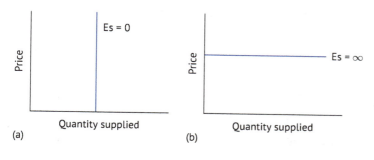

major sports, such as football, baseball, and soccer, as well as arenas for hockey and basketball games or concert halls for music and theater. The real-world implications for this shape of the supply curve is that if the demand shifts upward, it will only keep increasing the market price at successive intersections between the vertical supply curve and the increasing demand curve shifting upward (not shown here). That is the reason the market prices for big sporting events like the Superbowl or rock music concert events have such high price tags per tickets sold in the secondary market (price is driven up by demand shift only).

In panel (b) of Figure 6.4, the supply curve is just the opposite shape of panel (a). This perfectly horizontal shape (parallel to the horizonal axis) is known as the infinitely elastic supply curve. This infinite supply elasticity means that at a fixed price, a firm can produce as much as it likes to sell as long as the demand curve from consumers intersects at a point on the horizontal supply curve. In other words, if the downward-sloping demand curve keeps shifting to the right (not shown here) and intersects at different points on the supply curve, then the firm can sell more and more quantity with no change in price. The real-world examples could be the mass-scale production of milk and dairy products, small-size school supplies and sporting goods, some processed food items, or fast-food chain items. It is recommended that students draw their own demand curves on both panel (a) and (b) to do some exercises in the context of changing the equilibrium prices of major sports and entertainment events. Such practices will help with connecting the relationship between changes in the equilibrium prices of goods and services at different price elasticities of supply when the demand curve increases or decreases. The shape of the price elasticity of supply is mostly determined by the market conditions that change over time when the degree of competition rises as more and more substitute products and services emerge in the market. The analysis of such an effect is presented in more detail in the discussion of tax and tariff policy implications in Section 6.5.

6.5 Price Elasticity of Demand/Supply and Implications for Government Tax and Tariff Policies

There are many implications for government policy on changes in taxes and tariffs in terms of the policy effect on the welfare (loss or gain) of consumers and producers. In this section, the focus is on analyzing the effect of changes in tax/tariff policies depending on different values of price elasticity of demand and supply. This analysis also provides a deeper understanding of projecting the outcome of tax increases or decreases on certain goods and services by using the concept of the price elasticity of demand and supply.

6.5.1 Price Elasticity of Demand and Tax/Tariff Policies of the Government
The effects of the government's imposition of taxes and tariffs on market prices of goods and services depend on the price elasticity of demand for those goods and services. Since the nature of goods is different based on whether they are of necessity or luxury or their degree

of substitution, the distribution of tax effects on consumers and producers is different. The distributional effect of taxes/tariffs between producers and consumers and producers and sellers is called **tax incidence**. There are various types of taxes that the government charges, such as sales tax, excise tax, property tax, gas or carbon tax, tariffs (taxes on imported goods), and surcharges on airport securities, travel, and car rentals. The incidence of tax from this long list of taxes is driven by the demand and supply elasticity. However, taxes are not only imposed on spending (and sales) transactions in the market. Taxes are also imposed on household and individual incomes, corporate profits, capital gains, interest earnings, and dividends earned by shareholders' equity of corporate stocks.

A clear understanding of the economic incidence of so many taxes and tariffs helps policy makers and taxpayers to measure the welfare maximization for consumers and producers. Since taxes are necessary for the government to collect to provide public goods and security protection for citizens, measuring the optimum efficiency of these taxes is extremely complex. Although no one likes to pay taxes, tax is a necessary policy tool for maximizing economic well-being for society. Therefore, tax categories and their structure on both the spending and income sides are socially and politically sensitive areas of government policy. Table 6.3 provides a summary of the tax incidence of both the income and spending sides of tax policy. The role of the study of economics is to explore the efficiency measures of the tax incidence so that the goals of tax policy are optimum. The analysis of the tax incidence based on different types of price elasticity of demand and supply is the way to measure such economic efficiency.

Table 6.3: Tax Types and Tax Incidence

	Tax Types	Tax Incidence	Policy Implications	Examples
Income Taxes	Progressive income tax	The higher the income, the higher the tax rates	Expected to reduce income inequality	Individual income taxes
	Regressive income taxes	The higher the income, the lower the tax rates	Expected to increase income inequality	Social Security taxes at a fixed rate regardless of income level
	Flat tax on income	Same tax rate across the board	Expected to distribute tax burden equally	Medicare and Medicaid taxes
	Corporate tax: progressive	The higher the profit, the higher the tax rate up to a maximum limit of tax	Expected to reduce income inequality	Corporate profits, dividends
	Capital gain tax: flat rate on dividend received	The same tax rate across the board	Expected to increase income inequality	Sale proceeds from stocks, bonds, real estate, and other assets

Spending Taxes	Regressive spending system	Flat tax rates regardless of the volume of spending	Expected to generate an unequal tax burden with more on the lower-income group	Sales tax, tariffs, real estate property taxes, gas tax, surcharges
	Progressive spending tax	The higher the sales, the higher the tax rate	Expected to distribute the tax burden equally	Carbon tax as a disincentive to preventing an increase in CO_2 emissions

The various types of income and spending tax structures and their scope and limitation in measuring the efficiency of tax incidence is the key focus of the economic policy of the government. The complexity of the tax structure comes from the progressive and regressive nature of tax rates imposed by the government on both the income and spending sides. Depending on the rates of taxes in the previous list, typical households end up paying a substantial percentage of their gross incomes in the form of all types of taxes. The percentage share of all taxes combined can vary from 25 percent to 45 percent of every dollar of gross income earned by households. For example, on average, the typical American household pays up to 25 percent plus of their gross income in taxes. For Canada and the United Kingdom, the average tax burden might go up as high as 40 percent to 45 percent of their gross income. Since a detailed economic analysis of this phenomenon is beyond the scope of this introductory textbook, the focus of this section and the next is limited to the incidence of spending taxes based on the price elasticity of demand and supply.

Incidence of Spending Taxes with Different Price Elasticities of Demand

The incidence of taxes and tariffs is measured by the distribution of tax burdens between buyers and sellers from whom the government collects the tax revenue. The share of the tax burden is not necessarily equally distributed between buyers and sellers. The distribution of the tax burden depends on the relative price elasticity of demand (and that of supply). For example, if the price elasticity of demand is inelastic for a good, such as gasoline, cigarettes, electricity, or similar goods and services, then the tax burden will fall on consumers more than sellers. The opposite effect is expected in the case of the Ed curve, such as luxury items of goods and services and similar goods with more substitutes. This distributional pattern of tax incidence is illustrated in Figure 6.5.

In panel (a) of Figure 6.5, we can see that the imposition of a fixed tax $ per unit of sales of Good X_1 has shifted the supply curve to the left (note: shifting either the supply or demand curve to the left will produce a similar incidence). If the tax $ amount is $P_1 - P_2$, the movement of the supply shift to the left will be that position on the demand curve so that the vertical distance between the new equilibrium point on the new supply curve and down to the old supply curve is exactly equal to the tax $ amount of $P_1 - P_2$. Since the elasticity of the demand curve in panel (a) is inelastic (<1), the distribution of the tax burden (the tax incidence) falls more on the buyer than on the seller. The total tax burden is the $P_1 - P_2$ amount, and the increase in the price paid by the buyer is equal to $P_1 - P_0$, and the revenue loss by the seller before tax is $P_2 - P_0$. It clearly indicates that ($\$P_1 - P_0$) > ($P_2 - P_0$). In other words, the revenue lost by the seller ($P2 - P_0$) because of a higher price and less quantity sold ($Q_2 < Q_1$) is relatively less than the amount of the price increase paid by the buyer ($\$P_1 - P_0$). It is also important to notice that the increase in price because of the new tax imposed is less than the total amount of tax collected by the government ($P_1 - P_0$) < (Tax $P_1 - P_2$). To express it more clearly, the incidence of tax burden also indicates that the buyer does not end up paying the full tax amount in terms of price increase (as long as the demand curve is downward sloping and the supply curve is upward sloping.

In panel (b) of Figure 6.5, a similar analysis of tax incidence can be made with a case of price elasticity of demand greater than (Ed > 1) for Good X_2. In this scenario, the increase in price caused by tax per unit imposed on sales is P_1, which again is less than the tax amount

Figure 6.5 Tax Incidence with Different Price Elasticities of Demand

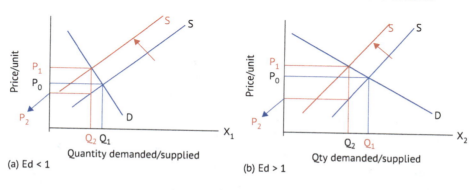

(a) Ed < 1

(b) Ed > 1

of $P_1 - P_2$. However, unlike panel (a), the burden of tax on the seller is more than the pro-portionate burden on the buyer. From panel (b), students may notice that the price increase paid by the buyer, $P_1 - P_0$, is less than the loss of revenue incurred by the seller, as shown by $P_2 - P_0$. In other words, with a price elasticity of demand greater than one, the burden of taxes falls more on sellers than buyers, as both parties share the burden of taxes. Also, as mentioned earlier in this chapter, price elasticity of demand could be different at different segments of the same downward-sloping demand curve. Therefore, the tax incidence on buyers and sellers would be determined by the position of the equilibrium price and quantity on a specific point on the demand curve from where the tax is imposed.

Tax and Tariff Policy Implications

Based on the previous discussion on the types of taxes and their incidence on buyers and sellers based on different values of elasticity of demand, understanding the distributional pattern of taxes and tariffs is very important for making a forecast of the possible consequences of a tax policy from the government prior to that policy being imposed. The key four purposes of the government imposing taxes and tariffs are as follows:

1. Increase tax revenue to finance government spending on public goods and security
2. Discourage spending on certain consumption habits, such as the use of cigarettes and alcohol
3. Prevent environmental damage with a carbon tax on products that emit greenhouse gases
4. Protect domestic industries against foreign competition of similar goods and services imported

To achieve these key objectives of the government policy, identifying the price elasticity of goods and services must be the key strategic task before a tax is imposed. For example, if the demand for goods and services is price elastic, and they are domestically produced, then the tax imposition on those goods and services will significantly reduce the quantity produced, and the sellers will not have the ability to pass along the higher price to the consumers to maintain the profit. As a result, the government will not only lose revenue targeted from the proposed tax, but it will also create unemployment from the significant loss of production. On the other, if the government wants to place import restrictions on foreign goods to protect the jobs and production of domestic industries, it is desirable to place tariffs on imports of Ed curves. For example, if the US government wants to impose tariffs on imports from China in retaliation of unfair trade practices based on China's policies on US exports, then the tariff policy should be focused on imports of goods and services with a higher price elasticity of demand and many substitutes produced domestically. Otherwise, imposing tariffs on imports with low elasticity of demand, such as medical equipment, textile products, and similar necessary products not produced domestically, won't be effective. Conversely, the imposition of higher taxes on luxury goods produced domestically is expected to backfire because it would reduce production and employment more than the proportionate tax revenue collected.

Students are encouraged to practice this phenomenon by drawing their own graphs using the analysis made from Figure 6.5. If the government wants to change consumer behavior regarding the consumption of certain goods and services or to prevent carbon emission in a

Figure 6.6 Tax Incidence with Different Price Elasticity of Supply

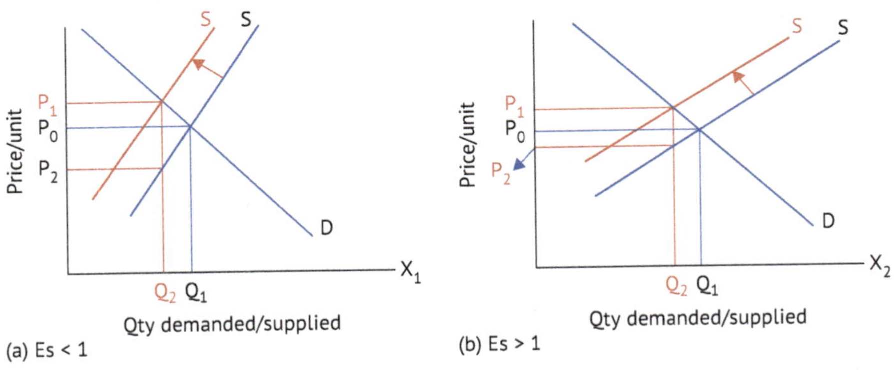

(a) Es < 1

(b) Es > 1

Microeconomics Principles, Applications, and Policy Implications

year, the effective tax policy must be based on the existing magnitude of demand elasticity of those products. The last section of this chapter is based on the similar concept of tax incidence in the case of different price elasticities of supply.

6.5.2 Price Elasticity of Supply and Tax/Tariff Policies of the Government

In the previous section, the analysis of tax incidence on consumers and producers was made by considering situations concerning the inelastic demand and Ed curves. In this last section, analysis is focused on the different price elasticities of the supply curve with the relatively normal shape of the downward-sloping demand curve. When the price elasticity of supply is different, the share of tax incidence falls disproportionately between buyers and sellers. For example, if the price elasticity of supply is inelastic ($Es < 1$), then the supply curve is a relatively steeper slope. The price increase caused by a tax increase or new tax imposed will negatively affect producers more in regard to losing sales revenue than the increase in the price paid by consumers. On the other hand, with the elastic supply curve ($Es > 1$), the burden of taxes falls more on consumers than the loss of revenue to producers. Figure 6.6 illustrates this scenario with its important policy implications.

As illustrated in panel (a) with $Es < 1$, tax burden falls on consumers much less than the loss of revenue to sellers, as indicated by the spread of the tax amount $P_1 - P_2$, with $P_1 - P_0$ less than $P_2 - P_0$, where ($P_1 - P_0$) is the increase of price (less than the tax amount as well), which is much less than the loss of revenue ($P_2 - P_0$). In panel (b) of Figure 6.6, the supply curve is drawn as an elastic supply condition with a flatter shape than that drawn in panel (a). The tax incidence in panel (b) shows that it is just the opposite of what is observed in panel (a). The price increase paid by the buyer in the amount of $P_1 - P_0$ (again less than the total tax/unit) is greater than the loss of revenue by the seller in the amount of $P_2 - P_0$. In other words, the magnitude of the price increase paid by the consumer ($P_1 - P_0$) is more than the magnitude of the revenue lost by the seller ($P_2 - P_0$).

From the analysis of price elasticity of supply and incidence of taxes illustrated in Figures 6.5 and 6.6, a general conclusion about this topic can be drawn as: with low price elasticity of the supply curve (the same for the high price elasticity of demand), the tax burden falls more on sellers than on buyers, and vice versa. Therefore, the policy makers must be careful in understanding the price elasticity of supply and demand and the consequence of taxes on buyers and sellers, and thus tax revenue, before a new tax is imposed.

Chapter Summary

The content of this chapter is divided into five sections summarized next:

Section 6.1 focused on the concept of the price elasticity of demand and types of elasticity of demand:

Ed = (% change in quantity demanded)/(% change in price per unit), algebraically expressed as

Ed = (ΔQ/Q)/(ΔP/P),

which indicates the degree of responses by consumers toward purchase decisions when the price of goods and services changes by a certain percentage. The ranges of price elasticity values are between zero and infinity in absolute terms. Based on that range, there are five types of elasticity: (1) Ed >1 price elastic, (2) Ed <1 price inelastic, (3) Ed = 1 unit elastic, (4) Ed = 0 infinitely inelastic or zero elastic, and (5) Ed = ∞ or infinitely elastic (graphs are illustrated in Figure 6.1). Real-world examples of goods and services with different elasticity values are also listed in Section 6.1.

In addition, a graphical illustration with an explanation is made in Section 6.1 with different values of elasticity of demand on different points of a straight-line demand curve. The applications of the difference between the constant slope of a linear demand curve and the different elasticities are also explained in the same graph (Figure 6.2).

Section 6.2 presented important relationships between types of elasticity and firms' strategies for maximizing TR = P × Q by changing the pricing of their products. The important connection between Ed and TR are explained by logical theories and applications summarized next. This chart has important applications for the marketing strategies of firms for revenue maximization.

Elasticity Value	Price Change	Change in Sales Revenue
Ed < 1	Increase Price	Increase TR
Ed > 1	Increase Price	Decrease TR
Ed < 1	Decrease Price	Decrease TR
Ed > 1	Decrease Price	Increase TR
Ed = 1	Increase or Decrease Price	No Change in TR

In the same section, concepts of other types of elasticity of demand, such as cross-price elasticity of demand and income elasticity of demand, are introduced and explained with their real-world applications.

For example, cross-price elasticity demand is the degree of responses to the change in quantity demanded to changes in price other than the own price of goods, which are either substitute or complementary goods. The equation for cross-price elasticity of demand is presented as

Ed_{xy} = % change in quantity demanded for x ÷ change in price of y.

A positive value of Edxy indicates that goods are substitutes, and the higher the value of Edxy, the closer the substitutes are. Conversely, a negative value of Edxy indicates that goods are complementary, and the higher the value of Edxy, the higher the degree of complementarity.

Income elasticity of demand is expressed by the following equation:

Ed_i = (% change in quantity demanded) ÷ (% change in income).

Depending on that preference pattern, the nature of a good is classified as *normal*, *inferior*, or *luxury*. For a normal good, the value of Edi is expected to be greater than zero but less than one. For an inferior good, Edi is less than zero (a negative value), and for a luxury good, Edi is supposed to be greater than one. The economic interpretations with real-world examples are given next.

For a normal good, the value range is between 0< Edi <1, a positive value but less than one, which means as income rises (or falls), the quantity demanded of normal goods and services increases (or decreases) as well but not at the same proportion of income change.

For an inferior good, the value is Edi <0, a negative value, which means as income rises (or falls), the quantity demand for inferior goods and services does actually decrease (or increase) at any given level of price of those goods and services.

For a luxury good, the value is Edi >1, which means as income rises (or falls), the quantity demand for luxury goods is expected to increase (or decrease) greater than the proportionate increase in income at any given price level.

Section 6.3 introduced multiple factors that affect elasticity values and discussed them in more detail with real-world examples. Those factors affecting the elasticity are as follows:

- Proportion of income spent on specific goods and services
- Degree of substitutability and complementarity
- Necessities versus luxury goods and elasticity
- Time length of products in the Market
- Share of input cost of production by the producers
- Category of consumers

Section 6.4 explained the concept and applications of price elasticity of supply with its policy implications in understanding market behavior from the producers' perspectives. The equation for price elasticity of supply is given next:

Price elasticity of supply = Es = (ΔQs/Qs) ÷ (ΔP/P), with o< = Es< = ∞

Similar to price elasticity of demand, the applications of supply elasticity are discussed in detail in the context of different shapes of supply curves and their implications for changes in sales revenue because of changes in the demand curve and thus changes in the equilibrium price.

Section 6.5 introduced tax and tariff policies and their implications for different types of price elasticity of demand and price elasticity of supply. The discussion focused on how the strategy of government policy on taxes and tariffs can be effective by clearly understanding the elastic and inelastic demand and supply curves before changes in tax policy or a new tax policy is imposed on certain goods produced domestically and tariffs on imported goods. The distributional effect in the form of tax incidence on consumers and producers was discussed with different price elasticities of demand and supply. Figure 6. 5 and Figure 6.6 demonstrated tax incidence with real-world examples.

Application Activities

1. Use the hypothetical demand schedule in the following table to answer the questions. The table describes the number of visits per day to the New York Zoo in Bronx, New York, with their corresponding prices as admission ticket prices per day.

Ticket Price/Admission	Visits per Day
$50	200
40	400
30	600
20	800
10	1,000

2. Explain briefly why the price elasticity of demand for luxury goods and services plus many substitutes of normal goods and services tend to be greater than one (elastic) as compared to necessities that have a price elasticity of demand that is less than one. Give a specific example from the real world.

3. Suppose the price elasticity of demand for subway trains in Boston and New York City is almost close to zero. If the city authority raises the fare of Massachusetts Bay Transportation Authority (MBTA) passengers by 20 percent over its current prices to cover the loss of operation for MBTA, how much increase in revenue do you expect because of a fare increase of 20 percent? Give reasons to substantiate your answer.

4. Suppose you are an attorney representing two large corporations that filed for legislative approval to merge two companies that produce very similar products or services. The court authority tries to prevent the proposed merger on the grounds that the two companies, if merged, would occupy major market share with more market power to jack up the prices on consumers. Given your knowledge on cross-price elasticity of demand, what would be your evidence to argue against the court to make your case for merger approval?

5. Briefly explain why the local city authorities in major cities of tourist destinations in the United States and US territories impose extremely high surcharges (between 20 and 30 percent) on car rentals and hotel rooms while imposing low taxes on local residents. The purpose of high surcharges is to raise enough revenue to improve and maintain local roads, bridges, airports, and other infrastructure. Is this economically and politically justified? Why or why not?

6. Explain briefly why the owners of grocery stores and other supply stores distribute discount coupons to some selected groups of shoppers who have a price elasticity of demand less than one for those goods and services.

7. Suppose the case for Donald Trump's proposed tariffs on China is the retaliation of unfair trade practices being conducted as a result of China's trade policy on US exports and because of their continued piracy of US business intelligence. In pursuing these proposed tariffs, what type of imported goods or services with price elasticity of demand would be appropriate to impose tariffs on without much negative effect on US consumers? Give specific examples to substantiate your answer.

8. Explain briefly why the government should avoid imposing tax increases on luxury goods

if the government wants to raise the tax revenue based on social and economic justifications of tax increases on luxury items usually purchased by high-income households.

9. Suppose the government has imposed a new increase in gas taxes by imposing $1.00 per gallon of gas at the retail level to increase tax revenue to finance a growing budget deficit and to reduce the level of greenhouse gas emissions. Also, assume that the price elasticity of gasoline at the time of the increase in taxes by $1 per gallon is about 0.3. Based on this information, and assuming other factors affecting the demand for gasoline remain the same, answer the following:

a. Do you think the gas price increase per gallon will be more than, equal to, or less than the $1.00 increase in tax per gallon? Give your reasoning either mathematically and with text or by drawing a relevant graph with an explanation in your own words.

b. Given your answer in 9a, briefly explain the incidence of this tax increase in terms of buyers and sellers sharing the tax burden.

10. Use the information given in the table to answer the questions that follow.

Income	Quantity of Good X Purchased	Quantity of Good Y Purchased
$40,000	4	25
$60,000	8	15

a. Using the midpoint estimation method, what is the income elasticity of demand of Good Y?

b. What is the income elasticity of Good X?

c. From your answers in 10a and 10b, which of the goods in the table is an inferior good and which is a normal good? Explain.

Chapter 7

Behavioral Economics and Consumer Choice Theories and Applications

Learning Objectives

As they read the chapter, students will learn the following:

▶ Introduction to Behavioral Economics and Application in Market Demand

▶ Consumer Choice Theories and Income and Budget Analysis

▶ MU Analysis of Consumer and Optimal Choice Criteria to MU

▶ Analysis of Utility Maximization and Derivation of the Demand Curve

Introduction

This chapter is the last chapter to discuss about the changes in consumer behavior in response to changes in prices and income in order to maximize consumer satisfaction from their alternative choice of spending decisions. The chapter begins with theoretical understanding of consumer behavior and that reflects in the demand function of a typical consumer. In explaining this important aspect of consumer behavior further, the consumer choice theory in terms of income and budgeting constraints is introduced. Given the income and budget constraints, and the marginal utility (level of satisfaction at the margin) of a typical consumer is explained with its application through analysis of how to maximize consumer's utility. The last section demonstrates the technique to analyze the utility maximization and thus derivation of demand function in response to changes in price of goods and services, consumers income, taste and preferences. The next chapter will start with supply side of this textbook focusing on production function and cost structure of firms and industry.

7.1 Introduction to Behavioral Economics and Application in Market Demand

The core of economics as one of the important fields in social science is primarily based on human behavior, which is extremely complex and unpredictable. But the unpredictable nature of human behavior is actually a good thing because the way we all process our changing behavior in our everyday lives is a mix of challenge and excitement. This mix of challenge and excitement forces us to explore ideas and creativity to maximize our happiness—the goal of every member of human society. As discussed at the beginning of this textbook, the opportunity cost of making alternative decisions to allocate our limited resources is an important part of measuring efficiency in production and consumption. The decisions we make when balancing production (the supply side) and consumption (the demand side) are basically driven by the complex nature of human behavior. Economists call this part of inter-active transactions the science of *behavioral economics*. When consumers and producers make choices as to what to buy or what to produce and for whom to produce and how to produce or why, they all have to make their best choices from many options to maximize their needs and goals. In other words, as consumers and producers, we intend to make the best choices from many options to maximize our satisfaction. Back in the 1760s, Adam Smith, the father of economics science, mentioned the puzzle of this choice of purchasing between alternative goods and services with an example of diamonds and water, with water being a necessity for our existence and diamonds being unnecessary. Placing relative weights in terms of which of these two products is worth more than the other is a puzzle we consumers need to figure out. A similar puzzle can be seen when college students make choices between the purchase of school supplies and clothing before the start of a semester. Given a limited budget, this choice can be difficult to make. This section intends to explore this puzzle of making decisions to maximize the happiness of consumers.

7.1.1 Behavioral Economics and Consumers' Choice Theory

From the puzzle introduced by Smith of making a choice between the purchase of diamonds or water—even though water is much less expensive and virtually free most of the time—is a theory of consumer preference that focuses on a consumer's ability to pay for diamonds versus a bottle of water or both given the tastes and preferences of a typical consumer. This choice must be driven by the consumer with a common objective: to maximize his or her sat-isfaction from either drinking water or enjoying the ownership of diamonds or a combination of both. The science of behavioral economics intends to make this decision more rational so that given the budget, a typical consumer can make the best trade-off as an act of rational behavior. As explained in earlier chapters related to demand theories and their applications, consumers make their purchasing decisions based on changes in prices given their income, preferences, and tastes. The demand curve explaining the phenomenon of purchasing the best combination of goods and services is the reflection of consumer behavior when making a rational choice. For example, given the budget constraints and knowledge of prices for school supplies needed and clothes to buy before a college session starts, students must make a rational choice when choosing the right combination of clothes and supplies. To analyze the behavioral aspect of this decision, the consumer choice theory of economics brings the concept of the marginal level of satisfaction for purchasing additional units of goods and services against the marginal value of money spent on them.

Since the common goal of all consumers is to maximize the level of satisfaction, the trade-off between the marginal value of money spent in exchange for the marginal value derived from goods purchased is important to analyze. The marginal satisfaction from purchasing additional goods and services in exchange for money is called **marginal utility (MU)**, originally theorized by philosopher Jeremy Bentham (1748–1832) in his theory of utilitarianism, which explained how to make a rational choice when maximizing a consumer's happiness and minimizing pain.[1] This theoretical foundation assumes that consumers are inherently rational when making spending decisions most of the time. However, this assumption does not necessarily imply that we as consumers never act irrationally in our spending behavior. But those irrational decisions are mostly random during times of uncertainty. Randomly made irrational decisions may not be intentional but the result of a lack of correct information. The bottom line is that random events of irrational choice made by some consumers are insignificant and, therefore, do not affect our society negatively. The study of behavioral economics explores the best possible scenario of consumer choice when balancing between MU of goods and services and MU of the money we pay for them. Therefore, it is important to minimize those random events of irrational choices so that we as consumers are able to maximize our level of happiness when making decisions to select the best bundle of goods and services.

7.1.2 Behavioral Economics and the Demand Curve

Given the concept of rational choice theory of consumer behavior explained earlier, it is obvious that the demand curve of a typical consumer is basically the display of different combinations of the prices and goods/services a typical consumer or a group of consumers chooses from. Therefore, every combination of price and quantity demand on the demand curve is called the *marginal willingness to pay (MWTP) approach*. This concept of MWTP is actually derived from the psychological aspect of consumer satisfaction from purchasing goods and services at different prices. This level of satisfaction for additional units of consumption is the **MU**. The values of the MU of consumers are actually the points of those

Figure 7.1   MU and Demand Curve

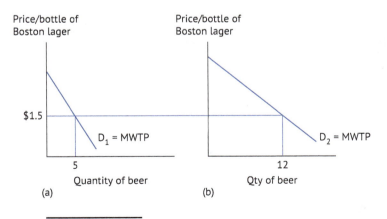

1   *Jeremey Bentham, Introduction to the Principles of Morals* (Oxford, Oxford University Press, 1789), pp.

combinations of price and quantity on the demand curve called MWTP. Figure 7.1 illustrates this process of consumer behavior on a typical demand curve in the market for an individual consumer.

Using Figure 7.1, suppose that two Red Sox fans are watching a game between the Red Sox and the New York Yankees at Fenway Park in Boston. Suppose these two individuals purchased bottles of **Samuel Adams**™ Boston Lager of different quantities with different slopes of their demand curves, with D_1 for individual A in panel (a) and D_2 for individual B in panel (b). The D_1 curve is relatively inelastic as compared to the elastic D_2 demand curve. Since the preference patterns and consumption tastes are different for different consumers, the different shapes of D_1 and D_2 drawn in the figure are reasonable and close to reality. Suppose that individual A ended up drinking 5 bottles of Boston Lager at $1.50 per bottle and individual B ended up drinking 12 bottles of Boston Lager at the same price of $1.50 per bottle. So, individual A spent $7.50 (1.50 × 5) and individual B spent $18 ($1.50 × 12) while enjoying the game. The behavioral aspect of the beer consumption reveals the following: the total utilities (level of satisfaction from beer drinking) from these two combinations of price and quantity by individuals A and B must be different. Although it is not possible to accurately measure the psychological aspect of satisfaction that varies widely from one individual to another, it is reasonable to assume that as both individuals purchase more and more bottles of beer during the game, they will be willing to pay less and less for each additional bottle. The reason for this is the concept of **MU** (change in level of satisfaction from additional bottles of beer). The concept of MU is the change in total utility (TU) from successive units of consumption. Since MU from additional units of beer is less and less than the previous units, it is true for both individuals that the MU will decline with successive units of beer, even though TU may still continue to increase up to a certain point where MU = 0. This phenomenon of declining MU with additional units of beer consumption is called *diminishing marginal utility* (DMU), as expressed in the following equation.

$$MU = \frac{\Delta TU}{\Delta Q} \text{ declines as more and more quantity is purchased}$$

Since both individuals are getting less and less satisfaction from each additional bottle of beer, both will be willing to pay less for each additional unit. Therefore, the concept of DMU is the same thing as MWTP, as depicted in the downward-sloping demand curves for the Red Sox fans in Figure 7.1. In other words, the downward-sloping demand curve reflects two important aspects of the rational behavior of consumers: (1) to maximize the level of satisfaction from purchasing the right combination of goods and services at different prices and (2) to maintain a balance between the DMU and the price paid for additional units of goods and services purchased as the best value derived for the money spent. Combining these behavioral aspects of a typical consumer, it is reasonable to conclude that the MUs of both Red Sox fans A and B must be equal to the last price of $1.50 per bottle with a total consumption of 5 bottles for individual A and 12 bottles for individual B. In other words, MUs for the last bottle (5th for A and 12th for B) of beer purchased is equal to the price of $1.50 per bottle. Since the equality between MU and price are different at different points on the demand curves, the concept of DMU confirms the rational behavior of consumer to reflect the downward-sloping demand curve. This conclusion can be further extended to the following logical conditions if consumers allocate money to buy more than one commodity. From the example, we assume that both individuals allocated their fixed budget between beer consumption and food. In this case, the logical conditions for maximizing the TU and price combination can be expressed by the following equation:

Utility maximization for two goods: $\left(\dfrac{MUb}{Pb}\right) = \left(\dfrac{MUf}{Pf}\right)$, **where b = beer and f = food.**

An alternative expression of the equation can be rearranged as follows:

Utility maximization for two goods: $\left(\dfrac{MUb}{MUf}\right) = \left(\dfrac{Pb}{Pf}\right).$ **Eqn (7.1)**

Although the condition in Eqn (7.1) of utility maximization seems too abstract to measure the complex nature of the psychological aspects of consumer behavior when making spending decisions, this theoretical foundation developed by economists back in the eighteenth century has powerful implications for understanding the economic benefits of reallocating our money to buy different combinations of goods and services. This rule of the game for maximizing our total satisfaction given our limited budget does indeed help rationalize our behavior when it comes to achieving efficiency in consumption and in production. To clarify this phenomenon further in detail, another real-world application of the theory of DMU and pricing is provided in Section 7.1.3.

Figure 7.2 MU and Pricing

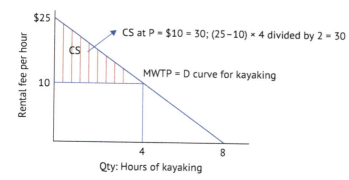

Qty: Hours of kayaking

7.1.3 Application of DMU, Consumer Demand, and Pricing

As explained in the previous section, DMU is derived from successive units of consumption of any good; this implies that MU for additional units of consumption continues to decline as more and more units are consumed. Therefore, MWTP reflects the rational behavior of a consumer to see a downward-sloping demand curve. The concept of MWTP is nothing but the best combinations of price and quantity on a demand curve where MU = P would be the rational sense of selecting the right quantity of goods and services to maximize the consumer's utility. Given this condition, another real-life example of outdoor activities, such as the demand curve for kayaking at a summer recreation, is explained with a visual illustration drawn in Figure 7.2.

Figure 7.2 indicates the hourly rental fee to determine the total spending on kayaking by a typical kayaker who will be willing to pay the price reflected on the D curve = MWTP schedule. The equality condition between MU and price shows that if the rental fee is $10/

hour, the kayaker will purchase four hours of boating. However, if she likes to kayak for more than four hours, then the rental fee must be less than $10 to rationalize her willingness to pay for additional hours of kayaking. This is because her experience during the fifth hour of kayaking may not be as enjoyable as the previous hours of boating. Therefore, the total expenditure of $40 for four hours of kayaking must be justified in the sense that the MU from the fourth hour of boating must be equal to the $10 rental fee. However, the MWTP schedule also indicates that the previous hours of boating (from one to three hours) must have an MU greater than the MU = 10 for four hours of boating. This logic clearly reflects the MWTP = D curve at rental fees above $10/hour. Assuming that at $25 per hour there will be no kayaker willing to rent a boat, the TU can be measured by taking the area of the triangle below the demand curve:

TU = ($25 × 8)/2 = 100 utils (units of satisfaction or utility)

From the area of the triangle below the demand curve for kayaking estimated at 100, it is reasonable to see the maximum TU or satisfaction equivalent close to 100, if not exactly 100, because at $25 per hour, the MU is zero. Given the TU concept, the MU for this demand curve can be estimated as equivalent to the slope of the demand as expressed in the following equation:

$$\text{MU} = \frac{\Delta \text{Rental}}{\Delta \text{Hour}} = \frac{25}{8} = \textbf{3.125}$$

This approximation of MU for the entire demand curve can be interpreted as the rate of DMU for successive hours of kayaking because at the hourly basis, the MU of boating is much higher than 3.125 utils, as reflected in the higher rental fee. This also explains why at every level of the rental fee on this MWTP schedule, the price and corresponding hours of boating will make the equality between the MU and price. This phenomenon has two important implications, as noted next:

(1) A typical kayaker will likely kayak either a minimum of four hours a day at a maximum price of $10 per hour or for more hours at less than $10 per hour. (2) It is also possible that the same kayaker may be willing to pay a fixed rental fee to boat for the whole eight hours at a maximum rate between $10 and $25 instead of paying an hourly rate of $10 or more.

Consumer surplus (CS): CS is defined as the difference between the maximum amount a typical consumer is willing to pay for particular goods and services and the amount actually paid for the same quantity of goods and services. The concept of TU explained earlier can be used as a real-world application in estimating potential CS. Given these two options or something in between, if the kayaker is happy with boating for four hours by paying $40 for the day, then the total potential utility for her is still close to the 100 utils or less estimated earlier. It has two implications, which are described next:

The maximum potential utility for the kayaker is (P × Q)/2 = ($25 × 8)/2 = 100 utils

The TU is the same as the total consumer satisfaction. It implies that a typical consumer, like the kayaker in this example, is willing to pay the maximum amount of money equivalent to each MU of additional units. Therefore, a consumer will not be willing to a pay price on the demand curve where MU is zero, and vice versa. Based on this rational behavior of consumer choice theory, the CS can be estimated from Figure 7.2 at a price of $4 per hour, which is shown next:

CS for this TU = TU − Actual $ spent (P × Q) at $4 = CS = [(25 − 10) × 4] ÷ 2 = 30.

The amount of CS at 30 indicates that the kayaker is actually able to generate a positive CS after spending $40 for four hours of happy boating. This positive CS is an incentive for consumers to purchase more units of goods, as long as the price is lower to match the DMU of additional hours of boating.

7.1.4 Pricing Scheme to Maximize Revenue

In the kayaking example, the owner of the boating club may capitalize on this consumer behavior of maximizing utility to maximize his or her revenue from each of the kayakers or canoers by undertaking an appropriate pricing scheme. The following is an example to try for this scenario of kayaking.

Option 1: Suppose the owner of the boating club charges MU = Price @ $3.125 estimated earlier with a minimum of four hours and maximum of eight hours with an additional charge of $3.125 for each additional hour after the first four hours. This hourly price with a minimum cap of four hours will maximize the revenue within the revenue range between $12.50 and $25 per kayaker. It is only possible to generate this revenue or a little less if the kayaker pays for the first four hours and the additional fees for extra hours of rental time. The success of this pricing strategy is highly unlikely because of the relationship between DMU and the declining MWTP approach. An alternative to this option may be more appealing, as described next.

Option 2: Instead of charging $3.125/hour for eight hours with a minimum of four hours of rental time, the owner may use the concept of CS and charge the appropriate rental fee rate that keeps the CS positive or just equal to the CS amount. From the example of CS provided earlier, the kayaker is happy with the $10 per hour rental for four hours boating because she generates a CS equal to the $30 rental fee, which she was willing to pay for extra hours of boating but not at the same rate of $10. This implies that if the club owner offers a flat fee for an all-day rental at a rate less than the CS or less than $25 (where MU is negative or zero), the same kayaker will be expected to spend more than $12.50 and less than $25 for a day pass while still happy with little positive CS left between the rental fees of $10 and $25/hour. This option is obviously better for generating more revenue without any additional work or cost and thus maximize profit for the club owner. This option is actually a common practice by many yacht and boat club owners and ski resort owners who offer a daily or weekly pass, or even a whole-season pass. The application of CS and MWTP is also useful for understanding the consequence of government regulations, tax policy, and travel and entertainment industries, thus making the appropriate changes for achieving an effective policy strategy. This process definitely has greater appeal when it comes to conducting extensive research on consumer preferences and behavioral patterns to improve their economic prosperity and living standards by making new investments in business enterprises. More details about this pattern of consumer behavior are discussed in Section 7.2.

7.2 Consumer Choice Theories and Income and Budget Analysis

Despite the unlimited desire to buy goods and services, we as consumers are bound to limit our desires within our income levels and the market prices of goods and services. With budgetary limitations and the given prices, the choice of the right combination of goods and services to purchase requires making a rational choice. Although not every consumer makes his or her choices rationally, understanding the limits of income and given prices, consumer preference patterns and tastes for different goods and services provide important tools for achieving the most desirable bundle of goods and services. This process of optimization starts with the analysis of the budget line for a consumer. To make this rational choice for the best combination, let me begin with a limited income left over for one of the two Red Sox fans (mentioned in Section 7.1.2), we'll call him Bobby. Suppose Bobby has $20 to spend on food and Samuel Adams beer during the game, with the price and quantity combination presented in Table 7.1 (of course the ticket was purchased in advance).

Table 7.1: Budget Line for Food and Beer

Price of Food	Quantity of Food	Price of Samuel Adams Beer	Quantity of Beer	Total $ Spent
$4/unit	5	$2/bottle	0	$20
$4/unit	4	$2/bottle	2	$20
$4/unit	0	$2/bottle	10	$20

Based on the possible combinations and more, the budget line for Bobby is illustrated in Figure 7.3.

The budget line shows the limit of the maximum possible alternative combinations of food and bottles of beer within the budget of $20. If Bobby prefers food only, then the maximum units will be five with zero units of beer, and for beer only, the maximum units will be ten bottles of beer. The combinations of both will be all other points on the budget line.

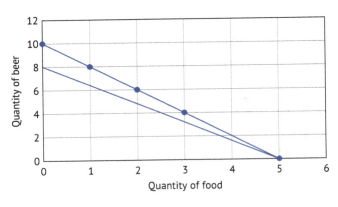

Figure 7.3   Budget Line for Food and Beer

Although it is possible to choose other combinations below the budget line with total spending less than $20, it is not possible to choose any bundles of food and beer beyond the budget line within the $20 limit and given prices. However, with relative price changes and budget-limit changes, the budget line can be shifted to the right or to the left depending on the changes in price and budget. Suppose the beer price increased to $2.50 per bottle. With the new price, given the same budget and no change in the price of food, the new budget line will be tilted inward, as shown by the budget line connecting five units of food and eight bottles of beer. With similar logic, if the price of food increases, the budget line will tilt leftward from the corner of food units at five on the horizontal axis. Conversely, if the budget increases from $20 to $25, $30, or any other higher amount, with no changes in relative price, the budget line will be shifted parallel to the right. Students may try these different situations by drawing on a piece of paper for practice. Using this limit in choices for a consumer on a budget line, the process of utility maximization will be explained in Section 7.3.

7.3 MU Analysis and Optimal Choice Criteria to Maximize Utility

With the understanding of the connection between the theory of consumer preference and the law of DMU discussed in Section 7.1 and budget analysis in Section 7.2, this section is extended to explore the optimum allocation of a given monetary budget or income in more than two goods to maximize TU (total satisfaction).

7.3.1 DMU and Utility Maximization

Since consumers do not really use all of their budgeted funds on a single good or service, two goods—food and bottles of beer—are considered here to analyze the optimum combination of the bundle of two goods for Bobby while watching the baseball game with his friend at Fenway Park. The purpose of this two-goods model of utility maximization for exploring the optimum choice of a consumer is to come up with the best combination of food (either slices of pizza or burgers or both) and bottles of beer that will maximize the utility of Bobby's budget on game day. This simplified model of utility maximization can also be generalized with more than two goods without much of a modification to the model because it will not make any difference as long as we can compare between one good versus the rest of the goods in the same model structure. However, for the sake of simplicity, this analysis is limited to two specific goods only: food and Samuel Adams beer. As the first step in the process of utility maximization, Table 7.2 offers a set of hypothetical data on prices of food and Samuel Adams beer and the quantity consumed by Bobby with total and marginal utilities from both food and beer consumption. It is also assumed from Section 7.2 that Bobby has a limited budget of $20 to spend on these two goods during the game with a price of $4 per unit of food and $2 per bottle of Samuel Adams beer.

Table 7.2: MU Analysis and Consumer Preference

Quantity of Food (1)	TU Food (2)	MU Food Utils (3)	MU in $s (4)	Quantity of Beer (5)	TU Beer (6)	MU Beer Utils (7)	MU Beer in $s (8)
0	0	–	–	0	0	–	–
1	60	60	6	1	80	80	8
2	110	50	5	2	150	70	7
3	150	40	4	3	200	50	5
4	180	30	3	4	220	20	2
5	200	20	2	5	230	10	1

7.3.2 MU Derivation from TU of Food and Samuel Adams Beer

In Table 7.2, the first column is the quantity of food (either slices of pizza or burgers or both) provides the increasing quantity of food consumption, and Column 5 includes the successive units of Samuel Adams beer consumed by Bobby during the entire game. Columns 2 and 6 provide the corresponding utils (the level of psychological satisfaction) against each of the units of food and beer, respectively. It is important to keep in mind that it is not impossible to quantify the psychological aspect of satisfaction into actual numbers by asking individuals about their preferences for those goods and services and the corresponding level of satisfaction they derive from them in numerical format. The values of MU ($\Delta TU/\Delta Q$) for both food and beer are shown in Columns 3 and 6, respectively. Since a typical consumer usually pays a price equal price per unit (explained in previous sections), the utility units are assumed to be worth 10 utils per dollar. Based on this restrictive but reasonable assumption, MU in utils in Columns 3 and 6 are converted into the dollar value of MU, as shown in Columns 4 and 8, respectively. Given the aforementioned set of MU with alternative combinations of food and beer, Bobby can rationalize the best combination of these two consumption items to maximize the utility by spending his maximum budget of $20. To rationalize this preference pattern, we can begin with the first item for consumption, which represents the highest MU. This will be the first beer with MU = 80 > 60; MU = 60 is for the first unit of food (pizza slice or burger). Therefore, it is reasonable to assume that Bobby will pay for the first beer of bottle by spending $2 out of the $20. For the second option of food or beer, that table shows that the MU of the second bottle of beer is 70 > 60. So, Bobby will buy the second bottle of beer, spending a total of $4. The next choice for him will be to buy the first unit of food because the MU of food at quantity 1 is 70 > 50, MU = 50 for the third bottle of beer. So far, it is shown that the Bobby spent $4 for two bottles of beer and $4 for one unit food with a total spend of $8, with $12 remaining in the budget of $20. The next choice for Bobby will probably be to buy both one unit of food and one bottle of beer because both give the same MU of 50. As a result, he will have three units of beer and two units of food, with a total spend of $14 (3 × $2 + 2 × $4) and $6 remaining. Bobby will continue to purchase either more food or drinks or both until the remaining $6 is fully spent. By looking at MU = 40 for the fourth bottle of beer as the same MU for the third unit of food, it makes sense for him to buy both at $4 for

Figure 7.4 IC and Utility Maximization

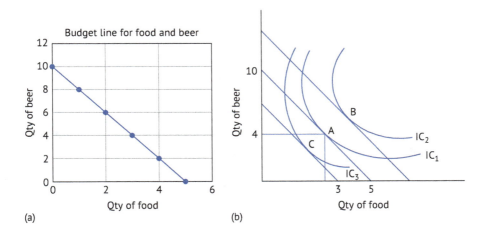

(a)

(b)

food and $2 for beer. This combination of the final purchase also indicates the equality of MU of 40 utils at three units of food and four bottles of beer. It is also the same case for MU in $s = 4 as we assumed 10 utils = $1. The TU for this combination of three units of food and four units of beer is 370 (150 + 220), as the highest possible utility given the budget of $20, the preferences for food and beer, and relative the prices. This process is the condition for the maximization of TU, as expressed by the following equation:

$$\frac{MU \text{ of Food}}{Price \text{ of Food}} = \frac{MU \text{ of Beer}}{Price \text{ of Beer}}, \text{ or } \frac{MUf}{MUb} = Pf/Pb, \textbf{40/20 = 4/2 = 2; this is the same as Eqn (7.1) in Section 7.1.2.}$$

The equation helps to rationalize the condition for the utility maximization of the subject to the budget constraint given the prices of two goods as the best possible combination of goods for consumption. This condition of utility maximization certainly helps a rational consumer like Bobby to feel indifferent when choosing the optimum combination. This condition can also be true for more than two goods as a tool for making a rational choice for typical consumers with their limited budgets and given market prices. The graphical representation of this rule of utility maximization is illustrated in Figure 7.4, where panel (a) is the *indifference curve (IC)* for Bobby and panel (b) is the combination of the *budget line* drawn and IC_1 showing the point of utility maximization at point A followed by an explanation.

The budget line in panel (a) is the same as the one drawn in Figure 7.3 with all possible combinations of food and beer for Bobby. Using this information from the budget line in panel (a) and the utility maximization condition in Eqn (7.1), Bobby's utility maximization for food and beer is illustrated at the tangency point between the budget line and the IC_1 at point A in panel (b). IC_1 is the indifference curve for Bobby, indicating his preference pattern of all possible combinations of food and beer along the IC_1, given the same level of TU for food and beer. In other words, Bobby is indifferent at any point on the IC_1 in terms of his total level of satisfaction regardless of what combination of food and beer he chooses to consume. However, it is also true that the marginal rate of substitution (MRS_{fb}) of beer for food along the IC_1 is different because MRS_{bf} of beer for food is the slope of the IC_1. As explained earlier, the law of DMU occurs as more and more of the same goods are consumed. Therefore, the different values of MRS_{fb} are consistent with the law of DMU as the slope declines on the IC_1. For example, as Bobby substitutes food for beer, his MRS or the slope of the IC_1 will continuously decline, which is the same as DMU. That is the reason the IC_1 is convex to the origin. On the other hand, IC_2 in panel (b) is another possible IC given the same preference pattern for Bobby, but it is not achievable within his maximum budget of $20 to spend on food and beer. Given that budget constraint, the budget line from panel (a) is redrawn in panel (b), which is tangent to the highest possible IC_1 at point A. At point A, the combination of three units of food and four units of beer is the best combination for achieving maximum possible TU. This combination of food and beer is exactly the one shown in Table 7.2 marked in red and blue. The conditions of utility maximization explained in Table 7.2 and illustrated in Figure 7.4 are summarized in Eqn (7.2).

$$\textbf{TU Maximization} = \frac{MUf}{MUb} = \frac{Pf}{Pb} = MRSfb \qquad \textbf{Eqn (7.2)}$$

Eqn (7.2) indicates that the three ratios (MU ratio, price ratio, and MRS ratio) must be equal at only one point of combination between food and beer, where the budget line is tangent to the highest possible IC. However, if the relative prices of both food and beer decrease by the same proportion and/or his budget is increased from $20 to a higher amount, the budget line can be shifted parallel to the right, and a new point of utility maximization will be achieved at point B, where the new budget line is tangent to the highest possible indifference curve IC_2. With the same logic, students may practice how to achieve another point of utility maximization if the prices of both food and beer decrease by the same proportion and/or Bobby's budget is reduced from $20 to a lower amount. In that case, the budget must be shifted parallel to the left, shown as IC_3 in panel (b) parallel to IC_1 or IC_2. The utility maximization with the budget line will be at point C, where the new budget line is tangent with IC_3. A group of ICs for Bobby shown by three different ICs is called the indifference map. The indifference map helps to determine changes in levels of TU maximization in response to changes in relative prices and/or budget constraints. Now, what if the price of one good relative to the other good has changed, say if the price of beer has increased given the same price of food, how do we determine the utility maximization with a new set of prices and no change in Bobby's budget? The analysis of this question is done in the next section.

7.4 Analysis of Utility Maximization and Derivation of the Demand Curve

Using the same ICs and indifference map illustrated in Figure 7.4 for the determination of utility maximization for Bobby, it is also possible to analyze the effect of changes in relative prices on his real income (change in purchasing power without an actual change in the budget itself) and reallocate his combination of food and beer to maximize his TU.

Figure 7.5 Relative Price Change and Utility Maximization

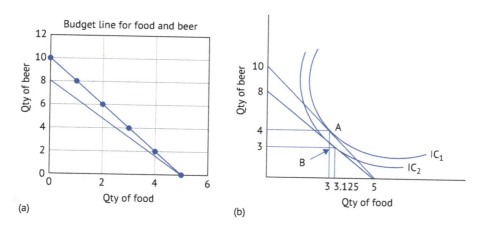

(a)

(b)

7.4.1 Changes in Utility Maximization from Changes in Relative Price

To be more specific, suppose the price of Samuel Adams beer has increased from $2 per bottle to $2.50 per bottle with no change in the price of food. Given this new price of food and beer, Figure 7.5 is redrawn from the same information depicted in Figure 7.4 in the previous section. In Figure 7.5, the new budget line with the price of beer at $2.50 per bottle and food still priced at $4 per unit, Bobby still has $20 to spend on food and beer, except the price of beer has increased from previous price of $2 per bottle. Obviously, with the new price, the budget constraint for Bobby will look like a different slope than what it was under the previous price. The slope under the old price was (10 − 0)/5 − 0) = 2 (absolute value ignoring the negative sign). With the new price ratio, the slope of the new budget line is (8 − 0)/(5 − 0) = 1.6, as shown in panel (a) in Figure 7.5.

Figure 7.5 includes a new budget line with eight bottles of beer on the vertical axis and five units of food on the horizontal axis. This new budget line has tilted inward from the previous level of ten bottles of beer because of the increase in the price of beer. With the new price, Bobby can buy a maximum of eight bottles of beer (2.50 × 8 = $20) with no food or a maximum of five units of food with no beer or both food and beer at other combinations between eight and five on the new budget line. Given the new budget constraint, if Bobby spends his full budget of $20 to maximize his TU for food and beer, his new combination of food and beer on this new budget line has to be different than point A illustrated under previous prices. To determine the new point of utility maximization under the new price of beer, the new budget line is redrawn from panel (a) to panel (b) in Figure 7.5. Given this new budget in panel (b), point A is no longer achievable by Bobby because it is beyond the new budget connected between eight units of beer on the vertical axis and five units of food on the horizontal axis. To maximize his utility under the new price and budget constraint, the new budget line must be tangent to the highest possible IC, as illustrated by IC_2 shifted parallel to IC_1. This new point of utility maximization is the tangency point at B, where the combination of three bottles of beer and a little more than three units of food will give the best scenario to maximize TU while spending his maximum budget of $20.

7.4.2 Relative Price Change, Utility Maximization, and Derivation of the Demand Curve

Integrating the effect of change in the relative price of beer and corresponding changes in utility maximization with the new price and quantity demand for beer are summarized next to derive the demand curve for beer. The price and quantity combination for both points A under previous prices and point B under new prices are calculated in Table 7.3.

Table 7.3: Relative Price Change and Bundle of Goods and Services

Old Price/ Unit	Quantity Demanded at Point A in Figure 7.5	New Price/Unit	Quantity Demanded at Point B in Figure 7.5
$2/bottle of beer	4	$2.50/ bottle	3
$4/food unit	3	$4/food	3.125
Budget spent	$4 \times 2 + 3 \times 4 = 8 + 12 = \$20$		$3 \times 2.5 + 3.125 \times 4 = 7.5 + 12.5 = \$20$

Figure 7.6 Utility Maximization and Derivation of the Demand Curve

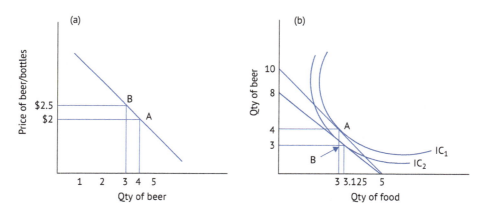

Using the price and quantity demanded for changes in the price of beer relative to the price of food, the information presented in Table 7.3 derived from points A and B from panel (b) of Figure 7.5 and the relevant demand curve for beer are illustrated in Figure 7.6 by redrawing panel (b) of Figure 7.5.

Figure 7.6 is the illustration of utility maximization redrawn from panel (b) of Figure 7.5 to derive the demand curve for beer against its two different prices of $2 and $2.50. This demand curve is derived from panel (b) and illustrated in panel (a) on the left side of Figure 7.6. This combination is also shown in Table 7.3 by taking the combinations of both food and beer from points A and B of utility maximization. As is shown in panel (a), all it needed was two points of coordinates between the prices of beer and their quantity demanded. For point A in panel (b), quantity demanded for beer is four units at $2 per bottle. It is plotted at point A in panel (a). From point B in panel (b), the quantity demanded for beer is decreased to three bottles of beer at $2.50 per bottle. This combination is plotted at point B in panel (a). Connecting these two points and expanding the line to the left and to the right is the derived demand curve for beer. Students are encouraged to practice similar techniques to derive the demand curve for assuming different changes in relative prices. It is also important to make a final note here that the movement from point A to point B in the process of utility maximization illustrated in panel (b) of Figures 7.5 and 7.6 has two implications for understanding and analyzing consumer behavior. This movement can be divided into two effects of consumer reaction because of changes in relative prices. One is called the income effect, and the other is the substitution effect. The income effect is the change in quantity demanded for beer because of the change in Bobby's real income or purchasing power because of the higher price of beer. The decline of quantity demanded for beer (from four units to three units) is part of this change in real purchasing power. The substitution effect is, on the other hand, the ability to purchase more quantities of food because of the rise in price of its substitute: beer. This is shown in the increase of quantity demanded for food just a little bit (from 3 units to 3.125 units). The mathematical mechanics and their graphical illustrations of these two effects and their real-world applications are much more tedious than the simple illustration shown in Figure 7.6 because they move from point A to point B. The details of the income effect and substitution effect are actually beyond the scope of this level of course learning. However, they are explained more systematically with higher levels of mathematical reasoning and relevant graphical illustrations in upper-level courses and in graduate schools. The chapter materials end here with the summary followed by application activities.

Chapter Summary

In Section 7.1, the concept of opportunity cost for making alternative decisions for the allocation of limited resources was discussed as an important part of measuring efficiency in production and consumption. The decision to allocate resources in the process of production and consumption is primarily a key part of human behavior. But the science of human behavior is extremely complex. Economists call this complexity the science of *behavioral economics*. Decisions made by consumers and producers come from many alternatives. Making the best choice from those alternatives is driven by a single motive: maximize satisfaction or profits, depending on whether we are consumers or producers. Given our limited resources, this section was dedicated to the analysis of maximizing satisfaction or utility for consumers, such as college students or professional workers, to make the best choice for buying different bundles of goods and services. Since this choice is not straightforward, the areas of exploring the best selection of goods and services from many alternatives are categorized next.

The rational choice theory of consumer preference is the concept of behavioral economics that deals with the rational and irrational decisions consumers make. Although the consumers are on average inherently rational, individuals make some random errors in their decisions.

Distinguishing those random errors from irrational actions is important to bring efficiency in production and consumption. The mechanics of maximizing our satisfaction from rational choice theory was discussed in this section, which explained how to minimize those random events of irrational activities if it is not possible to eliminate them.

The theory of the demand curve for individual consumers or the market demand theory and applications are actually integral parts of consumers' human behavior. The demand curve in the market for individuals or a group of consumers displays many combinations of price and quantity demands, reflecting the marginal willingness to pay (MWTP) approach of consumer behavior. This concept of MWTP is actually derived from the psychological aspect of consumer satisfaction from purchasing goods and services at different prices. This level of satisfaction for additional units of consumption is called marginal utility (MU). The values of MU of consumers are actually the points of those combinations of price and quantity on the demand curve, the same as the MWTP curve illustrated in Figure 7.1. The relationship between the demand curve and MWTP in terms of the DMU of goods and services from more quantities was explained in Figure 7.1, where some specific but hypothetical examples of beer consumption are given for a Red Sox fan called Bobby to maximize his utility maximization from beer consumption while watching the game. The utility maximization condition was thus derived by Eqn (7.1) rewritten as follows:

$$\textbf{Utility maximization for two goods:} \quad \left(\frac{MUb}{MUf}\right) = \left(\frac{Pb}{Pf}\right) \qquad \textbf{Eqn (7.1)}$$

In Sections 7.1.3 and 7.1.4, the concept of DMU was further extended to derive a demand curve and pricing mechanism for achieving optimum utility maximization and the best pricing scheme for business owners to maximize revenue. In these sections, a real-world example of the demand curve derivation and pricing scheme was applied to outdoor activities, such as kayaking. Figure 7.2. illustrated this mechanism of utility maximization and the best price scheme for kayaking. Section 7.2 presented the analysis of a consumer budget and utility maximization for two or more goods of consumption given a budget constraint and market prices. In this section, two goods were considered: beer and food for Red Sox fan Bobby while he watched the game in Fenway Park. Using the conditions of utility maximization for two goods, Figure 7.3 illustrated this condition with hypothetical data on food and beer consumption shown in Table 7.1. Section 7.3 analyzed the derivation of the MU from TU of Bobby from his combinations of beer and food within a given budget. The data of TU and MU used in Table 7.2 was graphically illustrated in Figure 7.4. The conditions for the utility maximization from two goods, beer and food, were based on the following equation:

$$\frac{\text{MU of Food}}{\text{Price of Food}} = \frac{\text{MU of Beer}}{\text{Price of Beer}}; \text{ or } \frac{MUf}{MUb} = Pf/Pb, \textbf{ same as Eqn (7.1) in Section 7.1.2.}$$

Furthermore, Figure 7.4 also integrated the consumer preference pattern by combining the indifference curve (IC), budget line, and relative price ratio for both goods, beer and food, to determine the utility maximization where the budget constraint is tangent to the highest possible IC fulfilling the utility maximization given next.

$$\textbf{TU Maximization} = \frac{\text{MUf}}{\text{MUb}} = \frac{\text{Pf}}{\text{Pb}} = \text{MRSfb} \qquad \textbf{Eqn (7.2)}$$

The equation is the condition of TU maximization at the tangency point between the IC and the budget line as the best possible combination of two goods for consumption. Figure 7.5 illustrated this utility maximization process for a typical consumer like Bobby. Section 7.4 explained the change in the tangency point between the budget line and highest possible IC when relative price changes. Changes in relative price, by assuming an increase in the price of beer per bottle and its corresponding change in the quantity demanded for beer, were illustrated in panel (a) of Figure 7.6 derived from panel (b) in the same figure. This derived demand curve for beer consumption validates the consistency of the law of demand, which states that if the price per unit of beer increases, then the quantity of demand will decrease if all other factors remain the same at that moment.

Application Activities

1. Suppose your friend in class has decided to purchase a pair of shoes that cost $150 or a dress shirt that costs $100. If she ends up purchasing the dress shirt, then it is possible to conclude that the MU of the dress shirt is higher than the MU of the additional pair of shoes. Explain this conclusion by describing the conditions of utility maximization in a two-goods case of consumption.

2. Consider the diagram that follows the demand curve for kayaking for a particular day in the summer or fall on the Charles River in Boston with the hourly rate of rental for a maximum of eight hours a day.

What is the total amount a kayaker will spend to boat for six hours?

Estimate the consumer surplus (CS) for the kayaker to boat for six hours?

Understanding the best possible scenario for the utility maximization for the kayaker and the CS and its relevant pricing scheme you, which you have learned in this chapter. What is the maximum price the kayaker will pay for kayaking all day for eight hours?

3. Suppose that a skier skiing in the White Mountains of New Hampshire in January is willing to pay for lift tickets for downhill skiing that reflects the MWTP = Demand

Image 7.1

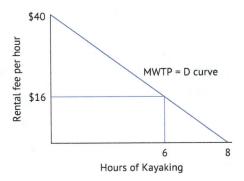

curve, as illustrated in image 7.2:

Based on the MWTP curve, select the correct answer for the multiple-choice questions that follow.

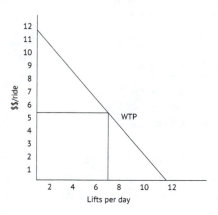

3.1. The willingness to pay (WTP; same as the demand curve) schedule slopes downward because

    a. There is DMU to additional ski runs on any given day.

    b. Since rational consumers only purchase items for which they expect to receive MU greater than or equal to the price, lower MU as quantity purchased expands implies lower WTP.

    c. Both a and b are true.

    d. None of the above is true.

3.2. Suppose all skiers had the same WTP schedule as this skier, and the resort operator charged $5 per ride up the lift. What is the price elasticity of demand at this price? Hint: Use the point elasticity of demand equation; do not use the midpoint arc elasticity equation.

    a. 1.0

    b. 0.714

    c. 0.5

    d. 2.5

3.3. The total revenue (TR) at price = $5 per lift is _____

    a. $35

    b. $50

    c. $60

    d. $55

3.4. The TR at P = $6 per lift is _____

    a. $72

    b. $55

    c. $ 36

    d. $30

3.5. Based on the relationship between the values of price elasticity of demand and the change in price and TR, the TR will be maximum in the ski resort at the elasticity value of ____

    a. 0.080

    b. 2.00

    c. 1.00

    d. 0.00

3.6. The CS at the price of $5 per lift is _____

    a. $24.5

    b. $36

    c. $42

    d. $49

3.7. If the ski resort owner eliminates the possibility of buying single-ride lift tickets and instead sells only all-day lift passes, entitling skiers to as many trips up the mountain as desired, what is the maximum price that could be charged (WTP) without discouraging skiers from coming to the ski resort? Hint: Skiers will pay the price up to where MU = 0 and MC of additional ski lifts is zero per as many lifts as skiers use at the single-ticket price.

    a. $72

    b. $55

    c. $48

    d. $36

Consider the following table with information regarding the preference and utility pattern of Red Sox fan Bobby when purchasing food and beer while watching a Red Sox game.

Consumption of Food			Consumption of Samuel Adams Beer		
Quantity	TU	MU	Quantity	TU	MU
0	0	–	0	0	–
1	120		1	160	
2	220		2	320	
3	300		3	440	
4	360		4	490	
5	400		5	520	

    a. Estimate the MU values for both food and beer and fill in the blanks in the MU columns.

    b. Suppose Bobby has $40 to spend on food or beer or both, and the price of beer is $4 per bottle and $5 for food/unit. What would be the best combination of beer and food for Bobby to maximize his TU?

    c. Suppose on another game day, Bobby found out that the beer price has gone up to $5 per bottle with no change in the price of food. With the new relative price, what will be the best combination of beer and food to maximize his TU?

d. Using the answers from 4.2 and 4.3, draw the corresponding demand curve for beer in a graph. You may skip the complexity of drawing the IC and tangency point.

e. Are beer and food close substitute goods? How did you figure it out? (Hint: Use the price elasticity of demand concept to calculate and apply the rule).

Chapter 8

Production Function, Cost Function, and Revenue and Profit Functions of Firms in Microeconomics

Learning Objectives

As they read the chapter, students will learn:

▶ Production Function and Measures of Productivities of Factors of Production

▶ Production Functions of Firms in the Short Run and in the Long Run

▶ Cost Functions of Firms and their Relationships in the SR and in the LR

▶ Economic Interpretation of Cost Efficiency and Economies of Scale

▶ Revenue and Profit Functions of Firms in the SR and in the LR

Introduction

Up to Chapter 7, the study materials covered were focused on the economics of consumer's behavior when dealing with the demand side of microeconomics. This chapter starts with the supply side of microeconomics, dealing with production function, cost functions, sales revenue, profit maximization, and cost minimization. Production is a technological relationship between outputs and inputs (factors of production) that relates to cost functions and the measures of efficiency in both production and cost of production. The primary goal of a firm is to manage production and costs and thus to maximize output while minimizing the cost of production. These simultaneous goals in the production process come down to the single-most-important objective of a firm: to maximize profit, the key driver for entrepreneurial investment. The economics of profit maximization is to analyze the process of measuring efficiency in production and cost. Measuring efficiency in production and cost involves understanding the technological efficiency, economic efficiency, and productivity of inputs—the factors of production. Setting aside the technological part of the production process, which is part of the engineering profession, economists focus on balancing between production efficiency and cost-efficiency so that overall economic efficiency is achieved. Before getting into the details of the production and cost functions in the next section, it is important to understand the difference between technological efficiency and economic efficiency—the core factors in this chapter and subsequent chapters for analyzing market competition. Technological efficiency measures the best possible combination of inputs and outputs to maximize profit subject to cost constraints. However, this criterion of technical efficiency does not necessarily guarantee economic efficiency because measuring economic efficiency needs to look at the pricing and consumers' ability to afford the output produced. As discussed in previous chapters, economic efficiency is quite relevant in understanding the difference between necessary goods and services and luxury goods. The efficiency of production and distribution of luxury goods is measured very differently than those of necessities. For example, traditional refrigerators and air conditioners we use in homes and offices are manufactured with a chemical substance called chlorofluorocarbons (CFCs) or another substitute substance called hydrofluorocarbons (HFCs), which are used as refrigerants, major ingredients to cool off the fridge and air-conditioning units. The problem with these chemicals is that they are extremely toxic and a thousand times more dangerous than carbon dioxide, causing greenhouse gases and thus damaging the ozone layer of the atmosphere. The replacement of these chemicals with better substitutes, such as thermoelectric technology,[1] to produce high-end refrigerators and air conditioners will be expensive, and it will take decades to bring costs down for the consumer market. Students are encouraged to read the article referenced in the footnote about the high cost of switching to new technology in order to manufacture a greener substitute for CFCs or HFCs.[1]

A similar example is relevant here about the efficiency of manufacturing plug-in electric motor vehicles as a substitute for the combustible engine powered by fossil fuel. The technology of producing fully electric cars or hybrid cars is not new; the first electric vehicle was invented by Scottish engineer Robert Anderson back in 1832, followed by American inventor Thomas Davenport in 1835. The reason that electric vehicles have not had much commercial success, even today with Tesla, is because of the lack of economic efficiency. Tesla, founded by Elon Musk, was highly subsidized by the US government to promote its commercial venture in 2008 when its first sports luxury model Roadster was sold at close to $100,000. Since then, Tesla has been struggling to make the company profitable by producing several models, including the Model S, Model 3, and Model X, with no significant commercial success. The answer to Tesla's unsuccessful commercial venture since the company started production in 2006 is simple: the absence of economic efficiency. The bottom line is that the technology

---

1   Jeremy Deaton, "A Clever Fix to the Biggest Climate Problem," Nexus Media, May 16, 2016, https://nexusmedianews.com/a-clever-fix-to-the-biggest-climate-problem-5d6362a0dbe8.

for producing plug-in electric vehicles is great but not so great in lowering costs for achieving economic efficiency. Until the costs and pricing are low enough to sell to mass consumers, Tesla cars, or any other electric vehicles, will not be close substitutes of traditional cars operated by fossil fuel. To dig further, electric vehicles are not even green in the sense that the production of lithium battery packs causes toxic emission to the air, and powering the cars overnight uses the electricity grid (unless it can be powered up by hydraulic or solar energy). There are several examples like these that we witness every day and realize how challenging it can be to transform production technology to a green economy by balancing between technical efficiency and economic efficiency. The Green New Deal initiative introduced by the Democratic Party of the US Congress in February 2019 will face the same challenge.

8.1 Production Function and Measures of Productivities of Factors of Production

To assist students with understanding the difference between the concepts of production, cost, and economic efficiency of production and distribution, this section starts with the basic theories of production function and productivity measures of factors of production for a typical firm.

8.1.1 Production Function

The theoretical definition of a *production function* is a technological relationship between total output and a combination of inputs (factors of production) to produce certain units of goods and services within a specified time period. This production function, either manu-facturing, service, or farm (agriculture), is an engineering project that economists use as the model structure to analyze its economic efficiency of production, cost, revenue, and profit. The general equation for production function is presented in Eqn (8.1).

$$\text{Total output} = q = F(K, L), \qquad \text{Eqn (8.1)}$$

where q = total output

    K = capital input (that is in a broad sense by considering all costs other than labor)

    L = labor input

Now it is important to note that this engineering production model is usually developed by a production engineer because of its capacity to produce certain units of total output in a fixed time period (weekly or monthly basis) by using a specified amount of capital and labor hours. Depending on the relative factor proportion used in the production process, technology of production can be *capital intensive or labor intensive*. For example, if the K/L ratio is greater than one in a particular technology of production, then the factor intensity of that production function is called capital intensive. Capital-intensive production function means that the technology of production requires more capital input than labor input. As a

real-world example, high-technology products such as software programming and development, microchip production technology of semiconductor industries, and hardware equipment
for computer-related and similar industries involve a highly capital-intensive production process. On the other hand, if the K/L ratio is less than one, then the production function is said
to be labor intensive, meaning the technology requires more labor hours than the amount of
capital. The classic examples of labor-intensive industries are textiles, shoes, shipbuilding,
steel manufacturing, traditional agriculture farming, and construction works In understanding
the technology and factor intensity, it is also important to measure the productivity of factors
of production function introduced in Eqn (8.1). Using this equation, Section 8.1.2 provides
some insights about the productivity of factors and rate of productivity of those capital and
labor inputs, with their economic implications.

8.1.2 Productivity of Capital and Labor: Measures of Marginal and Average Productivity

Marginal productivity of capital (MP$_K$) and *marginal productivity of labor* (MP$_L$) are defined as
additional outputs added to total output by each additional unit of capital and labor, respectively. By using simple differentiation techniques, students have learned from Calculus 101
that taking the partial derivatives of Eqn (8.1) will provide the equations for MP$_K$ and MP$_L$ in
Eqns (8.2) and (8.3), respectively, as shown next.

$$\text{Marginal productivity of capital} = MP_K = \frac{\delta q}{\delta K} \qquad \text{Eqn (8.2)}$$

$$\text{Marginal productivity of labor} = MP_L = \frac{\delta q}{\delta L} \qquad \text{Eqn (8.3)}$$

The two equations indicate the measures of efficiency of capital and labor as more and
more capital and labor inputs are added to produce more output. Specific examples with
hypothetical data will be presented in the next section.

The *average productivity of capital* (AP$_K$) and *average productivity of labor* (AP$_L$) are also
possible to measure by simply dividing the total output levels at different levels of input as
more and more inputs are added to produce more and more output. The relevant equations
for these productivity measures are shown by using Eqn (8.1). Specific examples with hypothetical data will be discussed in the next section.

$$\text{Average productivity of capital} = APK = \frac{q}{K} \qquad \text{Eqn (8.4)}$$

$$\text{Average productivity of labor} = APL = \frac{q}{L} \qquad \text{Eqn (8.5)}$$

Firm/farm versus industry/market: It is important to note here that the concepts of *firm* (in
service or manufacturing) and *farm* (in agriculture) are about an individual production unit
producing or delivering specific products or services to customers. On the other hand, *industry*
or *market* refers to all market activities of production and distribution in which individual
firms compete to gain market share by producing and selling similar goods and services.
The details of firm and industry relationships will be discussed in the next few chapters in
regard to market competition and its applications. At this point, it is important to note that

the size of a firm and/or farm widely varies depending on the scope and size of the industry and its relative market share. Small-size companies are mostly *partnership business entities*, and large-size firms are usually called *corporations*. The financial and accounting activities are taught in detail in business school courses focused on accounting and managerial finance.

8.2 Production Functions of Firms in the Short Run and the Long Run

This section is focused on short-run (SR) and long-run (LR) production functions and their analysis by using a production model with a production data schedule and their graphs.

8.2.1 SR and LR Production Functions

Production function is also defined as *SR production function* and *LR production function*. SR production function is considered to be a stage of the production process during which at least some inputs are fixed in quantity and some other inputs are variable as more output is produced by using more and more quantity of the variable input given the quantity of fixed input. For example, if a boat manufacturing company called the Boston Kayak Company (BKC) produces kayaks, it has already invested quite a bit of capital into its boat factory, along with all the ingredients it needs before staring the production of kayaks. This amount of capital already invested prior to the beginning of production is a fixed capital (K). The variable input in this case will be the labor input (L), such as the carpenters and their helpers who need to be hired to begin the production process.

On the other hand, LR production function is considered the stage of the production process during which all inputs of production are variable. In an example from the kayak production of the firm BKC mentioned earlier, the firm may have to increase its plant size to meet a growing demand from a regional or nationwide market. In this case, BKC will have to expand its plant size through capital expansion and more labor to meet the rising market demand for kayaks. In the LR, therefore, all inputs are variable. One important note here to emphasize is that there is no calendar time involved when comparing SR and LR. The time line between SR and LR depends on changing the plant size in response to industry or market demand after the initial start of the operation. In other words, we can say that SR is short enough to keep some inputs as fixed (usually capital input), and LR is long enough to expand the size of the firm with all inputs as variables.

8.2.2 Analysis of SR and LR Production with Data and Graphs

Considering the hypothetical boating company mentioned earlier, suppose the firm BKC is operating in the SR as a start-up enterprise. Table 8.1 shows the hypothetical data for the SR production process and its labor productivities (marginal productivity and average productivity). Using Eqns (8.1) through (8.5), Table 8.1 shows the estimation of total output (q) and measures of factor productivities in the SR production function followed by the analysis of the LR cost function. The data in the table represents total product, marginal product, and average product of labor input as variable inputs.

Table 8.1: Production and Productivity for BKC

Labor Input	Total Output* q = F (K, L)	Marginal Product $MPL = \dfrac{\delta q}{\delta L}$	Average Product $APL = \dfrac{q}{L}$
0	0	0	0
1	2	2	2
2	6	4	3
3	15	9	5
4	21	6	5
5	25	4	5
6	25	0	4.17
7	21	−4	3
8	16	−5	2

Total output is the quantity of kayak production per month given the fixed-capital input.

The input of the quantity of labor and quantity of total output of kayaks are illustrated in Figure 8.1, along with corresponding marginal product and average product as more and more labor inputs are added to produce more kayaks. The analysis of the relationship between output and productivities of labor input as variable factors of production (with capital input as a fixed cost of production) is shown in Table 8.1 and illustrated in Figure 8.1.

Starting with the production data in Table 8.1, students may notice that with successive labor inputs added to the production process with a fixed quantity of capital (not shown in the table for simplicity), the quantity of total output increases and reaches its maximum at 25 units of kayaks with the quantity of labor at five units. Additional labor inputs in the production process will not increase output, and total output starts declining at seven units of labor. This typical pattern of SR production function with fixed capital is common in

Figure 8.1 TP, MP, and Average Product (AP) of Variable Input Labor

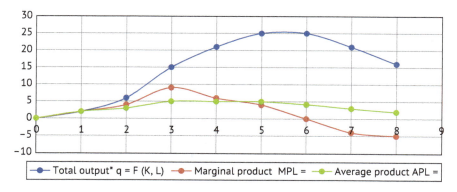

most of the technology regardless of the size of a firm. Applying the concept of MP_L, it shows the declining rate in Column 3 of Table 8.1. In the beginning of the production process, the quantity of MP_L rises at an increasing rate up to two units of labor and then at a decreasing rate up to three units of labor followed by a fall at a decreasing rate until it reaches zero at six units of labor. If the owner of BKC continues to hire more labor units, the MP_L becomes negative, as shown at seven and eight units of labor. This process of production efficiency in terms of declining MP_L is known as *diminishing marginal return (DMR)*. The law of DMR states that for an SR production function, the MP of the variable input (the labor in this case) increases at an increasing rate in the early stage of production and then decreases slowly and eventually becomes zero and negative as more and more labor is added without expanding the fixed quantity of capital. The reason for the decline of the MP_L is the loss of efficiency of productivity as more labor is added to the fixed capacity of production. It further implies that when the production capacity of a fixed size of a plant has a maximum limit with a maximum quantity limit of labor, hiring more labor beyond that maximum capacity will result in the loss of the efficiency of production because of an oversupply of labor.

The law of DMR is also illustrated in Figure 8.1, where the maximum point of MP_L is at three units of labor, and it reaches to zero at six units of labor when the total output is a maximum of 25 kayaks. We can also see that the further addition of labor to the production process reduces the total output production at seven units of labor, and its corresponding MP_L becomes negative beyond that point. On the other hand, the AP_L also declines after the point of maximum level of output at a slower rate than that of the MP_L. It is also worth observing that the AP of labor still shows a positive quantity even when MP_L is negative. It implies that using the MP concept is more important for measuring the efficiency of additional labor in its contribution to the production process. The measure of production efficiency by using the MP_L helps provide the owner of a firm with information to assist with making hiring decisions. In this case, the BKC owner should not hire additional labor beyond five or six units because further hiring of labor would generate negative MP_L as a result of the inefficiency of production in a crowded process. However, this constraint in hiring additional labor does not apply in the LR production process because capital input is expanded to a higher capacity of production. Therefore, in the LR, the productivity curve and total output curve shown in Figure 8.1 will shift upward with higher labor productivity in terms of both MP and AP of labor input.

8.3 Cost Functions of Firms and Their Relationships in the SR and the LR

In Section 8.2, analysis was made on the theory of the production function of a typical firm with its technological relationship with inputs (capital and labor) and productivity as a tool for measuring the factor efficiency of production. The concept of the cost of production embedded in the production function and factor productivity is an integral part of the entire production process. Understanding different cost concepts and their implications for achieving cost-efficiency to maximize a firm's total revenue and profit is as important as understanding the production function and its relevant technology. In this section, the focus is on the theories of various cost functions and their behavior of a typical firm in both SR and LR perspectives. At the end of this section, students are expected to know the sources of the supply curve in the market that we introduced in Chapter 3 and their application, which was covered in Chapter 4. The supply curve is basically derived from marginal cost behavior of a typical firm in both SR and LR production functions.

8.3.1 Types of Cost Function Derived from the Production Function

In reference to the production function stated in Eqn. (8.1), it is relevant to use the same production function to derive a theoretical cost function, which I present in Eqn (8.6) as a total cost (TC) function.

$$\text{Total cost (TC)} = TC = [q = F(K, L)] \qquad \text{Eqn (8.6)}$$

Eqn. (8.6) is a general expression of TC function as a dependent variable to changes with the increase in the quantity of output (q) as the independent variable. The restatement of output in Eqn. (8.1) in the right-hand side of Eqn. (8.6) also indicates that TC is actually dependent not only on output produced but also on how much capital input and labor input are used in producing different quantities of output. Therefore, it is clear that the connection between TC and quantity of total output (q) is such that TC will increase as more output is produced. And as more output is produced more quantity of inputs are needed, which would obviously add more costs to the production process. It also indicates that the prices of capital and labor are important factors for determining the behavior of TC increases as output increases. The price of capital is basically the price of funds needed to pay for the fixed cost in the SR. This price of capital funds is the interest rate or the opportunity cost of using funds in alternative investments or simply the cost of borrowing funds for a business venture. The price of labor is called wages and salaries. Since we are focusing on the behavior of various cost functions given the prices of capital (interest rates) and labor (wages), we will skip the price of inputs in this section. However, we cover the price of factors of production in Chapter 16. Using the equation for TC function expressed in Eqn (8.6), the types of various cost functions in SR and LR are listed next as simple algebraic definitions.

Given the aforementioned concepts and estimation methods of all types of cost functions, it can be easily observed that if we know the values of TC (FC + VC) and quantities of output as more and more output is produced, then we can estimate the rest of the cost functions in both SR and LR cost behavior. For example, if we know the TFC, which does not change in the SR production process, and the AFC is estimated by dividing the TFC (the same number at zero level of output) by successive units of output, then the variable cost kicks in the moment output starts in production. So, adding VC and FC gives you the TC at successive units of output produced. The rest of the cost functions are straightforward to estimate directly from TC and VC numbers that increase as more and more output is produced. The hypothetical data on all these cost functions are estimated in Table 8.2 for the firm BKC.

There are seven SR cost functions:

1. Total cost (TC) = Total fixed cost (TFC) + Total variable cost (TVC) as expressed in Eqn (8.6).
2. Total fixed cost (TFC) = The sunk cost (not recoverable) already incurred in fixed capital before the production starts. TFC does not change regardless of if the output increases or ceases to produce.
3. Total variable cost (TVC) = The cost that increases as output increases.
4. Marginal cost (MC) = The ratio of changes in TC to changes in quantity of output (q).

$$= \frac{\Delta TC}{\Delta q}$$

5. Average fixed cost (AFC) = The ratio of TFC to total output (q).
6. Average variable cost (AVC) = The ratio of TVC to output as output (q) increases.
7. Average total cost (ATC) = The ratio of TC to output as output (q) increases.

LR cost functions are reduced to three cost functions listed here:

1. LR total cost (LRTC) = LRTC increases as output increases, and TC is the same as the TVC because there is no fixed cost in the LR.
2. MC = The ratio of LRTC to output as output (q) increases = $\frac{\Delta LRTC}{\Delta q}$.
3. LR average total coast = LRATC is the ratio of LRTC to output (q).

Table 8.2 is the data set for all seven types of cost functions for an SR cost structure for BKC in manufacturing kayaks per month. The FC before production starts is $1,000 in capital cost, and it does not change in the SR as production units increase from zero to ten units per month. The TVC starts at $1,000 for the production of one unit and then continuously increases as the quantity of output increases, as shown in Column (3). Column (4) gives the data on TC by adding Column (2) and Column (3), which also increases as output increases. Column (5) provides the estimated value of MC as the ratio of changes of TC to changes of output by one unit. MC data starts with $1,000 and then drops significantly and reaches a minimum point of $400 at the output level of three units followed by a sharp rise to $5,000 at ten units of output. Similarly, the AVC data estimated in Column (7) starts at $7,000 and drops to its minimum point of $666.67 at the output level of three units and then rises sharply as output increases. Likewise, the ATC data in Column (8) starts with $2,000 and drops to its minimum point of $950 at four units of output followed by continuous rise as output increases. It is also worth noticing that the upward rate of increase in MC data tends to be equal to the minimum points of both AVC and ATC at output levels between three and four units (MC = AVC minimum) and between four and five units (MC = ATC at minimum point of

Table 8.2: SR Cost Functions for BKC

Output (q)	TFC in$	TVC	TC = (2) + (3)	MC $= \dfrac{\Delta TC}{\Delta q}$ $= \Delta(3)\Delta/((1)$	AFC = (2)/(1)	AVC = (3)/(1)	ATC = (4)/(1)
(1)	(2)	(3)	(4)	(5)	(6)	(7)	(8)
0	1,000	0	1,000	–	–	–	–
1	1,000	1,000	2,000	1,000	1,000.00	1,000.00	2,000.00
2	1,000	1,600	2,600	600	500.00	800.00	1,300.00
3	1,000	2,000	3,000	400	333.33	666.67	1,000.00
4	1,000	2,800	3,800	800	250.00	700.00	950.00
5	1,000	3,800	4,800	1,000	200.00	760.00	960.00
6	1,000	5,200	6,200	1,400	166.67	866.67	1,033.33
7	1,000	7,200	8,200	2,000	142.86	1,028.57	1,171.43
8	1,000	10,000	11,000	2,800	125.00	1,250.00	1,375.00
9	1,000	14,000	15,000	4,000	111.11	1,555.56	1,666.67
10	1,000	19,000	20,000	5,000	100.00	1,900.00	2,000.00

ATC), respectively. This crucial relationship between MC, AVC, and ATC will be further applied to profit maximization behavior in the next chapter. For now, the graphical illustration of this relationship among these three cost functions is shown in Figure 8.2 with more explanation to follow. Column (6) in Table 8.2 is the estimated data for AFC behavior by dividing Column (2) by Column (1). Since the fixed value of TFC is divided by higher and higher levels of output, the AFC values decline steadily as output increases. The data in the AFC column is plotted in Figure 8.4.

8.3.2. Graphical Representation of SR Cost Curves

Figure 8.2 is plotted by using the data from Columns (1), (2), (3), and (4), with output on the horizontal axis and TFC, TVC, and TC on the vertical axis. We see the clear relationship among these three cost functions, as TFC is a fixed straight line parallel to the horizontal axis at $1,000 fixed cost. The TVC cost curve starts from the zero level of output marked in red. The TC curve is the horizontal summation of TFC and TVC plotted above the TVC curve. The vertical distance between the TVC and TC curves is exactly the amount of TFC. The relationship among the other three cost functions, ATC, AVC, and MC, is illustrated in Figure 8.3.

Figure 8.3 shows a typical pattern of relationship among ATC, AVC, and MC functions in the SR production process. The graphs of these three cost functions are illustrated from the data in Table 8.2. First, students may notice that all three curves start from a high level of costs

Figure 8.2   TFC, TVC, and TC Curves

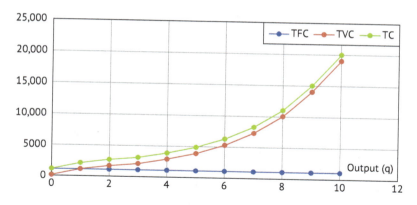

and drop sharply as more outputs are produced. Second, all of them reach their minimum points at different output levels before rising upward sharply. The minimum point of the MC curve occurs first at the output level of three units followed by the minimum points of AVC at close to four units of output and ATC curves at close to five units of output. They are all U-shaped, indicating the law of diminishing returns, which was explained earlier. Third, and most important to notice, the upward-sloping part of the MC curve cuts through the minimum points of both AVC and ATC curves from below. The three typical characteristics of these three curves have important implications for not only explaining the law of diminishing returns but also understanding the process of profit maximization in the SR. I will discuss and revisit this phenomenon in the next chapter. One more cost data for AFC is illustrated in Figure 8.4 from Column (6) in Table 8.2.

Figure 8.3   AVC, ATC, and MC Curves

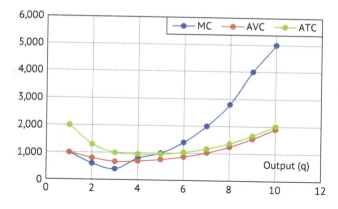

Figure 8.4   AFC Curve

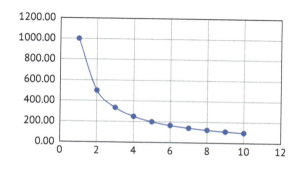

Figure 8.4 shows that the AFC curve is continuously in decline as the TFC is divided by successive units of output produced. In accounting terms, this rate of decreasing cost behavior of fixed costs of capital is called overhead cost per successive units of output. The unique shape of the AFC curve is steadily decreasing the cost function spreading over higher levels of output produced.

Chapter 8: Production Function, Cost Function, and Revenue and Profit Functions of Firms in Microeconomics

8.3.3 LR Cost Functions and Cost Efficiency

As mentioned earlier, there are three categories of LR cost functions: LRTC, LRATC, and LRMC. They are defined next and repeated from Section 8.3.1.

1. *LRTC* increases as output increases and TC is the same as the TVC because of no fixed cost in the LR. LRTC cost is the TC function associated with the production function of a firm when all inputs (both capital and labor) are variable as the plant size of a firm expands. The behavior of LRTC varies according to the relative size of a firm. For example, large-size firms, such as aircraft manufacturing companies or giant software companies; semiconductor firms, such as Intel; software operating system companies, such as Microsoft, Google, Apple, IBM; and similar companies have very high capital investments that constantly change as they continuously expand their size of operations to meet growing market demand. On the other hand, smaller companies do also grow faster in the LR, and their cost behavior changes but to a lesser degree in capital cost than large-size corporations. Therefore, depending on the relative size of the company, the speed of increase in output and related TC varies a great deal from firm to firm.

2. *MC = The ratio of LRTC to output as output (q) increases* $= \dfrac{\Delta \text{LRTC}}{\Delta q}$ is the simple derivate of LRTC with respect to the output level as output increases. Again, the larger the size of a firm, the greater the advantage it will have in decreasing its MC because major proportions of large-size firms need to invest more heavily in capital than the labor component. As the output increases, increasing cost as MC gets spread out across the board of production structure and thus MC continuously declines.

3. *LRATC is the ratio of the LRTC to output (q)* level as output continuously increases. Unlike in the SR, LRATC is the reflection of the efficiency of cost minimization of a firm that generates the lowest possible average cost of production. The process of cost minimization is mainly attributed to the declining rate of LRMC derived from the best combination of technology, labor specialization, and effective production and labor management.

Figure 8.5 summarizes the relationship between LRATC and LRMC curves (skipping the TC curve) stated earlier with its cost-efficiency implications for cost and labor productivity with a large capital investment.

Figure 8.5 illustrates the LR behavior of ATC and MC with a relatively flat portion of minimum ATC and MC as output increases. This cost-efficiency is achieved by

Figure 8.5   LRATC and LRMC Curves

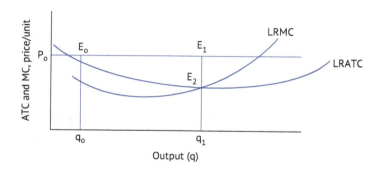

expanding the plant size with massive investment in the plant and equipment and the related capital component (both physical and human capital) with less intensity of the labor component. For this structure of high capital intensity of production technology, firms such as semiconductor companies, cloud computing companies, e-commerce companies, software companies, mobile operating systems (Apple, Android, Microsoft, IBM, and others), and similar entities take advantage of production and cost-efficiency by expanding the plant size rapidly in the LR. Cost and productivity management are the key driving forces in maintaining their low cost and high productivity in the complex nature of new plants and equipment demanded by new technologies. Economists call these forces *economies of scale* and *diseconomies of scale*. These two important concepts are briefly explained next.

8.4 Economic Interpretation of Cost-Efficiency and Economies of Scale

From the discussion on theories of cost functions and the analysis of data with their graphs in previous sections, the interpretation of cost-efficiency is presented here to compare the concepts of economies of scale, diseconomies of scale, and economies of scope with examples.

8.4.1 Economies of Scale

As total output increases, MC of production decreases very sharply in the beginning, and the longer the MC keeps declining, ATC also declines with increasing rates of output produced. This cost-efficiency of production is reflected in the downward-sloping ATC curve shown in Figure 8.5. In other words, when ATC (cost per unit) declines as more and more output is produced, this is called *economies of scale*. The key advantage of economies of scale of cost-efficiency is the firm's ability to keep cost per unit low and declining so that the profit margin per unit of output sold is stable and even increasing as ATC continues to decline as more output is produced. For example, with a fixed price per unit at P_o in Figure 8.5, the breakeven point (P = ATC) is achieved at output level q_o, where the corresponding price per unit and ATC intersects at E_o. As output increases beyond q_o, the advantage of economies of scale shows increasing profit margin by the vertical distance between the fixed price per unit and the declining rate of ATC. This increasing profit margin reaches to its maximum at output level q_1, where LRATC is minimum and the highest margin of profit (P-ATC) is the vertical distance between E_1 and E_2. This profit maximization process attributed to the advantage of economies of scale is also known as *minimum efficiency of scale (MES)*. It is also worth mentioning here that with the advancement of technology, this minimum efficient scale is further explained by shifting the entire set of ATC and MC curves in Figure 8.5 downward. The downward shift of the ATC curve with same price level helps increase a firm's profit margin further at a lower cost. Therefore, the LR production process of most firms, especially large-size corporations, tends to adopt new technology to take advantage of MES to lower the LRATC further by shifting LRMC and LRATC curves down and thus raising the profit margin. Students are encouraged to practice this MES concept from real-world perspectives while comparing large-scale firms and their strategies for buying out smaller rivals or just competing them out of the market by lowering their prices a little bit.

In this context, there is a little bit of history that explains how the dot.com boom and bust happened at the turn of this century. During the internet revolution of the late 1990s, more than 700 dot.com companies emerged simultaneously in the United States alone to take advantage of e-commerce opportunities. However, more than 90 percent of those dot.com companies started off with limited and small amounts of capital. Within a very short time span, the majority of those dot.com companies ran out of capital before they were able to reach the breakeven point, as illustrated in Figure 8.5. At that point, the value of their market capitalization started to decline. As a remedy, they needed more funds to continue their operations so that they could increase output and sells to lower their ATC and reach profitability. Unfortunately, the venture capitalist who had already funded them as start-ups declined their requests for more financing. Actually, some Wall Street analysts made a joke in their reporting at that time, staying, "Show me the money first before asking for more money" (a phrase borrowed from the punchline in the 1996 Hollywood movie *Jerry Maguire*). As a result of not obtaining more funds, most of the dot.com companies went bankrupt by early 2001, bringing a severe recession to the US economy that year. That recession was further aggravated by the tragic terrorist attacks on September 11, 2001.

8.4.2 Diseconomies of Scale

The concept of *diseconomies of scale* is said to be an increase in ATC as output increases. This increasing rate of ATC is mainly attributed to increasing MC and declining MP_L, as well as similar factors of production. This process is called the law of diminishing returns, as explained in Section 8.1. The upward portion of the LRATC curve in Figure 8.5 indicates the state of diseconomies of scale. This stage of inefficiency of production can happen even in very large-size firms because they cannot handle the growth and its challenge efficiently at certain points of expansion. As a result, mergers, acquisitions, and downsizing of many big firms are common organizational restructuring methods. However, the adoption of new technology does help many large-size companies to move into the MES level to survive and turnaround. As an example, Microsoft's restructuring of its business strategy at the beginning of 2010 was done by moving its key resources from its core stand-alone oper-ating system to cloud computing. Such a strategic move has saved and earned billions of dollars in recent years and, therefore, saved the company from potential financial trouble. It is also possible, how-ever, that some product divisions in corporations do rarely encounter diseconomies of scale. In that case, the LRATC curve would not be a U-shaped curve. It would rather be continuously downward sloping, as illustrated in Figure 8.6. As we can see, the ATC curve starts declining and stays downward sloping as more and more output is produced. In other words, as more output is produced, the ATC curve continuously declines—a case of economies of scale at all levels of output expansion.

Figure 8.6 Economies of Scale and the ATC Curve

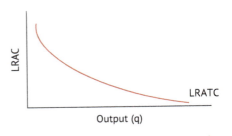

Microeconomics Principles, Applications, and Policy Implications

8.4.3 Economies of Scale and Economies of Scope

The last conceptual understanding presented in this section is the distinguish between the concept of *economies of scale* and *economies of scope*. As defined earlier, economies of scale are the declining rates of ATC (cost per unit) as output and plant size expand (see in Figures 8.5 and 8.6). This possibility of cost-efficiency is mainly attributed to using better technology and highly skilled specialized workers to produce a specific product or service. For example, cloud computing, antivirus software patch, microchip processing semiconductors, mobile apps, operating systems (for laptop and mobile phones), and similar products and services.

On the other hand, the concept of *economies of scope* is defined as the cost-efficiency generated from producing multiple products at a much cheaper rate under the same or similar technology and specialized workforce. Economies of scope refer to the strategy of cost reduction in MC and ATC by producing substitutes and complementary goods under the same management of operations. Large-size beer companies in the United States, such as Anheuser-Busch (which makes Budweiser) and its rivals Coors Brewing Company and Miller Brewing Company, make many brands of beer, along with many kinds of snacks with a very low cost to raise their profit margins. The largest consumer products manufacturing company Proctor & Gamble (P&G) has manufactured hundreds of different products for decades with a great deal of success in keeping their ATC at a low level. The motive behind mergers and acquisitions among many big corporations is nothing more than expanding their economies of scope to lower costs and increase profit margin. Several years ago, P&G acquired Boston-based Gillette with the same motivation. Economies of scope are basically derived from the concept of the MES of production discussed earlier. The following article was published by the *Wall Street Journal* in 2005 and explains the economies of scope for P&G in acquiring Gillette.

Case Study of Economies of Scale and Economies of Scope

P&G's Gillette Edge: The Playbook It Honed at Wal-Mart

Sarah Ellison, Ann Zimmerman, and Charles Forelle

If you have a digital edition of this book, please click on the following link to access the report by CBS Sports about the price increase for 2018 Super Bowl ticket sales.

https://www.wsj.com/articles/ SB110712811453540527

If you have a print edition of this book, please use your cell phone to scan the QR code to access the article:

8.5 Revenue and Profit Functions of Firms in the SR and the LR

In previous sections in this chapter, the theories of production and several types of cost functions were introduced and discussed in detail with real-world examples and policy implications. We will apply these production and cost concepts in the next chapter in relation to market competition and profit maximization process of firms and industries. But before we get to the analysis of market competition for profit maximization, the concepts of profit and revenue need to be explained. As mentioned earlier, the primary motivation of a firm's entrepreneurship is the maximization of profit and/or cost minimization in both the SR and the LR. In this last section, the basic equation for a profit function of a typical firm is introduced with conditions of profit maximization. The total profit function of a typical firm is expressed in Eqn (8.7).

$$\text{Total profit (q) = Total revenue (TR = p} \times \text{q) − TC (q),} \qquad \text{Eqn (8.7)}$$

where q in the parentheses in each of the components of Eqn (8.7) means that all these components depend on the quantity of output produced. TR is defined by price per unit multiplied by the quantity of output produced. In the SR, to maximize the total profit as the primary objective of a firm, it must continue to produce to a level of output where profit is maximized and/or cost is minimized to reach the optimal point of equilibrium. In this case, there are two possible ways to do it: (1) profit maximization subject to cost constraint (given cost of capital and labor) or (2) cost minimization subject to output target. These two possible options are based on the theoretical foundation of a firm's objective of profit maximization depending on which option fits the best with the firm's strategy. However, in the LR, there is no cost constraint, and the firm can continue its production to a level where the maximum possible profit is obtained. In either case, the general condition for profit maximization in both SR and LR would be at a maximum level of output where marginal profit is zero. In other words, as long as the marginal profit from each additional quantity of output produced is positive, the firm will continue to produce until the marginal profit becomes zero. This simple logic makes sense because a profit-maximizing firm will not produce up to a point where additional profit (marginal profit) falls into negative territory. By using a simple concept from basic calculus, it is possible to take the derivative of Eqn (8.7) with respect to output (q) and set the derivative equal to zero, as expressed in Eqn (8.8).

$$\text{Marginal profit = d(Total profit)/dq = d(TR = p} \times \text{q)/dq = d(TC)/dq = 0 (zero)} \qquad \text{Eqn (8.8)}$$

In the equation, the left-hand component of marginal profit is zero, d(TR)/dq is marginal revenue (MR), and the d(TC)/dq is MC. Therefore, Eqn (8.8) can be rewritten in as

$$\text{MR − MC = 0 (zero).}$$

Or, more precisely,

$$\text{MR = MC.} \qquad \text{Eqn (8.9)}$$

Eqn (8.9) derived from Eqn (8.8) implies that the condition for profit maximization, the maximum output level, must be produced at the point of equilibrium output where MR = MC, with marginal profit equal to zero. This general condition of the profit maximization rule is called the golden rule **MR = MC** for both SR and LR production and cost behavior. This golden rule will be used frequently in analyzing the market competition in the next three chapters.

At this point, one more thing is important to highlight: in the MR component in Eqn (8.8), students may notice two items for TR as price (p) and output (q).

When both p and q are variables in monopolies and imperfect competition, we must differentiate them twice to get the value of MR, **[P × (dq/dq)] − [q × (dp/dq)]**. In that case, MR value will be different and less than price. On the other hand, when price (p) is fixed by a firm, such as in perfect competition, differentiation of the fixed price with respect to output is zero (the derivative of any fixed number is zero), which means the second part of the MR derivative (q × dp/dq) is zero. In other words, we can conclude that when price is fixed in case of perfect competition, MR = Price (dq/dq = 1). This important concept of MR and its relationship with price under different competitive market structure will be applied in the next few chapters. For now, we have learned this important golden rule of profit maximization of output where MR = MC. This concludes our analysis of the principles of production and cost functions and their applications. The summary of this chapter is given next followed by practice questions.

Chapter Summary

Section 8.1 introduced production function as a technological relationship between inputs and outputs produced, along with measures of productivity of inputs (labor and capital). The concepts of marginal productivity and average productivity of variable input, such as labor, were introduced with their economic interpretations for diminishing returns. Also, factor intensity was explained as the capital labor ratio with different technology for different goods and services to produce. If the K/L ratio is greater than one, then the production is said to be capital intensive, and if the K/L ratio is less than one, this means the production function is labor intensive.

In Section 8.2, the SR and LR production functions and their implications for productivity were explained with specific data in Table 8.1 and an illustration of the data in Figure 8.1. The law of diminishing returns in the SR production function was further explained with its economic implications for production efficiency of a firm's production process.

Section 8.3 introduced various cost functions of a firm for both SR and LR production functions. The unique relationships among ATC, MC, and AVC were introduced with their interpretations in the context of cost-efficiency. The cost data of all cost categories were introduced in Table 8.2 and illustrated in Figures 8.2, 8.3, 8.4, and 8.5.

Section 8.4 discussed measures of cost-efficiency in terms of economies of scale, diseconomies of scale, and economies of scope, along with their applications in the real world of business and operations management in the production process. An article featuring the case study for Gillette's acquisition by P&G was also referred to as an example of economies of scope.

Section 8.5 introduced the equation for total profit as a function of TR minus TC. The profit-maximizing condition of the **MR = MC** threshold was derived from the total profit equation, setting the marginal profit equal to zero so that profit-maximizing output can be determined. This golden rule of **MR = MC** as the condition for profit maximization of a firm will be applied in the next few chapters.

Application Activities

1. Briefly, but clearly, explain the concept of production function and cost function of a typical firm in both LR and SR.

2. How many cost functions in the SR, and how many cost functions in the LR? Why do they differ?

3. Suppose you quit the job that you started after completing your college education and start your own business. After a year of successfully operating your own business selling clothes online, you have the following data about your business operations for the first year.

Annual Sales Revenue (TR)	Annuals Cost Items of Clothes Sold	$ Costs per Year
$100,000	Lease of your office	$18,000
	Domain and website usage cost and internet web housing fee	$10,000
	Transportation and shipping costs	$12,000
	Electricity, phones, and other utilities	$5,000
	Other sales related expenses	$10,000

    a. From this chart of the TR and TC amounts, what is your total gross profit? Is it accounting profit or economic profit? Why or why not? Explain.

    b. Calculate the fixed cost and compare with variable costs.

    c. What is your accounting profit, and what is your economic profit as you have found in your answer to Q3.a?

4. How do you distinguish between SR and LR cost functions? Example?

5. Explain the concept of the law of diminishing returns in SR production and cost function and its implication for the U-shaped MC curve.

6. Explain by drawing a hypothetical diagram why a firm in the LR must produce its maximum output level, where MC must be equal to its minimum ATC, but that is not necessarily the case in the SR profit maximization.

7. Distinguish between the concepts of economies of scale and economies of scope with real-world examples in case of mergers and acquisitions.

8. Explain briefly why advanced technology and specialization of the labor force in the LR reduces the MES point of economies of scale. Does this scenario shift the LRATC curve downward or upward or stay the same? Give reasons by drawing a hypothetical diagram.

9. What is the concept of the cost of capital from the point of view of economists' definition of the normal rate of return (same thing as interest rate on capital) on fixed investment (considered as fixed cost or sunk cost)? Give an example from SR production and cost function.

10. Consider the following data on SR production and costs for a small boating firm manufacturing kayaks for summer recreation on the Charles River in Boston to answer the questions that follow.

Output (q)	TC	TFC	TVC	AFC	AVC	ATC	MC
0	400						
2	2,000						
4	3,000						
6	3,500						
8	4,200						
10	5,000						
12	6,000						
14	7,200						
16	8,600						
18	10,500						
20	12,500						

a. Fill out the rest of the column based on the information in the first two columns.

b. At what level of output does the law of diminishing returns start?

c. At what level of output does the firm show the least cost-efficiency?

d. At what level of output does MC = AVC and MC = ATC, and why?

e. Graph the data for output on the horizontal axis against AVC, ATC, and MC on the vertical axis. You can use an Excel spreadsheet to graph it easily.

Chapter 9

Introduction to the Market Structure of Firms and Industries in Microeconomics

Learning Objectives

As they read the chapter, students will learn the following:

▶ Concept of Market Structure and Types of Market Structure

▶ Introduction to Market Structure under Perfect Competition

▶ Derivation of a Firm's Demand Curve from Market/Industry Demand Curve under Perfect Competition

▶ Profit Maximization of a Firm under Perfect Competition and SR and LR Equilibrium

▶ Derivation of SR and LR Supply Curves of a Firm and Industry under Perfect Competition

▶ Changes in SR and LR Supply Curves because of Changes in Technology, Costs of Production, and Regulations

Introduction

Understanding the theoretical foundation for economics of production and cost functions of typical firms and related industries in the previous chapter, this chapter focuses on application of production and cost theories in the process of profit maximization of firms under perfect competition market structure. To begin with, the chapter introduces the concept of market structure in terms of degree of competition among rival firms within the industry. There are four types of market structure: perfect competition, monopoly, monopolistic competition and oligopoly.

This chapter focuses economics of perfectly competitive market structure. Focus is made on the economic analysis of profit maximization techniques of firms to determine optimum quantity of output and equilibrium price. The analysis includes the relationship between firms and industry as well as the derivation of a firm's demand curve from the market/industry equilibrium price and quantity. The profit maximization process was discussed in the context of both short run and long run perspectives based on the knowledge on cost and revenue functions learned from previous chapter. The chapter ends with explanation on the role of technological change, changes in cost of production and productivity to determine profit, loss, price and output of firms and industry in the long run.

9.1 Concept of Market Structure and Types of Market Structure

In the previous chapter, students learned the cost structure of the production function and its relationship with inputs/factors of production in both SR and LR. Given the foundation of the various cost functions of a typical firm, this chapter introduces the theoretical foundation of production and supply decisions of a typical firm under different market competition that economists call *market structure*. Market structure is typically characterized by the degree of competition among firms producing and selling similar substitute goods and services. In business literature, those substitute goods and services are called brands or rival goods and services. The supply and production decisions of competing firms depend significantly on the degree of competition they encounter in the market. In the field of microeconomics, such competitive behavior in the supply decisions of firms is categorized by four market structures:

1. **Perfect competition**
2. **Monopoly**
3. **Monopolistic competition**
4. **Oligopoly**

9.1.1 Characteristics of Market Structure and Market Competition
The four categories of market structure listed earlier are distinguished by many market forces, such as the number of competitive firms in the industry/market producing and selling their substitutes, percentage of market share by each firm, industry type (luxury or consumer goods, services, or manufacturing; software; or hardware), degree of barriers to entry of new firms into the industry, level of market power by individual firms, length of presence of a firm in the industry, type of product (newly invented product or has been around for a long time), and size of the industry. Given these several factors to determine the market structure, Table 9.1 is the summary of the four categories of market structure.

Table 9.1: Types and Characteristics of Market Structure

Types	Firms in the Industry	Degree of Substitution	Information Availability	Barriers to Entry
Perfect Competition	Large number of firms	Close substitutes or almost identical	Easily available with no information asymmetry	Easy to enter and exit firms in the LR
Monopoly	Only one firm	No substitute	Imperfect information	Strong barriers to entry
Monopolistic Competition	Many firms	Close substitutes but not identical, differentiated by brand names	Imperfect information	No barrier in the LR
Oligopoly	A few firms	Close substitutes but differentiated by brand names	Imperfect information	Strong barriers to entry

The business and economic implications of the characteristics of the four market structure listed in Table 9.1 are basically the price and cost differences, which are predominantly determined by the structural differences in market competition. For example, under perfect competition market structure, there are a large number of buyers and sellers in the market selling almost identical products. In that situation, an individual firm as a seller or an individual consumer as a buyer has no influence over the price of the product. Then the question becomes, who does control the price? The answer is the interaction of market demand and supply that Adam Smith called the "invisible hand" in his book *The Wealth of Nations* (1776). On the other hand, under the monopoly market structure, a single firm with no substitute controls the entire market. This means the monopoly firm controls the price completely with no competition. Given imperfect information about the technological know-how of production and related knowledge, it is difficult for new firms to enter and compete with an existing monopoly.

The *oligopoly* and *monopoly* market structures with a few firms and many firms, respectively, indicate strong barriers to entry for new firms, mainly attributed to technological barriers and size of capital and cost structure. The characteristics of oligopoly and monopolistic competition basically fall in between the two extreme cases of perfect competition and monopoly. Looking at real-world examples of goods and services, most agricultural products, such as fruits and vegetables, grains, corn, cooking oils, wheat, dairy products, rice, soybeans, and related products, fall under the category of perfect competition. Although a pure monopoly firm is hardly found in today's competitive market, there are a few monopoly firms that still exist because they represent a natural monopoly (to be discussed in the next chapter) or have patent law protection and high technology with cost-efficiency. The firms operating under monopolistic competition and oligopoly are the most common entities we find in today's competitive market environment with constantly changing innovation and new product development in both old industry and newly emerged products and services.

The degree of substitutability among rival products is a great influence for determining price and availability of products. The supply decisions by competing firms are also highly influenced by the degree of substitutions. If the products are homogenous, then price difference cannot sustain for long in the free market where price is determined solely by demand and supply. But with product differentiation, brand loyalty of different products makes it possible for firms to control the prices charged to their buyers. More details are discussed in next several sections of this chapter and subsequent chapters regarding market structure.

Information availability for each of the categories is also important to notice because perfect information about techniques of the production process and technological know-how makes the market highly competitive. As a result, price becomes a driving force to efficiently allocate resources for the benefit of consumers to buy products and services at the lowest possible prices. On the other hand, imperfect information or information asymmetry makes it difficult for consumers to bargain at a lower price and for potential firms to enter the market.

Barriers to entry for new firms depends on the level of technology and capital needed to start the business and compete with existing firms in the industry. For example, for perfect competition market structure, there are no barriers for new firms entering the market. However, for other market structures listed in the previous table, there are high barriers to entry involving price and nonprice factors of competition. We will discuss each of these four categories with their distinct models and applications starting with perfect competition in this chapter, followed by monopoly in Chapter 10, monopolistic competition in Chapter 11, and oligopoly in Chapter 12.

9.2 Introduction to Market Structure under Perfect Competition

Although the existence of perfectly competitive market structure is highly desirable (for its efficiency in the determination of price, maximizing quantity of output, and minimizing cost of production), there are not many industries actually operating under perfect competition. As mentioned earlier with some examples of agriculture products and listed in Table 9.1, the key characteristics under which the market structure of competition is said to exist is explained with their implications in the following subsections.

9.2.1 Conditions for Perfect Competition

Perfect competition market structure is considered to exist under the following four characteristics:

1. Large number of buyers and sellers
2. Products are homogeneous or almost identically produced by all firms
3. Perfect information regarding production, distribution, and reliability
4. Free entry into and exit out of firms in and out of the industry in the LR

9.2.2 Examples of Industries and Price Implications

Given the aforementioned conditions, most of the agriculture products (fruits and vegetables, grains, corns, soybeans, rice, wheat, milk, and dairy products) and financial assets, such as loanable funds and treasury securities issued by the US government) do seem to satisfy the previous four conditions of perfect competition. The implications for price dynamics under these conditions seems to be desirable by the consumers and government legislators because of low prices and low cost of production. Because of the existence of a large number of buyers and sellers, an individual buyer or seller cannot possibly control the supply or price for the entire market. The nature of the "invisible hand" of market demand and supply will determine the price and quantity for the entire industry at the point of equilibrium, as determined in Chapters 3 and 4. An individual firm out of so many firms and an individual consumer out of so

Figure 9.1   Derivation of Firm's Demand Curve

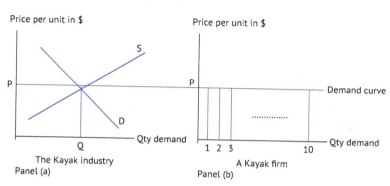

many consumers will have to accept the market price as given. Therefore, firms and consumers under perfect competition are price takers. It also implies that at a given price signaled from the industry/market equilibrium price, a firm can sell as much as it wants as long as the cost conditions allow the firm to maximize its profits. Any price charged at higher than market price will not be feasible for a firm to sell its products. Any price lower than the market price will not make it possible for a firm to reach its maximum level of profit. That is why the demand curve for a typical firm under perfect competition is different than the market demand. This unique demand curve for a competitive firm is derived in the next section with its economic implications.

9.3 Derivation of a Firm's Demand Curve from the Market/Industry Demand Curve under Perfect Competition

As mentioned previously, the firms under perfect competition are price takers. In this section, only one firm is considered as a representative of several firms operating in the industry. Since the market demand curve is usually downward sloping and the corresponding supply curve is upward sloping, a typical firm under perfect competition will accept the equilibrium price from the point of intersection between market demand and supply for a particular product or service. In developing this concept for deriving a firm's demand curve, let us consider the kayak industry as an example of a perfectly competitive market. Figure 9.1 shows the connection between the market equilibrium price and a firm's demand curve derived from that equilibrium price of the market.

In Figure 9.1, panel (a) shows the equilibrium price (P) and quantity produced (Q) at the point of intersection between market demand and supply. Since an individual kayak firm is a price taker, the firm takes this market price as a given signal to sell as many units of kayaks at this market price that is can. As shown in panel (b), the kayak firm can sell either one unit or ten units or even more with no change in price. Therefore, the demand curve for the kayak firm is illustrated as the horizontal demand curve at price P. However, if the demand and/or supply curves of the market in panel (a) shift to any directions caused by some external factors with a new equilibrium price (not shown here), then the firm would take the new equilibrium price to sell its products. Of course, the new demand curve for the firm would horizontally shift up or down, depending on the new position of the market equilibrium price.

9.4 Profit Maximization of a Firm under Perfect Competition and SR and LR Equilibrium

The profit-maximization strategy of a firm is not only to maximize total revenue but also to make sure that the total revenue earned minus total cost of goods sold is the maximum. This section will develop that strategy to achieve the best possible level of output to maximize total profit.

9.4.1 Profit-Maximizing Conditions

The profit function of a typical firm is restated here in Eqn (9.1) from Eqn (8.7) in Chapter 8.

Total profit (q) = Total revenue (TR = p × q) − Total cost (q)   **Eqn (9.1)**

Also, the corresponding marginal profit for the profit-maximization setting is equal to zero and gives the profit-maximizing condition in Eqn (9.2) (repeated from Eqns (8.8) and (8.9) in Chapter 8).

$$\text{Marginal profit} = \frac{d(\text{Total profit})}{dq} = \left[\frac{d(\text{TR} = p \times q)}{dq} - d(\text{TC})/dq \right] = 0 \text{ (zero)}$$

In the equation, marginal profit is zero, and d(TR)/dq is MR, and the d(TC)/dq is MC. Therefore, it can be rewritten as

MR − MC = 0 (zero).

Or, more precisely,

MR = MC.   **Eqn (9.2)**

9.4.2 Equality of MR and the Price under Perfect Competition

Now, it is also important to understand the relationship between MR and the price per unit (P) under the operation of a perfectly competitive firm. Since the price is given for a firm as a price taker, the MR equation can be derived by the use of a simple calculus solution from the equation of TR (p × q) as shown next.

TR = P × q, where q is output produced by a competitive firm.

The MR is the derivative of TR, as derived next:

$$d(TR)/dq = d(P \times q)/dq = P \times \frac{\partial q}{\partial q} + q \times \frac{\partial p}{\partial q}, \text{ where } \frac{\partial q}{\partial q} \text{ and } \frac{\partial p}{\partial q} \text{ are partial derivatives}$$

of q and p, respectively.

Since P is fixed or given constant value under the assumption of perfect competition, the term $\frac{\partial p}{\partial q}$ is equal to zero (as you may recall from Calculus 101, the derivative of any constant value is always equal to zero). Therefore, the MR equation derived earlier can be expressed as in Eqn (9.3).

$$MR = P \qquad \textbf{Eqn (9.3)}$$

From Eqns (9.2) and (9.3), it can be established that in a perfectly competitive firm, the condition for profit maximization is not only the equality between MR and MC, but it is also equal to price, as provided by Eqn (9.4) here.

Profit-maximizing condition under perfect competition:

$$MR = MC = P \qquad \textbf{Eqn (9.4)}$$

Equation (9.4) clearly implies that the per unit price taken by a firm from the industry equilibrium price is always equal to its MR. Graphically, it can be seen in Figure 9.1 that the rectangle for each unit of output multiplied by the same price per unit is exactly the MR of BKC (one of the firms in the kayak market) for each of the additional units produced. The next few subsections will expand on this concept for profit-maximizing decisions in both SR and LR for BKC introduced in Chapter 8.

9.4.3 Profit Maximization in the SR

Establishing the *golden rule* for the profit maximization of a typical firm under perfect market competition provided in Eqns (9.3) and (9.4), this section will provide the actual process of profit maximization by incorporating the complete model structure for price, revenue, cost, and profit or loss introduced in Chapter 8 and in this chapter so far. To begin the process, a hypothetical set of data based on these relevant variables of a typical firm are given in Table 9.2. Assuming the market price taken by BKC is $1,000 per kayak produced and sold in the market, the firm is a price taker.

Table 9.2: Data for Profit Maximization of a Firm

Quantity of Kayak per Month	TFC	TVC	TC	MC	AFC	AVC	ATC	TR @$1,000	MR	Total Profit	Marginal Profit
0	1,000	0	1000	–	–	–	–	–	–	–	–
1	1,000	1,000	2000	1000	1,000.00	1,000.00	2,000.00	1,000	1,000	–1,000	–1,000
2	1,000	1,600	2600	600	500.00	800.00	1,300.00	2,000	1,000	–600	–400
3	1,000	2,000	3000	400	333.33	666.67	1,000.00	3,000	1,000	0	600
4	1,000	2,800	3800	800	250.00	700.00	950.00	4,000	1,000	200	200
5	1,000	3,800	4,800	1,000	200.00	760.00	960.00	5,000	1,000	200	0
6	1,000	5,200	6200	1400	166.67	866.67	1,033.33	6,000	1,000	–200	–400
7	1,000	7,200	8200	2000	142.86	1,028.57	1,171.43	7,000	1,000	–1,200	–1,000
8	1,000	10,000	11000	2800	125.00	1250.00	1,375.00	8,000	1,000	–3,000	–1,800
9	1,000	14,000	15000	4000	111.11	1,555.56	1,666.67	9,500	1,000	–4,500	–1,500
10	1,000	19,000	20000	5000	100.00	1900.00	2,000.00	10,000	1,000	–9,000	–4.500

Note: Total Profit = TR – TC; Marginal profit = (Delta of total profit)/(Delta of quantity produced)

The students may note that the cost structure of this table is simply extracted from Table 8.2 in Chapter 8. The only additional information added to this table is the market price per kayak at $1,000 to estimate the values of TR (P × q) and MR ($\Delta TR/\Delta q$). Since the explanation of the SR cost structure of BKC was already made in Chapter 8, students are already familiar with the cost behavior of various cost types as they are reflected in this table. Now we can focus on the process of profit maximization by applying the *golden rule* from Eqn (9.4) in the previous section to determine the optimum level of output that BKC must produce and sell to maximize its total profit. The golden rule for this purpose is where its *marginal profit is equal to zero*. In Table 9.2, that magic level of optimum units of output is highlighted in blue at five units of kayak per month. At this level of output, TR – Total TC = 5,000 – 4,800 = 200, and, obviously, marginal profit is equal to zero. Students may also notice that at four units of kayaks produced, the total profit is also 200, but the marginal profit is still greater than zero and MR > MC (1,000 > 800). Therefore, BKC will expand its kayak production until MR is equal to MC and marginal profit is zero, which is at five units of kayak production. This equilibrium point is the optimum level of output produced by BKC in its SR production process. Producing beyond five units of kayaks will, of course, increase its revenue, but because of the law of diminishing returns in the SR production process, the marginal profit becomes negative and the loss amount continues to rise if the firm intends to continue producing more products. This hypothetical process of SR production and profit maximization is the best scenario of the firm given the economic cost structure and market price taken from the market demand and supply. Figure 9.2 illustrates the graphical representation of the table to represent the whole process for a typical competitive firm in a perfectly competitive market.

From Figure 9.2, the consistency of the relationship among three important SR cost functions—(1) average variable cost (AVC), (2) ATC, and (3) MC curves as explained in detail in

Chapter 8—is clear. In this graph, what is new is the fixed price given at $1,000 per kayak = MR curve. The profit-maximizing output produced at five units of kayaks, where MR intersects the MC curve to fulfill the golden rule of profit maximization at MR = MC. Since the MR = Price, the Price = MR curve is also the demand curve for the firm, it is a perfectly elastic demand curve shown as parallel to the horizontal axis. The shape of the firm's demand curve under perfect competition was already explained in the previous section with the help of Figure 9.1.

To determine the maximum amount of profit (TR − TC at q* = 5 units), we can see from both Table 9.2 and Figure 9.2 that the ATC (per unit cost of production) at five units of kayaks is around $960. Given the price at $1,000 per unit, the per unit profit is $40 per unit (P-ATC). The total profit is estimated by multiplying the per unit profit by the optimum level of output (five units here) to calculate the total profit at $200 = (1000 − 960) × 5. In Figure 9.2, we can also carefully observe that MR = MC = price against five units of kayaks did not actually intersect at the minimum point of the ATC curve. The point of intersection is just a little before the minimum point of the ATC curve against five units of output. It also sits just below the price corresponding to the level of ATC's downward-sloping segment (ATC is at $960). The same pattern can be observed in Table 9.2 against five units of output. That is why the profit margin per kayak is $40 per unit (1,000 − 960) with a total profit of $200.

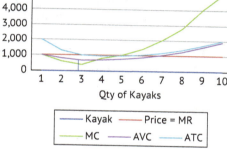

Figure 9.2 SR Profit Maximization

Analysis of Changes in Profit or Loss When Market Price Changes

The next step is to analyze the changes in profit or loss when the market price changes because of the changes in demand and supply in the entire industry. As discussed earlier, because of the shift of market demand and supply in the competitive market structure, the equilibrium market price will change, and a firm like BKC will have to use the new market price to sell its kayaks. Suppose the market price has fallen to $800 per kayak (not shown by drawing a change in market demand and supply). Given the new price of $800 and keeping the same cost structure for the simplicity of the model, the profit/loss estimation from Table 9.2 comes out be as explained next:

At a price of $800 per kayak, the MR is also now $800. To determine the profit-maximizing level of output at P = MR at $800, the MC must be equal to $800 at that level of optimum output. This optimum level or profit-maximizing level of output is at four units of kayaks in Table 9.2. The profit or loss estimate can be made by subtracting TR earned from selling four units of output at 800 × 4 = 3,200 against its total cost of 3,800. Therefore, it will be a loss of 600 (3,200 − 3,800). The question is now to ask whether the firm should shut down its operations or continue to produce four units of kayaks per month with a loss of $600. Before we can figure that out to make a rational decision, we have to first keep in mind that the cost structure is the same in this SR operation. Second, the firm cannot change the price either because it is a price taker and the price signal comes from the entire industry's market equilibrium. Given this position, if the firm shuts down its operation, it will still incur the variable cost (total fixed is not a factor because it is already spent as a sunk cost). So, it is important to see the variable cost per unit (AVC) at four units of kayaks to produce. The data in our table and the corresponding Figure 9.2 indicates that the AVC at four units of production of kayaks is $700 per unit. It implies that if the firm continues to produce and sell four units at $800, it can still cover more than its variable cost per unit (AVC = $700). Based on this scenario, the

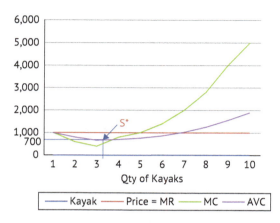

Figure 9.3 Shutdown Point in SR

decision-making process as to whether the firm should shut down or continue to operate with the loss is explained next.

The Shutdown Decision Process of a Firm in the SR

The economic rationality in shutting down the operation of a firm in the SR is based on whether the firm can cover its variable cost (in the business sense, it is called operating cost) by the existing price. As long as the market price is equal to its AVC or above AVC, the firm should continue its operation to minimize its losses (when it actually incurs losses caused by a decline in market price). From the previous example of BKC decision whether to shut down or continue its operation at $800 price per kayak, it is economically rational to continue its operation at that price because the price is still more than covering its corresponding level of AVC at $700.

However, if the price continues to decline further to the point of minimum AVC, which would be somewhere between three and four units of kayak production, as illustrated in Figure 9.2. At that point, the MC curve intersects through the minimum point of AVC. This minimum point of AVC is the *point of shutdown*. At any price falling below this shutdown point, the firm must cease its operation in the SR for the time being and wait for the higher price signal to get back to operations again. The reason for shutting down at a price below the minimum point of AVC is the firm's inability to cover its variable costs or operating costs at that low price. The relevant graph for shutdown is illustrated more clearly in Figure 9.3 by indicting S* as the point of shutdown.

9.4.4 Profit Maximization in the LR

In the previous section, we analyzed the process of profit and loss determination of a typical firm operating under SR conditions of perfect competition. In that analysis, we established conditions that state when the market price is higher than ATC, the firm makes a positive economic profit greater than zero (P-ATC) *q > 0). We have also seen that when the price

Microeconomics Principles, Applications, and Policy Implications

Figure 9.4   LR Adjustment of Firm's Output and Profit

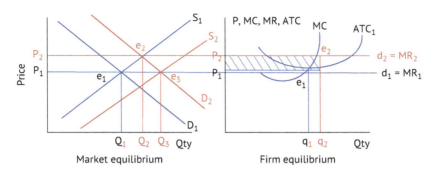

Market equilibrium   Firm equilibrium

is equal to the ATC at the profit-maximizing level of output, the firm's economic profit is considered to be normal, with zero economic profit implying that the accounting profit for the firm is still greater than zero. It was also established that if the price falls below its ATC level at profit-maximizing output, it will still stay in business while operating at a loss as long as the price is high enough to cover the variable cost, implying P > or = AVC. However, if the price falls below the AVC, then the firm must shut down its operation temporarily to minimize its loss just equal to its fixed cost or sunk cost. In this section, the focus is on the process of determination of the profit-maximizing output and price in the LR, where the free entry and exit of firms in and out of the market are guided by profit or loss situations when all costs are variable.

In the LR situation of perfectly competitive market structure, if firms making positive economic profit from being at a market price greater than the ATC, new firms will enter the market to compete freely with existing firms. Given the same cost structure we have seen in previous sections, except no fixed cost in the LR, the existing firms are also expected to expand their outputs in the LR to maximize their profits with all costs that are variable. On the other hand, if some existing firms experience economic loss because of the market price being less than their ATC, then those firms will exit the market permanently because individual firms cannot control the market price. This free entry and exit of firms in and out of the market in the LR creates the adjustment process influenced by changes in market price, as determined by the industry demand and supply functions. When the changes in the market price signal come from the shift of industry demand and/or supply curves, the firms take the new equilibrium price of the market and thus adjust their profit-maximizing output accordingly. This adjustment process in the LR is illustrated in Figure 9.4 with an assumption that the market demand curve shifted outward to the right because of higher market demand, resulting in an increase in market price, as explained in Figure 9.4.

The left-hand side graph in Figure 9.4 shows the changes in equilibrium from point e_1 to e_2 because of an upward right shift of the market demand curve from D_1 to D_2. In response to the new equilibrium price at P_2, the firm's reaction is shown in the right-hand side of the graph in the same figure by shifting its profit-maximizing output level from q_1 to q_2 at equilibrium point e_2. If the ATC_1 stays the same after a change in price from P_1 to P_2, then the existing firm with its new output produced at q_2 will end up making positive economic profit by the shaded area shown in blue. Given this positive economic profit, new firms will enter the market to make some profit out of this higher price. As a result, the market supply curve is expected to shift outward to the right, as shown in the left-hand side of the graph as S_2 with an increase in the market supply of quantity produced at Q_3 at the new LR equilibrium point e_3 with a new equilibrium price back to P_1. This new equilibrium price at P_1 is actually the LR minimum ATC for the firm at equilibrium point e_1. Given the decline in price in the LR caused by an increase in the quantity of market supply, existing firms either have to lower their production to make sure they are at least making zero economic profit (accounting profit is still greater than zero, of course) or some of the firms may have to exit out of the market if the cost conditions are not favorable to stay in business. This adjustment process is shown in Figure 9.4, bringing the production from q_2 to its original level of q_1. A similar analysis can be shown if the market supply curve shifts to the right to start with no shift in the market demand curve from D_1.

Students are encouraged to do this exercise by using the same process of LR adjustment, keeping the price P_2 level, assuming that the initial equilibrium price and quantity in the market at the point of intersection at e_2. Given the same cost structure of the firm, the LR adjustment will be straightforward to practice. In either case, the LR equilibrium condition for competitive firms under perfect competition will settle at a profit-maximizing level of output where each of the firms will end up producing at the minimum point of ATC.

To summarize this result, the LR equilibrium condition is MR = MC = P = Minimum ATC. It is important to note here that this LR equilibrium condition has several economic and policy implications. A few of those are noted next in the context of economic efficiency derived from market competition.

Cost-efficiency: The LR condition of minimum ATC at the profit maximization for each of the firms is certainly cost-efficient to sell at the same price equal to its ATC and MC. This MC pricing is economically efficient for both producers and consumers at the economic profit level for firms.

Production efficiency: Given the condition in the LR, the firms are able to produce the maximum level of output with the minimum possible cost of production per unit with the lowest price possible to charge their buyers. This is the best scenario for the efficient allocation of resources with maximum capacity utilization.

Distributional efficiency: The benefits of cost-efficiency and production efficiency mentioned earlier certainly generates a great advantage for the consumer by charging the lowest price at the MC pricing level. This MC pricing is considered the minimum opportunity cost incurred by both consumers and producers. The consumers end up paying the lowest possible price and get the highest possible benefit from consumer surplus (CS). Therefore, from the perspective of the highest CS at the lowest price, the previous condition of cost and production efficiency can be expanded further by adding the MU we discussed in Chapters 5 and 6. The complete efficiency equation for market competition in the LR can be rewritten as MR = MC

= P = Minimum ATC = MU. Any reallocation of resources as an alternative to this optimum condition may not be possible without the loss of efficiency of some economic agents in society. We will discuss this further in more detail in the context of the role of government policy in the presence of market power and externality in later chapters of this textbook.

Despite the consumers' satisfaction and production efficiency under market competition, the profit maximization for all firms is not always possible in a fiercely competitive market environment. Since the market prices are highly volatile, caused by unpredictable changes in internal and external factors, such as constant change in technology and cost of production, natural calamities, changes in government tax policies and environmental regulations, workers' strikes, and wage increases, many firms face tough challenges to stay in business. The common industries under this scenario are dairy farms, soybean, coffee, tea, corn, wheat, fruits and vegetables, and peanut farms, as well as many other grains. The farm owners in these industries are extremely vulnerable to the internal and external factors mentioned here. Under those circumstances and the interruptions caused by the technological shifts and changes in government policy have profound influence on the constant shifting of demand and supply conditions in the market. We will discuss these issues in the last section of this chapter.

9.5 Derivation of the SR and LR Supply Curves of a Firm and Industry under Perfect Competition

The market supply curve and firm supply curve are basically combinations of price and quantity supplied at various prices. To be more specific, a firm's supply curve or supply function reflects the profit-maximizing decision of a firm to produce the quantity of output at a given price determined by the market demand and supply interaction. When price changes in the market, the firm reallocates its resources to maximize its profits in response to the new market price. This adjustment process provides various combinations of profit-maximizing output and a price that constitutes the supply functions and the supply curves. The mechanism of deriving the supply functions are different in the SR than the LR production process under perfect competition. In this section, the derivation of both SR and LR functions are explained separately.

9.5.1 Derivation of the SR Supply Function

As we can recall from previous sections, the firm under competition cannot change the price, a profit-maximizing firm is a price taker of a predetermined market price. However, when the market price changes, the

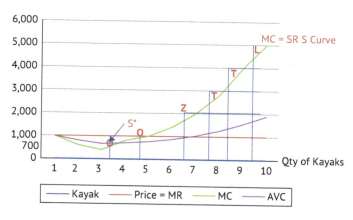

Figure 9.5   SR Supply Function

firm adjusts its production decision to make sure the profit-maximization rule is not compromised. Accordingly, the new equilibrium price and quantity combination would be different than the previous equilibrium point. To construct this supply function in the SR, we will use the same data set and the graph introduced in Section 9.4.3. To make the construction of the SR curve simple, the same cost and revenue curves in Figure 9.3 are redrawn in Figure 9.5 to focus on deriving the SR supply decisions of the firm at various prices.

As we can see in Figure 9.5, the shutdown point of a firm is S*, where the market price is $700 per kayak. It implies that the firm BKC will shut down its operation if the market price falls below $700. However, if the market price rises above $700, suppose a new price determined by the market demand and supply is increased to $1,000 per kayak, then the profit-maximizing output level for BKC would be at five units of kayaks, where MR = MC = P intersect on the horizontal demand curve. With the same profit-maximizing rule of MR = MC, if the market price continues to rise from 1,000 to 2,000 to 3,000, 4,000, and 5,000, then the corresponding profit-maximizing output level of kayak production would be at seven, eight, nine, and ten units, respectively (assuming the same cost structure). Those price and output combinations are indicated by the red dots on the MC curves in Figure 9.5. Therefore, the segment of the MC curve starting from the shutdown point at S* and above along the red dots is precisely the SR supply curve of this firm. It is also important to note that the segment of the MC curve below the shutdown point is not part of the supply function because the price below $700 is not high enough for the firm to stay in business. In other words, the SR supply curve of a competitive firm is the segment of the MC curve starting from the minimum point of the AVC curve and above. Now, what about the SR supply curve of the market as a whole? The answer to this question is straightforward. Since there are large number of firms in the market, the horizontal summation of the SR supply curves for each of the firms as derived earlier would be the SR supply curve for the market as a whole. Students are encouraged to practice this simple step to derive the market supply curve by assuming that a certain number of firms exist in the whole industry.

9.5.2 Derivation of the LR Supply Function

Unlike the adjustment process of profit-maximizing output and price in deriving the SR supply curve for a firm, LR adjustment in the supply function of the industry depends not only on changes in the prices of the output but also on the changes in the cost conditions of the production process. As mentioned earlier at the end of Section 9.4, demand and supply in the market are shifted because of several internal and external factors, such as changes in government regulations, taxes, weather-related issues, climate change, technological change, and innovation. Those changes significantly affect the cost of productions, and, therefore, firms must respond to those changes in the cost of production to maintain their profitability. The structural changes in cost functions widely vary from industry to industry depending on the nature of the industry. Economists consider those different cost structures by using the concept of economies of scale and diseconomies of scale introduced in Section 8.4 of Chapter 8. Economies of scale imply the downward-sloping ATC curve in the LR as the firms produce more and more units of output with a continuous decrease in the MC of production.

Figure 9.6   LR Industry Supply Functions

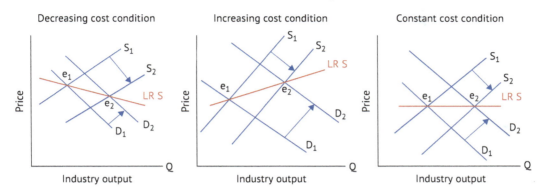

Diseconomies of scale imply just the opposite; MC continues to increase as more output is produced and thus the upward-sloping ATC curve. On the other hand, if the ATC curve stays the same (flat) at its minimum point as production increases, it is called a constant scale of cost condition or simply constant returns to scale. By the same token, production processes with economies of scale are called increasing returns to scale, and with diseconomies of scale, this is called decreasing returns to scale.

In the LR adjustment of supply functions, if the industry structure is characterized by economies of scale of the production process, the shifting of demand and supply functions in the market will form a new equilibrium price and quantity combination at a lower price than the previous condition of equilibrium. As a result, the LR supply curve in the market will be a downward-sloping supply curve. On the other hand, if the industry structure faces the cost condition of diseconomies of scale, then the shift in market demand and supply functions will form an upward-sloping LR supply curve. And, finally, with constant cost condition or constant returns to the scale of the industry, the LR supply curve would be a horizontal shape. A simplified comparison of these three different possible supply functions of the competitive market supply functions in the LR is illustrated in Figure 9.6.

In the set of graphs in Figure 9.6, the first panel on the far left is an industry with economies of scale of the production process. In this graph, we notice that because of the rightward shift of demand and supply curves, the adjustment of the cost of production and profit maximization with a new equilibrium price, the LR profit-maximizing output and price combination has moved from e_1 to e_2, where price at e_2 is lower than the previous equilibrium price at e_1. Connecting the two points of equilibrium e_1 and e_2 and expanding, the supply curve derived, as marked in red, is the LR supply curve for the industry.

The second panel in the middle of Figure 9.6 indicates the industry with increasing cost conditions and thus diseconomies of scale of the production process. Using the same adjustment process from the shifting of the demand and supply curves in the same direction, the equilibrium point has moved from e_1 to e_2 at a higher price and output combination. Connecting the two points of equilibrium and expanding gives the upward-sloping LR supply curve as marked in red. Likewise, the third panel on the far right, the industry cost condition, is characterized by constant returns to scale. Therefore, the LR adjustment from equilibrium point e_1 to e_2 gives the LR supply curve at a constant price with the horizontal shape of the LR supply curve. In this condition of the constant cost industry, the market price does not tend to change in the LR in response to the SR price or cost fluctuations. Students are encouraged to practice some other scenarios using these three cost conditions by shifting the demand and/or supply curves in opposite directions.

9.6 Changes in the SR and LR Supply Curves because of Changes in Technology, Costs of Production, and Regulations

The changes in the SR and LR supply curves of both the firms and industries we explained in Sections 9.4 and 9.5 are attributed to several factors that significantly affect the direction of cost functions both in the SR and in the LR. Some of the common factors that constantly change the supply functions are mentioned next.

Technological change and innovation: The dynamics of technological advancement and innovation of the production process improves labor productivity and lowers the cost of production in both fixed costs and variable costs over time. As a result, all cost functions of the firms we have discussed so far in Chapters 8 and 9 do change with shifts of the curves to achieve a new equilibrium. It is also important to note that new technology may have much higher fixed costs for building new infrastructure and more capital-intensive production infrastructure. However, as production expands with the advantage of economies scale in reducing cost per unit from declining MC, the ATC functions continuously decline. The increasing efficiency in cost minimization and production maximization will thus eventually shift the market supply curve outward to the right with decreasing cost conditions. This process is illustrated in Figure 9.6. For example, the firms in the cloud computing industry, e-commerce industry, and mobile operating system industry have to start with very high fixed costs to develop their software and network infrastructure. But when the operations start with the expansion of their deliveries to their customers, the MC function is expected to decline continuously and so is the ATC—a great example of economies of scale and favorable shifts of the market supply curve in the LR with decreasing cost conditions. Students may think of many other similar high-technology firms in industries such as mobile phone devices, laptops, music and video streaming devices, internet hosting, browser services, big data management and storage facilities, microchips and computer operating systems.

Changes in the cost of fixed inputs of production: It is also common to notice a constant trend of changes in prices of fixed variables the firms that must incur upfront called sunk costs or fixed costs. Although we have assumed previously that the fixed costs do not change in the SR, they are not necessarily constant for a very long time. For example, the rise in prices on rental equipment and workspace, price of land, opportunity costs of capital, lease of office space, and taxes on property will increase the fixed costs of production. As a result, the total cost of production and ATC functions will shift upward. Thus the profit volume of firms will be negatively affected in both the SR and in the LR. The opposite will occur when the prices of fixed costs decreases and thus the profit of firms will increase to reflect the shift of the market supply curve in both the SR and in LR. The key challenge to this process is that to survive in a successful operation with profitability, the firm size must be large enough to stay cost-efficient with economies of scale. The smaller-size firms will have to exit out of the industry because of their lack of economies of scale. Therefore, in the LR, the firms with their ATC above its price will continue to incur loss and exit in the LR.

Changes in variable costs: The major elements of variable costs mainly come from raw materials, utilities, transportation, worker wages, and taxes. Since these costs are never fixed, any changes in the cost structure of these cost items will definitely impact the MC and ATC of the production process. The resulting shift of the related variable costs of production will eventually shift the SR supply curve of firms and industry. With the decline in variable costs, the firm's supply curve would shift outward to the right and the rising variable cost will do the opposite. This process of shifting the cost functions of a typical firm will change the profit volume of firms in both the SR and in LR.

Changes in cost functions because of changes in government legislation: Changes in legislation by the government on consumer safety, taxes, investment incentives, environmental protection, minimum wage laws, and other related policy implementations, such as antitrust laws, do have a direct effect on the cost of production of firms. In complying with those changes in legislation, the firms' fixed costs and variable costs will increase. As a result, the price and output combinations shift because of the shift of cost structure at a higher level. Those changes in the SR output and supply decisions eventually affect the shift of the LR supply curves in the industry.

Chapter Summary

Sections 9.1 and 9.2 introduced market structure. Market structure is characterized by the degree of competition among the existing firms in the industry that are producing and selling close substitutes of goods and services to maximize their profits. Based on the degree of competition and strength of substitutability of competing goods and services, the market structure is classified into four different categories:

1. Perfect competition
2. Monopoly
3. Monopolistic competition
4. Oligopoly

Perfect competition consists of a large number of buyers (consumers) and sellers (firms) producing almost identical goods and services with free entry and exit in and out of the industry by the firms in the LR and with no information asymmetry. Under this condition, the market price is determined by industry demand and supply functions as price takers by the firms, as well as by consumers.

The monopoly market is a sole producer and seller of goods and services with no substitutes or competitors in the market with a large number of buyers. The monopoly power makes the monopolist responsible for changing the price and output to maximize his or her profit with no worries about market reaction. Therefore, a monopolist is a price maker, with strong barriers to entry for new firms to enter and compete.

Monopolistic competition market structure consists of many firms (not as many as under perfect competition) and a large number of buyers. The goods and services are close substitutes but not identical. Therefore, the substitutability of competing goods and services is characterized by differentiated products with imperfect information. However, free entry and exit of new firms are possible in the LR, allowing new firms to enter the competition easily.

Oligopoly market consists of a few firms with close substitutes dominating a vast market size with a large number of buyers. The imperfect information and interdependence among a few firms in making supply decisions makes the profit-maximization strategy a distinct and complicated challenge for oligopoly firms as compared to the other three types of market structure. There are several alternative strategies for profit maximization that are possible under oligopoly. They are price leadership, collusion, cartel, and game theory, and Nash equilibrium and massive advertisement are also common practices that oligopoly firms pursue with a strong barrier to entry for new firms to enter the market in the LR.

Examples of perfectly competitive industries are fruits and vegetables, grains, corns, soybeans, rice, wheat, milk, and other dairy products. The financial assets, such as loanable funds and treasury securities (issued by the US government) do seem to satisfy the previous four conditions of perfect competition. The implications for price dynamics under these conditions seem to be desirable by consumers and government legislators because of low prices and low cost of production. Because of the existence of a large number of buyers and sellers, an individual buyer or seller cannot possibly control the supply or price for the entire market. The nature of the "invisible hand" as a force in market demand and supply determines the price and quantity for the entire industry. An individual firm out of so many firms and an individual consumer out of so many consumers would have to accept the market price as given.

Section 9.3 discussed how the pricing structure under perfect competition is determined by demand and supply interactions in the market, and the firms in the market are price takers. Therefore, the demand curve for a competitive firm under perfect competition is perfectly horizontal, as derived in Figure 9.7 by redrawing Figure 9.1 under Section 9.3.

Figure 9.7 also indicates that the change in the equilibrium price in the industry because of a shift in market demand and/or supply will be taken by firms as a new price signal. This change will shift the firm's demand curve up and down depending on the direction of the price changes in the entire market (industry). For example, in Figure 9.7, as a result of the leftward shift of market supply curve in panel (a) of the figure, the new equilibrium price P_2 has translated the firm's demand curve by shifting upward, as illustrated by demand curve on the right-side panel (b). Unlike the downward-sloping market demand curve representing the consumers, the horizontal demand curve for the firm in panel (b) represents the firm's demand curve as a perfectly elastic demand curve. This difference in shape between the market demand curve and the firm's demand implies that the firm as a price taker can sell as much of its output at the given price as desired. Further implication is the response to the new equilibrium price at P_2; the firm will take the new price and be able to sell as much as desired along the new horizontal demand curve shifted up parallel to the demand curve at P_1.

Section 9.4.1 and 9.4.2 presented the profit-maximization process of a typical competitive firm and provided a detailed analysis for production and cost-efficiency conditions starting with the golden rule for profit maximization repeated next in Eqn (9.2).

$$MR = MC \qquad \text{Eqn (9.2)}$$

Figure 9.7 Derivation of a Firm's Demand Curve

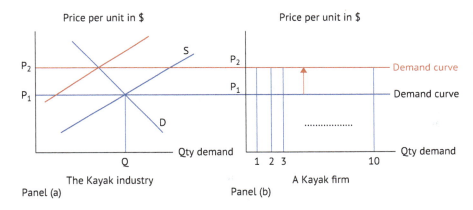

The Kayak industry — Panel (a)

A Kayak firm — Panel (b)

Since the price is given under perfect competition, implying P = MR, the golden rule in Eqn (9.2) is also expanded to additional conditions of profit maximization repeated in Eqn (9.4).

$$MR = MC = P \qquad \text{Eqn (9.4)}$$

Figure 9.2 SR Profit Maximization

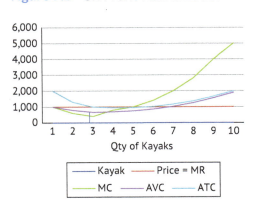

Qty of Kayaks

Legend: Kayak — Price = MR — MC — AVC — ATC

Section 9.4.3 presented the rule of Eqn (9.4), the graphical representation of profit maximization of a typical firm under perfect competition, which was redrawn from Figure 9.2.

The relevant data for this graph is referred to in Table 9.2 in Section 9.4.3. The equilibrium output for profit maximization is derived from Price = 1,000 at five units output on the horizontal axis. The total profit or loss is now determined from the difference between price and ATC at five units of output (per unit profit = 1,000 – 960) multiplied by 5 = 40 × 5 = $200, as shown in Table 9.2 in Section 9.4.3. If the market price moves up and down from the price in Figure 9.2, then the firm must adjust its price and output combination to follow the profit-maximization rule of MR = MC = P.

In Section 9.4, the shutdown decision of a firm in the SR production process was explained when the market price falls below the ATC. Our analysis has established that as long as Price ⩾ to AVC in the SR, the firm will continue its operation at a loss because the price above or equal to its AVC is sufficient to cover its operating cost. Therefore, the shutdown point will be the minimum point of AVC. At a price falling below the minimum point of AVC, the firm will shut down. The shutdown process in a graph is redrawn here from Figure 9.3 with S* as the point of shutdown.

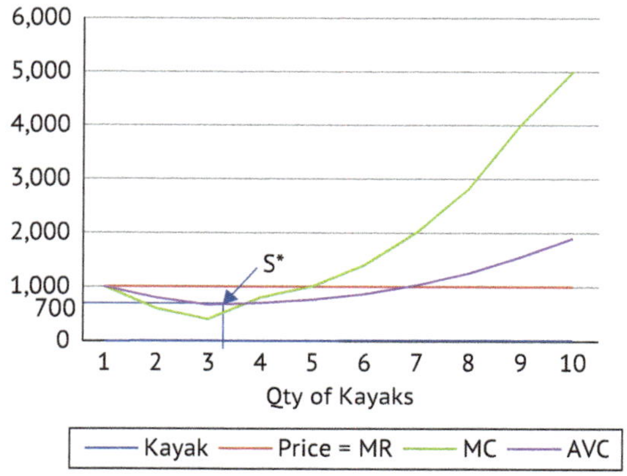

In Section 9.4.4, LR determination of price and output was explained by the condition of free entry and exit of firms in the LR. When market price allows firms to make positive economic profit, new firms will enter the market, and the quantity of market supply will increase by shifting the market supply curve outward to the right. As a result, the market price will fall. The opposite will happen when firms are losing money; some firms will exit the market by shifting the market supply curve inward to the left. This process of free entry and exit of firms in the LR will force firms to make a normal economic profit at the equilibrium point where MR = MC = P = Minimum ATC, the condition for zero economic profit. The zero economic profit is still good for the firms to operate with because accounting profit is still greater than zero for the firm to stay profitable and efficient. The LR equilibrium process is reillustrated next from Figure 9.4. A detailed explanation is provided in Section 9.4.4. Students are encouraged to think of similar situations from changes in price in the industry for practice in deriving LR zero economic profit for a firm.

Figure 9.3 Shutdown Point in SR

(Chart: Qty of Kayaks on x-axis 1–10, values 0; 700; 1,000; 2,000; 3,000; 4,000; 5,000; 6,000 on y-axis. S* marked. Legend: Kayak — Price = MR — MC — AVC)

Figure 9.4 LR Adjustment of a Firm's Output and Profit

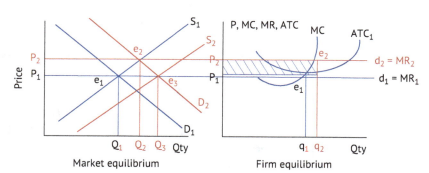

Market equilibrium   Firm equilibrium

Figure 9.5   SR Supply Function

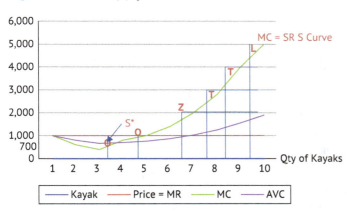

Section 9.5.1 explained the systematic derivation of the SR supply function of a typical firm under perfect competition. The segment of the SR MC curve starting from the minimum point of AVC moving upward is derived as the SR supply curve of a firm. At different price signals from the market, the firm will produce along the MC cost function from the minimum AVC and above. The graphical derivation of the SR supply curve is illustrated next from Figure 9.5. The SR curve derived in the figure is the dotted line, which is the segment of the MC curve from the shutdown point and above.

In Section 9.5.2, the derivation of the LR supply function was explained based on different cost conditions of industry type. Three different conditions were defined: (1) decreasing cost conditions with economies of scale of production, (2) increasing cost conditions with diseconomies of scale of production, and (3) constant cost conditions with constant returns to scale. These three different cost conditions will determine the shape of the LR supply functions of firms and industries. The graphical representation of all these cost conditions with their corresponding LR industry supply curves are redrawn from Figure 9.6.

In Section 9.6, factors that shift SR and LR supply functions for firms and industries were listed and explained. Those factors are changes in technology and innovation of the production process, changes in variable costs, changes in fixed cost components, and changes in government legislations. The details of the process concerning how those factors affect the changes in the supply functions and firms' profit-maximization processes are explained in the last section. Students are encouraged to double-check the learning process in this chapter by reading this summary with their cross references to relevant sections in the chapter.

Figure 9.6   LR Industry Supply Functions

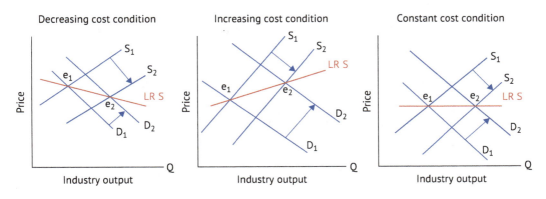

Application Activities

1. Critically, but briefly, explain why the four characteristics of the perfectly competitive market make the demand curve for a competitive firm perfectly horizontal and equal between MR and price per unit.

2. Does a competitive firm necessarily maximize its profit in the SR at a level of output where ATC is at its minimum point? Why or why not? How about in the LR?

3. Explain briefly why the free entry and exit of firms in the LR ensures cost and production efficiency with the efficiency criterion of MR = MC = P = Minimum ATC.

4. Using the same cost structure of the small boating manufacturing firm introduced in Question 10 of Chapter 8, consider the following set in regard to the SR production and costs for manufacturing kayaks for summer recreation on the Charles River in Boston. Using the data in the table, answer the questions that follow.

Output (q)	TC	TFC	TVC	AFC	AVC	ATC	MC	TR at Price = $700	MR	Profit
0	400									
2	2,000									
4	3,000									
6	3,500									
8	4,200									
10	5,000									
12	6,000									
14	7,200									
16	8,600									
18	10,500									
20	12,500									

a. Fill in the blanks in the table with a given market price of $700/kayak.

b. Suppose the boating is selling at a given market price of $700 per kayak, determine the profit-maximizing level of output and the amount of profit the firm will make at that price.

c. If market price falls to $500 per unit, what will be the profit-maximizing output and total profit.

d. What is the point of shutdown for this boating firm in the SR?

e. Below what price will the firm shut down its operations and why?

5. Use the figure that follows to answer the questions.

Image 9.1a–b

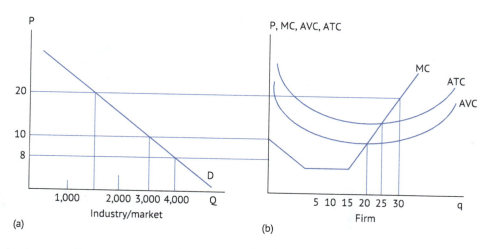

(a)

(b)

In the diagram, panel (a) on the left-hand side is the market demand curve for the entire industry (assume). The panel (b) on the right-hand side represents one firm's operations out of many firms in the industry. Assume that the MC curve in panel (b) intersects the AVC curve at $10 and quantity q = 20, and the same MC curve intersects at the ATC curve at P = $15 and quantity q = 25. Also, consider that the minimum MC is at five units output for the firm. For the market demand curve in panel (a), consider that for a price of $20, the quantity demanded is at 1,500 units and at a price of $8, the quantity demanded is 4,000 units.

a. Determine the profit-maximizing output of the firm at $20.

b. Is the firm making a positive economic profit at P = $20?

c. If the market price is at $8, will the firm stay in business? Why or why not?

d. At what market price will the firm shut down? Why?

e. Suppose there are 50 firms in the industry. Draw the SR supply curve of the market in panel a.

f. If the rental cost of manufacturing facilities rises, how will the change in cost functions in panel (b) take place, and which cost curve(s) will be affected and in what direction? If the wages of workers rise because of a new bargaining agreement with the owner, what cost curve(s) will be affected in panel (b) and in what direction? Note: Just explain briefly in your own words.

Chapter 10

Introduction to the Market Structure of Monopoly

Learning Objectives

As they read the chapter, students will learn:

▶ Concept of Monopoly and Conditions for Monopolies to Exist

▶ Derivation of the Monopoly Demand Curve and Marginal Revenue Curve

▶ Profit Maximization of Monopoly

▶ Monopoly Pricing and Output Determination and Measures of Efficiency

▶ Monopoly and Perfect Competition Compared to Antitrust Laws against Monopolies

10.1. Concept of Monopoly and Conditions for Monopolies to Exist

In Chapter 9, we introduced four types of market structure based on the degree of competition and the type of product substitution produced and sold by competing firms in each industry of goods and services. Unlike the perfect competition market structure discussed in Chapter 9, the monopoly market structure is just opposite competitive firms. The characteristics of the monopoly market are listed next.

- A single firm in the entire industry producing and selling a product with no close substitutes with a large number of buyers
- Imperfect information about technology and related aspects of production and distribution to both consumers and potential firms that may enter the industry

- Strong barriers to entry by new firms because of information asymmetry and the amount of capital and risk needed to compete even in the LR
- Market power as a dominant market share makes a monopoly firm a price maker instead of a price taker. That means a monopoly has complete control over deciding what price to charge consumers

Although there are not many pure monopoly firms in today's market environment under the previously listed characteristics, there are several monopoly firms we see in many industries, such as pharmaceuticals, software and hardware industries, internet browser industry, cloud computing industry, sports and entertainment industries, utility and communication services, biotechnology industry, and many mining industries (with rare substitutes). The sources of monopoly power are primarily attributed to barriers to entry (with enormous market power in technology and factors of production), economies of scale (cost advantage), and patent laws (regulated by the government to encourage investment in research and development [R&D] of new products and innovation).

Out of several examples of near or complete monopoly firms in the US economy, Table 10.1 provides a short list of monopolistic industries and firms with their respective sources of monopoly.

Table 10.1: Examples of Monopoly Markets

Sources of Monopoly	Industry Type	Types of Barriers to Entry	Strength of Market Power	Examples of Monopolies
Economies of scale (a case of natural monopoly)	Utilities, high technology, such as software, hardware, cloud computing	Cost advantage, technology, and information asymmetry	Very strong	Electricity grid, cable companies, internet browser, operating systems
Patent laws	All industries	Regulated by the government to protect monopoly power for 20 years	Complete monopoly by regulation but diminishes once patent law expires	Pharmaceutical companies, biotech industries, software, and communications
Control on technology and factors of production	High technology, such as medical equipment, mining products, and software industry	Information asymmetry and technological superiority and massive capital requirement	Moderate market power but may diminish in the long run	Precious metal industries, such as gold, diamond, silver, copper, aluminum, computer operating systems, search engines

From the list of monopoly sources and examples of monopolies, we can easily identify the giant monopoly firms in those industries, such as Microsoft and Intel in the software industry, Alcoa and DeBeers (aluminum and diamonds, respectively), local telephone and electricity companies, Pfizer and Johnson & Johnson in the pharmaceutical industry, Google in the internet search engine industry, the NFL in the sports industry, and P&G in the consumer products industry. These specific firms have enormous power in controlling the market share and pricing of their products to maximize abnormal profits. To understand monopoly power, the next section of this chapter discusses the steps for deriving a demand curve of a typical monopoly and its corresponding MR function and MR curve.

10.2. Derivation of the Monopoly Demand Curve and Marginal Revenue Curve

As we mentioned earlier, a monopoly firm is the dominant market power producing and selling its product with no close substitutes. It is reasonable to say that a monopoly firm is the same as an industry with no competitors. It implies that the market demand curve and a firm's demand curve are exactly the same because a monopoly firm itself is the industry. By digging deeper into the concept, we can say that the shape of the monopoly demand curve as the market demand curve must be downward sloping. It is also important here to keep in mind that monopolies are price makers instead of price takers under perfect competition. In other words, unlike the fixed price for a firm under the competitive market, the price under the monopoly market structure is variable. Based on this fundamental difference between monopoly and perfect competition, the derivation of the MR function from the total revenue (TR) function along a downward-sloping demand curve is explained next.

TR function and corresponding MR function are as follows:

TR = P × Q; where, TR = Total revenue, P = Price per unit; Q = Output Eqn (10.1)

MR = d(TR)/dQ = d(P × Q)/dQ, where dQ is the total derivative of TR with respect to output increase (delta Q). It can be expressed by using a partial derivative, such as

MR = P *($\partial\partial/\partial Q$) + Q × ($\partial P/\partial Q$), where the lower-case delta is used for partial derivates of both output and price, respectively, because both price and quantity of output are variables under monopoly. To simplify this MR derivation, the MR equation expressed next is the direct derivation of the TR function from Eqn (10.1):

MR = P + Q × (–$\partial P/\partial Q$), where P/Q = the slope of the demand function of a monopoly. Since the demand curve is downward sloping, the slope P/Q must be negative. Putting this concept in an equation, we can express the MR in Eqn (10.2).

$$\textbf{MR = P – Q × (}\partial P/\partial Q\textbf{)} \qquad\qquad \textbf{Eqn (10.2)}$$

In Eqn (10.2), MR is equal to P per unit minus output quantity times the slope of the demand function. Since the multiplication of the positive and negative slope of the demand curve gives a negative sign, we must use a negative sign after P on the right-hand side of Eqn (10.2). Eqn (10.2) as the MR function implies that the value of MR is less than its corresponding level of TR for each level output produced. This is because to produce and sell more and more, a monopoly, with its downward-sloping demand curve, must lower its prices and, therefore, the MR function will fall right below the price on the demand function (the price is always on the demand function). To explain this relationship between the TR and MR function of a typical monopoly, consider a hypothetical software development firm as a monopoly, say Mustang Software Corporation (MSC) in Boston. Table 10.2 is a set of hypothetical data for MSC on the price and quantity of a software development package for its clients and its related cost structure (MC and ATC).

Table 10.2: Revenue and Cost Structure of MSC as a Monopoly Firm

Price (P) (1)	Output (Q) (2)	TR (3)	MR (4)	TC (5)	MC (6)	ATC (7)*
$5,000	0	0	0	4,000	–	–
4,500	1	4,500	4,500	6,500	2,500	6,500
4,000	2	8,000	3,500	8,000	1,500	4,000
3,500	3	10,500	2,500	9,500	1,500	3,167
3,000	4	12,000	1,500	11,000	1,500	2,750
2,500	5	12,500	500	12,500	1,500	2,500
2,000	6	12,000	−500	14,000	1,500	2,333
1,500	7	10,500	−1,500	15,500	1,500	2,214
1,000	8	8,000	−2,500	18,000	2,500	2,250

Some numbers in the ATC column have been rounded off to skip the decimals.

In Table 10.2, the demand function of MSC is the price and quantity of the output produced shown in the first two columns on the left. Column (3) gives the TR function by multiplying P and the quantity of output from Columns (1) and (2). Using Eqn (10.2) for the MR function, MR data is estimated from Columns (3) and (1). MR data shows a lower value than the TR, as the firm has to lower its price to produce and sell more output. It is also important to notice that after five units of output are produced, the MR becomes negative as more output is produced. Therefore, the firm will not have incentive to produce more than five units. On the other hand, given the cost structure shown in Columns (5) to (7), the profit-maximizing output and price for MSC will be determined where **MR = MC** as the golden rule of profit maximization. Before providing a detailed discussion about the profit-maximization process for MSC in the Section 10.3, let us illustrate the demand and MR curve from Columns (1) to (4) in Table 10.2, as shown in Figure 10.1.

In Figure 10.1, we see that the MR curve falls below the demand curve for MSC. Under normal circumstances for a straight-line demand curve like this one, the slope of the MR curve would be twice the steepness of its corresponding demand curve. It is also shown

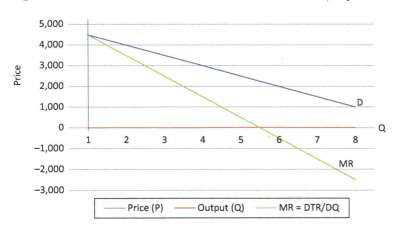

Figure 10.1 Demand and the MR Curve of a Monopoly

that the negative values of MR in Table 10.2 reflect the MR curve in Figure 10.1, sloping downward below the five and half units of output. A monopoly, obviously, will not produce below that level of output unless the demand condition changes. Using the demand and MR curve and the cost structure from Table 10.2, the profit-maximizing output level is explained and illustrated graphically in the next section.

10.3. Profit Maximization of a Monopoly

Using the golden rule of the MR = MC principle for profit maximization, the monopoly firm MSC will produce the optimum level of output where total profit is maximized. In other words, a monopoly will produce at the level of output where its marginal profit will be zero and total profit is maximum. The equality between MR and MC will fulfill that objective for profit maximization. Looking at the cost structure data of MSC in Table 10.2, we see that the MC reaches to a minimum point of 1,500 at two units of output and remains at that level up to seven units of output. This sustained value MC at a low level also explains why the ATC is continuously falling as more output is produced. The phenomena of DMC and the ATC cost structure are known as economies of scale of a monopoly, which were explained earlier in this chapter, as well as in the previous two chapters. Economies of scale are one of the key sources of a natural monopoly that creates strong barriers to entry by new firms to compete with the existing market power of a monopoly. The MC value in the same table starts rising after seven units of output, and thus the corresponding value of the ATC starts rising from its minimum point of 2,214.

Following the profit-maximization rule of MR = MC, the firm MSC maximizes its profit at four units of output, where the values of MR and MC are at 1,500 with a total maximum profit of 1,000 (TR − TC = 12,000 − 11,000). Students can also observe that the firm will expand output beyond three units because MR > MC at that level of output. The firm will not produce beyond four units because total profit will fall to zero. Therefore, output at four units is the optimum level of output for the firm with its equilibrium price at $3,000 per unit. The graphical illustration of this process of profit maximization from Table 10.2 is drawn in Figure 10.2. The total maximum profit for the firm is shown by the shaded area with blue lines in the box between the price of $3,000 and the ATC of 2,750 against four units of output (P-ATC as profit per unit) multiplied by four.

The contents of our discussion on the data in Table 10.2 and their corresponding graphical illustration in Figure 10.2 provide a foundation of monopoly behavior for maximizing its profit. The shaded area of total positive profit shown in the previous diagram may increase or decrease depending on the degree of power a monopoly has in the market. That power is determined by the size of the market and barriers to entry. The higher the entry barriers and larger the size of the market

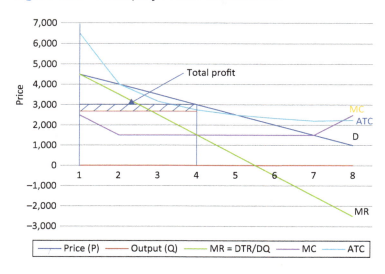

Figure 10.2   Monopoly Profit Maximization

share, the steeper the demand curve (with less price elasticity of demand) of a monopoly. For example, given the same cost structure of the previous monopoly diagram, if the demand curve is steeper than this one, then the profit margin would be much larger than shown by the shaded area. The higher profit margin would come from charging a higher price and producing less output by using the same profit-maximization rule of MR = MC. Students are encouraged to practice by drawing similar diagrams with different elasticities of the demand curve and the corresponding MR curve with the hypothetical MC and ATC curves. In doing the practice, no specific data is needed to fit the diagram. The next section of this chapter provides the techniques for measuring the efficiency of monopoly pricing and output determination plus the pros and cons of monopoly power in the context of consumer benefit and the effect on society as a whole.

10.4. Monopoly Pricing, Output Determination, and Measures of Efficiency

From our analysis of price and output determination of a monopoly to maximize its profit, we have seen that the monopoly has the market power to charge higher prices and offer lower production as it wishes. A monopoly also enjoys the cost advantage from economies of scale to create strong barriers to entry and thus retain its monopoly power for a long period of time. In addition, the patent laws of the government that encourage investments in R&Ds for new products and innovations do help create a large number of monopolistic firms in pharmaceutical industries, biotech firms, software and similar high-tech industries, and transportation and communication industries. In pharmaceutical industries, for example, companies with new drugs for some complicated diseases related to cancer, immune deficiency, metabolic, cardiovascular, and other genetic disorders are protected by patent laws for about 20 years. These drug companies charge hundreds and thousands of dollars (ranging from over $300,000 to $1 million per year per treatment) to patients, thus making super-abnormal profits after paying taxes. Some of those companies actually end up paying very few taxes or no taxes at all by using the tax loopholes and reinvesting their profits into R&Ds as tax deductibles. Given this general scenario of monopoly power, the following are some specific areas that focus on the loss of economic efficiency and social benefits under monopoly practice.

10.4.1. Monopoly and Efficiency Loss in Production and the Cost of Production

A typical monopoly firm will never have a tendency to produce more output than the level of output where MR = MC. Since the monopoly demand curve is downward sloping and relatively steeper than a regular market demand curve, the MR curve is below the demand curve to intersect with the MC curve. As one may notice in Figure 10.2, MR = MC is at the output level of four units to maximize profit. But the price is to be determined from the demand curve by going up to the demand curve and then going across to the vertical axis at $3,000. This means P > MR (= MC). The efficiency is measured by Price = MR = MC, like we saw in the case of perfect competition. That is not the case in the monopoly equilibrium, where price is not only higher than MR and MC but also produces lower output than the condition under MC pricing. In Figure 10.2, we see that it is possible to produce five units of output with MC pricing and still have zero economic profit for the firm with positive accounting profit. But a monopoly has the power to make above normal profit by producing fewer products and charging higher prices. This practice of making an abnormal profit means the loss of a consumer surplus (CS) with higher prices and less use of resources.

10.4.2. Monopoly and Barriers to Entry

As explained earlier, the barriers to entry mechanism of monopoly power prevents new firms from competing. These barriers are considered a loss of potential benefits to consumers and society in the sense that market competition is always desirable for lowering prices, more output and jobs, and improving the quality of products and services through competition.

10.4.3. Monopoly and Corporate Lobbying: Rent-Seeking Practice

The practice of monopoly firms of lobbying the elected legislators by financing their election campaigns is called corporate lobbying or *rent-seeking practice*. Once they get elected, the representatives become obligated to initiate and pass legislations in favor of the monopolies to protect their powers from the competition. In most cases, corporations hire lawyers and environmental and accounting professionals to keep lobbying until they are protected by preventing competition. This rent-seeking practice involves multibillion-dollar expenses for monopoly firms to protect their profits by maintaining their market shares. It is expected that this legally permitted lobbying practice compromises social and economic desires for low prices by consumers, consumer safety, and quality of goods and services. Some pundits dub this practice *crony capitalism*. It also has the potential to lose the quality and innovation of products and services because corporate management will not have incentive to invest in new products and/or service improvements. Many monopolies are also involved in causing greenhouse gas emissions by using old technologies. They have no desire to adopt greener technology to internalize the negative externality of causing pollution. They actually lobby to not change their operations to higher-cost, greener, and more efficient technology.

10.4.4. Monopoly and Price Discrimination

Monopoly firms not only have the power to charge higher prices and produce less quantity of output; they also have the power to arbitrarily fix different prices for different customers categorized by location, type of customer, price elasticity of demand and income elasticity of demand, difference in taste, and necessity of the products. This practice of charging different prices to different groups of consumers for the same product and services is called *price discrimination* under a monopoly. For example, airline companies charge different fares to different travelers for the same destination depending on whether the passengers are students, vacationers, or business travelers. Monopolies also offer their services based on the ages of their customers, such as senior discounts for specific products and times of service. The circumstances described here under which monopolies practice **price discrimination** are categorized by economists into three degrees of price discrimination: **first degree, second degree, and third degree.** These three common practices of monopoly price discrimination are briefly explained next.

First-degree price discrimination is charging the maximum price a consumer is willing to pay; thus, a monopoly firm can exploit the whole amount of CS for its profit. This is also called perfect price discrimination. Suppose the previously mentioned MSC in Boston has a monopoly power over its software product with virtually no competitors. Figure 10.3 is illustrated to explain how MSC can practice perfect price discrimination of the first degree by exploiting the potential CS.

In Figure 10.3, the profit-maximization output and price combination for MSC would be Q_1 and P_1, where the MR and MC curves intersect at point D. The CS for this normal monopoly pricing would be the area of the triangle P_0P_1B with the firm's profit of the area of the rectangle P_1BDP_2 (initial profit before price discrimination). However, if MSC charges piece by piece for its product, then quantities sold by single units starting from one unit and extending to Q_1 or even Q_2 means the firm is able to take away the CS of the P_0P_1B for its profit by charging higher than P_1 for selling fewer units than Q_1 and charging P_1 at Q_1 and then lowering the price below P_1 to sell higher quantities of output beyond Q_1. Let's assume this firm has a cost structure of constant MC and the same ATC. The MC = ATC curve is shown as a perfectly horizontal curve. If this firm does practice perfect first-degree price discrimination, then it has the power to take away the entire CS of the area in the upper-most triangle in Figure 10.3, plus more profit by selling more than Q_1 at a lower price than P_1. In Figure 10.3, we notice the additional maximum profit this firm can make is the area of BCD, showing a total profit of MSC equal to the area of the triangle P_0P_2C.

Figure 10.3 First-Degree Price Discrimination of Monopolies

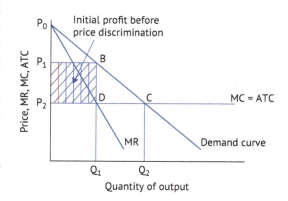

Second-degree price discrimination is the monopoly practice of charging different prices to customers based on different volume or units of output at a time. The lower volume or lower units of quantities are charged at a higher price than if purchased in a bulk. The utility companies, cable companies, internet service providers, cell phone data usage services, software development products, and various consumer items are priced by this pricing scheme of second-degree price discrimination. This practice lowers the marginal cost of sales and increases profit further by avoiding the discount pricing scheme. To illustrate this pricing scheme, Figure 10.3 is redrawn in Figure 10.4, showing the process as a little bit different than first-degree price discrimination.

Figure 10.4 Second-Degree Price Discrimination of a Monopoly

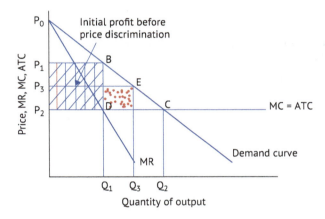

In Figure 10.4, the firm can offer a bulk amount of Q_3 at a lower price of P_3 than its usual profit-maximizing price of P_1. With the price break at P_3, the firm's profit margin has increased by the area of the rectangle indicated by the red dots in Figure 10.4.

Third-degree price discrimination is a frequently common practice of a monopoly based on different price and income elasticities of different groups of customers. For example, the lower the elasticities of demand, the MR = MC rule of profit maximization gives the leverage of charging a higher price than the customers of higher price elasticities of demand are willing to pay. The price difference in hotel industries, car rentals in different tourist destinations, casino industries, and online ticket prices for major sports events, music concerts, and movie tickets are key examples of third-degree price discrimination. These examples are also seen in many software companies that charge a discounted price to some of the customers who have not shown their willingness to pay at the profit-maximizing price charged to relatively big clients. This way, the firm can make additional profit by taking advantage of different willingness to pay approaches of their clients with different price elasticities of demand. This example is graphically illustrated in Figure 10.5. This figure is an extension of the Figures 10.3 and 10.4, except two different price elasticities of demand and their corresponding MR curves are drawn in two sets of diagrams with the same cost structure of the software firm MSC.

As we notice in panel (a) and panel (b) in Figure 10.5, the demand curves for two different groups of customers have different price elasticities of demand, with lower price elasticity of demand in panel (a) than that in panel (b). It implies that the MR = MC rule of profit maximization indicates that MSC clients in panel (b) have less willingness to pay than the clients in panel (a). As a result, the profit-maximizing price for panel (b) at P_1 is less than the price at P_1 in panel (a). This strategy of market segmentation by a monopoly firm like MSC can maximize its profit even more by charging different prices. The lower price charged to the panel (b)

Figure 10.5 Third-Degree Price Discrimination of a Monopoly

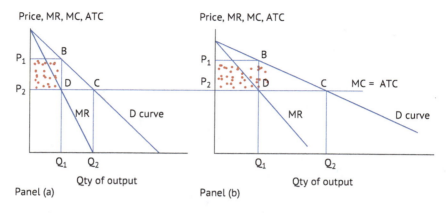

Panel (a)

Panel (b)

group is basically a discounted price based on a lower willingness to pay by that group of clients, reflecting their higher price elasticity of demand. A similar example can be applied to online ticket agents for major sports events and music concerts where the event hosts select only one or two agents to sell the tickets online. Those agents identify the fans based on their willingness to pay at different prices, as reflected in their price elasticity of demand and ability to pay. The market segmentation process based on this elasticity difference helps online ticket agents charge different prices to the ticket buyers and thus maximize their revenue and profits. The implications of these three types of price discrimination are many in the context of efficiency versus equity perspectives of monopoly power. Given the trade-off between efficiency at the expense of equity, price discrimination is definitely a powerful tool to take away the CS from consumers and move it to the profit side of a monopoly firm.

10.5. Monopoly and Perfect Competition Compared to Antitrust Laws against Monopolies

In previous sections of this chapter, we have noticed the power of a monopoly to maximize its abnormal profit by not only charging higher price than it would in a competitive market but also through the practice of three different degrees of price discrimination. A monopoly has also the power to create strong barriers to entry by taking advantage of economies of scale derived from its cost-efficiency with the decline of MC and ATC as the company expands to produce more output. Given those monopoly powers, monopoly firms are price makers or price fixers as opposed to price takers under perfect competition. The barriers to entry mechanism of monopoly firms from the advantage of economies of scale also creates a situation called *natural monopoly*. The position of natural monopoly is commonly seen in utility industries, such as electricity, water, heating oil and gas, telephone, cable and internet services. The examples of a natural monopoly are also common in high technology products, such as cloud computing for data management; software operating systems for PC, laptop, and mobile devices; and search engines like Google. The source of their monopoly power is mainly attributed to their advantage of economies of

Figure 10.6 Economies of Scale and Barriers to Entry for a Monopoly

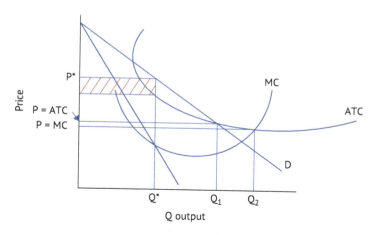

scale, which we discussed several times in previous chapters. The phenomenon of barriers to entry created by monopoly power from economies of scale is illustrated in Figure 10.6. The diagram shows how a monopoly has the leverage to raise its price as opposed to a competitive firm, in which price taken by a firm from the market will always be equal to the MC and minimum ATC in the LR.

The diagram in Figure 10.6 is presented with the assumption that the monopoly firm is the same as the industry demand curve, and, therefore, the corresponding MR is drawn right below it as twice the slope of the market demand curve. Given the economies of scale advantage of this monopoly, the monopoly will tend to produce at Q* at MR = MC and charge a price of P* against the demand curve with its total profit shaded in red. However, if new firms make an effort to enter the industry to compete with this monopoly by offering a much lower price than P*, this monopoly can easily match the lower price with probably not much loss of profit because of its downward-sloping ATC curve and continue with enough room for more output of produce at a price as low as P = ATC. In the diagram, it is shown where the firm will end up making a normal profit (P = ATC). But this aggressive price reduction would be the SR move to make sure that potential competitors cannot possibly enter the market. Once the threat of entry of competitors is eliminated, the monopoly firm will have the opportunity to raise the price again to start making abnormal profit. This strategy of creating barriers to entry is obviously a loss of efficiency in production and consumer welfare, although the firm could still be cost-efficient with its downward sloping-ATC. This situation is fairly common in private-sector natural monopolies in industries such as software operating systems (Microsoft is a good example), internet search engines (Google), microchips (Intel), some airline routes with hub and spoke networks with exclusive license by the government, cloud computing, and cable companies.

Utility companies have the same scenario of natural monopoly with the advantage of **economies of scale**. Those companies are actually better off as single producers that are more efficient than allowing competitors because of the cost advantage at least. However, the pricing mechanism by utility companies is regulated by government legislation so that monopoly firms cannot charge a high price by using the profit-maximizing rule of MR = MC. The government regulations usually try to use two alternative options instead of allowing the monopoly to charge by the MR = MC rule.

The first alternative is the *marginal cost pricing rule*. It means that a utility company must charge a price per unit to its MC. This option is shown in the diagram in Figure 10.6 at a price of P = MC with an output level at Q_2 at the minimum level of ATC. The problem with this price rule is the significant loss of profit for the utility monopoly. A firm usually does not welcome such MC pricing legislation from the government. To implement this pricing scheme, the government must subsidize the monopoly firm so that it can stay profitable.

The second alternative legislation for lowering price is the ATC pricing rule. This option is indicated in Figure 10.6 as P = ATC with the output level at Q_1. This second alternative is more common to implement with much less loss of profit by a monopoly. This is a sort of compromise between the MR = MC rule and MC pricing rule. However, the government still needs to subsidize the monopoly so that it can stay in business. Since the implementation of regulations to control price and quantity produced is difficult and costly, there are some other alternative forms of legislative rule pursued by the US government. Some of them are known as the rule for guaranteeing certain rates of return on capital investment, maximum price rule, and fixed-plus variable pricing based on usage by individual customers. The legislative detail of these rules is much more complicated, and discussion of those areas is beyond the scope of this introductory principles of economics textbook.

On the issue of monopoly power in the private sector, the US government has enacted a number of antitrust laws with the first of its kind called the Sherman Antitrust Act of 1890, which punished attempt at monopolization of market activities as an act of felony. This land-mark antitrust act was followed by the Clayton Act of 1914 intended to punish companies for the intentional practice of price discrimination by a monopoly power, and it established the Federal Trade Commission in the same year to monitor unfair business and trade practices by monopolies and other conglomerates. Since then, US legislators passed and implemented several more antitrust laws in the 1930s (Glass Steagall Act of 1933 focused on banks and financial institutions) and more laws in subsequent decades aimed at the financial market, banking industry, consumer safety in transportation industries, communication industries, and housing industries, as well as the areas of mergers and acquisitions. Students are encour-aged to read some of the most recent antitrust cases that government took actions against, including AT&T, Microsoft, Facebook, and Google.

Chapter Summary

Section 10.1 described the monopoly market structure as the sole producer and seller of a product or service to a large number of buyers with no close substitute of its product or ser-vice. Therefore, a monopoly firm is the same as the industry or market entity. The conditions under which a monopoly firm exists are listed next:

- A single firm in the entire industry producing a product with no close substitutes
- Imperfect information about production technology and distribution of product
- Strong barriers to entry by new firms because of information asymmetry and the amount of capital and risk needed to compete even in the LR
- Market power as a dominant market share makes a monopoly firm a price maker instead of a price taker.

Examples of monopolies: Real-world examples of monopoly firms are pharmaceuticals, software and hardware of computer industries, internet browser industry, cloud computing industry, sports and entertainment industry, utility and communication services, biotechnology industry, and many mining industries with rare substitutes as major inputs and precious metals. The existence of monopoly power is primarily attributed to barriers to entry (with enormous market power in technology and factors of production), economies of scale (cost advantage), and patent laws (regulated by the government to encourage investment in R&D for new products and innovation). A detailed list of sources of monopolies provided in Table 10.1 at the beginning of this chapter.

In Section 10.2, we learned that as a sole producer and with a dominant position in the industry, a monopoly firm is a price maker and, therefore, it has the power to change its price as it wishes to maximize profit. The implication for this market position with no competitor is that a monopoly demand curve is the same as the industry demand curve. In other words, unlike the fixed price for a firm in the competitive market, the price in a monopoly market structure is variable. From this fundamental difference between monopoly and perfect competition, the derivation of the MR function from the TR function along a downward-sloping demand curve is given next.

TR function and corresponding MR function:

TR = P × Q, where TR = Total revenue, P = Price per unit; Q = Output Eqn (10.1)

MR = d(TR)/dQ = d(P × Q)/dQ, where, dQ is the total derivative of TR with respect to output increased (delta Q). It can be expressed simply as follows:

MR = P */Q + Q × (P/Q), where the lower-case delta is used for partial derivates of both output and price, respectively, because both price and quantity of output are variables under a monopoly. The simplified derivation of the MR function from the TR function in Eqn (10.1) is expressed next.

MR = P + Q × (−P/Q), where P/Q = the slope of the demand function of a monopoly. Since the demand curve is downward sloping, the slope P/Q must be negative. Putting this concept in an equation, we can express the MR in Eqn (10.2):

$$\text{MR} = \text{P} - \text{Q} \times (\text{P/Q}) \qquad\qquad \textbf{Eqn (10.2)}$$

In Eqn (10.2), MR is equal to P per unit minus output quantity times the slope of the demand function. Since the multiplication of the positive and negative slopes of the demand curve is equal to negative, we must use a negative sign after P on the right-hand side of Eqn (10.2). Eqn (10.2) as the MR function implies that the value of MR is less than its corresponding level of TR for each level output produced. This is because to produce and sell more and more, a monopoly with its downward-sloping demand curve must lower its prices and thus the MR will fall right below the price on the demand function (the price is always on the demand function). To explain this relationship between the TR and MR functions of a typical monopoly, consider a hypothetical software development firm as a monopoly: MSC in Boston. A set of hypothetical data of the TR and MR functions of MSC and its cost structure are shown and explained in Section 10.2. The corresponding graphs for demand and MR curves of the data set in Table 10.2 are illustrated in Figure 10.1 under Section 10.2.

Using the rule of MR = MC for profit maximization, Section 10.3 explained how the hypothetical monopoly firm MSC will produce the optimum level of output for its profit maximization. Given that rule of profit maximization and using the total profit function as TR – TC (total cost) for a monopoly will produce at a level of output where its marginal profit will be zero and thus total profit is maximum. Concerning the total derivative of this profit function with respect to the expansion of output, the monopoly firm MSC will produce output where MR = MC to maximize its profit given the cost functions for MC and ATC. The revenue and cost data in Table 10.2 are used to analyze the process of profit maximization in a monopoly in Section 10.3. The concept of economies of scale as one of the key sources of a natural monopoly by creating strong barriers to entry is also discussed in Section 10.3. Using the revenue and cost data in Table 10.2, the corresponding graph for monopoly profit maximization is illustrated in Figure 10.2 in Section 10.3. Students are encouraged to read the data analysis from Table 10.2 and review the graphs drawn in Figure 10.2.

From the detailed analysis of price and output determination of a monopoly in Section 10.3, the measures of efficiency in production, cost, and distribution of consumer and producer surpluses are critically discussed in this section in four different subsections briefly summarized next:

Since a monopoly uses the MR = MC rule for profit maximization, and MR is below the downward-sloping demand curve, as shown in Figure 10.2, the profit-maximizing output is lower than it would be under perfect competition. On the other hand, the corresponding price under a monopoly on the demand curve is higher than it would be under perfect competition. Students may notice in Figure 10.2 that MR = MC is at the output level of four units to maximize its profit. But the price is determined from its demand curve by going up to the demand curve and going across to the vertical axis at $3,000. It means P > MR (= MC). The efficiency is measured by Price = MR = MC like we have seen in case of perfect competition. That is not the case in monopoly equilibrium, where price is not only higher than MR and MC but also produces lower output than the conditions under MC pricing. As explained in detail in Section 10.4.1 with the help of the graph in Figure 10.2, a monopoly has the power to make above normal profit by producing fewer products and charging higher prices. This practice of making abnormal profit is the loss of CS with higher prices and less use of resources.

As explained earlier, the barriers to entry mechanism of monopoly power prevents new firms from competing. These barriers are considered a loss of potential benefits to consumers and society in the sense that market competition is always desirable for lowering prices, more output and jobs, and improving the quality of products and services through competition.

The practice of monopoly firms lobbying elected legislators by financing their election campaigns is called rent-seeking behavior of monopoly and oligopoly firms. Once they get elected, the representatives are obligated to initiate and pass legislation in their favor and at the expense of consumer welfare. In most cases, corporations hire lawyers and environmental and accounting professionals to keep lobbying until they are protected by preventing competition. This rent-seeking practice involves multibillion-dollar expenses to protect their profits by maintaining their market shares. It is expected that this legally permitted lobbying practice compromises social and economic desires for low prices by consumers, consumer safety, and quality of goods and services. Many monopolys are also involved in causing more greenhouse gas emissions by using old technologies. They have no desire to adopt greener technology to internalize the negative externality of causing pollution. They actually lobby to not change their operations to higher-cost, greener, and more efficient technology. Students are encouraged to read this subsection and related peer-reviewed publications to learn more about this major economic and social issue in the country.

Monopoly firms not only have the power to charge higher price and produce less output, but they have also the power to arbitrarily fix different prices for different customers categorized by location, type of customers, price elasticity of demand and income elasticity of demand for different customers, difference in tastes, and necessity of the products. This practice of charging different prices to different consumers for the same product and services is called price discrimination under monopoly. Some real-world examples of price discrimination under different circumstances are given in Section 10.4 with three different types of price discrimination a typical monopoly uses in the US market. They are listed next with brief descriptions. The details are discussed in Section 10.4.

First-degree price discrimination is charging the of maximum price a consumer is willing to pay, and thus a monopoly firm can exploit the whole amount of CS for its profit. This is also called perfect price discrimination. Figure 10.3 in Section 10.4 illustrated this practice and explained how a monopoly can practice perfect price discrimination of the first degree by exploiting the potential CS from its clients.

Second-degree price discrimination is the monopoly practice of charging different prices to customers based on different volume or units of output at a time. The lower volume or units of quantities are charged at a higher rate than the purchase of higher volume or quantities in bulk. The utility companies, cable companies, internet service providers, cell phone data usage services, software development products, and various consumer items are priced by this pricing scheme of second-degree price discrimination. This practice lowers the marginal cost sales and increases profit further by avoiding discount pricing schemes. Figure 10.4 in Section 10.4 illustrated this type of price discrimination.

Third-degree price discrimination is a frequently common practice of a monopoly based on different price and income elasticities of different groups of customers. For example, the lower the elasticities of demand, the MR = MC rule of profit maximization gives the leverage of charging a higher price than the customers of higher price elasticities of demand are willing to pay. The price difference in hotel industries, car rentals in different tourist destinations, casino industries, online ticket prices for major sports events, music concerts, and movie tickets are key examples of third-degree price discrimination. These examples are also seen in many software companies, which charge a discounted price to some of their customers who have not shown a willingness to pay at the profit-maximizing price charged to relatively big clients. This way the firm can make additional profit by taking advantage of different willingness to pay approaches of their clients with different price elasticities of demand. This example is graphically illustrated in Figure 10.5. Students are encouraged to find other examples similar to this type of price discrimination and practice by using the same model structure shown in Figure 10.5.

Section 10.5 provided a comparison between monopoly and perfect competition with respect to measures of efficiency in production, cost of production, and distribution of consumer and producer surpluses. From our discussion in previous sections about the power of a monopoly to maximize its abnormal profit, we have seen that a monopoly, in addition to practice of price discrimination, also has the power of creating strong barriers to entry by new firms. This barriers to entry comes from the advantage of economies of scale derived from its cost-efficiency with the decline of MC and ATC as it expands to produce more output. Given this monopoly power, monopoly firms are price makers or price fixers, as opposed to price takers under perfect competition. The barriers to entry mechanism of monopoly firms from the advantage of economies of scale also create a situation called a natural monopoly. Some real-world examples of the phenomenon of barriers to entry created from economies scale are given in Section 10.5 and illustrated in Figure 10.6. Students are encouraged to review the diagram and practice by selecting a similar scenario from the market behavior of a monopoly industry. Government legislation in the form of antitrust laws of the US government are discussed in Section 10.5.

Application Activities

1. In a perfectly competitive market structure, a competitive firm has the given price as a price taker and, therefore, its price is equal to its MR, shown on the same demand curve as the perfectly elastic demand curve. On the other hand, a monopoly firm has a downward-sloping demand curve, and its equilibrium price is always larger than MR (P > MR). Briefly explain why. Use both equations and diagrams.

2. Define and explain the concept of a natural monopoly and give the conditions under which a natural monopoly exits with real-world examples.

3. Briefly explain the concept of price discrimination under a monopoly and the conditions under which a monopoly practices price discrimination. In your explanation, give examples of three different types of price discrimination and the effects of the discriminatory practices on consumer welfare.

4. Why are the antitrust laws important for controlling the behavior of monopoly pricing? Also, why does the government protect some monopolies under patent laws? Give examples of both sides.

5. Is the Google search engine a monopoly in the digital internet search industry? Why or why not? Give your own thoughts in the answer that reflect a conceptual understanding from the materials you studied in this chapter.

6. Using the graph for a monopoly software firm called MSC, answer the questions.

Image 10.1

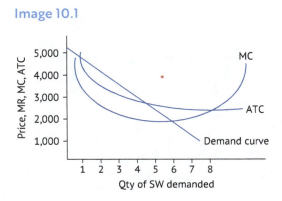

a. Draw the MR curve from the demand curve. You may recall from previous discussions at the beginning of this chapter that the MR curve is twice as the steep of the demand curve.

b. Using the MR curve from Q6.a and the MC curve in the diagram, indicate the profit-maximizing output and price combination for this firm.

c. From your answer to Q6.b, show the level of maximum profit in the diagram.

d. Looking at the shape of the ATC curve, explain briefly if this firm enjoys economies of scale.

e. How can this firm prevent any attempts by new firms to enter its market?

7. After reading the *Wall Street Journal* article about the monopoly behavior of Tyco International, critically, but briefly, explain how this plastic hanger company can raise its price and increase its profits. Given market position, do you think Tyco International can stay in its monopoly power for a long time by creating barriers to entry?

8. Provide a list of monopoly corporations from the pharmaceutical industry and internet plus software industries and provide a brief critical analysis of how these monopolies create their barriers to entry and remain monopolies for a long period of time.

9. From your own experience, provide an example of a specific degree of price discrimination of a monopoly with examples.

10. Do you think Google is a monopoly, and how does it maintain its monopoly position in the US market?

Chapter 11

Introduction to the Market Structure of Monopolistic Competition

Learning Objectives

As they read the chapter, students will learn the following:

- ▶ Monopolistic Competition and Its Conditions to Exist

- ▶ Product Differentiation and the Demand Curve under Monopolistic Competition

- ▶ Profit Maximization and Price-Output Determination in the SR and in the LR

- ▶ Case Studies of Monopolistic Competition and Nonprice Competition

- ▶ Price-Output Decision and Measures of Efficiency in the SR and the LR

Indroduction

In Chapter 9, we saw the economic analysis of perfect competition as the point of efficient allocation of resources under the assumption of the laissez-faire market system. In Chapter 10, on the other hand, we saw the operations of a monopoly firm as the sole market power, quite opposite the perfect competition. Until the 1930s, economists were not quite familiar with the other two types of market systems operating between these two extreme forms of market structure. The other types are known as *monopolistic competition* and *oligopoly*. In the 1930s, two economists, Edward Chamberlin at Harvard University in Cambridge in the USA and Joan Robinson at Cambridge University in the United Kingdom, introduced the concept of *monopolistic competition* through their separate and independent research work (Baumol and Blinder 2016, 230[1]). Their research analysis helped develop the theory of market structure as a distinct market system with more realistic applications in rapidly increasing industrial growth and business expansion. This market structure, by its own characteristics, falls between perfect competition and monopoly as a hybrid market structure. Over the next several decades, since the end of World War II, the majority of market competitions have fallen under the categories of monopolistic competition and oligopoly. The development of these two distinct market structures was mainly attributed to the rapid rate of industrial expansion and revolutionary development of new technology and innovation in major industries. More than 90 percent of total market competition falls under monopolistic competition and oligopoly. In this chapter, we focus our discussion on price and output determination under monopolistic competition, and the same will be covered on the oligopoly market structure in Chapter 12.

11.1. Monopolistic Competition and Its Conditions to Exist

Unlike the perfect competition with homogenous products and monopoly with a single product, the firms under *monopolistic competition* market structure compete among many small and medium-size firms with differentiated substitutes for goods and services predominantly recognized by brand names and their distinct features. Four such characteristics of this market structure are listed next.

1. Many firms and a large number of buyers in different size market segmentation
2. Products and services produced and served by each firm are close substitutes, but they are differentiated with respect to brand names and other related features
3. Perfect information of business and technology and market behavior
4. Free entry and exit of firms in and out of the industry/market in the LR

By comparing the aforementioned characteristics with those of perfect competition discussed in Chapter 9, we may notice that the third and fourth characteristics here are the same as perfect competition. The first one also seems similar to perfect competition, except the number of firms under monopolistic competition are not as many as there in under perfect competition. The second characteristic is the key difference between perfect competition and monopolistic competition. This distinct condition of product differentiation is marked by the attributes of difference in quality, brand recognition, features and packaging, and other forms of product information to create consumer loyalty through advertisement and word of mouth spreading excellent customer service and perks. As mentioned in the introduction, with rapid industrial innovation and recent decades of digital revolution, product quality and services have improved significantly while the average cost of production and services have declined at the same time. These twin developments in most of

---

1   William J. Baumol and Alan S. Blinder, *Microeconomics: Principles & Policy* (Mason, OH: South-Western, Cengage Learning, 2016), 230.

the industrial products and services have made these industries extremely competitive. Most of these industries have similar products and services but product differentiation falls under monopolistic competition.

A few of the real-world examples include national fast-food chain stores, such as Subway, McDonald's, Burger King, and Wendy's; local restaurants of different ethnic food types in major cities around the globe; various beauty products and shoe and fashion clothing industries with top name brands; wine industries and beer markets; local convenience stores; gas stations by location; some brands of motor vehicles; and airline services. Despite the fierce competition among firms in each industry, the product differentiation for brand loyalty make each firm a bit of a market power, so they can fix their own price to charge to their customers. This power of independence in controlling its own price makes a monopolistic firm a price maker. Therefore, like a monopoly, a monopolistic competitive firm's demand curve is downward sloping but a little more elastic than a monopoly's demand function in the face of competition with many other firms. The more substitutes, the flatter (more elastic) the demand curve will be, and vice versa. This concept of *product differentiation* and the shape of the demand curve are further explained with the help of a diagram in Section 11.2.

11.2. Product Differentiation and the Demand Curve under Monopolistic Competition

With the existence of product differentiation of each firm under monopolistic competition because of brand specialty and distinct features, market segmentation is obvious for each firm. This market segmentation implies that the price elasticity of a downward-sloping demand curve for each of the firms will be different in values. Given several examples of this scenario in fashion, shoes, wine and beer, fast-food chains, and local restaurants, the two diagrams in Figure 11.1 illustrate the case of two ethnic restaurant chains in Cambridge, Massachusetts, as close approximation to realistic demand curves in the food industry.

Figure 11.1 Demand Curves for Monopolistic Firms in the Restaurant Industry

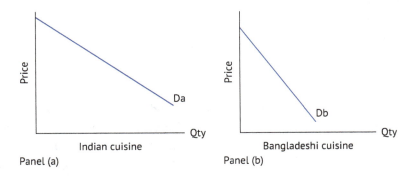

In Figure 11.1, suppose panel (a) represents an Indian restaurant in the city of Cambridge competing with many other ethnic restaurants serving Indian cuisine. Since the number of competitors serving ethnic Indian cuisine are many, the demand curve Da is expected to be much flatter, as illustrated in panel (a) with relatively higher price elasticity of demand than the demand curve Db for a Bangladeshi restaurant illustrated in panel (b) with a steeper demand curve. The reason for a relatively steeper demand curve for Bangladeshi cuisine is because the recipes and taste of Bangladeshi food is distinctly different from similar food items served by Indian restaurants. In addition, the number of Bangladeshi restaurants is only a few as compared to many Indian restaurants in the city and its vicinity. This distinct difference in taste and recipes clearly reflects a difference in the shape of the demand curves for competing restaurants, not only in this example of Indian versus Bangladeshi restaurants, but also it applies to other ethnic restaurants, such as Thai, Chinese, Mexican, Korean, Middle Eastern, Italian, Japanese, and French restaurants. The product differentiation in monopolistic competition is the key factor for a near monopoly position during the determination of price and output, at least in the SR. However, the free entry and exit of firms in the LR do change the position of market power by changing the price elasticity of the demand curves. The price and output determination of ethnic restaurants in both the SR and LR for a typical ethnic restaurant as shown in Figure 11.1 is analyzed in Section 11.3.

11.3. Profit Maximization and Price-Output Determination in the SR and LR

The process of profit maximization under monopolistic competition is similar to that under the monopoly market, where the MR curve is derived from its downward-sloping demand curve at twice the steepness of the demand curve. The profit-maximizing rule is also the same as MR = MC in both the SR and LR. However, the key differences between a monopoly and monopolistic competition are that the demand curve is relatively flatter for a monopolistic firm, and there are no barriers to entry for new firms in monopolistic competition. The relatively flatter demand curve for a monopolistic firm becomes even flatter in the LR as new firms enter the market to capture a piece of the profit being made by existing firms. On the other hand, a monopoly firm's demand curve stays at its steeper position because of its barriers to entry, even in the LR. Given this market environment of monopolistic competition, Figure 11.2 is shown as the process of price and output determination for a typical Bangladeshi cuisine restaurant introduced in Figure 11.1.

11.3.1. Price and Output Determination of a Profit-Maximizing Firm in the SR

Consider a Bangladeshi cuisine restaurant called Darul Kabab (DK), which is currently operating in Cambridge and serving ethnic Bangladeshi food with its distinct tastes as compared to competing restaurants serving similar ethnic cuisines, such as Nepalese and West Bengal (India) cuisines. Although their foods are close substitutes, they are not identical in taste and recipe. Also, assume that DK cuisine, with its distinct taste and specialty recipes, has

Figure 11.2 Profit Maximization of DK in the SR

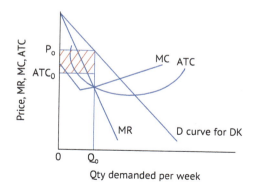

gained popularity in the busy neighborhood where it is located. In the face of very little competition from only a few similar restaurants in the area, the demand curve is expected to be relatively inelastic, as illustrated in Figure 11.1 in the previous section. The same demand curve for DK and its corresponding MR curve are illustrated in Figure 11.2.

With a relatively steep demand curve for DK, Figure 11.2 represents its market position as a near monopoly with a relatively low elasticity of demand. The hypothetical cost structure is also drawn as MC and ATC in the diagram to illustrate the profit-maximizing price and output determination with the MR = MC rule of profit maximization. We notice that DK serves its quantity per week, say at Q_o at an average price per unit at P_o, with its total profit shown in the shaded area as $(P_o - ATC_0) \times Q_o$. Its advantage in product differentiation and near monopoly position gives the restaurant solid leverage to make a positive abnormal profit, as indicated in the shaded area. It is also easy to observe from the diagram that the steeper the demand curve, the higher the profit margin DK can make. The opposite would be the case for a flatter curve. This near monopoly position is only possible to hold on to in the SR. As the time passes and potential rivals (usually called imitators in the monopolistic industries) will try to enter the market in an attempt to get a piece of this profit-making business in the LR. The Section 11.3.2 analyzes the process of LR adjustment of this restaurant business as a representative case for monopolistic market behavior.

11.3.2. Price and Output Determination of Profit Maximization in the LR

With abnormal profit being made in the SR by DK, as shown in Figure 11.2, a new firm will try to enter the competition in Cambridge by imitating the same model of product differentiation in the LR. With the gradual entry of new firms into the restaurant business, two consequences of market behavior are expected to happen. First, there will be more choices for existing customers currently eating at DK and other existing Bangladeshi restaurants. As a result, DK customers will see more substitutes in newly opened restaurants serving similar items with similar tastes. That means DK will probably lose some of their customers to newly opened rivals in the city. This consequence of having more substitutes will change the shape of the demand curve for DK with higher elasticity of demand. As we know from basic theory of demand and supply elasticity the more substitutes, the flatter the demand curve. As a result, the existing demand curve for DK shown in Figure 11.2 in Section 11.2.1 will tend to tilt inward with a flatter shape. The second consequence will be the LR adjustment of price and cost behavior for DK by lowering the price to keep its customers. Combining these two consequences in the LR, the amount of profit maximization of DK will shrink to a point where price will be equal to its level of ATC, thus making a normal profit. This LR process of profit maximization is illustrated in Figure 11.3.

From the diagram in Figure 11.3, we may notice DK's prices have been lowered because of the entrance of more substitutes, which is reflected in its flatter demand and MR curves. The profit-maximizing output and price combination at the MR = MC intersection are shown at Q_o and P_o with its corresponding ATC curve tangent with its flatter demand curve at P_o level (at T_o). This is the LR equilibrium solution for DK with the loss of the abnormal profit it was making in the SR, as shown in the diagram. The normal profit of zero economic profit is calculated as $(P_o - ATC_o) \times Q_o = 0$. However, it is also important to keep in mind that DK is still making accounting profit greater than zero because the cost structure used in this model is the economic cost, including the opportunity cost not shown in the accounting cost. Therefore, the monopolistic firm DK is still profitable by making a positive accounting profit. As time passes, many other possible adjustments can happen in the market. One of the possible cases may be some of the newly entered competitors are experiencing accounting losses (P < ATC) because of changes in market conditions and rising cost conditions for serving high-quality of food. With that possibility, the losing restaurants will quit and exit the competition over time. As a result, DK's demand curve will reverse its shape by tilting into a direction other than the one shown in Figure 11.3. With changes in the shape of the demand curve, DK will enjoy its market near monopoly position again with the possibility of making abnormal profit, as shown in Figure 11.2. This process of LR adjustment continues to operate in all other industries under monopolistic competition. Students may also try to select other industries such as fast-food chains, wine and beer industries, fashion design, and beauty products industries to practice similar behavior of profit maximization. Section 11.4 provides some realistic examples of monopolistic competition followed by the method of measuring efficiency of production and pricing under monopolistic competition in Section 11.5.

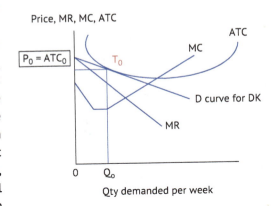

Figure 11.3 Profit Maximization of DK in the LR

11.4. Case Studies of Monopolistic Competition and Nonprice Competition

Similar to the example of monopoly market behavior discussed in Chapter 10, a firm under monopolistic competition behaves very much the same, except the latter does not have full control over prices. Therefore, to create their own brand loyalty, firms undertake different market strategies, such as senior discounts in grocery stores, movie theaters, airline services, and sport events. Other forms of pricing strategies include charging different prices for the same product and services to different groups of customers based on the consumers' preferences, patterns, ability to pay, time of the sale or services, and the most

Microeconomics Principles, Applications, and Policy Implications

difference in price elasticity of demand. This is called price discrimination—classifying customers based on their behavioral patterns as consumers. As mentioned in the monopoly case of price discrimination in the previous chapter, there are three types of price discrimination that are commonly practiced by the monopoly market. They are first-degree, second-degree, and third-degree price discrimination. Unlike the monopoly practice of first-degree and second-degree price discrimination in the form of negotiations (the first degree) and bundling of bulk prices (second degree), third-degree price discrimination is the most commonly practiced strategy in both monopoly and monopolistic competition. Since third-degree price discrimination is based on consumer preference and difference in price elasticity of demand, monopoly and monopolistic competitive firms can easily exploit CS to transfer to their profitability without facing any possible violation of anti-trust laws. Some of the examples of third-degree price discrimination by a monopolistic firm is explained next.

Since the practices of first-degree and second-degree price discrimination are complicated and may increase the MC of firms, monopolistic competition firms prefer third-degree price discrimination to the other two alternatives. The reasons for this are primarily the zero MC increase and the ease of implementation. For example, the owners of a ski resort charge different prices for ski lifts based on the number of lifts, by the hour or bundle of hours, morning versus afternoon rates, and weekdays versus weekend rates. This different pricing mechanism does not incur any extra MC for the firm but easily exploits all preference patterns of skiers to maximize the revenue and thus transfer almost the entire amount of CS (under a single pricing mechanism) to their profit. In addition, the ski resort owners can also charge different rates for all-day skiing versus half-a-day skiing. Another option they can use is charging lower rates for young skiers and higher rates for adult users because the price elasticity of demand is larger for young skiers than that is for the adult skiers. Similar techniques of third-degree price discrimination are commonly used by casino and vacation resort owners, airline services, movie theaters, and music concert events. For a more specific example, Table 11.1 includes a hypothetical example of cost, revenue, and profit data for a casino resort focused on identifying two groups of casino goers to stay in the hotel over the weekend for their gambling mission. Assume that these two groups of customers are identified on the basis of difference in price elasticity of demand derived from their family's composition and ability to pay and their gambling habits. Suppose that, based on research work, Group A was identified with high price elasticity of demand for staying in a casino hotel for gambling. Group B was identified with the same gambling habit but with a lower price elasticity of demand for hotel rates. The relevant data on elasticity, cost, and changes in revenue and profit are provided in Table 11.1 as numerical examples.

Table 11.1: Third-Degree Price Discrimination and Profit Maximization

(1)	(2)	(3)	(4)	(5)	(6)	(7)
Hotel/ Casino Guest Groups	Single Rate for Hotel Room/ Night	Price Elasticity of Demand	Variable Rate for Hotel Room	% Change in Quantity Demanded as the Area of a Rectangle*	MC for Each Hotel Room	Change in Revenue and Profit as the Area of the Triangle*
Group A	$200	2.0	Decrease 20% = $160/night	2 × 0.2 = 0.4 = 40% increase	$0.00	Revenue increase by 20% (40/2)
Group B	$200	0.5	Increase 20% = $240/night	0.5 × 0.2 = 0.10 = 10% decrease	$0.00	Revenue increase by 5% (10/2)

* Please note that on the downward-sloping demand curve, the quantity demanded increase or decrease multiplied by the change in price will generate a change in demand by the area of the rectangle. This is shown in the fifth column in the table. However, to calculate the actual change in revenue for a downward-sloping demand curve, the change in quantity demanded needs to be divided to find the area of the triangle. In other words, the actual change in revenue is the area of the triangle below the demand curve as the half of the rectangle (the other half is outside the demand curve). This is shown in the seventh column on the right side.

Looking at the numbers in Table 10.1 for third-degree price discrimination, commonly practiced by a typical casino hotel, it is interesting to see how the owners can increase revenue by 20 percent from Group A guests with a price elasticity of demand >1 at 2.0 by lowering the room rate by 20 percent. On the other hand, they can also increase revenue by 10 percent from Group B guests with a price elasticity of demand <1 at 0.5 by increasing the room rate by 20 percent. The MC of adding more guests in the hotel is virtually zero in both cases because the hotel rooms are already there with or without occupancy (with no change in fixed costs) and no increase in variable cost either (the hotel staff are already paid to maintain the rooms and guests anyway). So, it is evident that the estimation of changes in revenue from both groups of hotel guests will be equal to 25 percent total (with no change in cost structure). This increase in revenue estimate is shown in the last column on the right side of Table 11.1. Since there is no change in MC and ATC for adding additional guests, then the total profits will be exactly equal to a 25 percent increase in revenue. The 25 percent increase in revenue is actually transferred from potential CS if the hotel management charged the single rate of $200 per room to both groups instead of lowering it for Group A to $160 and increasing the rate for Group B to $240. This is the best alternative pricing scheme for the use third-degree price discrimination by monopolistic firms to maximize profits without changing its current cost structure and with no legal violation of the antitrust laws. However, the real challenge for the marketing wing of hotel management is to accurately identify and separate the customers, like the example, on the basis of difference in demand elasticity. Students are encouraged to practice similar techniques of measuring profit increase by using the specific information of another firm or using the same example with different values of elasticity and price mechanism to see the changes in revenue and profit. It is also possible to illustrate the numbers in a diagram with specific numbers plugged into the graph (not drawn here). Section 11.5 focuses on the techniques used to measure the efficiency of monopolistic competition with respect to consumer welfare and allocation of resources.

11.5. Price-Output Decision and Measures of Efficiency in the SR and the LR

This last section of the chapter is focused on measures of efficiency of a firm operating in both SR and LR. Starting with the SR profit-maximization rule of MR = MC, we have seen in Figure 11.2 that a firm has the ability to make abnormal profit at P > ATC against the optimum equilibrium output level. Compared to the MR = MC = Price rule under a perfectly competitive firm, a monopolistically competitive firm charges higher prices and produces less. As a consequence, it is fair to conclude that price and output decisions made by monopolistically competitive firms are not efficient with respect to price and resource allocation. On the other hand, a firm under perfect competition may or may not make abnormal profit in the SR. However, a monopolistically competitive firm is able to raise its price with its distinct product differentiation from its rival substitutes to ensure that it can make a profit in the SR. Therefore, it is almost certain that a firm under monopolistic competition is able to make an abnormal profit in the SR.

In Section 11.4, we have also seen that a monopolistically competitive firm can practice third-degree price discrimination by identifying different groups of customers with different price elasticity and ability to pay. By practicing third-degree price discrimination, they charge different prices to different groups while selling the same product to increase its revenue and profit by exploiting the CS to its profits. For increasing such profits, the firm doesn't have to incur additional costs or increase the level of output a bit to increase its revenue. From the efficiency point of production and pricing, it is not really so bad thing. However, from the consumers' perspective, it is definitely not desirable with respect to consumer utility maximization.

In the LR process of profit maximization, monopolistically competitive firms face free entry and exit of new firms because existing firms do not have the ability to create barriers to entry. With the free entry and exit of firms, there is the challenge of staying competitive in terms of quality and feature improvements and innovation, which may cause the cost of production to increase. At the same time, with the new entry of firms, more product substitutes will emerge. As discussed in Section 11.3.2 and shown in Figure 11.3, the increase of substitute products and services will make the existing demand curves of individual firms flatter with higher price elasticity of demand. As a result of the increasing cost of production and higher elasticity of demand, the profit-maximizing output and price competition will be at the price equal to ATC with zero economic profit. In other words, as we have seen in Figure 11.3, the ATC curve is just tangent to the demand curve against the optimum output level to maximize profit in the LR. However, despite the P = ATC position in the LR, a monopolistically competitive firm is not cost-efficient because the output produced at ATC is actually higher than the minimum point of ATC. It also produces less output than what it should under the MC = Price = Minimum ATC rule, as seen in the LR condition under perfect competition. Therefore, production, cost, and pricing under monopolistic competition are still not efficient, even in the LR with zero economic profit. In other words, the firm shows its excess capacity with a higher price equal to ATC at a higher than minimum level of ATC. This inefficiency of production and cost per unit does not allow the firm to take advantage of economies of scale, even in the LR. However, it is also possible for a firm to keep lowering the price close to its minimum point of ATC in the face of continuous entries of new firms into the industry. This kind of price war seems to be common, as we may know from reading the *Wall Street Journal* article that follows, which provides a real-world business example of monopolistic competition in New York City. Several years ago, one of my colleagues shared this article with me, and I saved it to share with students reading this chapter.

Chapter Summary

Sections 11.1 and 11.2 discussed firms under the monopolistic competition market structure and how they compete among many small and medium-size firms with differentiated substitutions of goods and services predominantly recognized by brand recognition and distinct features. The four main characteristics of this market structure are listed next.

1. Many firms and a large number of buyers in different size market segmentations
2. Products and services produced and served by each firm are close substitutes, but they are differentiated with respect to brand names and other elated features
3. Perfect information about business and technology and market behavior
4. Free entry and exit of firms in and out of the industry/market in the LR

The real-world examples are national fast-food chain stores, such as Subway, McDonald's, Burger King, Wendy's, local restaurants of different ethnic food types in major cities around the globe; various beauty products and shoe and fashion clothing industries with top name brands; wine industries, beer markets; local convenience stores; ethnic restaurants; gas stations by location; some brands of motor vehicles; and airline services.

Because of the nature of the differentiated products of all substitute goods under monopolistic competition, the demand curve of a firm is more elastic than that under a monopoly

A Case Study of Price War under Monopolistic Competition: Successful Product Differentiation

Article: A Drugstore Fights the Major Chains with Its Own Provocative Chains

Devon Spurgeon

If you have a digital edition of this book, please click on the following link to access the article:

https://www.wsj.com/articles/SB950573420101921043

If you have a print edition of this book, please use your cell phone to scan the QR code to access the article:

market structure. With detail explanations, such a demand curve for a typical monopolistic firm is illustrated in Figure 11.2.

Section 11.3 focused on the profit-maximization principle for monopolistically competitive firms, which is the same under a monopoly at MR = MC, and P > MC because the MR curve is below the demand curve and twice as the steep. Therefore, a firm charges higher prices and produces less output than monopoly. A firm under this market structure can also manipulate price changes as the degree of competition changes in the market because of changes in cost condition and the number of close substitutes. Based on that limited power in the market, a firm can make abnormal profit (P > TC) at the equilibrium price and quantity at the profit-maximization level. However, not every firm in the market is guaranteed to make abnormal profit in the SR. With close substitutes and different cost conditions, some of the competitors may have to shut down even in the SR because of incurring losses. The details of the explanations and graphical presentation for profit maximization are shown in Figure 11.3.

The LR process of profit maximization is determined by the free entry and exit of firms in and out of the industry. This is because of easy information gathering and technological know-how for products and services to be delivered. As a result of the free entry of new firms, price falls with more competition adding more substitutes, along with increasing the price elasticity of demand. The per unit cost (ATC) may also go up because of additional investment in product development and improving service quality. In combination of such declining prices and increasing costs, firms may end up making a normal profit (P = ATC). The details of this LR adjustment are explained and shown in Figure 11.4. They are also explained with the help of the diagram in Figure 11.4, which shows that despite the normal economic profit solution in the LR, a firm is not cost-efficient: it still produces at a higher than minimum ATC. It is also not efficient in production because excess capacity of production remains even in the LR. The detailed explanation is provided in Section 11.3.2.

In Section 11.4, real-world examples are provided for alternative sales and marketing strategies, mostly as nonprice competition, such as advertisements, discounts, and third-degree price discrimination based on consumers' tastes, preferences, ability to pay, and price elasticity of demand. Those examples were provided in detail in this section. Table 11.1 in this section also provided some numerical examples of third-degree price discrimination based on difference in price elasticity of demand in casino hotels.

In Section 11.5, the strengths and limitations of a monopolistically competitive firm were discussed. Since existing firms do not have the ability to prevent the entry of new firms into the market in the LR, they face greater competition than a monopoly. As a result, they end up producing a level of output at P = ATC. However, the ATC level is still at a higher than minimum ATC. Therefore, firms under monopolistic competition are not cost or production efficient. They could have produced MC = Price if they were near perfect competition with more production and less price. In addition, the practice of third-degree price discrimination of monopolistic firms intends to transfer most of the CS to firms' profits as compared to charging a single price to all consumers. The details of such inefficiency were provided in this section. Students are encouraged to use the examples of inefficiency and relate them to real-world case studies of similar situations under this market structure.

Application Activities

1. After reading the market conditions under which monopolistic competition exists, identify one or two industry examples of real-world business operations in which a firm is considered a monopolistically competitive entity.

2. Knowing the second characteristic of monopolistic competition market structure concerning differentiated products, briefly explain why a firm cannot make abnormal profit in the LR.

3. Similar to the hypothetical example of the ethnic restaurant explained in Section 11.3, suppose that an ethnic Moroccan restaurant in the same city enjoys a near monopoly position by gaining popularity. Assume that with its great reputation, it is making significant profits. Knowing the SR and LR adjustment in the market, make a prediction about the changes in the level of competition in the SR and LR. As part of your explanation, illustrate the adjustment process in both the SR and LR as discussed in Sections 11.2 and 11.3.

4. Briefly explain why institutional subscribers, such as school and college libraries, public libraries, business entities, and government offices end up paying much higher subscription prices for newspapers and magazines than individual subscribers of the same periodicals.

5. Briefly explain why the new entry of firms into the market under monopolistic competition forces the shape of the existing firms' demand curves to tilt outward to the right or become more elastic (flatter).

6. Briefly explain the situations under equilibrium conditions in the LR for the monopolistically competitive firm noted next.

   a. Why does a firm charge P = ATC, but P is still > ATC?

   b. Why is it that a firm cannot or doesn't use its full capacity of production, even in the LR? In other words, why does a firm's excess capacity remain in the LR?

7. After learning the challenges and opportunities for a monopolistic competition firm, provide a few realistic strategies of a firm to gain and strengthen its market power, even in the LR.

8. Assume that a monopolistically competitive airline service has successfully divided its passengers into two groups with one group (say Group A) as vacationers and other group (say Group B) as business flyers. The airline service company also estimated the price elasticity of demand for Group A as 3.0 and that for Group B as 0.75. Knowing this difference in the price elasticity of demand for these two groups of flyers, assume that the airline service intends to use third-degree price discrimination by charging different prices for these two groups. If the airline company increases the airfare from its current single rate for both groups (no need to know the actual current rate), estimate the net increase in revenue for the airline company with a decrease in rate by 10 percent for Group A and simultaneous increase in rate by 10 percent for Group B. Hint: You may use the estimation model used in Section 11.4, which includes Table 11.1.

Chapter 12

Introduction to the Market Structure of Oligopoly

Learning Objectives

As they read the chapter, students will learn the following:

▶ The Concept of the Oligopoly Market Structure and Its Conditions to Exist

▶ Profit Maximization and Price-Output Decisions under Oligopoly

▶ Interdependence of Oligopoly Firms in Making Decisions on Pricing: The Game Theory

▶ Cartel, Price Leadership, and Collusion under Oligopoly and Antitrust Law

▶ Nonprice Competition and Advertisement Under Oligopoly: Some Case Studies

Introduction

In the previous three chapters, students learned about the process of price and output determination by firms under three different market structures: (1) *perfect competition* (Chapter 9), (2) *monopoly* (Chapter 10), and (3) *monopolistic competition* (Chapter 11). This last chapter on market structure introduces the *oligopoly* market structure, which is the largest market structure in terms of the size of competing firms and their volume of production, revenue, and profits in the industry. The oligopoly market is also very distinct in its characteristics as compared to the other three markets discussed so far. Unlike the many firms operating in monopolistic competition, there are only a few firms that dominate the industry occupying most of the market share with a market size that is not only nationwide but also global in scope of sales and distribution. The most commonly visible industries under oligopoly are computer hardware and software devices (desktop, laptop, operating systems, mobile phones), airlines, social media, internet search engines, microchips, cloud computing, e-commerce, some models of motor vehicles, beer and wine industries, tobacco industry, cable companies, video-streaming services, news media, sports broadcasting, internet service providers, telephone and utility companies, and transportation services, and just to name a few.

From the list of oligopoly industries, it is easy to get a sense of the degree of substitution of goods and services provided by oligopoly firms. The firms compete with either homogeneous products and services or differentiated goods and services. Therefore, the nature of the competition and model structure of oligopoly is not so straightforward. The first section starts with the concept and common characteristics of the oligopoly market.

12.1 The Concept of the Oligopoly Market Structure and Its Conditions to Exist

The way an *oligopoly* works is basically as a club of big business operations covering not only the nationwide market operation but also the global market in many cases. The large market share under oligopoly is predominantly controlled by a few firms, by only four or five firms in most of the industries occupying more than 80 to 90 percent of the market share. For example, the mainstream beer market in the United States is dominated by three beer brands: (1) Budweiser or Bud Light (owned by Anheuser Busch-InBev), (2) Miller Light (owned by Miller Brewing Company), and (3) Coors Light (owned by Coors Brewing Company). They dominate the US market as a classic example of an oligopoly that still exists. The brands of light beer and all other brands manufactured by these three beer companies occupy more than 80 percent of the beer market in the United States alone. In sports broadcasting, ESPN, ABC, NBC, CBS, and Fox occupy more than 90 percent of all major sports events in the US sports entertainment industry. To understand the concept of an oligopoly more clearly, let us describe the five common characteristics (listed next) under which the firms operate.

1. A few firms dominate the entire industry despite the existence of many smaller firms with either similar or a bit differentiated products
2. Imperfect information about technical know-how and other product-related logistics
3. Interdependence among the firms in the price and output decision-making process mainly attributed to vast market dominance by only a few firms
4. Product differentiation is a gray area of complicated characteristic of the oligopoly market where some products are homogenous and some are differentiated
5. Strong barriers to entry represent one of the key characteristics in the LR mainly attributed to the high cost of advertisement, amount of fixed cost, and economies of scale

Among the five characteristics, the degree of *interdependence* among competing firms is the key driver in making strategy a critical success factor for maintaining market dominance.

Given that interdependence is the main challenge for each dominating firm, several strategies are undertaken for successful marketing and sales by setting appropriate prices and output levels through massive advertising budgets. Such strategies also create strong barriers to entry of new firms into the industry. In addition to the high cost of advertising, the firms also invest heavily in brand recognition to maintain brand loyalty so that each firm can successfully differentiate its products and qualities from its rivals. However, the nature of interdependence makes these strategies extremely challenging because a set of strategic actions by one firm may create a similar reaction by other firms to stay on a par with the group.

For example, if Anheuser-Busch-InBev advertises more heavily to promote its key brand, Budweiser, then Miller Light and Coors Light may follow suit to stay competitive. To cover the increasing cost of advertisement, however, it may be necessary for Anheuser-Busch-InBev to increase the price of Budweiser. The company's two rivals may not increase their price. As a result, Budweiser's sales volume may decline because some beer drinkers will substitute Miller Light or Coors Light for Bud Light. The inherent nature of interdependence and strong barriers to entry make marketing and product design strategies extremely challenging for oligopoly firms. The possible reaction to any strategic moves undertaken by another firm must be taken into account by each of the firms before taking any action. This phenomenon of interdependence forces existing firms to use a number of alternative pricing and output strategies for the best possible solution to maintain market dominance. Some of the common alternatives are cartel and collusion, kinked demand curve model, price leadership, and game theory. The relevant general equations for understanding the degree of independence under oligopolistic competition are provided next without any of the mathematical jargon used in game theories commonly used in the oligopoly industry.

Suppose there are three dominant firms in an oligopoly industry, such as the three beer brands in the US domestic market for beer mentioned earlier. The reaction functions of interdependence for these three beer brands are expressed next in the form of general profit equations as functions of their price and quantities.

$$\text{Firm 1: Profit function } \Pi_1 = \Pi_1 (P_1, Q_1) \qquad \text{Eqn (12.1)}$$

$$\text{Firm 2: Profit function } \Pi_2 = \Pi_2 (P_2, Q_2) \qquad \text{Eqn (12.2)}$$

$$\text{Firm 3: Profit function } \Pi_3 = \Pi_3 (P_3, Q_3), \qquad \text{Eqn (12.3)}$$

where the symbol Πs are respective expressions for profit strategy as dependent variables and the symbols Ps and Qs are, respectively, price and quantities of each of the firms as independent variables.

Now the interdependence among these three firms in the determination of the optimum level of price and quantity combinations to maximize profit implies that none of the three firms can solely rely on their own price and quantity decisions without considering the price and quantity decisions made by their two rivals, and vice versa. To express this interdependence on each other's strategies more clearly, it is logical to say that each of the profit strategies of the three beer brands not only depend on their own price and quantity combinations but also on the price and quantity combinations of their rivals' decisions. Given that realistic scenario of interdependence, the three equations are not realistic without incorporating the price and quantity combinations of each of the firms in all three profit functions. To reflect the interdependence of this strategic phenomenon of price and output decisions to maximize profit, the relevant profit equations as appropriate strategic reactions by each of the firms are rewritten in the equations that follow.

Firm 1: Profit function II1 = II1 (P1, Q1, P2, Q2, P3, Q3)   **Eqn (12.4)**

Firm 2: Profit function II2 = II2 (P2, Q2, P1, Q1, P3, Q3)   **Eqn (12.5)**

Firm 3: Profit function II3 = II3 (P3, Q3, P1, Q1, P2, Q2)   **Eqn (12.6)**

In the set of Eqns (12.4), (12.5), and (12.6) are basically the replacement of the independent Eqns (12.1), (12.2), and (12.3). The later set of three equations are more realistic for representing the true level of interdependence in the sense that all three pairs of price and quantity of each of the three firms are incorporated in their respective profit functions. It is also worth noting that in this set of three profit functions, three are dependent variables II_1, II_2, **and** II_3 on the left-hand side. On the other hand, there are six independent variables on the right-hand side for each of the equations: P_1, Q_1, P_2, Q_2, P_3, Q_3—a total of nine variables in three equations. To determine the equilibrium solutions for the maximization of profits for each of the firms, the puzzle of these three equations is complicated because the strategic management of these firms will need to have nine equations to achieve all possible optimum combinations of nine variables. This is due to the mathematical and logical rules, as the number of variables must be equal to the number of equations to solve the puzzle. The details of the mathematical simulation of these reaction functions for profit maximization are beyond the scope of this introductory textbook. Therefore, it is logical to say that the conventional rule of profit maximization that relies on the golden rule of $MR = MC$ is not good enough to solve this puzzle. Therefore, there are several alternative techniques of profit maximization commonly and frequently practiced by oligopoly firms. Some of those are cartel, collusion, price leadership, kinked demand curve solution, and game theory. Section 12.2 explains some of these alternatives in the process of price and output determination under oligopoly.

12.2 Profit Maximization and Price-Output Decisions under Oligopoly

This section is focused on analyzing the behavior of pricing and output determination under the strategies of cartel/collusion, kinked demand curve, and price leadership. The game theory strategy is discussed in Section 12.3 in more detail with its various applications that go beyond economics and business.

12.2.1 Profit Maximization of Oligopoly by Cartel and Collusion
In this section, we are considering a case for the oligopoly market with a few firms and almost homogeneous products, such as refined petroleum oil supplied by major oil companies. The most notable examples will be ExxonMobil, Chevron, Conoco Phillips, and Occidental

Petroleum Industries, as the top-four petroleum oil companies dominate the oil supply in the United States the rest of the world with their total market value more than $550 billion per year, with more than $350 billion from ExxonMobil alone. The pricing strategies for these major energy firms are not independent of each other. The price setting by one firm, say ExxonMobil, will affect the sales of the other three firms immediately. Therefore, the other three firms must adjust their pricing strategy as well. We will start with price and output determination under the cartel strategy followed by a combination of cartel and collusion. Although cartel and collusion are illegal in the United States and European Union, there are not many countries in the rest of the world that have antitrust law against cartel and collusion. Besides, the tactics of cartel and collusion can be practiced by oligopoly firms, even in the United States and European Union, as long as the companies act within the loopholes.

Price and output determination under cartel: Cartel is a formally agreed upon contract among the competing oligopoly firms to set the production quota distributed among the cartel members. Of course, an explicit cartel is illegal in the United States and the European Union, but a tacit form of cartel may still occur in those markets. Using the four dominant oil companies mentioned earlier, we will explain the process of price and output determination with a restrictive assumption that the four dominant firms charge the highest single price possible given the market demand and its corresponding MR function as drawn next. The realistic analysis of this sort of cartel (and collusion) model is highly mathematical and complex and beyond the scope of this introductory textbook. Therefore, the simplistic approach is illustrated in Figure 12.1.

The diagram in Figure 12.1 is a hypothetical illustration that explains how pricing and output are determined under cartel behavior in the oligopoly market. Suppose there are four major oil-producing firms that dominate the oil supply in the United States. Also assume that they supply an average of 12 million barrels of crude oil per day in the US market, which is close to actual production in the United States in 2019. Now, if each of the four firms has MC and ATC curves, as shown by blue MC and ATC curves in Figure 12.1, the profit-maximizing output for each of the firms will be at three million barrels per day (assuming they all produce an equal

Figure 12.1   Cartel Behavior of Oil Companies

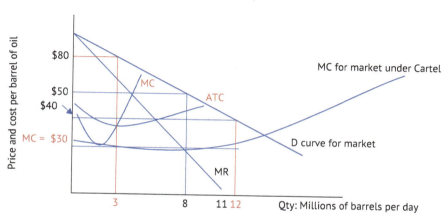

quantity per day). The market price per barrel for the production of up to three million barrels by each firm can be determined by the corresponding price from the demand curve shown at $80 per barrel. If each of the firms produces 3 million barrels, then the total production per day will be 12 million barrels per day. This scenario is without the formation of the cartel. However, each of the firms cannot really charge $80 per barrel because they supply a total of 12 million barrels to the entire market, as shown in the diagram. With 12 units against the MC cost of production at $30 per barrel, the maximum price they can charge will be $40 per barrel, as determined by the demand curve against 12 units of output. If individual firms want to produce more than 3 units meaning, a total production of more than 12 units per day for the market, then their MCs will rise above the current constant level of $30 per barrel.

Using the cost and pricing structure of the hypothetical oil market in the United States, the diagram also shows the industry MC curve at a constant rate of $30 at 3 units, staying the same up to 12 units as combined production by four firms in the market. Now, instead of increasing the production of each firm with increasing MC, forming a cartel will reduce the output level for the entire market from 12 units to 8 units, and the profit-maximizing price will be $50 per barrel, where MR = MC intersects, and $50 per barrel is determined from the corresponding point on the demand curve. Under this cartel agreement, if a firm reduces its output from three million barrels per day to two million barrels per day (equally distributed production quota), then each firm will increase total profit to $20 million ($50 − $40) × 2 million, with no change in MC or ATC. However, if some of the members of this cartel cheat and sell oil under the table, then the profits of the cheating firms will increase temporarily. But if everyone cheats, then the power of the cartel will breakdown with a price that declines to its original level of $40 or even lower if the total production rises above 12 million barrels per day.

Price and output determination under collusion: Collusion is the simultaneous increase in price and reduction in production by cartel agreement between firms. The explanation is made by focusing on cartel only when reducing the output level to 8 units from 12 units, while using the MR = MC rule of profit maximization at a price of $50 per barrel per unit. However, in the real-world practice of collusion as defined here, it may be seen as a common practice by reducing the output to eight units and increasing the price arbitrarily above $50 per barrel. This collusion price mechanism and possible cheating behavior will be discussed in more detail under game theory later in this section. Our next alternative solution of interdependence characteristic of an oligopoly is the kinked demand curve solution. In the absence of antitrust laws against explicit cartel and collusion, this example is a common practice for maintaining high profits as long as no member in the pack cheats.

A classic example of this type of cartel and collusion is the Organization of Petroleum Exporting Countries (OPEC) cartel initiated in the 1970s consisting of 12 member countries, mostly in the Middle East and North Africa. The OPEC cartel is led by Saudi Arabia (the largest oil-producing nation in the world at that time the organization was established), which retaliated against US support of Israel in the wake of the Arab-Israel conflict. OPEC was very successful in raising oil prices from $4 per barrel to $30 per barrel on a single day, and prices continued to rise up to $100 per barrel in the next few years. This skyrocketing oil price caused worldwide hyperinflation with the sudden increase in the cost of production and services for those using oil as a major source of raw materials. However, over the next decade in the 1980s, the power of OPEC in controlling oil prices faded significantly because of the increase in oil production by non-OPEC countries, such as the United States, Canada, Mexico, China, Norway, England, and Brazil. The cheating practices by some members within OPEC also made the OPEC cartel ineffective over the years. Currently, OPEC doesn't have that much power in manipulating market price because non-OPEC countries supply more oil than ever before, with the United States alone producing almost 12 million barrels of crude oil per day, satisfying more than 80 percent of its domestic demand for oil. There is a prediction that the United States will probably become a net oil exporter in the next five years. The declining power of OPEC in controlling price and quantity of output is nicely explained in an article[1] (the URL is in the footnote) published in the media on November 29, 2014. Students are encouraged to read the details of the time line that describes how the power of the OPEC cartel has collapsed over the years.

12.2.2 Kinked Demand Curve Solution

This alternative model of oligopoly pricing is theoretically a bit complicated but easy to understand from the real-world practice in the sense that it gives a logical view of the sticky price of some products supplied by oligopoly firms. Some examples are the pricing of cell phone devices, laptop computers, mobile data usage charges, cable services, and some high-end car models. The kinked demand curve model is based on two assumptions: (1) an oligopoly firm will tend to match the decrease of price by its rivals but (2) it will not increase its price when the rival increases its price. These assumptions, not far from reality, imply that prices at these firms do not tend to change, or they remain stable at least in the SR. The theoretical explanation of the kinked demand curve solution is illustrated in Figure 12.2.

In Figure 12.2, suppose there are two dominant cell phone service companies in the market, such as AT&T represented by the D_a demand curve and Verizon Wireless represented by the D_b demand curve, with price elasticity of demand for AT&T higher than that of Verizon Wireless. The corresponding MR curves are drawn as marked by MR_a and MR_b, respectively. Also, the

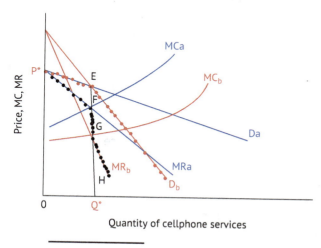

Figure 12.2 Pricing under the Kinked Demand Curve of Oligopoly

1   Patrick Watson, "OPEC Is Collapsing, With Oil Prices Right Behind," NewsMax Finance, November 25, 2014, http://www.moneynews.com/StreetTalk/opec-oil-energy-gasoline/2014/11/25/id/609516/?ns_mail_uid=41810005&ns_mail_job=1597088_11252014&s=al&dkt_nbr=9lsv6etb#.

MC curves are drawn for both companies as MC_a and MC_b, respectively. Now, given the two assumptions about the reaction of one firm to price changes made the rival firm, suppose that an increase in price by Verizon Wireless from P^* won't be matched by AT&T, but lowering the price below P^* will be matched by AT&T. As a result, combining these two demand curves into a single market behavior, we can fairly assume that the portion of the D_a demand to the left of point E and the portion of the D_b curve to the right of point E is the relevant combination of the market demand curve, creating a kink at point E. This kink market demand curve combining the two individual demand curves for A&T and Verizon Wireless is denoted by P^*-E-D_b. The corresponding MR curve of the kinked demand curve will be the MR portion below that portion of the D_a curve and the portion of the MR_b curve below the point G. The vertical distance between points F and G is also the part of the derived MR curve from the MR_a and MR_b curves. This combined MR curve derived from the kinked demand curve is denoted by the line P^*-F-G-H, as marked in blue dots. We may also notice that as long as the MC curves for both AT&T and Verizon Wireless pass through points F and G of the derived MR curve, then the equilibrium price for profit maximization for both firms will be stable at P^* with no change in Q^*. This **price stickiness** solution under the kinked demand curve model is common in the case of two dominant firms in an oligopoly called duopoly pricing. The interdependence between the two firms under duopoly can also be explained by an alternative marketing strategy called game theory with its many applications. We will see that behavior under the game theory section later in this chapter. Before going into that explanation, let's review the next section, which is an extension of the kinked demand curve solution called price leadership.

12.2.3 Price Leadership under Oligopoly

Price leadership under oligopoly is a common practice in a market of two or more dominant firms with the largest and most financially stable rival firm in the pack acting as the price leader. When the kinked demand curve solution explained earlier doesn't work effectively or the price is hiked up by one firm (presumably the price leader) followed by its rivals, this is called price leadership. This practice will make the kink scenario in Figure 12.2 go away, and we will end up with the relatively less elastic demand curve and MR curve charging higher prices, thus leading to all firms in the industry making a more abnormal profit. This practice of the single-most dominant firm raising prices is also called *tacit collusion* because there is no open conversation or explicit understanding among the rivals before the price is raised by the leader. The moment the price hike is announced by the leading firm, the smaller firms usually follow suit almost immediately. If they don't follow the leader's action, then the leader can easily lower the profits of its rivals significantly with a drastic decrease of its own price the next time around. Therefore, to minimize the risk of losing profit in the future, the smaller firms follow the suit immediately with no loss of profit expected. Nevertheless, because of the advantage of economies of scale and economies of scope, price stickiness or price increase through the price leadership model keeps the price way from the above minimum ATC level to maintain abnormal profit. Even with the new entry of firms in the LR, the pricing strategy of price stickiness and price leadership tend to remain strong. We will discuss the LR behavior of an oligopoly with product differentiation in the last section of this chapter. Section 12.3 explains various aspects of game theory derived from the inherent interdependence among firms for profit-maximizing price and output determination.

12.3 Interdependence of Oligopoly Firms in Making Decisions on Pricing: Game Theory

We have mentioned and explained in previous sections that interdependence among firms regarding decisions about price and output determination, product design, and marketing strategy, such as nonprice competition of advertising, provides many alternative techniques to maximize their profits. *Game theory* is one of those alternatives that is frequently pursued by each of the oligopoly firms. Game theory is the analysis of strategic actions of individual firms to improve goals of profit maximization while their rivals' actions or reactions may eventually affect the outcome of initial strategies taken. There are many examples of game theory in practice, not only in economics of imperfect competition like oligopoly or monopolistic competition but also widely used in sports, political campaigns, arms deals between countries for defense strategy, trade dispute, high-technology services, such as social media networks and high-profile legal proceedings. We will discuss a few of these applications, starting with examples of oligopoly firms in next subsections.

12.3.1 A Game Theory of Airfare Discount Strategies

Depending on the time of occurrence of playing game theories in business strategies, game theory can be broadly classified into two categories: sequential or simultaneous games. A *sequential game* is the game played by one firm first followed by the other rivals. A *simultaneous game* is the actions and reactions played by the rivals at the same time. The increase or decrease of airfare strategy by airlines service companies are sequential games, where if one airline gives a discount, its rivals do not follow suit immediately. They wait a bit to see the outcome before they join or not join the discount price war. Depending on reactions to the initial discount strategy by the first airline, the outcome will be different for all firms regardless of if they join the price war or not. The game tree of outcome for such sequential strategy is illustrated in Figure 12.3.

In the diagram in Figure 12.3, the first two trees on the left side are the alternative strategies of Airline A with either a discount or no discount. If Airline A, with its relatively dominant position in the network of flight routes, decides if it will give the discount or not, then Airline B will follow suit depending on the action taken by the former. The outcomes of this sequential game strategy are four combinations for both airlines, as shown

Figure 12.3 Sequential Game Tree for Airfare Discount

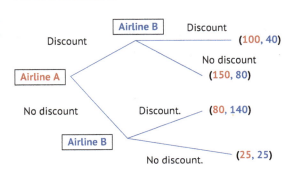

as to the end of the second set of trees indicating the increase in payoffs for Airline A in red and that for Airline B in blue. The different outcomes for providing a discount or no discount can be summarized as follows.

If Airline A provides a discount, it has two sets of payoffs: 100 with a discount by Airline B or 150 with no discount by Airline B. So, in this case, it would be better for Airline B not to give a discount because without its discount, the payoff is 80, which is larger than 40 with the discount. On the other hand, if Airline A does not give the discount, then Airline B should give the discount with the payoff combination of 80 for Airline A and 140 for Airline B, which means 140 is much larger than without the discount, with a payoff at 25. For Airline A, its best strategy would be to give discount because the payoff with the discount is 150, which is the largest when compared to other payoffs without a discount at 80 and 25. The equilibrium of payoffs thus comes to a combination of 150 for Airline A with the discount and 80 for Airline B with no discount. In this case, the dominant company Airline A has the upper hand to give the discount. However, it may also be possible to see if a smaller or less dominant company like Airline B can gain the upper hand. Another is example is when of a smaller player like T-Mobile in smartphone services takes the initiative to provide a discount, and the larger or more dominant company, such as Verizon Wireless or AT&T, does not respond with a discount of its own services. The logic is that the revenue volume the dominant company will lose will be much higher than the gain or there will be no gain at all with the discount. So, they are expected to ignore the discount imitated by smaller rivals. The next subsection analyzes a game theory for the simultaneous occurrence of action and reaction of a trade dispute between two countries, such as the US and China trade war in 2019 initiated by Donald Trump.

12.3.2 A Game Theory of Trade Disputes between China and the United States

Simultaneous game strategies are frequently played by the majority of oligopoly firms and policy makers in international trade and arms conflicts. The notable examples of industries involved in simultaneous games are food industries, pharmaceutical companies, consumer products and household appliances companies, beer and wine industries, cell phone companies, computer hardware and software companies, and many more similar entities. In this section, the payoff combinations of simultaneous trade disputes between China and the United States are illustrated in Table 12.1.

Table 12.1: Simultaneous Game Theory for Trade Disputes

			CHINA	
			Agree	Don't Agree
			↓	↓
USA	Agree	⟶	No Tariff	NO RESOLUTION
	Don't Agree	⟶	NO RESOLUTION	Tariff by Both Countries

Microeconomics Principles, Applications, and Policy Implications

From the simultaneous occurrence of trade disputes between China and the United States since 2018, the four possible outcomes of relevant game theory are listed in Table 12.1. Assuming that neither side of the Sino-American trade disputes knows for sure about the specific strategies the other side is considering for bilateral negotiations before they can sit at the table, the four possible outcomes are wide open with a great deal of uncertainty. The only information announced publicly by the United States was the threat of imposing tariffs of hundreds of billions of dollars on Chinese exports to the United States. China has also announced its possible retaliation by imposing similar levels of tariffs on US exports to China if the United States sticks to its threatened trade war. We notice from the game table that if both parties agree, both side will lift the tariffs, and business will go on as usual. However, if neither side agrees, there will be no resolution. The other extreme outcome if neither side agree is the imposition of tariffs by both countries on each other's imports. The uncertainty contained in the earlier game table with the collapse of trade negotiations between China and the United States actually caused China's stock market crash in May 2019, while the US stock market was almost about to crash. The consequence of not agreeing on trade disputes regarding US imports from China and Chinese imports from the United States have already declined significantly. Given the collapse of the trade negotiations, many economists and trade experts at the International Monetary Fund have made a forecast of the global decline of GDP in 2019 and 2020. Students are encouraged to play this game theory model to figure out why the second summit between Trump and North Korean President Kim Jong-un failed in early March of 2019 during their negotiations over North Korea dismantling its nuclear facilities.

An Example of Game Theory Application: Nash Equilibrium

The *Nash equilibrium* was developed by economist John Nash (his model was applied to the free-trade agreement between the United States, Canada, and Mexico enacted in 1993 called NAFTA) by explaining that the best outcome in a game theory can be achieved when each participant in the game takes the best strategy by knowing the best possible strategy by its opponent. In other words, given all possible outcomes are known in the game table, those outcomes can be converted into expected payoff by multiplying each of those outcomes by its respective probabilities of the outcomes. These probabilities are estimated by knowing the information of the best possible strategies of the opponents. By using the Nash equilibrium model, it is possible to figure out the optimum combination of payoffs on the game table and, therefore, no other alternative will be of benefit without a loss to one's opponent. The mathematical estimation for the Nash equilibrium is intentionally skipped for this introductory textbook as it is taught and practiced in upper-level microeconomics and graduate schools of economics. However, it is fairly easy for the students to play the game on the US-China trade disputes illustrated in Table 12.1 by assigning hypothetical but reasonable probabilities to those outcomes and thus estimate the payoffs to compare. However, it is important to keep in mind that in the world of imperfect information, the theory of the Nash equilibrium may not be achievable because of the conditions of noncooperation in which both parties may end up much lower than the optimum outcome. The dominant strategy we discussed earlier is a situation in which the Nash equilibrium may not be optimum in some cases, such as in the classic example of the prisoner's dilemma.

What is the prisoner's dilemma? The classic example of game theory is actually the game of the *prisoner's dilemma* in which two prisoners were accused of the same crime with no proof that the crime was committed. This situation is explained by the game theory dominant strategy. Suppose the legal authority is trying to convict those two prisoners by using game theory in a state of noncooperation. The legal team can put these two prisoners in two different prison cells with no cooperation or talking between them and then offer both of them the same bargaining chip. Table 12.2 is this classic example of how the prisoner's dilemma may be useful in real activities, such as business competition, campaign finance, merger-acquisition, arms conflicts, and trade wars (as shown in Table 12.1).

Table 12.2: Prisoners's Dilemma

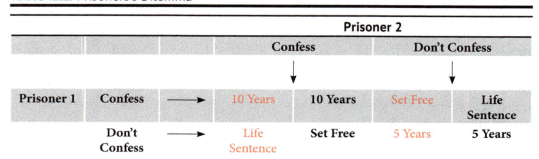

			Prisoner 2			
			Confess		Don't Confess	
Prisoner 1	Confess	→	10 Years	10 Years	Set Free	Life Sentence
	Don't Confess	→	Life Sentence	Set Free	5 Years	5 Years

The legal authority offers the same bargain to both prisoners secretly so that prisoner 1 doesn't know if the authority offered the same deal to prisoner 2, and vice versa. The alternative offers and their outcomes are illustrated in Table 12.2. The summary of the offer goes like this: if both prisoners confess to committing the crime, each will get ten years in prison. If one of them confesses and the other one doesn't, then the prisoner who confessed will be set free, and the prisoner who did not confess will get a life sentence, and vice versa. If neither of them confesses, then both of them will get a five-year sentence. Given the sets of offers listed in the table, if we assume that every human being is guided by his or her self-interests, both of these prisoners are expected to accept the deal that will minimize the length of their sentences. The game theory of rational behavior expects that both prisoners will confess with no risk taking if the other prisoner doesn't confess. The confession by both prisoners is actually the best strategy, despite the fact that if neither one confesses, this will bring their sentences to five years. It is basically the result of minimizing the risk of the unpredictable response from the other prisoner. Students may use this classic model of the prisoner's dilemma to apply to real-life cases, such as advertisement budget for cell phone services companies, pricing strategies of beer companies, election campaign advertisements, and arms conflicts between the United States and Russia, just to name of a few.

12.4 Cartel, Price Leadership, and Collusion under Oligopoly and Antitrust Law

The US government antitrust laws prohibit cartel, collusion, and any forms of explicit agreement among the existing oligopoly firms to prevent entry of new firms. Therefore, the practice of collusion and cartel are illegal in the United States. However, there is no international law against collusion or cartel, thus OPEC (as discussed in Section 12.2.1) has been practicing this solution for more than 40 years. To prevent collusion or cartel activities in the United States, the government has a policy to allow smaller firms to enter the market freely by issuing them easy licenses. The terminology they use is called *perfectly contestable* opportunities for new firms to enter or existing firms to exist with no extra capital cost to enter or no loss to exit. The antitrust laws are strictly enforced in the United States against the anticompetitive behavior of oligopoly firms to maintain the policy of freely contestable opportunities for new firms to enter the market. Therefore, existing firms are under constant threat of new entries of firms who might be capable of producing better quality products with better technology while offering lower prices. To safeguard their market share from this constant threat, existing companies usually undertake many alternative strategies, such as a tacit form of price leadership, massive advertisement as nonprice competition, and improving the quality of their products. These strategies have two implications: first, they make the entries more expensive to compete and, second, the products and services have strong brand loyalty. Therefore, entry or exit of firms is hardly a case of free contestable competition. The case of economies of scale is another advantage of existing firms that also works as a strong barrier to entry.

In the case of mergers and acquisitions between oligopoly firms, the antitrust laws administered by the Federal Trade Commission and the Federal Communication Commission, along with the Securities Exchange Commission. The agencies work jointly as watchdogs to make sure that the market share of total sales revenue after a merger or acquisition doesn't exceed the federal guidelines to prevent the creation of a virtual monopoly power. These three agencies are responsible for preventing any form of explicit agreement among firms to create a monopoly and/or prevent contestable entries. The case study of the merger between Boston-based Gillette and P&G noted in Chapter 8 is a real-life example for this discussion.

12.5 Nonprice Competition and Advertisement under Oligopoly: Some Case Studies

This last section focuses on the strategy of *nonprice competition* of existing oligopoly firms to maintain a *barrier to entry* for new firms without violating the antitrust laws. As mentioned in the previous sections, a few existing oligopoly firms occupy the bulk of the market shares of revenue; the size of each of the competing firms is large enough to maintain their *economies of scale* with a very low constant level of ATC and MC. To maintain its barrier to entry, they do not prefer a price war against each other because the application of game theory we discussed previously would be a lose-lose game. The best alternatives to the price war are to increase their state of *economies of scale* so that new firms will have less incentive to compete, and to create brand image by improving the quality of products and services and provide correct information to customers. In doing the second alternative, the firms have to engage massive advertisement through all possible media, including major sports events on TV networks. This strategy of cost increase with innovation and advertisement costs for improving the brand name image increases the fixed cost of production and thus improves the conditions for economies of scale (lowers the per unit cost). The improvement of economies of scale makes the new entry of firms extremely risky with large investment outlays that include the fixed cost or sunk cost. The examples of these nonprice competitions to maintain barriers to entry include beer companies mentioned previously (Budweiser, Miller, and Coors), fast-food chain, large-scale food processing companies, and cell phone companies. Students are encouraged to select one of those industries to make a list of strategies that companies undertake to maintain their barriers to entry. The nonprice competition of firms under oligopoly is a fairly common practice in US big business.

Chapter Summary

In Section 12.1, the oligopoly market structure was mainly characterized by the existence of a few firms dominating the bulk of the total market share, with imperfect information regarding technological know-how and the supply chain, similar substitutes, and strong barriers to entry in the LR. One of the critical factors for the oligopoly market structure is the interdependence among existing firms in making decisions about the optimal price and output level to maximize their profits while maintaining individual market shares. The interdependence thus forces the firms to pursue many alternative solutions for profit-maximizing price and output determination. Some of the key alternative models were discussed in Section 12.2.

In Section 12.2, a number of oligopoly models were discussed to deal with the interdependence among existing firms to maintain their profitability and market shares. Some of the models are listed next, and the details of those were discussed in Section 12.2.

In Section 12.2.1, the cartel was described as a formal agreement among the oligopoly firms to limit their production quotas and thus maximize the revenue and profit by forcing the price to go up given the rise in demand for their products and services. Collusion is, on the other hand, a formal agreement on both production quota and price fixing by the firms for profit maximization. Sometimes, cartel and collusion can occur simultaneously. Examples and graphical representations were given in Section 12.2, including the real-world example of OPEC as a classic case for cartel and collusion. Although cartel and collusion are illegal in the United States, that doesn't necessarily mean that they cannot happen. Tacit forms of cartel and collusion do actually occur to avoid violation of the antitrust laws of the United States. This tacit form of collusion is called price leadership.

The kinked demand curve model, featured in Section 12.2.2, explained the behavior of price stickiness of oligopoly firms when firms do not increase their prices if one leading firm raises its price. But they will lower their prices on a par when the leading firm decreases its prices. The key assumption for this model is that the competing firms have their differentiated goods and services with different price elasticity of demand. The result of this solution is the tendency of all competing firms to stick to the same price, even with different cost conditions in the firms. The graphical illustration and detail explanation were made in Section 12.2.2.

AS with collusion and cartel, which are illegal for firms to practice in the United States, the dominant firm can engage in a price leadership role as a tacit form of monopoly-style price fixing. Once a dominant firm increases its prices, the other rivals follow suit almost immediately. The details of the analysis of this model with illustration were given in Section 12.2.3. The extended model of the interdependence nature of oligopoly firms was discussed under game theory in Section 12.3.

In Section 12.3, the analysis of the complexity from the interdependence nature of oligopoly firms and their alternative solutions to maximize profits was further extended to another commonly used business and economics model called *game theory*. Game theory is the analysis of strategic actions of individual firms to maximize their goals of profit maximization while their rivals' actions or reactions may eventually affect the outcome of initial strategies taken. The examples of game theory in practice are found not only in economics of imperfect competition, such as oligopoly or monopolistic competition, but also widely used in sports, political campaigns, arms deals, trade disputes, high-technology services network, and high-profile legal proceedings. In the subsections in Section 12.3, the theoretical models and applications were discussed in regard to international trade disputes, such as the US-China trade war in 2019; the Nash equilibrium; and the prisoner's dilemma.

In Section 12.4, the policy implications for the antitrust laws of the United States were discussed in detail regarding how the US government implements its antitrust legislation to prevent the practice of cartel and collusion and thus promote more competition in the market. A detailed discussion was made on legislative and legal implications for promoting market competition through the free contestable entry and exit of firms in the LR.

The last section of the chapter (Section 12.5) discussed the real-world implications of the strategy of nonprice competition of firms in the form of massive advertisement. Because of price rigidity under the interdependence among firms and the continuous threat of new entries of rivals into the competition, the firms usually engage massive advertisement campaigns to promote their products and services. These massive advertisements, by increasing the fixed cost of marketing, also serve as LR strategies to create strong barriers to entry of new firms into the industry. The high cost of marketing makes it virtually impossible for new firms to enter and compete and a make profit. The advantage of the economies of scale for existing firms makes it easier to make up for the high advertisement costs so that firms can remain profitable. But for new firms, it is usually risky to compete with high initial capital costs. The details of this scenario were discussed in Section 12.5 with real-life examples of this nonprice competition, such as top beer companies, mobile phone companies, software companies, and other related high-tech firms engaged in advertising campaigns.

Application Activities

1. How does the oligopoly market structure differ from the characteristics of monopolistic competition? Provide a chart that compares the four market structures we have discussed in Chapters 9–12 by highlighting the key differences and their implications for efficiency and equity for consumers and society.

2. What role does the government play in carrying out antitrust laws against monopoly and monopolistic competition and oligopoly? Provide a list of key points, highlighting the pros and cons of antitrust legislation against a monopoly and oligopoly in particular.

3. What are cartel and collusion, and how do they form to determine price and output combinations? What are the effects of practicing cartel and collusion? Give a real-world example in your responses.

4. Since cartel and collusion are illegal in the United States, provide a real-world example of an alternative solution that oligopoly firms can practice in the United States to get around the antitrust laws.

5. Critically explain why OPEC, as one of the most effective and successful cartels in the 1970s, lost its influence in recent years.

6. What is the concept of interdependence among firms under oligopoly? From that concept, critically describe the similarities and contrasts among the solutions for firms, such as cartel, collusion, price leadership, and kinked demand curve solution.

7. Why is the concept of game theory so relevant and useful to practice in the oligopoly market structure? Give an example of a specific component of game theory and its application in a specific industry as an example.

8. What is the Nash equilibrium? Do you think the Nash equilibrium could be useful as the key guideline for successful negotiation between the United States and North Korea to make North Korea dismantle its nuclear facilities?

9. What is the best alternative solution to the price wars in existing monopoly firms? Give an example.

10. With the brand name image creation, how does an oligopoly firm differentiate its products and services and thus create a barrier to entry?

11. Critically explain how an oligopoly firm maximizes its profits when a few other existing rivals produce and compete with virtually homogeneous products or services (no product differentiation). Assume that there a fixed number of firms in the industry. You may use a diagram to explain the behavior of a typical oligopoly firm in this situation.

Chapter 13

Market Competition, Efficiency of Imperfect Competition, and Government Regulations

Learning Objectives

As they read the chapter, students will learn the following:

▶ Comparison of the Efficiency of Production and Distribution under Different Market Structure

▶ Effect of Government Legislation on the Production, Cost, and Pricing for Imperfect Competition

▶ Case Studies of Government Legislation's Effect on Monopoly Practice

Introduction of Efficiency of Production and Distribution

In the last four chapters (Chapters 9–12), the economic analyses were presented on the market structure of goods market behavior in both perfect competition and imperfect competition structures. The focus of analyses was to demonstrate the firms' decision-making processes when determining the optimum combination of price and output produced while maximizing profits by those firms in the industries. While demonstrating the best combinations of price and output levels, our previous discussions were dedicated to measuring the efficiency of allocating limited resources for production, cost of production, pricing, consumer satisfaction, and profit maximization of firms in different industries. Measuring the efficiency criterion in those areas of production and distribution of limited resources, it was necessary to make certain restrictive assumptions to develop workable theoretical models and their real-world applications and policy implications. The contents of this chapter will revisit those assumptions underlying economic efficiency conditions to analyze the technological, allocative, and distributional efficiency in the context of regulatory importance further. The analysis of efficiency criterion and its application is intended to dig further into the understanding of the business and economic implications for government policy intervention in free market behavior.

13.1 Comparison of Efficiency of Production and Distribution under Different Market Structures

In the world of unregulated market competition, the assumption of the invisible hand under *laissez-faire* has been the driving force for understanding the concept of free market behavior. The concept of laissez-faire (leave the market alone) helped economists and business experts to rely on the power of demand and supply models when figuring out the price and output combinations as the best market signals for measuring efficiency. As we have learned from the last four chapters, however, free market behavior (laissez-faire) doesn't necessarily provide the most efficient combination of price and output that is compatible with the maximization of profits for firms and satisfaction for consumers. This section will discuss measuring the efficiency of production and distribution of resources based on the assumptions made in the previous four chapters and by revisiting those assumptions here.

13.1.1 Conditions for Measuring the Economic Efficiency of Market Structure

The concept of economic efficiency is actually focused on the theory of *Pareto efficiency*, which refers to the efficiency theory of income distribution originally developed by Italian engineer and economist Vilfredo Pareto in the late nineteenth century. Pareto's contribution to the field of economic distribution is still significant in the twenty-first century with income inequality rising at an alarming rate and the rapid growth of economic activities fueled by advanced digital technology production and services. The basic idea of the Pareto efficiency refers to a point of allocation of resources in production and distribution as efficient only if any alternative point of reallocation from that point of efficiency will make someone better off at the expense of making someone else worse off. In other words, the Pareto efficiency of resource allocation is the only point considered efficient because any departure from that point would not be equally satisfactory for everyone in society. The real-world example of the Pareto efficiency condition is as follows: if Apple Inc. diverts some resources from its iPhone production to its laptop production because of increasing demand for laptops, then the supply of iPhones will decline. As a result, the new iPhone users will end up paying a higher price for the iPhone and may have to unwillingly move to purchase the Google Pixel or Samsung phone. This simple example provides an understanding of properly connecting the theoretical concept of the Pareto efficiency with real-world economics and society. Economists like to explain this important concept in the area of economic efficiency under three major categories as explained next.

The efficiency conditions of market structure discussed in Chapters 9 through 12 are revisited here as listed next in three types of efficiency: (1) production efficiency, (2) distributional efficiency, and (3) technological efficiency.

Efficiency in production and cost of production: Output is produced where price (P) is equal to minimum average total cost or per unit cost (ATC).

P = Minimum ATC

Efficiency in distribution of resources: Output is produced at where MC is equal to MU and price (P).

MC = MU = P

Efficiency in technology of production: Technological efficiency refers to the management of the production process, not the technology of production itself, in which the maximum level of production and price combination will be determined at a point where the per unit cost (ATC) will be minimum. As we have seen in our LR profit-maximization process, this technological efficiency means that the combination of capital (both physical and human capital) and labor will be a point of production where ATC will be minimum. The utilization of capital and labor by firm management is the key driving force to expand its output level in the LR where the technological efficiency will ensure the condition that follows:

P = Minimum ATC = MC = MR = MU.

We discussed the previous LR conditions of profit maximization for a perfectly competitive firm in Chapter 9. However, these theoretical conditions depend on certain restrictive assumptions briefly explained here. The underlying assumptions to establish the previous three efficiency conditions for production and distribution are based on two key assumptions as stated next.

Assumption one: Absence of *information asymmetry* between producers/sellers and consumers about the product and price

Assumption two: Absence of *externality* in transactions between consumers and sellers

The first assumption of the absence of information asymmetry means that the consumers have the perfect knowledge about the safety and quality of goods and services; they are willing to buy from the suppliers who serve the best interest of consumer satisfaction. It is also assumed that the suppliers or producers are fully aware of consumers' need to receive the right quality and safety of products, causing no harm or negative side effects from consuming them. For example, when mobile devices and wireless services are offered to users, the information provided by mobile phone device makers for the consumers must reflect the true value to match with the consumers' preferences, tastes, and ability to pay the price for the device. On the contrary, the lack of perfect information, the demand and supply behavior for mobile phone devices, would not be efficient enough to reflect true social scarcity of resources.

The second assumption of the absence of externality means there are no spillover benefits or costs to the third parties from the transactions between buyers and sellers. In other words, the transactions occurring from the interaction between market demand and supply will benefit only the buyers and sellers involved in transactions with no extra benefit or cost to third-party members of society who were not invited to that party. In the case of the mobile phone device, no externality assumption means that the benefits of production and distribution of cell phone devices will be limited to the buyers and sellers in the market without causing any spillover effects (positive or negative effects) to the community members who are not part of that transactions. On the other hand, if there is an externality effect from those transactions, the cost structure of cell phone makers in the form of MC and ATC will not reflect the true value to the device makers. By the same token, with externality, the price offered will not be able to reflect the true value to consumers concerning what they are willing to pay for the devices.

The economic implication for the two restrictive assumptions is that the measure of production and cost-efficiency is derived from free market conditions called **laissez-faire**. These assumptions are also useful for understanding the market conditions under which the Pareto efficiency criteria are applicable. However, in reality, these restrictive assumptions do not seem to perfectly fit into the market structure, not even in the perfectly competitive market. Before we get into that world of perfect and imperfect market behavior for measuring efficiency, let us demonstrate the working mechanism of economic efficiency for production, distribution, and technological efficiency illustrated in Figure 13.1.

Figure 13.1 is a hypothetical illustration of efficiency measures that demonstrate the conditions for Pareto efficiency by comparing efficiency of production and prices of different firms with their own demand functions. This theoretical model structure is very similar to the kinked demand curve model analyzed in Chapter 12, except we will skip the case of the kinked equilibrium solution here. Although a number of companies other than Apple and Google manufacturer cell phone devices, such as Samsung, Nokia, Motorola, HTC, and smaller companies, we are using this two-firm model for the sake of simplicity in explaining the behavior of market price and output allocation to understand the measures of economic efficiency under the Pareto conditions. We also assumed that the demand curve for Google Pixel is relatively more elastic than that for the Apple iPhone device. This is a reasonable

Figure 13.1   Measures of Economic Efficiency of Production and Distribution

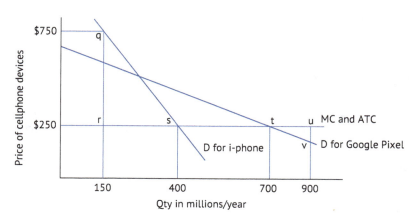

Microeconomics Principles, Applications, and Policy Implications

assumption in the sense that Google Pixel is a relatively new device integrated with its own Android mobile operating system.

To start the analysis of Figure 13.1, suppose Apple and Google are guided by the efficiency conditions of production and distribution as P = Minimum ATC = MC = MR = MU. If that is the case and the LR minimum ATC and MC for the industry is at a constant rate of $250, it seems clear that the optimum level of cell phone devices produced by Apple and Google are 400 million and 700 million per year, respectively, where the efficiency criteria of production and distribution are satisfied. The technological efficiency is also satisfied at the same points because $250 is the lowest possible cost per unit of devices produced.

Now, if Apple and Google do not follow the principles of Pareto efficiency of production and distribution at the price of $250, then any other pricing strategies than $250 by any of these firms will violate the efficiency criterion of the Pareto conditions. For example, suppose Apple has increased its price per iPhone device to $750 and Google did not change its price from $250 per unit. As a result, the quantity demanded for iPhone devices would fall to 150 million per year and quantity demanded for Google Pixel would rise to 900 million per year. Under this scenario, the CS lost by iPhone users is shown by the area below the line between q and s. On the other hand, the gain in CS by Google Pixel users is the area below the line connecting t and v. The CS gained by an increase in the production of the Google Pixel from 700 million to 900 million is much lower than the loss of CS by increasing the price of the iPhone from $250 to $750 by the decrease in production of iPhone from 400 million to 150 million. Students may practice this model by reversing the pricing strategy demonstrated here with the increasing price for Google Pixel from $250 per unit and keep the same original price of $250 for iPhone to increase output. The results will still be suboptimal when compared to the Pareto efficiency point at P = $250, and quantity produced for iPhone and Google Pixel at 400 and 700 million, respectively.

Now, if we include more competing firms that are active in the mobile device market with equal status of Google and Apple position, it is likely that we will see the price decline to close to the minimum ATC in the LR. However, that is only possible if competition in the market transforms from an oligopoly market structure to a state of monopolistic competition or pure competition. The next subsection demonstrates the effects of price and output efficiency when the previous assumptions of Pareto efficiency are violated in the case of monopoly, oligopoly, or monopolistic competition.

13.1.2 Comparison of the Efficiency of Production and Distribution under Perfect and Imperfect Competition

In Section 13.1.1, we saw the possible achievement of Pareto efficiency under the conditions of perfect information and knowledge of consumers about products and services, as well as no externalities involved in the transactions. However, as also mentioned earlier, in a world of imperfect competition, those two restrictive assumptions are far from reality. In reality, the difference in consumers' income levels, tastes, preferences, and ability to pay show a continuous departure from the assumptions of the Pareto efficiency. From the supply side, it is also realistic to notice that many competing firms in most industries are far from being cost and production efficient. In addition, some dominant firms under imperfect competition, such as oligopoly and monopoly market structures, have price setting that are much higher than MC and ATC. From this realistic view of the imperfect world of production and distribution, a comparative analysis is made here by considering efficiency measures between perfect competition versus monopoly and between monopolistic competition and oligopoly market structure.

Measuring Efficiency in Perfect Competition versus Monopoly

As we have seen in our discussion on price and output determination under perfect competition and monopoly in Chapter 9 and Chapter 10, respectively, the conditions for profit maximization are different for these two market structures. In perfect competition, the profit-maximization rule is MR = MC = P in both SR and LR. In the LR, this profit-maximization criterion is further extended to equality with the minimum ATC and MU. Therefore, the LR price and output determination of perfect competition satisfies the Pareto optimum conditions of MR = MC = P = Minimum ATC = MU. On the other hand, the monopoly profit maximization rule in both SR and LR is only MR = MC, with price at greater than MR and MC even in the LR. On the consumer side, MU = P because consumers will be willing to pay up to Price = MU. Since P > MC = MR, MC is less than MU. This condition of inequality between MU and MC, with MU being greater than MC, means efficiency is lost under monopoly pricing. This loss of inefficiency remains even in the LR under monopoly because a monopoly firm has the ability to maintain higher prices than MC to increase its abnormal profit by producing lower-level output than that it would have been under perfect competition. Therefore, it seems fair to say, that an unregulated monopoly pricing and output determination may not be a condition of Pareto optimum, even in the LR. Any reallocation of resources toward equality between MC and price level is expected to improve the MU of consumers and thus for the society with more production and better allocation of resources. The government regulations on monopoly pricing can help improve this inefficiency. We will discuss the effect of regulation in the next section. At this point, however, we demonstrate a clear comparison of efficiency in Figure 13.2 for monopoly market interaction as opposed to what it could have been under perfect competition.

Figure 13.2 illustrates that being a monopoly, say the Windows operating system of Microsoft (MSFT), with its near monopoly position in global market has its market demand curve and corresponding MR curve below its market demand curve. The profit-maximizing rule of MR = MC, the output produced by MSFT, is shown at Qm with its price at Pm from the

Figure 13.2 Efficiency Comparison between Perfect Competition and Monopoly

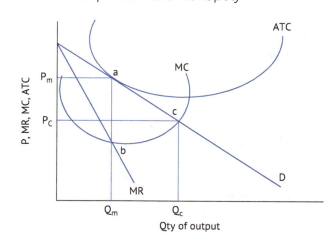

demand curve. As explained earlier, this monopoly price > MR = MC shows a loss of efficiency in resource allocation by reducing output from its potential output under near competition, which could have been close to Qc. CS would be much higher under near competition if the P = MC = Minimum ATC at point c against output Qc (under competitive market). The gain in CS is the area shown by "abc" below the line "ac" on the demand curve. The public utility companies, such as electricity, water supply, gas and heating oil, telephone and cable, Wi-Fi, and other essential service companies, are operating under a natural monopoly with the advantage of the economies of scale. As we discussed in Chapter 10, these service companies are natural monopolies and are usually subject to government regulation, making them charge prices near the MC and ATC. Therefore, government regulations may play a significant role in improving the efficiency conditions that are not usually achieved by monopolists in the absence of government policy intervention. A similar situation is discussed next in the case of monopolistic competition and oligopoly.

Measuring Efficiency in Monopolistic Competition versus Oligopoly

As we have demonstrated the process of profit-maximizing price and output determination for monopolistic competition in Chapter 11 and the same for oligopoly in Chapter 12, we have seen that price is always greater than MR and MC in both SR and LR. Although firms under these two market structures compete with both price and nonprice market strategies, their equilibrium price and output at profit maximization are far below the efficiency points to satisfy the Pareto conditions. The marketing strategies used by firms under these two market structures are massive advertising to create a barrier to entry of new firms, economies of scale for barriers to entry, price leadership, and tacit forms of collusion/cartel. These strategies are real-world examples of inefficiency of production and distribution to take away the CS from customer's pockets and put it in the pockets of firms as profits. Even in the absence of barriers to entry in the LR for monopolistically competitive firms, we have demonstrated in Chapter 11 that the firms do not usually produce at the full capacity of production and distribution. If we recall from the discussion in Section 11.3.2 and its illustration in Figure 11.3, monopolistically competitive firms have the ability to keep price greater than MC even in the LR with excess capacity remaining. They also produce at an output level before the minimum ATC. Therefore, monopolistically competitive firms are not considered Pareto efficient in production, cost, and allocation, even in the LR. This is similar to the situation of inefficiency we found in Chapter 12 for the price and output determination under oligopoly both in SR and LR.

The barriers to entry through massive advertisements, tacit forms of collusion, and price leadership are examples of oligopoly industries. Some of those industries under this category are airline services, pharmaceuticals, beer and wine brands, software and hardware products, mobile services, cloud computing, web browsers, search engines, and many other high-technology industries. Firms with inefficiency of production and allocation are also found under monopolistic competition markets, such as beauty and fashion industries, brand-name apparel, hotels, sports and entertainment, local and ethnic restaurants in cities, and fast-food chain stores nationwide. Although efforts to create barriers to entry through advertisement and tacit forms of price leadership/collusion are a source of inefficiency, it is also theoretically argued by many experts that advertisement may also improve consumer knowledge about the product. However, there has never been a straightforward case about learning the safety and quality of the products through advertisement alone. In this case, government regulations are sometimes considered important as an alternative policy intervention to be socially and economically desirable, as discussed in next section.

13.2. Effect of Government Legislation on Production, Cost, and Pricing for Imperfect Competition

From the examples given earlier about the inefficiency in production and distribution caused by the existence of monopoly, monopolistic competition, and oligopoly, government intervention to implement the antitrust laws seems desirable to make those firms act like near competition or at least to operate at a point that is socially desirable and economically efficient. The antitrust laws have the ability not only to prevent firms' efforts to create barriers to entry and inefficiency but also to help promote competition in the market to maximize consumer welfare. In this case, a landmark legal settlement between MFST and the US Justice Department is a great case study example that occurred in October 2001, which was implemented on November 2, 2001. The section that follows includes an excerpt of this settlement published in the *Wall Street Journal* on October 31, 2001.

Article: A Tenacious Microsoft Emerges From Suit With Its Software Monopoly Largely Intact

John Wilke

If you have a digital edition of this book, please click on the link to access the article:

https://www.wsj.com/articles/SB1005255211920328640

If you have a print edition of this book, please use your cell phone to scan the QR code to access the article:

13.3. Case Studies of Government Legislation's Effect on Monopoly Practice

Several years ago, a colleague of mine shared this case study article published in the *Wall Street Journal* on October 31, 2001. The students are encouraged to view the excerpt of the article as an example of legal implication for improving the inefficiency created by imperfect competition market powers. The practice questions for application activities for this chapter are asked at the end of this case study article.

In another case of antitrust laws, the European Union Commission has fined the search engine giant Google three times since 2017 for multibillion dollars in each of the cases for violating the European Union laws of antitrust activities. The violations cited by the European Union Commission were Google's continuous efforts to preventing competing firms from entering the competition with Android OS, search engine browsers, and related online advertising. For more information on this case, students can read about this accusation and the verdict by the European Union Commission against Google (Google occupies more than 70 percent of market share in European Union search engine related advertisement). Students are encouraged to use the URL link in the footnote to read the details of Google's antitrust activities in the European Union market.[1]

Chapter Summary

In the absence government regulation, the assumption of the invisible hand under ***laissez-faire*** has been the driving force for understanding the concept of free market behavior. Economists and business experts appreciate the power of demand and supply models in figuring out the price and output combinations as the best market signals for measuring efficiency. As we have learned from the last four chapters, however, free market behavior (laissez-faire) doesn't necessarily provide the most efficient combination of price and output to be compatible with maximization of profits for firms and the satisfaction of consumers. In Section 13.1 of this chapter, the conditions of efficiency of production and distribution were discussed, along with the highlights that follow.

The concept of economic efficiency is based on Pareto efficiency, which refers to the efficiency theory of income distribution originally developed by Italian engineer and economist Vilfredo Pareto in the late nineteenth century. Pareto's contribution to the field of economic distribution is still significant in the twenty-first century as income inequality is rising. The Pareto condition of efficiency was further explained on the basis of three types of efficiency: (1) production efficiency, (2) distributional efficiency, and (3) technological efficiency.

Efficiency in production and cost of production: Output is produced where Price (P) is equal to minimum average total cost or per unit cost (ATC).

$$P = \text{Minimum ATC}$$

Efficiency in distribution of resources: Output is produced where MC is equal to MU and Price (P).

$$MC = MU = P$$

Efficiency in technology of production: The utilization of capital and labor by firm management is the key driving force for expanding its output level in the LR, where $P = \text{Minimum ATC} = MC = MR = MU$.

---

1   Kelvin Chan and Raf Casert, "EU Fines Google $1.7 Billion for Abusing Online Advertising Market," *USA Today*, March 20, 2019, https://www.usatoday.com/story/money/business/2019/03/20/google-fine-eu-online-advertising/3224834002/.

The underlying assumptions to establish the three efficiency conditions for production and distribution are based on two key assumptions, as stated next.

Assumption one: Absence of information asymmetry between producers/sellers and consumers about the product and price

Assumption two: Absence of externality in transactions between consumers and sellers

The implications for these two important assumptions were explained in Section 13.1.1, with their real-world implications illustrated in Figure 13.1. In Figure 13.1, the application of Pareto efficiency in the case of imperfect competition, such as the mobile phone industry, indicated that the Pareto efficiency is unlikely to be achieved under conditions of the oligopoly market structure. Therefore, government regulations may be necessary to minimize the loss of CS from the higher than normal price setting behavior of oligopoly firms.

The loss of efficiency under imperfect competition was explained further in this section by comparing the process of price and output determination under perfect competition versus monopoly and the same for monopolistic competition and oligopoly. The analysis was also illustrated in Figure 13.2.

Section 13.2 offered a brief description of the positive effect of government regulation on improving efficiency in production and distribution guided by the Pareto conditions of efficient allocation of resources. The explanation tends to justify the rationale for government intervention in the imperfect competition market structure to improve the inefficiency in production and distribution caused by the existence of market power of oligopoly and monopoly.

Section 13.3 provided the case studies of government verdicts on antitrust laws against MSFT in 2001 and by the European Union Commission against Google between 2017 and 20019. Students are encouraged to read the articles referred to in this section.

Application Activities

1. Briefly explain the concept of *laissez-faire* as the key driving force in a free market system of competition. Why does the economics literature prefer the laissez-faire market system for pricing and production to alternative market mechanisms? Give a real-world example as part of your answer from your reading experience in this chapter.

2. Provide at least two important reasons for the justification of government legislation to implement antitrust laws that allow the free entry and exit of firms.

3. What is the Pareto condition for efficiency of production and distribution of resources? Do you think the Pareto condition is still relevant to use in today's state of economy to improve the economic efficiency discussed earlier? Give an example as part of your explanation.

4. Explain three conditions of efficiency discussed in this chapter plus the key assumptions upon which these conditions could be satisfied. What happens to efficiency conditions if those assumptions are not realistic in an imperfect market structure?

5. From your understanding in answering Q4, briefly explain why the existence of oligopoly and monopolistically competitive market structures are expected to create inefficient allocation of resources. Do you think strict enforcement of antitrust legislation from the government can improve this inefficiency of production and allocation of resources? Why or why not?

6. Using the explanations illustrated in Figure 13.1, draw a diagram to analyze the efficiency of production and distribution for another industry of your choice. Critically explain the rationale for regulation to improve the efficiency from the diagram you will have drawn.

7. Why do economists consider utility companies natural monopolies that can operate efficiently rather than have competition? Given your logic, why does the government need to regulate those natural monopolies?

8. From the case study of the MSFT settlement story told in Section 13.3, do you think MSFT is a natural monopoly with its Windows operating system? If so, how is it different from the natural monopoly of utility companies that the government regulates?

9. How does advertisement as a nonprice competition strategy create inefficiency in production and distribution under oligopoly and monopolistic competition? Is regulation of advertisement desirable to improve efficiency? Why or why not? Give an example as part of your explanation.

Chapter 14

Public Goods and Private Goods

The Role of Government Welfare Programs

Learning Objectives

As they read the chapter, students will learn the following:

▶ Concept of Public Goods and Private Goods and Free-Rider Problems of Public Goods

▶ The Role of Government Policy on Welfare Programs and Provision of Public Goods

▶ Price and Output Determination of Public Goods

Introduction: Public Goods versus Private Goods

In the previous chapter, our discussion mainly focused on the issues of economic efficiency and how to achieve the best alternative solution from demand and supply interactions under different market structures. We have learned that the economic efficiency guided by the Pareto conditions can only be achieved under the competitive market structure with two key assumptions to hold: *perfect information* and *no externality*. However, we have established the reality about the nature of imperfect market structure, such as monopoly, oligopoly, and monopolistic competition, where economic efficiency defined by the Pareto criterion is not possible. Even under perfect competition, where the efficiency condition P = MR = MC = Minimum ATC = MU holds true, the assumption of no externality doesn't hold true. As a result, the government has been found to play a significant role in the regulation of firms under any market structure to improve the economic efficiency and thus to maximize social welfare by reducing prices and expanding output levels to a point where P = MC. The entire process of understanding the production and allocation efficiency under four market structures, however, was predominantly driven by private-sector production and distribution. But there are certain goods and services that may not be economically or commercially viable to be produced and distributed by the private sector. These products and services are known as *public goods or common pool goods*. The nature and characteristics of public goods are the polar opposite of those of private goods. There are two key characteristics of public goods: nonexclusiveness and nonrivalry, which clearly distinguish public goods from what we understand as private goods. The classic examples of public goods are national defense, toll-free highways, restoration of environmentally damaged public property, or water sources. These examples do satisfy the condition of nonrivalry (never depletes by increasing the number of users) and nonexclusiveness (cannot exclude anyone from its benefit who does not pay for it). There are also other goods classified as near public goods, which may include losing nonrivalry property by repeated use but is still nonexcludable. These goods are called common pool goods. National parks, state parks, water reservoirs, lakes, and fishing areas of the ocean are good examples of common pool goods. This chapter demonstrates the economic analysis used to find optimal solutions for the supply of public goods for the interest of society at a minimum cost and the related policy implications.

14.1 Concept of Public Goods and Private Goods and Free-Rider Problems of Public Goods

The concept of public goods in general can be defined as any goods and services that belong to everyone regardless who uses them or not with no price to pay by the users. More specifically, public goods cannot be claimed by any individuals as his or her owned property. On the other hand, private goods are excludable and rivals in the sense that whoever owns it has his or her ownership rights to exclude others. It is also rival in the sense that one person's use can reduce its use by others, either partially or completely. For example, if you purchase a car for yourself to drive, no one else has the right to drive your car. It will also deplete over time with a constant rate of depreciation. In other words, all goods and services that individuals and organizations buy and sell everyday are called private goods. Table 14.1 provides a comparison of private goods, public goods, and common pool goods.

Table 14.1: Private Goods and Public Goods—Comparison

Characteristics of Goods	Nonexcludable	Excludable
Nonrival	**Public Good** Examples: Highways, national defense, lighthouse, streetlights, restoration of damaged environmental property	**Near Public Good** Need to pay for access Examples: Cable TV, radio
Rival	**Common Pool Good** Examples: National and state parks/ forests, lakes, and ocean fishing	**Private Good** All goods and services bought and sold in the open market

In Table 14.1, there are four combinations of goods and services based on two key characteristics for classifying four categories of goods and services: *rivalry* or *nonrivalry* and exclusiveness versus *nonexclusiveness*. Based on these two characteristics, the four combinations of goods and services are shown in four boxes in Table 14.1. The goods in the box for public goods satisfy the characteristics of both nonrivalry and nonexclusiveness. The other extreme is the box for private goods where the combination of rivalry and exclusiveness determine the classification of private goods. The goods listed in the box for near public goods are non-rival but excludable with restricted access. For the box of common pool goods, the goods are rival but nonexcludable. Since the public goods are characterized by nonrivalry and nonexclusiveness, the private sector with profit motivation will have no incentive to provide public goods because of the *free-rider problem*. The free-rider issue implies that the private sector won't be able to collect a price to deliver the goods because of nonexclusiveness for those who would refuse to pay for the goods. As a result, public goods, such as national defense, are provided by the government and duly financed by tax revenue and/or borrowing. However, not everyone pays an equal amount of taxes (low-income families do not even have to pay taxes), but they are equally protected by national defense spending. Therefore, the free-rider problem is real in the case of justifying the government providing public goods. The next section discusses the role of the government in budgeting for the provision of public goods.

14.2 The Role of Government Policy on Welfare Programs and Provision of Public Goods

Since the public goods must be provided by the government, it is expected that the government must collect enough revenue to finance the cost of providing all public goods and near public goods for the benefits of all citizens. The policy question concerning financing the public goods is more of a political and social debate than an economic debate. The economics of financing public goods is straightforward in a sense that the efficient allocation of public goods should follow the same efficiency criteria of MR = MC = P at the minimum ATC. However, the real demand for public goods does not have its corresponding MR revenue because of the free-rider problem and government provisions. We also discussed this efficiency criteria in the previous chapter in the context of private goods determined by private-sector firms in four different market structures. In the case of public goods, however, the supply side is decided by the government through a political process. On the demand side, it is different than the market demand for private goods. But one thing is common in both cases: the efficiency point of utility maximization for consumers for public goods should be MR = MC = P = MU = Minimum ATC. Since the supply of public goods is the responsibility of the government, MC and ATC are expected to rise as the quantity of public goods produced keeps increasing. Examples of public goods and near public goods are national defense, poverty and hunger reduction, climate change to restore clean air, education funding for needy students, health care, maintenance of national and state parks and forests, and much more. The funding of these essential services by the federal, state, and local governments required more than 30 percent of total GDP for the US economy in 2019. Therefore, the rule of MC pricing in the determination of optimal public goods is extremely complex, as the willingness to pay by individuals doesn't really exist because of the free-rider problem. On the other hand, the US government borrows money by issuing bonds to finance the bulk of its national defense budget and other public goods for social welfare. Therefore, the solution for the determination of the optimal mix of public goods is broad and complicated. The complexity of analyzing the government budgeting for the provision of public goods is thus beyond the scope of this introductory textbook. However, a simple theoretical model of demand and supply behavior is demonstrated in the next section to give us a basic understanding of price and output determination for finding an optimal solution for public goods to maximize the social and economic benefits for everyone.

14.3 Price and Output Determination of Public Goods

Unlike the demand and MR curves for private goods, the demand curve for public goods is different in the sense that the nonrivalry and nonexclusiveness nature of public goods. These two properties of public goods make the marginal social benefit equally available to everyone (regardless of if they pay it or not) once additional units are supplied by the government. The process gets further complicated by the free-rider problem because the willingness to pay approach by users is not easy to determine. As a result, measuring MU from the willingness to pay approach is difficult. Given this complexity, the simplified version of the theoretical model of demand and supply for public goods is illustrated in Figure 14.1 by skipping the issue of MU and adding the individual demand curves vertically for three individuals Dk for Kevin, Da for Al, and Ds for Sam.

Suppose that the three outdoor-loving friends Kevin, Al, and Sam are willing to lease a public landscape in the valley of a mountain in the New Hampshire White Mountain area attached to a lake for fishing and kayaking, as well as hiking in the nearby mountains. The yearly price per acre on the vertical axis and the corresponding willingness to pay as the demand curves are drawn with Dk, Da, and Ds, respectively, with their different preferences. The MC curve is considered upward sloping because in addition to the fixed cost for the lease of the land, additional costs of maintenance and interest rates are expected to increase from year

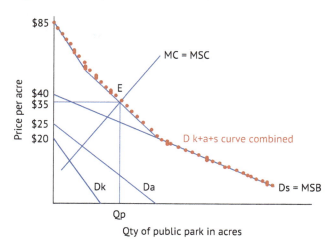

Figure 14.1   Optimal Solution for Public Goods

to year. The combined demand for Kevin, Al, and Sam is derived by vertically adding upward instead of horizontal summation because of the nonexcludability characteristic of this public land. This combined market demand is shown by a dotted line, assuming that they are the only three individuals living in the area. The point of intersection between the MC curve and the combined demand curve Dk + a + s at E is obviously the optimal solution for the determination of the equilibrium quantity of land and price, respectively, at Qp and $35. At this equilibrium point, MSB is the combination of three individuals' willingness to pay reflected at the point of intersection where MC, assumed to be equal to MSC, cuts through the combined Dk + a + s curve.

In the context of financing this public land, there are a number of options the government may choose from. One of the commonly practiced methods is the ability to pay approach through the imposition of taxes at different rates. However, given the different preference patterns of these three individuals, and no clear knowledge about willingness to pay, the imposition of taxes won't be equitable because of the free-rider problem. One of the options might be to impose a rate of payment based on the marginal benefit of each individual. The problem with this second option is the expected sense of unhappiness from the majority of individuals because of their differences in preference patterns. As of now, the government does collect taxes on the ability to pay regardless of if that matches with the pricing solution for the optimal combination Qp and $35 at the equilibrium point E shown in Figure 14.1.

Chapter Summary

In Section 14.1, the concept of public goods is defined as the goods and services that fulfill two characteristics: nonexclusiveness and nonrivalry. Nonexclusiveness implies that the users of public goods cannot be excluded whether they pay for it or not. This is a case of the free-rider issue. Nonrivalry means there is no depletion no matter how many users use the public goods. In other words, one individual's use of public goods does not reduce the use or consumption of the same goods by others. Examples of public goods are national defense, restoration of degraded environmental damage, toll-free highways, streetlights, and lighthouses. Private goods, on the other hand, are characterized by exclusiveness and rivalry, with exclusive property rights and ownership by each individual. There are other types of goods called near public goods with exclusions, such as cable TV and radio signals, that require certain costs to access them but nonrivalry exists. The other type of goods and services are called common pool goods, which may deplete over time from excessive usage but the nonexclusiveness nature of the goods still exists. Examples of common pool goods are ocean and lake fishing, national and state forests. A comparison of these categories of goods and services were listed in Table 14.1.

Section 14.2 briefly described the significant role of government policy in providing public goods because the private sector will not have any incentive to provide these because of the issue of the free-rider using public goods. Since the budget expenditure for providing public goods is a political process in the government, the price, cost, and output determination for public goods is decided by the government during the voting process by the legislator. So the profit-maximization rule of determination of private goods does not apply in the case of public goods. The budgeting process and financing of public goods through tax revenue is complicated. The technical aspect of finding optimal solutions for financing public goods is beyond the scope of this textbook. However, a simplified version of the theoretical model was illustrated and explained in Section 14.3.

Section 14.3 illustrated the derivation of the theoretical demand curve for public goods by assuming that all individuals in society know their preferences in terms of obtaining the best combination of price and quantity of public goods. By vertical summation of individual demand curves for specific public land use, the optimal solution of pricing and quantity combination was shown through the intersection of the upward-sloping MC curve and aggregated individual demand curves. The graphical solution of this theoretical model was illustrated in Figure 14.1 to satisfy the condition of equilibrium by the equality between the MSC of providing public goods and the MSB from the demand curve for public goods. The financing option for public goods was also discussed at the end of this section, with one of the best options being the ability to pay approach in the form of taxation.

Application Activities:

1. Distinguish between the concept of public goods versus private goods. How do they differ from common pool resources? Give examples for each of these three types of goods from the reading at the beginning of the chapter.

2. Critically and briefly explain the issue of the free-rider problem in the context of public goods. Why is it not possible for the private sector to provide public goods?

3. In 2018, Donald Trump proposed a bill for the privatization of all national parks by auctioning off the management and services to the private sector. From your learning experience about the efficiency of production and distribution of public goods and common pool resources, explain briefly if you agree with Trump's proposal. Why or why not?

4. Using the same model illustrated in Figure 14.1, use the example of leasing the national parks to private contractors to determine the optimal solution for equality of MSC and MSC for national parks.

5. Use the diagram that follows to answer the questions. This diagram is related to the theoretical model for finding an optimal solution for national defense spending for the United States, where national spending is the largest volume of public goods spending in the economy. Suppose the two demand curves Da and Db are represented by the entire population of the United States divided equally into two groups with Group A for the demand curve Da and Group B for the demand curve Db. Each of the two groups of the population has different preferences for the defense budget. The MC curve is considered upward sloping with the expectation that the rate of federal spending on national defense will accelerate from 2020 in the wake of geopolitical tension with Russia and ongoing trade wars with China in 2019 and beyond.

Figure 14.2   Optimal Solution for Defense Spending

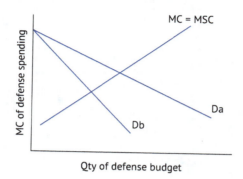

a. Draw a combined demand curve from the two individual demand curves D_a and D_b.

b. Given the MC curve, what will be the optimum solution for the defense budget?

c. From the optimum level of the defense budget, what are the alternative options for financing national defense spending?

d. What option in your answer to Question 5.c would be the most satisfying for both groups of the US population?

e. If the optimum level of defense spending you determined in Q5.a is financed by income tax, which of the two groups would be happy or unhappy, or would both groups be happy or both unhappy? Give reasons to justify your answer.

Chapter 15

Economics of Externality, Environmental Pollution, and Policy Implications

Learning Objectives

As they read the chapter, students will learn the following:

▶ Concept of Externality: Positive and Negative Externality

▶ Sources of Externalities: Causes and Consequences of Externalities and Market Inefficiency without Regulation

▶ Externalities and Pollution: A Case for Government Regulation to Minimize Greenhouse Gas Emissions

▶ Externalities and Property Rights: A Case for the Regulation on Property Rights

▶ Policy Implication and Strategies on Climate Change: A Case for a Global Strategy for Achieving Sustainable Development Goals

Introduction

In the previous two chapters, we focused our economic analyses on the techniques of achieving economic efficiency (in Chapter 13), in producing and distributing private goods (Chapter 13), and determining the optimal price and quantity for public goods (Chapter 14). In our discussion about attaining economic efficiency in Chapter 13, the key purpose was to analyze the Pareto conditions for measuring efficiency in production at the lowest possible cost of production and deliver the product to the consumer at its highest value. In the same analyses, we also found that the efficiency conditions in production and distribution require two restrictive assumptions: *perfect information* and *no externality*. In the market structure of perfect competition, we have concluded that the Pareto conditions for efficiency were satisfied except for the assumption of externality. In the other three market structures of imperfect competition, we concluded that the Pareto efficiency is difficult to achieve in an unregulated market structure. In Chapter 13, we explored another area of economic goods known as public goods as opposed to private goods with its distinct characteristics of nonexclusiveness and nonrivalry. These two characteristics of public goods call for the government to be actively involved in providing the public goods because the private sector has no incentive to produce public goods. Therefore, we have realized from both of the previous chapters that government policy must play a significant role in not only providing public goods efficiently but also regulating the externality problems caused by a rapid increase in production and distribution in both the private and public sectors. From the understanding of the importance of government policy in achieving economic efficiency and budgeting for public goods, this chapter intends to explore and analyze the economics of externalities. The aspects of externalities covered here are listed next.

- Concept of externalities: positive and negative externalities with examples
- Sources of externalities in the absence of government regulations
- Analysis of economic models to internalize the externality
- Connection between the law of property rights and externality
- Role of government regulation in externalities for sustainable economic growth and development

15.1 Concept of Externality: Positive and Negative Externality

Having introduced the concept of externality in one of the two assumptions made in Chapter 13, almost each and every delivery of goods and services has spillover effects to the third parties in society. The spillover effect impacting the well-being of the third parties who were not directly invited to that party of production and distribution is called the *externality*. In other words, the externality is an external effect on others in society who are not directly involved in the interaction between demand and supply of production and distribution of specific products or services. The externality effect could be positive or negative depending on how it affects third-party well-being. If the spillover effect benefits the third party, then it is called *positive externality*. Education and technological advancements are great examples of positive externality because of their profound positive effects on economic growth and prosperity for improving economic and social lives. If the external effect causes harm or reduces their well-being, it is called *negative externality*. Pollution is a classic example of negative externality because the greenhouse gas emissions and other toxic wastes generated by the use of fossil fuels and related chemicals adversely affect people's health and the environment. Positive externalities are also called *external economies* and, likewise, negative externality is called *external diseconomies*.

To elaborate more on the examples of positive externality given earlier, the values generated by providing high-quality education and technological progress have tremendously improved the economic lives of the global society since the Industrial Revolution took place in late eighteenth-century England. The new technology in computer software and hardware and its eventual spillover invention of the internet in the late twentieth century have shown tremendous economic growth and prosperity globally. That spillover effect also paved the way for the invention of the iPhone in 2007 by Apple to generate even more positive externality to the digital economy of the twenty-first century. The progress in development of technological and digital skill, literary enrichment, and computer skill in software and hardware technology increased the productivity of labor and human capital at a rapid rate. This high rate of productivity helps increase GDP growth rate and thus creates more jobs with higher income levels for the educated and skilled labor force. The increase in income through better education and technological progress thus increase the living standard in society. The increase in the living standard is not only limited to the higher educated workforce but also benefits others in society by making further progress on education and training to develop more quality and productive jobs for a sustainable trend in economic prosperity.

Adding more to the example of the negative externality of pollution, it is an undeniable fact that the tremendous growth of economic goods and thus the increase in income over decades have caused society a huge amount of negative externality. The trade-off between rapid economic growth and its negative externality in the form of greenhouse gas emissions has become one of the most hotly debated economic, social, and political issues in recent decades. Since the climate change problem is real, the economics of negative externality has become one of the most important areas of research as a distinct branch of the economics discipline. The reason for our growing interest in negative externality caused by pollution is very straightforward: it is causing ozone layer depletion of the atmosphere and making the clean air polluted by emitting CO_2 from our cars and sulfur dioxide from electricity grids. Since we cannot change our present lifestyle of driving cars and using electricity for almost everything, the increasing threat of global warming and its adverse effects will continue to negatively affect our quality of life and progress for a very long time before we can reverse the trend for a better future. Therefore, understanding the sources of externality and finding the solutions to internalize the externality through economic models is an important part of the field of sustainable economic development. The next few sections demonstrate this field of microeconomics and its policy implications.

15.2 Sources of Externalities: Causes and Consequences of Externalities and Market Inefficiency without Regulation

From our discussion in Section 15.1, it seems we are convinced that the sources of positive and negative externalities are the results of our economic activities in a modern industrialized system of production and distribution of economic and social goods. It is also clear that the way resources are allocated under unregulated market activities seems to cause inefficiency in resource use. Causing externalities (either positive or negative) is a big part of that inefficiency because limited resources are not allocated efficiently to maximize the highest value of resources at minimum cost and to the maximum level of consumer utility. Therefore, increasing externality, along with the growing power of oligopoly and monopoly in the market, causes the market failure in the modern capitalist market system. For example, the current market system has the problem of information asymmetry: using the right technology, right product, and right management to minimize the inefficiency in cost, price, and quantity produced. The current price system is also faulty in the sense that it doesn't reflect true social scarcity of resources for the correct signal of the social price. In other words, the true social price in many cases is either greater or smaller than the current market price, even in a competitive market. Also, the factors of production used for the production system are either the wrong mix of capital and labor for the technology or the excessive use of both capital and labor. This inefficient use of factors of production seem to generate negative and positive externalities. It is also possible that the market system has failed to realize that resources can be reallocated by diverting more resources from industries, thus causing negative externality to those industries causing positive externality. In other words, producers/sellers and consumers do not take into account the external cost from their production/service and consumption in their pricing mechanisms to reflect the true social MC of their activities. The explanation of marginal social cost (MSC) is based on this concept of true social scarcity of resources. Similarly, the benefits that consumers receive from paying the market price must reflect the true value of their MU from additional units of output purchased. This point of efficiency of price equal to the true value of MU is called marginal social benefit (MSB). In the next two paragraphs, we will demonstrate the conditions under which negative externality from pollution generated by the electricity grid shows less MSC than MSB at the point of market equilibrium (by drawing a diagram). We will then introduce the policy implications that will internalize the externality of pollution in subsequent sections.

In order to understand the equilibrium condition for efficiency in production and consumption discussed earlier, the equality between MSC and MSB defined earlier is stated in the equations that follow.

$$\text{MSC} = \text{MC} + \text{Marginal cost of externality (MCE)} \qquad \text{Eqn (15.1)}$$

$$\text{MSB} = \text{MU} + \text{Marginal benefit of externality (MBE)} \qquad \text{Eqn (15.2)}$$

For equilibrium condition for efficiency without externality remains or minimized would the equality between Eqn (15.1) and Eqn (15.2) as stated in Eqn (15.3).

$$\text{Optimum efficiency condition: MSB} = \text{MSC} \qquad \text{Eqn (15.3)}$$

Since unregulated market behavior does not include the second parts of Eqns (15.1) and (15.2) on the right-hand side (MCE and MBE, respectively), the market equilibrium price, even in a competitive market structure, doesn't reflect the equality between MSB and MSC stated in Eqn (15.3). To understand this phenomenon more clearly in the context of pollution generated by the electricity grid, the simple diagram of demand and supply is illustrated next with a further explanation to follow. In this figure, the diagram is a hypothetical production unit of the electricity grid showing units of production on the horizontal axis and the price and MC (= S curve) are on the vertical axis. The upward-sloping MC curve, which is the same as the supply curve, is considered the increasing cost condition of the electricity grid industry. Assuming that this hypothetical grid company causes sulfuric acid called acid rain pollution in the clean air from burning coal fired sulfur for generating electricity.

Figure 15.1 Sources of Negative Externality—Electricity Grid

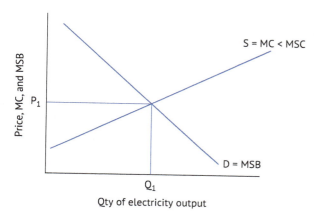

In Figure 15.1, the demand curve represents the consumers' willingness to pay with the assumption of no external benefit. That means the demand curve is the same as MU = MSB. On the other hand, the producer of electricity is the polluter causing acid rain (a combination of sulfur dioxide compound and air vapor in the atmosphere) in the clean air. Therefore, from Eqn (15.1), the MC curve of producing electricity is the actual MC of output expansion with no additional external cost showing on that curve. In other words, the MC = the supply curve of the firm doesn't reflect the actual value of MSC. On every level of output vertically drawn upward to the MC = S curve is the MC less than the additional cost of pollution, the cost of externality borne by the third parties. So, we can conclude that MC at the point of equilibrium at the P_1 and Q_1 combination is the suboptimal point in the presence of negative externality. At this point of equilibrium, MSC > MC. The internalization of this externality would be possible by reallocating the resources to produce an alternative combination of quantity and price, where MSC = MSB. This equality between MSC and MSB can occur in two different ways: (1) by the adoption of a new green technology with a minimum or zero emission of acid rain in the air or (2) by enforcement of government regulation to reduce output with existing technology. Either of the alternative measures or a combination of both would shift the existing supply curve to the left to achieve the optimal combination of price and output where MSB = MSC. Section 15.3 will demonstrate these two techniques for the internalization of externality.

15.3 Externalities and Pollution: A Case for Government Regulation to Minimize Greenhouse Gas Emissions

In order to internalize the externality caused by pollution as explained in the previous section, we will examine a few techniques, including two major options mentioned at the end of Section 15.2. The internalization of externality through the market system alone is difficult to achieve because the producer and supplier wouldn't have incentive to cut the greenhouse gas emissions voluntarily. The voluntary initiative would increase MC and thus decrease their profits. However, adoption of new and cleaner technology (dubbed so-called green technology) by potential competitors may supply substitute goods with less or no pollution. This option, however, cannot be expected to replace the polluting firms in the SR. It is also more expensive to adopt green technology, meaning a higher priced new product with less or no externality. Therefore, the efficiency criteria to satisfy at MSB = MSC would have to be settled at a higher price.

The second option is the imposition of government regulations in the form of taxes, or production limits at a reduced level, or a combination of both. The pros and cons of different types of regulations will be discussed in a later part of this section. At this point, it is easy to conclude that either of these two options would raise the MC of production and reach to an efficient point of price and output level where MSB = MSC, a point of complete internalization of negative externality. This process of internalization is illustrated by redrawing the diagram from Figure 12.1 and adding the MSC curve, as shown in Figure 15.2.

In the diagram in Figure 15.2, the equilibrium point E_1 represents the price and output combination of electricity with negative externality at MC at less than potential MSC before internalization of this externality from pollution. After internalization either from the adoption of greener technology or from regulation or both, the MC curve has been shifted to the left and continued to shift to the left until the new equilibrium point E_2 was reached, where MSB = MSC at the lower quantity of output at Q_2 from Q_1 and at a higher price of P_2 from P_1. The optimum combination of price and output at E_2 is possible to achieve by undertaking two different options: (1) adoption of new technology or (2) government regulation. However, these

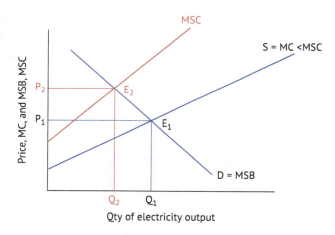

Figure 15.2 Internalization of Externality of Pollution

are not the only two solutions for internalizing the pollution externality. Economists have developed some other solutions for internalization that have potentially less in MSC while keeping the output at higher levels instead of reducing it. It is also important to keep in mind here that internalization of externality from pollution at the optimum point is not necessarily a point of zero pollution. It is a solution, rather, that shows an economically efficient point at the right price and right quantity to minimize the level of pollution. The limitation of this optimum solution is also the loss of the consumer surplus (CS) equivalent to the area of $P_1E_1E_2P_2$.

15.3.1 Other Regulations for Internalization of Pollution Externality

In addition to government regulation for limiting the production level by polluters from the diagram in Figure 12.2, there are a few other alternative government policy implications to reduce pollution effectively. A few of them are briefly explained here with their limitations.

Pollution Tax Policy

Instead of imposing taxes on the output level of polluters, a certain rate of pollution tax (also called effluent tax) on per unit of pollution emitted by firms seems to be more effective. The key advantage of this effluent tax that it imposes a levy on the level of marginal rate of externality caused by the polluters. The second advantage of this tax is that it creates an incentive for firms to not only save tax payments by reducing pollution but also switch to greener technology for production if there are more tax breaks offered for transformation. As long as the tax amount is less than the MC of additional pollution, then the policy of pollution tax is expected to be effective, at least in the SR. Despite the theoretical appeal of the effectiveness of a pollution tax, resistance generated by vested interest groups in big businesses and political lobbying have made this policy rarely effective in the United States in recent decades.

Marketable Pollution Permits

As an alternative to pollution tax policy, a more appealing policy has been developed by economists called marketable pollution permits. Under this policy, the government issues a certain number of pollution permits to the existing polluters to trade freely once they have bought the permits from the government-selected agency such as the Chicago Board of Trade as the auctioning agent. **The key advantage** of this marketable permit policy is the implementation of a limited quota of pollution allowed by existing polluters. If one polluter has too many permits, then they can produce pollution; they will be free to sell the surplus or unused permits to other polluters who are short of the needed permits to produce more pollution. **The second advantage** is the incentive it creates to use the permits with a great deal of flexibility to spread the limited allocation of permits based on the needs by all polluters through the market system. **The third advantage** is that the market price is the driving force for determining the use of permits by constant changes in demand with a fixed supply of permits. This process seems to be better fair play with no resistance by the permit users. **The fourth and the most important advantage** of this policy is that it works the same way a pollution tax would, except it seems to be much more effective without so much resistance. The internalization of pollution externality is determined by the equality between the number of pollution permits issued = the amount of pollution allowed, which is the same as we have provided in the condition of MSB = MSC. This policy has been proved to be very effective in the United States, reducing the level of acid rain since its implementation at the beginning of the 2000s.

Marketable permits can also be applied in cases of common pool goods to work as lease systems on a long-term basis. The advantage of this permits in common pool resources such natural aquifer and ocean fishing is kind of giving a temporary but long-term ownership to create an incentive to preserve and use the resources in a sustainable pace for future use.

The only limitation for marketable permits is the possible concentration of permits being used in the limited areas of the country instead of being dispersed across the country. As a result of this clustering of permit use, pollution concentration in the limited areas are called **hot spots**. In order to eliminate this problem of clustering, some complicated models were developed. Those models are taught in upper-level economics classes.

Command and Control Policy

This form of regulation is the government policy that is set up at a standardized level of pollution to create each type of industry while at the same time a technological specification is mandated to use and transform to a more efficient technology within a set grace period. The regulation is enforced by the US government in all sources of pollution, including common pool resources, such as in ocean fishing, lakes and forest conservation, national park services, and freshwater resources. The key advantage of this nationally dominant regulatory policy achieving the goal of equality between MSB and MSC, as discussed in Section 15.3 and illustrated in the internalization process in Figure 15.2. The effectiveness of this policy is mostly reliant upon the standardization of pollution levels across all industries. The drawbacks inherent in the standardization and corporate lobbying against this policy has been the reasons for the limited effectiveness of this policy for decades. Economists have described four limitations for limited effectiveness of this policy. **First**, lobbying firms have been arguing that standardization of pollution control requires the kind of technology that is simply not available to meet the time line of the grace period. **Second**, it is very expensive to transform the production process to meet the standard, and in many cases, the mark up price is too high to cover the increasing MC to maintain profits. **Third** is that the scope of reducing pollution is limited to a point where the standardized guidelines are met. There is no extended policy formulation to set the pollution level lower or at least stop from rising the greenhouse gas emissions. **Fourth**, and not the last, the standardized policy guideline has been called noncompatible across the industries because of the wide differences in technology. Therefore, this policy calls for major reform while other alternative polices are at work already, as discussed earlier.

Internalization of Positive Externality:

In previous discussions in this section, we concentrated our focus mostly on the techniques of internalization of negative externality, especially in the pollution control process. Internalization of positive externality is also very important to allocate the limited resources more efficiently. In this paragraph, we will revisit the value of a higher education and technological skill that was mentioned in Section 15.1 as an example of positive externality. Since positive externality is a spillover of knowledge and technical skill of labor force and human capital to spread out for more economic growth and prosperity, reallocation of resources to internalize the positive externality seems to benefit the society as the third party more equally as well as more efficiently. The phenomenon of internalization of positive externality is illustrated in Figure 15.3.

The diagram in Figure 15.3 demonstrates a simplified illustration of the internalization process for positive externality generated by higher education in postsecondary and graduate-level education, as well as advanced technological training. Suppose

Figure 15.3 Internalization of Positive Externality of Higher Education

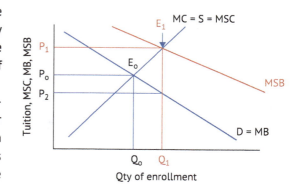

the actual equilibrium point of higher education is at the point of intersection between D = MB and S = MSC curve. The price (the tuition cost) and quantity of enrollment at this initial level of equilibrium is marked as P_o and Q_o, respectively, at point E_o. Since the enrollment of higher education generates a benefit to individuals who acquired the knowledge at the cost of P_o, the D curve is the same marginal benefit of higher educated individuals. The benefit generated from this higher education would reflect in their higher wages from better-paying jobs. However, the contributions made by the higher-educated and more skilled workforce to society in terms of raising their productivity and other aspects of knowledge-sharing and training would have positive spillover effects. The value generated from such spillover effects would be the MSB, which is higher than the initial equilibrium at E_o. To determine the efficient point of internalization of this positive externality, the D = MB curve has to be shifted to the right and continue to do so until the external benefit from higher education is added fully to the vertical distances of the demand curve. Such shifting of the original demand curve to achieve the equality between MSC on the supply curve and MSB curve (MB + Marginal benefit from higher education) at the point of intersection at point E_1. The equilibrium point E_1 is the optimal solution for internalization of positive externality from higher education. We also may notice that the optimum rate of tuition at P_1 is higher than the actual tuition paid against the initial equilibrium point at E_o. The quantity of enrollment is also expanded to Q_1 from its initial quantity of Q_o.

The optimum solution discussed earlier from the diagram in Figure 15.3 has several economic and policy implications. First, the marginal social value from higher education is larger than the actual cost of education. That explains why the demand for higher education is so high and keeps increasing over time with very little expansion of facilities for higher education. This theoretical argument seems to make sense in the context of the reality of benefits and costs in higher education industry. The second implication comes from the expansion of enrollment at a higher tuition cost that actually benefits more by extending the opportunity of accessing higher education to more students seeking to develop their skills for better- and higher-paying jobs. The third implication is the added benefit to society as a whole toward more growth and prosperity.

However, the key policy question remains unanswered: Who is willing to pay the increase in tuition equivalent to $P_1 > P_o$ after internalization of this external value to society? Of course, the D = MB curve indicates that students seeking higher education at the enrollment level at Q_1 won't be willing to pay the tuition at P_1. They will actually be willing to pay P_2. The difference between P_1 and P_2 should be subsidized by government funding for education or by charity or a combination of both. In the US higher education system, both federal and state governments provide funding for higher education and research that includes low-interest student loans, scholarships, special funding for veterans, and many other programs in the private sector. However, given the rising demand for education, the supply side is still limited in making education costs socially and economically desirable for all income levels. Education funding by the government in the United States is not sufficient to make higher education affordable for everyone regardless of their income levels. Investment in education as a percentage of GDP must be increased significantly by the government for education support. The policy makers must realize the importance of higher education for sustainable and long-term economic prosperity, thus maintaining socioeconomic and sociopolitical stability and peace for the nation and the world.

15.4 Externalities and Property Rights: A Case for the Regulation of Property Rights

There are certain resources that are not owned by any firms or individuals, such as ocean fishing banks, or lake water, or natural aquifers or national parks and state forests. They are called common pool goods. These resources are nonexcludable by users, and the service providers do not actually own them. The government owns them and fully preserves via strict rules of preservation through codes of law. Nonetheless, people can use them with no fee paid or at a very minimum charge with a gain of much higher MU and CS. But excessive use of those limited resources can deplete them. This eventual depletion of valuable natural resources under loosely defined ownership is called the tragedy of the commons. In order to prevent "the tragedy of the commons," economists recommend providing proper ownership with the right pricing mechanism, which would reflect the true social and economic value of the resource. That way, the owners will have incentive to preserve the resources for an efficient price and quantity combination as an optimal solution for present and future users. Regulatory mechanisms by the government have great potential to internalize this externality of the common pool goods to prevent the tragedy of the commons.

15.4.1 Coase Theorem of Pollution Reduction at Zero MSC?

Economist Ronald Coase, a Nobel Laureate in economics, developed an intriguing theory of minimizing the social MC for internalization of externality from pollution. His idea was to achieve the optimal level of pollution by open bargaining between the polluters and the victims with very low or zero MC of transactions. Coase stated that this optimum solution with zero MC to society can be achieved by reducing the output level to a socially optimum level where both parties agree regardless of polluters' right to pollute and the victims' willingness to be free from pollution.

Although the Coase Theorem has contributed an interesting concept to the process of internalization of externality, especially in the case of pollution reduction, there are some serious limitations in his theorem. **The first problem** with the theorem is the lack of a mechanism to negotiate openly and freely between the parties when the victims are practically dispersed; sometimes it is impossible to make a connection without agency support. But agency support or legal support is not free of MC when needed to negotiate. **The second problem** with the Coase Theorem is ignoring the level of rights to pollute by property owners and/or giving freedom to the victims to accept whatever comes in the negotiation. This nonbinding condition doesn't seem to be effective in reducing pollution. **The third problem** is that the theorem does not suggest any guiding principles of standardization for pollution reduction through two-party bargaining. Government regulation is still required to standardize the level of pollution as socially and environmentally acceptable. **The fourth problem** is the uncertainty about the rational behavior of the negotiating parties. If some members from either party do not act rationally because of a lack of information about the crisis, negotiation is bound to fail. In this case, Coase's assumption of perfect knowledge does not guarantee a negotiation in good faith.

15.5 Policy Implications and Strategies on Climate Change: A Case for a Global Strategy for Achieving Sustainable Development Goals

From our learning experience from Sections 15.1 through 15.4 in this chapter, students are expected to acquire a basic understanding about the concept of externalities and the importance of analyzing the economics of externality to find ways to internalize and thus improve efficiency in production and distribution. One of the most striking lessons learned from the contents of these sections is the issue of the rising pollution from man-made industrialization using toxic chemicals without paying any attention to their negative externality effects on the environment. The effect of rising pollution in the form of CO_2, methane gas (Ch_4), nitrous oxide (N_2O), fluorinated gas (F), and sulfuric acid (H_2SO_4) is responsible for today's global warming. The issue of global warming and its effects on climate change has already threatened our stability in production, consumption, industrial lifestyle, and the way we live and how we will move forward. The United States and China alone are causing 45 percent of the world's CO_2 emission, with 25 percent by China and 20 percent by the United States. The consequence of greenhouse gas emissions is the increasing rate of global warming in recent decades. The symptom of climate change caused by global warming has been noticed in melting ice sheets in both the North and South Pole regions, rising sea levels, decline in balanced biodiversity, extreme forms of unpredictable weather, adverse effects on poor and disadvantaged residents in developing countries, urban pollution, and frequent flow of smog in densely populated cities in many countries in the world. This ongoing problem also spreads the diseases caused by the acid rains and smog in those cities.

The policy implications for addressing the issues of global warming and climate change must start from the rapid internalization of externalities we have discussed in this chapter. Since the responsibility of preventing climate change starts by reducing the externality from the existing production and distribution system fueled by fossil fuels and coal-burning energy, it is a major task for policy makers to reverse this trend of the industrial system of the old economy. Ignoring this dangerous trend without disruption will make our way of life unsustainable. Therefore, sustainable development policy must be the top priority of each of the governments of every country to address this issue on a global scale. Economists and environmental experts have already focused their research studies on the best ways to promote sustainable development policy globally, transforming corporate social responsibility to use energy that is an alternative to fossil fuels and coal for mass production, promotion of the development of renewable energy, such as wind turbine, hydraulic and solar source of energy, hybrid vehicle production, and production of substitute goods for those using fossil fuel and other toxic materials. Since the policy actions and implementations of climate change are multidimensional, appropriate policies must be coordinated globally to make a significant impact on the internalization of global warming before it is too late. Students are encouraged to read the 17 sustainable development goals of the United Nations that are to be achieved by 2030, which seems to be overly ambitious if not impossible.

Chapter Summary

In Section 15.1, the concepts of positive and negative externality were introduced. Positive externality is the spillover effect from the production and consumption that benefits third parties at no cost. The best example of positive externality is the investment in education and technology that generates a highly productive skilled labor force that contributes to external positive effects to GDP growth and prosperity. Conversely, negative externality spillover effects third parties and causes harm or negative outcomes for the victims without them being compensated. The classic example of negative externality is the environmental pollution causing global warming and climate change problem.

Section 15.2 described the sources of externalities and discussed the effects of externalities on the economic efficiency of production, consumption, and distribution of limited resources. To explain the inefficiency in allocation of resources in unregulated market system of demand and supply, the efficiency conditions for achieving optimum solution by reallocating resources are introduced next:

In order to understand the equilibrium condition for efficiency in production and consumption discussed earlier, the equality between MSC and MSB defined earlier is stated in the equations that follow.

$$MSC = MC + MCE \qquad \text{Eqn (15.1)}$$

$$MSB = MU + MBE \qquad \text{Eqn (15.2)}$$

For the equilibrium condition for efficiency without externality remains or minimized would the equality between Eqn (15.1) and Eqn (15.2) as stated in Eqn (15.3).

$$\text{Optimum Efficiency condition: } MSB = MSC \qquad \text{Eqn (15.3).}$$

Based on the efficiency criterion listed in this section, the case for the internalization of externality is explained in detail. In addition, the inefficiency in the form of negative externality caused by pollution is explained under the unregulated demand and supply model of market interaction. This explanation is illustrated in Figure 15.1.

Section 15.3 analyzed the detail of techniques for internalization of externality by using the efficiency condition introduced in Section 15.2 as **MSB = MSC** as the optimal condition for internalization of externality. The techniques for achieving optimal solution is explained in detail and illustrated in Figure 15.2.

In addition, a number of policy alternatives for regulating the pollution externality were discussed in this section. They are the imposition of a production quota to reduce pollution called command and control policy, including a requirement of the use of more efficient production method, pollution tax, marketable permits, and reward and incentives for the adoption of greener production technology.

This section also explained the techniques for internalizing positive externality with the example of investing in education and technological advancement. The external benefits from higher education and training are explained with alternative pricing of education and expansion of accessibility to education for everyone. The analysis of optimal solution for higher education and training is explained and illustrated in Figure 15.3. Based on that solution, a policy recommendation is suggested for the government to provide more funding to subsidize the rising cost of higher education and to expand the facilities for education with equal access to all citizens regardless of their income levels.

Section 15.4 explained the issues of externality from the common pool goods with no clearly defined ownership of those goods and services. In an unregulated environment with a lack of proper use and preservation, the excessive use of those common pool resources could deplete the resources for future use. This is called the **"tragedy of the commons."** A number of policy recommendations were discussed in this section and it was explained how those policies can be implemented to prevent the consequence of "the tragedy of the commons." The importance of regulation is explained to preserve natural aquifer, water resources in lakes and ocean, ocean fishing banks, forests and national parks, and other similar common pool goods and services.

Section 15.5 explained the problem of global warming and its negative effects on climate change as one of the most economic, social, and political issues in recent decades. The sources of greenhouse gases were explained in this section with their negative externality problems threatening our lifestyle. The importance of global collaboration and policy recommendations were made at the end to make a positive impact in earth's atmosphere. The importance of internalization of global warming is explained and thus called for effective regulations to be undertaken by governments of every country in the world. Implementation of a long-term sustainable development policy is not a choice but necessity to internalize the externality of climate change. Students are encouraged to read and review the United Nations' 17 sustainable development goals to achieve by 2030.

Application Activities

1. Define and briefly explain the concept of external economies (positive externality) and external diseconomies (negative externality) as two sides of the same concept of externality in the context of economics and society. Give real-world examples of both types of externality from your own observations in society.

2. By drawing a diagram, explain briefly how unregulated market behavior, even in perfectly competitive market environments, doesn't seem to satisfy the conditions of economic efficiency because of the existence of externality.

3. In the same diagram drawn in Q2, illustrate the techniques to internalize the negative externality to achieve optimal solutions and thus to satisfy the conditions of economic efficiency at MSB = MSC.

4. Draw another diagram to illustrate the internalization of positive externality to satisfy the condition of economic efficiency of resource allocation.

5. Critically explain some existing regulatory measures put in place by the government to reduce pollution and related environmental issues that threaten the sustainability of economic growth and stability. What are the pros and cons of those measures in terms of effectiveness for reducing pollution? Do you have your own set of recommendations for effective policies for minimizing the social cost?

6. In the case of common pool goods, what are the situations under which we may expect "the tragedy of the commons" in the absence of government regulation? Using real-world examples of common pool goods, what is the most effective form of regulation you suggest for preventing the possible "tragedy of the commons"?

7. Is the regulation for property ownership and zoning laws necessary to preserve and maintain the economic value of private goods, public goods, and common pool goods? Briefly explain, with examples, each of your own observations.

8. Use the diagram that follows to answer the questions. This diagram is related to increasing CO_2 emissions in the atmosphere, causing the ozone layer depletion. This depletion of the ozone layer reduces its capacity to absorb the sun's ultraviolet radiation. The environmental danger of the depletion of ozone layer is a great threat to the stability of Earth's atmosphere above the planet's surface. The increasing global warming is the effect of this depletion of the ozone layer. Suppose the downward-sloping curve is the MSB of reducing CO_2 emission, and the upward-sloping curve is the MSC of reducing CO_2 emission.

Image 15.1

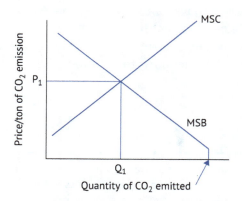

a. From your reading materials in this chapter, determine the optimum level of CO_2 reduction that satisfies the economic efficiency condition from a social MC perspective.

b. Compare and contrast the relative effectiveness of government regulations in the form of pollution tax versus marketable permits using the diagram. From your analysis, which of the two regulations do you prefer and why?

c. Suppose the use of alternative renewable energy has been on the rise. In that case, how would it change the conclusion you have drawn in Q8.b? Briefly explain.

Chapter 16

Market Structure of Factors of Production and Labor Market Behavior

Learning Objectives

As they read the chapter, students will learn the following:

▶ Introduction to Factors of Production: Land, Labor, Capital, Technology

▶ Derivation of the Demand Curve for Labor: Marginal Product and Marginal Value Product

▶ Determination of Labor Market Equilibrium Wages and Labor Quality

▶ Wage Determination under Imperfect Completion

Introduction

Up to Chapter 15, we have become familiar with basic theories and applications of consumer behavior (Chapter 1 to Chapter 7), cost of production and profit maximization of firms and industries (Chapter 8 to 12), and economics of externality and policy prescriptions in Chapter 13 to 15. This penultimate (the last but one) chapter introduces the factors of the production process and their economic implications for efficiency and policies. The factors of the production process are classified into four main categories: (1) land, (2) labor, (3) physical capital, and (4) entrepreneurship (also called human capital). This extended branch of microeconomics is very broad and complicated in the sense that the integration of all these factors of production into a final production process with rapidly changing technology is enormously challenging. The key challenge obviously comes from complicated labor market diversification with different skill levels and their wage structure, different entrepreneurial ability, changing technology, and compliance with government legislation on consumer safety, labor law, and environmental issues. The development of theories on factors of production and their pricing mechanisms have brought significant understanding about the comparative cost structure among land, labor, capital, and human capital to analyze the efficiency of production and cost of production. The theories on factor market behavior have also had important policy implications, especially on labor market behavior, which is rapidly changing because of the emergence of the digital economy and its by-product labor market called "the gig economy." Since the discussion of theories and policy implications of all four of these factors of production is beyond the scope of this textbook, the focus is narrowed down to capital and labor markets with the assumption that capital input can be used as a combination of land, physical capital, and human capital. However, since the labor cost accounts for almost two-thirds of the US GDP, most of our discussion in this chapter is devoted to labor market behavior and its pricing mechanism.

16.1. Introduction to Factors of Production: Land, Labor, Capital, Technology

This section analyzes the working mechanism of the production function with its technological relationship between output (final goods and services) and different factors of production (inputs) required to produce the quantity of output. In order to establish the relationship between inputs and outputs, we start with a general expression for the production function.

16.1.1. Production Function and Factors of Production

As the readers may recall, our introduction to the production function came in Chapter 8, Eqn (8.1), during the production process of the Boston Kayak Company (BKC). With the same production function equation, we will analyze the economics of inputs and outputs to derive the demand function for labor input while keeping capital input fixed in the SR production function.

$$\text{Total output} = q = F\ (K, L), \qquad\qquad \text{Eqn (16.1)}$$

where q = Total output,

K = Capital input (that is in a broad sense by considering all costs other than labor), and

L = Labor input.

The capital input (K) here is considered a combination of all other factors (such as land, building, machine and equipment, and human capital) and is assumed to be fixed in the SR. The only variable input here is labor to increase the quantity of kayaks. As we explained in Chapter 8, Eqn (16.1) is a general expression of the kayak production process as a technological relationship between kayak output and its inputs capital (K) and labor (L). We also assume that the kayak firm BKC is operating under competitive market conditions in which a large number of buyers and sellers of kayaks exist with perfect information on technology, pricing, and availability with free entry and exit of firms (in the market) in the LR. These assumptions of perfect competition also imply that both buyers and sellers are price takers from the equilibrium market price.

In addition to the assumption of the perfectly competitive output market for kayaks, we also assume that the capital and labor markets for kayak production are also perfectly competitive with perfect information about the market wages for labor, and cost of capital, productivity of labor and availability of labor with no discrimination in hiring decision by the owner of the firm. Based on these assumptions in both the output and input markets, we will derive the demand and supply functions of labor inputs by using the hypothetical set of data we used in Chapter 8. The demand function for labor is derived from the concept of marginal productivity of labor and consumer demand for kayak supply. The supply function of labor is derived from the existing wage rates for labor and the trade-off between work hours and leisure given the existing market wage rates per hour.

16.2. Derivation of the Demand Curve for Labor: Marginal Product and Marginal Value Product

We will use the same hypothetical data of the production process of BKC from Table 8.1 in Chapter 8 and presented here in Table 16.1 to derive the marginal product of labor (MP_L) and marginal value product of labor (MVP_L)—the demand function and the demand curve for labor.

16.2.1. Production Function, MP_L, and MVP_L

Table 16.1 shows the hypothetical data for SR production and labor productivities (MP_L) with the competitive price of kayaks (output price) and wages (input price). Using Eqn (16.1) and the marginal productivity equation $\textbf{MPL} = \dfrac{\delta q}{\delta L}$, Table 16.1 shows the estimation of total output (q) and the corresponding marginal productivities of labor [Columns (1) to (3)]. Column (4) shows the competitive price of kayak per unit as a price taker sold at $1,000 per unit of kayak. Column (5) shows the MVP_L = MP_L * Price of kayak. Column (6) shows the fixed wage rate of $4,000 per month in a competitive labor market. Lastly, Column (6) is the marginal profit for BKC for every additional laborer hired as estimated by subtracting wage from corresponding MVP_L.

It is important to observe in the table that Column (3) and Column (5) indicate the law of diminishing return of the marginal physical product (MP_L) and MVP_L as explained in Chapter 8 for a SR production function with fixed capital input. The economic implication of this declining value of MVP_L is as follows: given the fixed capital input, the efficiency of the labor productivity declines as more labor input is added to the existing plant size of the production process. Looking at the values of marginal profit for every additional labor input hired depicted in Column (7), the marginal profit becomes zero at five units of labor hired. Any additional labor hired afterward indicates negative marginal profit. It implies that maximum number of labor hours should be hired up to five units where marginal profit is zero. It is also

Table 16.1: Production and MVPL of BKC*

Labor Input (1)	Total Output* q = F (K, L) (2)	Marginal Product MPL = $\frac{\delta q}{\delta L}$ (3)	Price Kayak in $s (4)	Marginal Value Product MVPL = MPL*P (5)	Wages in $s monthly (6)	Marginal Profit MVPL-W (7)
0	0	0	1,000	0	0	–
1	2	2	1,000	2,000	4,000	−2,000
2	6	4	1,000	4,000	4,000	0
3	15	9	1,000	9,000	4,000	5,000
4	21	6	1,000	6,000	4,000	1,000
5	25	4	1,000	4,000	4,000	0
6	25	0	1,000	0	4,000	−4,000
7	21	−4	1,000	−4,000	4,000	−8,000
8	16	−5	1,000	−5,000	4,000	−9,000

*Total output is the quantity of kayak production per month given fixed capital input.

important to keep in mind that the labor input at two also shows marginal profit at zero. However, at labor input of two units, the MVP_L is greater than the fixed wage. Therefore, the owner of firm BKC will continue to hire more labor to increase its marginal profit until MVP_L and wage becomes equal again at five units of labor, after which marginal profit becomes negative. The value of estimated MVP_L as such in Column (5) is the derived demand for labor illustrated in Figure 16.1.

Figure 16.1 reflects the derived demand curve illustrated from the hypothetical data of labor hours to hire by the firm BKC to the point of efficiency where MVP_L equals the existing fixed wage rate. This efficiency point is denoted by E* where the horizontal labor supply curve S_L intersects with $D_L = MVP_L$, where five units of labor is hired at the wage rate of $4,000 per month. However, if the wage rate in the competitive labor market falls to below $4,000,

Figure 16.1   Derived Labor Demand Curve and Wages

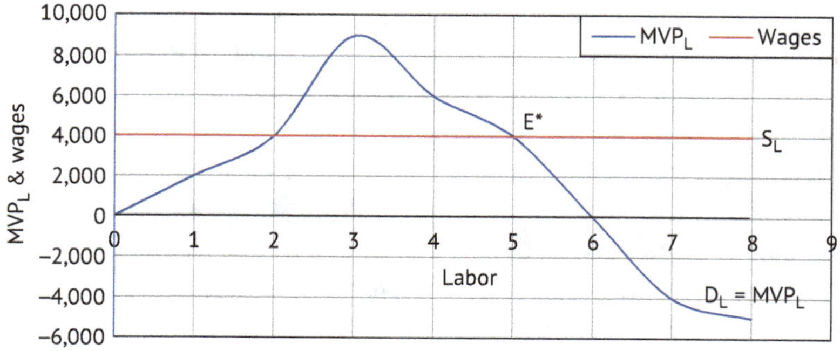

say to $2,000, then the number of labor inputs hired will increase to six units, where the new labor supply curve = W = $2,000 will intersect. Please note that this horizontal labor supply curve is only for the firm's labor supply with the fixed wage rate at which the firm can hire as many labor inputs as it wants as long as marginal profit is equal to or greater than zero. However, the market supply curve behavior is more complicated than the firm's supply curve shown in Figure 16.1. The shape of the market supply curve is usually upward sloping because in the entire labor market, changes in wage rates and willingness to work by the labor force move together. In other words, with the increase in wage rates, more labor hours will be offered to the labor force up to a certain point to trade with leisure hours, and vice versa, *ceteris paribus*. More details of this behavior of the labor supply function are provide in the later subsections. On the other hand, the market demand curve for labor is even more complicated because of the difference in skill level and demand for specialized labor for specialized industries. Therefore, the derivation of the market demand curve is beyond the scope of this textbook. But it is sufficient to say that the market demand curve for labor for each type of industry is also downward sloping in most cases. At this point, we will discuss further the factors that change the labor demand curve we just derived from Table 16.1 and illustrated in Figure 16.1.

16.2.2 Factors to Change the Labor Demand Curve and Equilibrium Wages

As the learners have noticed, the derived demand curve for labor depends on the consumers' demand for the final output of kayaks and labor productivity. There are also external factors other than those two internal factors (product price and productivity of labor) that change the labor demand function and thus the labor demand curve to change the equilibrium wage rate and labor quantity hired. Those factors are briefly discussed next.

Changes in marginal productivity of labor MP_L: The changes in labor productivity have a significant effect on the value of the MVP_L. If the marginal productivity falls, so does the MVP_L, and thus the demand curve shifts to the left and changes the equilibrium wage rate and quantity of labor. On the other hand, with the increase in labor productivity, MVP_L does increase to shift the demand curve for labor to the right and increases equilibrium wages and quantity of labor hired.

Changes in product prices: The change in price of final goods and services also changes the value of MVP_L and thus shifts the demand curve for labor in the same way explained for changes in the MP_L. The changes in prices of final goods and services are determined by the changes in demand and supply of the entire industry of a particular product.

Changes in shape of the labor demand curve (wage elasticity of labor demand): The wage elasticity of the labor demand curve is an important factor in determining the shape of the labor demand curve. The wage elasticity of the labor demand curve is expressed by the equation that follows:

$$EDL = (\% \Delta \text{ in labor demand}) / (\% \text{ in wages}) = (\Delta L/L)/(\Delta W/W) \qquad \text{Eqn (16.2)}$$

Eqn (16.2) indicates that if $E_{DL} < 1$, then the labor demand curve is inelastic, implying that a rise in wages is relatively insensitive to changes in quantity demanded for labor. On the other hand, if $E_{DL} > 1$, then the demand for labor curve is elastic or more sensitive to changes in wages and, therefore, changes in wage rates significantly alter the quantity demanded at more than proportionate changes in the wage rate.

Changes in input prices: Changes in input prices other than labor input, such as capital, land, rent, or raw materials, may also change the demand for labor to shift left or to shift right and thus change the equilibrium wage rate and quantity of labor. The relative price change of other inputs not only changes the demand but also may affect the wage elasticity of demand for labor. The combination of changes in relative prices of inputs and degree of substitution between factors of production, such as labor and capital, affect the changes in elasticity and shift of the demand curve.

Changes in technology: In a world of rapidly changing technology, the relative factor intensity of production is constantly changing from more labor-intensive production (K/L ratio < 1) toward capital-intensive production (K/L ratio > 1). This rapid transformation of factor intensity lowers the demand for labor input and increases the demand for capital input and thus lowers the wage rate of relatively unskilled workers in labor-intensive industries.

16.2.3 Derivation of Labor Supply Function and Factors to Change the Labor Supply

Based on what we learned about the behavior of the labor demand curve in previous sections, we now turn to the supply function of labor in a competitive market as assumed at the outset of this chapter. To understand the supply side of the labor market, it is worth explaining the psychological aspect of human labor in terms of willingness to work at different wage rates. The common psychology of every human being is to respond positively to work more as wages or income increases. Accepting that fundamental behavior of human labor as normal, the supply curve of labor in terms of wage rates is upward sloping. In other words, the higher the wage rate, the more hours will be offered to work by human labor, and vice versa, *ceteris paribus*. However, studies performed by economists indicate that this law of labor supply function may be true only up to a certain extent, followed by making a trade-off between leisure and work. This typical behavior of the individual labor supply function implies that within a limited time for all individual workers, they must choose the best combination between work and leisure to maximize their satisfaction derived from the value of their earnings and the value from spending their earnings during their leisure time. This fundamental trade-off between work and leisure is a great dilemma that we all face during our entire work life. Economists explain this dilemma of finding the right combination under *income effect* and *substitution effect* of change in wage rates, as explained next.

As most of the workers work about 40 hours a week in a typical workweek, with some exception of more or fewer hours of work, depending on the specific profession or industry type. Considering the average work hours per week as 40 hours of work and the remaining hours are left to eat, sleep and, other do activities, such as as leisure time, the preference pattern of a typical worker to work more than 40 hours and spend less time doing leisure activities, or vice versa, depends on many factors. One of the most measurable factors is the rate of increase of wages, which may give more incentive to prefer more work hours over leisure hours, as long as that worker's marginal value from additional earnings is more than the marginal value of leisure he or she has to give up. On the other hand, another worker may find that the marginal value of leisure time exceeds the marginal value of additional earnings and prefers leisure to additional work hours. This trade-off between earnings/wages and leisure shows an important implication in the effects on work and leisure relationships called *substitution effect* and *income effect* of the labor supply function.

Substitution effect of the increase in wages is assumed to be positively related with the willingness to work more by a typical laborer. If this assumption is correct up to a certain level of earnings, then the labor supply curve against the wage rate is upward sloping.

Income effect of the increase in wages, on the other hand, is assumed to be negatively related to a willingness to work by the same workers. In this scenario, after an increase in earnings to a certain level, typical workers would prefer more leisure to work hours.

In measuring the trade-off between work and leisure for the entire labor market in the United States, economics research studies found the following:

1. The degree of responses to higher wages by low-wage earners is positively related to an increase in work hours to be consistent with the principle of the substitution effect. Therefore, the substitution effect outweighs the income effect defined earlier.

2. The degree of responses to higher wages by high-wage earners is negatively related to changes in work hours, which is consistent with the income effect. Also, the income effect in this case outweighs the substitution effect for high-wage earner. The combination of these two opposite forces of work-leisure trade-off is called the backward-bending labor supply curve, and it is as illustrated in Figure 16.2.

Figure 16.2 helps explain the principle and empirical study of the US labor market as a backward-bending labor supply curve. At a wage rate of W_0, a typical worker will tend to work more if wages rise above W_0 and will gradually trade leisure for work hours up to the wage rate of W_1. So, the movement from point A to point B is the substitution effect. However, as the wage rate increases further beyond W_1, the same worker would tend to trade work hours for leisure, which is the income effect that out-weighs the substitution effect. Therefore, when the wage increases from W_1 to W_2, the backward-bending supply curve indicates the value of substitution effect exceeds the value of the income effect.

Figure 16.2 Backward-Bending Labor Supply Curve

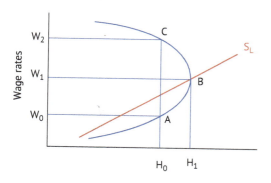

Market labor supply curve behavior: Although a typical individual worker's labor supply curve indicates the ABC curve illustrated in Figure 16.2, the realistic data of the labor supply curve for the entire labor market has shown a continuous upward-sloping curve, as shown by the S_L curve in Figure 16.2. The upward-sloping supply curve for the entire labor market is mainly attributed to the diverse characteristic of labor market composition and the nature of specialization that widely varies from industry to industry. The factors other than wage rates affecting changes in the market supply of labor are briefly explained next.

16.2.4 Factors Affecting the Shift of the Labor Market Supply Curve

Given the vast diversity and specialization of labor market conditions, there are numerous factors, both internal and external, that constantly influence the existing labor market supply curve to shift to the right or left. The direction of shifting would depend on factors affecting the relative extent of changes. Some key factors are labor force growth rate, population growth rate, growth rate of the aging population, labor force participation, wage structure for skilled and unskilled workers, nonwage factors, and technological advancement and educational institutions. Some of these factors are briefly explained here.

Labor force growth rate: This is one of the most important factors to shift the labor supply curve in either direction that widely varies from country to country. The labor force growth rate is measured by the simple equation $\frac{\Delta L}{L} \times 100$, where delta L is the change or increase in the newly entered labor force in the labor market looking for a job in a particular time period, say annually. In a high population growth country, this percentage of growth in the labor force is much higher than the labor force growth rate in the US labor market. The most recent data for the US labor force growth rate shows about 1 percent only because of the low growth rate of the population for the last several decades. This low trend tends to shift the labor supply curve very slowly to the right.

Population growth rate and immigration: These two factors go hand in hand in a country of immigrants like the United States. Given the low rate of the labor force growth rate, the immigration policy has a profound effect on both skilled and less skilled labor force growth and their effect on changes in the labor supply curve. The recent tight federal immigration policy has significantly reduced the supply of labor in the US labor market. Experts predict that in the next several decades, the majority of the labor supply available to meet the growing demand for labor will depend on an immigrant labor force coming from other countries.

Labor force participation rate: This is an important factor affecting the supply curve because the age composition actively looking for a job and/or currently working indicates the percentage of the total population participating in the labor force. Current data compiled by the US Department Labor shows that there are about 165 million civilians aged 16 plus years who are actively participating in the labor force. That is exactly the 50 percent of the total estimated population of 330 million in 2020. If the rate of retirement increases in the aging population currently working, such as the baby boomer generation, then the labor supply curve is expected to shift to the left in the coming years given the current rate of immigration and low population growth rate. Nonwage factors also significantly affect the labor force participation. The nonwage factors are health benefits, pension fund, and other forms of retirement funds; vacations; family leave; and sick leave. The next section of this chapter will analyze the combination of labor demand and labor supply labor functions to determine labor market equilibrium wages and quantity of labor.

16.3 Determination of Labor Market Equilibrium Wages and Labor Quantity

Based on the assumption of competitive market structure in both the product market and input market (labor and capital market), we derived a downward-sloping demand curve and upward-sloping supply curve in the previous section. This section analyzes the equilibrium condition under which efficiency of wage rates and labor quantities hired are measured. The equilibrium condition of the labor market is the point of intersection between labor demand and labor supply functions, as illustrated in Figure 16.3.

Figure 16.3 demonstrates the determination of the equilibrium wage rate and labor quantity demanded equal to labor quantity supplied at the point of intersection between demand and supply. At the equilibrium point E_1, the equilibrium wage rate is shown as W^* on the vertical axis and corresponding equilibrium quantity of labor as Q_L^* on the horizontal axis. The equilibrium point E_1 determines the best possible scenario of the labor market equilibrium condition under the assumption of a competitive labor market. The equilibrium point E_1 is also based on change in wage rates only, keeping other factors of labor supply and demand unchanged *(ceteris paribus)*. Those factors of demand and supply are explained in Sections 16.2.2 and 16.2.4, respectively. Changes in those factors will actually change the equilibrium wage rate and quantity of labor by shifting the labor demand and/or labor supply curve either to the right or to the left to reach a new equilibrium wage and quantity. For example, if the technological advancement improves the labor productivity and thus lowers the marginal cost of production, both the supply and demand curves for labor would shift to the right and thus the equilibrium wage rate will decrease with more quantity of labor hired. This possibility is shown in Figure 16.3 at the equilibrium point E_2, if only the supply of labor shifts to the right. At E_2, the equilibrium wage declined to W_2 and quantity increased to Q_2. On the other hand, if the demand curve for labor shifts to the right simultaneously because of an increase in marginal labor productivity of labor, one of the possible points of equilibrium would be as depicted at E_3, with wage at W_3 and quantity at Q_3. The actual new equilibrium wage rate would depend on the relative

Figure 16.3   Labor Market Equilibrium and Wage Determination

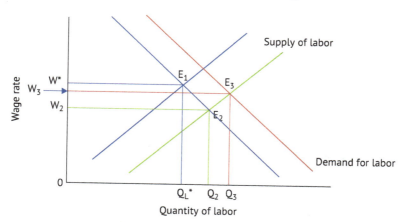

magnitude of the shifts of both supply and demand curve, which is indeterminate here because of the absence of actual data for changes. Students may try to use other factors on the demand or supply side of labor discussed in Sections 16.2.2 and 16.2.4 to shift the demand curve and/or supply curve in appropriate directions for reaching a new equilibrium wage and quantity.

16.4 Wage Determination under Imperfect Competition

In the previous section, we analyzed how to determine equilibrium wages and quantity of labor with the assumption of competitive market conditions in both the goods market and input market. But the ideal condition of competitive market behavior is far from reality in a world of market imperfection, not only in the goods market but also in the input market (labor and capital market). For example, in Chapters 10, 11, and 12 we discussed the price and output determination under imperfect competition of monopoly, monopolistic competition, and oligopoly, respectively. In those imperfect competitions, we have seen that the price of the product is variable. So, the demand for labor changes not only because of the diminishing MP_L but also because of changes in prices to changes in output with the downward-sloping demand curve of firms, where the MR curve is less than the demand curve. Therefore, the data on MVP_L we estimated in Table 16.1 and thus derived the demand curve for labor in Figure 16.1 would be influenced by changes in product prices, marginal productivity of labor, and other related factors. Under these imperfect products or goods markets, the employers do necessarily give equal wages to all employees. The wage differentials actually vary widely among employees based on level of relative skills, specialization, experience, managers' discretion in deciding wages for different employees even with the same level of skill and experience, and efficiency of wage differential for the shortage of labor for highly skilled workers.

16.4.1 Wage Determination under Monopoly and Monopsony Market

With the relaxation of conditions of perfect competition in both the product market and input market (as explained earlier), some specific theoretical models are presented here. One possibility is a monopoly in the output market and competition in the input market; another possibility is a monopoly in the input market to hire (called monopsony or buyer's monopoly) and competition in the output market; the third possibility is the existence of both a monopoly in the output market and monopsony in the input market at the same time. With the help of three diagrams, we will demonstrate the determination of the equilibrium wage rate under these three imperfect market conditions.

16.4.1.1 Wage Determination under Monopoly in Output Market but Competition in Labor Market

This condition of dual market condition with monopoly market structure in the output market and competition in the labor market is illustrated in panel (a) in Figure 16.4.

Figure 16.4 Wage Determination Under Monopoly and Monopsony

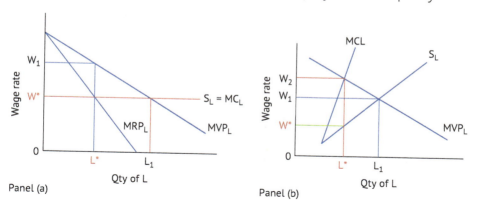

Panel (a)

Panel (b)

In panel (a), monopoly condition in output market shows the demand curve for labor from employer by the curve MVP_L, and its corresponding marginal revenue for labor is shown by the MRP_L curve. Since the labor market is assumed to be under a competitive condition, the relevant supply curve of labor input will be the horizontal supply curve with fixed wage rate shown by the $S_L = MC_L$ curve. Unlike in Figure 16.1 where the equilibrium wage rate was determined at the point of intersection between horizontal SL curve and MVPL curve, this monopoly case of output market equilibrium wage rate would be at the point of intersection between MRP_L and SL, with wage W^* and quantity of labor at L^*. So, it clearly compares the monopolist's exploitation by paying less than W_1 and hiring at L^* instead of L_1. As illustrated in panel (a), monopoly power in output market can get away with paying existing wage rate under competitive labor market at W^*, which is much lower W_1.

16.4.1.2. Wage Determination under Competition in the Output Market but Monopoly in the Labor Market

On the other hand, in panel (b) in Figure 16.4, we can see the same pattern of exploitation under the monopsony power of the employer hiring in the labor market, even the output market is under condition of competition. As illustrated in the figure, the monopsony (buyer's monopoly power of employer to hire) position of employer with its supply curve of labor as S_L and corresponding marginal cost of labor as MC_L to the left of S_L curve. The equilibrium condition to determine the wage rate under this monopsony market is found by the point of intersection between the MVP_L curve and the S_L curve by the wage rate of W^*. The labor exploitation in terms of wage differential in this case is even greater than we have seen in panel (a) as the difference between W_1 and W^* when the MVP_L is at W_2. The employers do not pay much less wage in the competitive market; they also hire less labor than they would under competition, as shown by the difference between L^* and L_1. Under competition, the quantity of labor would have increased to L_1.

16.4.1.3. Wage Determination under Monopoly in the Output Market and also Monopoly in the Labor Market

To demonstrate the third case scenario of wage determination under monopoly conditions in both the output market and labor market, the relevant diagram is illustrated in Figure 16.5. Labor exploitation by monopolies in the output market with monopsony power in the labor market is shown by the wage differential between W_2 and W^*. W^* is the wage rate determined by the point drawn straight down from the point of intersection between MC_L and $D_L = MVP_L$ curve, which is a much lower wage rate than the competitive wage rate at W_2. On the employment side,

Figure 16.5 Wage Determination Under Monopoly and Monopsony

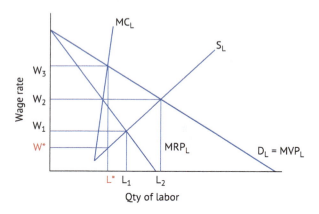

the employer hires L^* quantity of labor, which is much less than the quantity hired under the competitive market at L_2. It should be noticed here that the combination of the equilibrium quantity of labor L^* and wage rate W^* is even lower than that under monopsony and competition shown in Figure 16.4 in panel (b). Therefore, from the efficiency point of view, the competitive market in both input and output is much more desirable because coemption in both markets not only generates more employment but also pays higher wage rates, which is almost equivalent to MVPL.

16.4.2. Other Sources of Wage Differentials

Aside from the input and output market imperfection, the input market behavior in practice is not dictated by the assumptions of perfect competition in most cases. For example, the imperfection in the labor market comes from labor market segmentation, especially in a high-level diversified labor market. The labor market segmentation is mainly attributed to the difference in skill level classified as high-wage versus low-wage workers; union versus non-union workers for collective bargaining power; occupational differences; gender preferences; discrimination based on gender, sexual orientation, and ethnicity; superstar status in sports, music, and entertainment industries. These are the reasons why we see that the corporate CEOs and other top executives earn thousand times higher wages than the lower- or middle-wage earners of the employees in the same corporations. We also see that some NBA, MLB, and NFL players earn over $30 million per year in recent years. Some top actors in Hollywood earn more than $25 or $30 million per motion picture. This wide range of wage differentials and the way they are determined with a wide range of different earnings are not purely based on the principle of the value of marginal productivity of workers (MVP_L) that we have discussed in previous sections. The sources of these difference in wages are primarily attributed to the imperfect nature of market behavior in both the goods market and labor market (so is the capital market). Some of those factors are briefly explained next.

Wage Discrimination by Hiring Managers

It is common to see the actual evidence of wage discrimination not only based on differences in skill level but also workers are discriminated against based on race, gender, ethnicity, religion, national origin, sexual orientation, and the people in their lives. Although the federal and state law in the United States for equal opportunity act and the law of affirmative action are in place to eliminate these types of man-made discriminations practiced by managers, the US Department of Labor statistics indicate that the wage differential based on these categories are still far from over. For example, the recent statistics of 2019 shows that every woman on an average earns 80 cents of every dollar earned by their male counterparts with the same education and experience. The wage differential between a white male and African American male is an even higher percentage. The same statistics show a wage differential between Latinos and their white counterparts.

Labor Union

Although the labor union workers for collective bargaining are only about 10 percent of total American labor force, a tension still persists between employers and employees when compared with union versus non-union workers across the industries. Unlike European countries, where 99 percent of workers are union members, the relationship between employers and union employees in the United States has not been so productive in recent years. This political and cultural tension in the small-scale union environment in the United States shows mixed outcome as compared to non-union members in many industries, especially traditional factory-based industries union such as UAW for auto industry, Teamsters Union in the tracking industry, and other small-scale unions in construction industries. The wage structure negotiated through bargaining process under these unions do not actually fit to the competitive models of wage determination we discussed in Section 16.2.

Entrepreneurship and Human Capital

The role of entrepreneurship and human capital in increasing productivity is a separate input factor that most economists try to explain in advance level economics. For the simplicity of our production function at the outset of this chapter, we included this factor entity into the physical capital and land factor. However, the compensation for entrepreneurs and human capital can never be measured by their enormous marginal value contribution to the economy. The reason can be put simply this way: the productivity of founders of big corporations, inventors and innovators of high technology applications, researchers in academia, and by many more scientists are extremely high in terms of positive externality to the society. Their valuable contributions to economic prosperity since the Industrial Revolution of late eighteenth century have been priceless. They have done those contributions not because of just getting material rate of return for themselves but also, they loved dedicating themselves to create something new and useful for the generations to come. Therefore, higher rewards in terms of monetary compensations for them seem very fair and reasonable to see the earning differential. In reality, however, majority of the human capital did not receive that much high rewards during their lifetime.

Labor Market Segmentation

The labor market segmentation theory suggests that wage differential is attributed to not only the imperfect competition but also the factors such as the division of labor by specialization, occupational differences, growing service sectors, and changes in preference pattern of job seekers with a variety of options to choose from. With the growth of division of labor and specialization, rise in economic growth has opened up many alternative jobs that fit to the preference and taste of labor to choose from. Therefore, understanding the opportunity cost of choosing from alternative job offers over the last several decades of economic prosperity has paved the way of creating more labor market segmentation. Such a rising trend of labor market segmentation into different parts has created a wide array of wage differentials. The wage differential due to market segmentation is found to be true even in the competitive labor market environment. For example, difference in preference in different occupations by women only versus men only is found to be very common in market segmentation across industries.

16.4.3. The Emergence of the Gig Economy and Future Labor Market

Since the beginning of the internet revolution in the late 1990s and its subsequent impact on the invention of smartphone industry and cloud computing industry in the late 2000s has opened up a new industry called the e-commerce, the online retail entities such as Amazon, eBay, Alibaba, and so many others. The revolutionary concept of e-commerce has changed the traditional labor market structure since the mobile app has become the daily mode of transaction in the mainstream. The newly emerged *gig economy* labor market is characterized by short-term contract basis job with the employers at all categories of job starting from plumbing, ride sharing (Uber and Lyft), lodging sharing, information technology (IT), and data analytics internet-based consulting. These jobs are very different than traditional nine to five desk jobs. It derives several benefits for both employers and gig economy workers. For employers, they prefer gig workers to take the advantage of saving cost from not to give benefits and medical coverage with no long-term commitment, less office space, and thus less legal obligation to comply with the labor law. For the gig workers, the advantages are even greater for enjoying personal freedom in managing their work and leisure time on their own control, opportunity to use their specialized skill to sell at a higher rate of return in terms of compensation, and more time to look for better opportunities while in the short-term contracts. This new pool of gig workers is a game changer in the labor market structure of the twenty-first-century digital economy. The rapid rise in independent contractors among young college graduates in recent years is good evidence of this gig economy labor market.

The wage differential is obviously seen as a major change in this segment of the labor market. This newly emerged gig economy and its gig workers will continue to transform the future labor market from working in fixed office desks to telecommuting work environment. The infrastructure for telecommuting environment for across the industries is already here due the heavy investment in Wi-Fi and cloud computing technology. The greatest example of this quick transformation has been witnessed during the mandatory policy of taking shelter-in-place and social distancing in the winter and spring of 2020 to combat the coronavirus (COVID-19) pandemic across the world. During this unprecedented health crisis, the telecommuting option (working from home over the internet) for all office workers and academic teaching was one way for people to continue to work while stopping the spread of COVID-19 virus. This transition to working from home to keep the economy functional across the world is a new way of thinking and adopting to the telecommuting work environment. If this transition becomes successful—it seems to be working very well—it will be a major starting point toward the complete transformation from the traditional labor market structure to the gig economy work environment. It seems clear that the future labor market structure powered by the gig economy is already here in its full potential in 2020.

Chapter Summary

Chapter 16 introduced the factors of production process and their economic implications for efficiency and policy implications. The factors of production process are classified into four main categories: Land, labor, physical capital and entrepreneurship (also called human capital). As an extended branch of microeconomics, this chapter analyzes process of integration of all these factors of production considering the both output and technology in combination with factors of production. Due to the complexity of integration so many variables in a single model of production function, effort is made to narrow down the focus of our discussion into broad categories factors of production: Labor (L) and capital (K). The understanding about the comparative cost structure among land, labor, capital and human capital has been the primary focus in the analysis. The policy implications of the theories on factor market behavior have also been discussed in later sections of this chapter, specially on labor market behavior. We also have also highlighted the importance the implication of e-Commerce revolution and connection with gig economy labor market to transform the traditional labor market structure. The key areas of all the sections discussed in the chapter are briefly summarized next as a recap for the students.

Section 16.1.1 reintroduced the production function from Chapter 8, Eqn (8.1) for the production process of BKC. With that production function equation, Eqn (16.1), detailed analysis was made to make the coordination among input-output relationship to derive labor productivity and labor demand function.

Total output = q = F (K, L),   **Eqn (16.1)**

where, q = Total output,

      K = Capital input (that is in broad sense by considering all other costs than labor), and

      L = Labor input.

Eqn (16.1) is a general expression of kayak production process as a technological relationship between kayak output and its inputs capital (K) and labor (L). We assumed that the kayak firm BKC is operating under competitive market condition where large number of buyers and sellers of kayak exist with perfect information on technology, pricing, and availability with free entry and exit of firms (in the market) in the LR. These assumptions of perfect competition also imply that both buyers and sellers are price takers from the equilibrium market price. We have also assumed a state of perfect market for inputs capital and labor market for kayak production with perfect information about the market wages for labor, and cost of capital, productivity of labor and availability of labor with no discrimination in hiring decision by the owner of the firm. The demand function for labor is derived from under these assumptions by introducing the concept of diminishing marginal productivity of labor. The supply function of labor is derived from the existing wage rates for labor and the trade-off between work hours and leisure given the existing market wage rates per hour.

Section 16.2.1 presented a set of hypothetical data to fit the production function in Table 16.1 and estimated the value of the marginal product and MVPL of the kayak firm BKC along with its marginal profit behavior in the last column of Table 16.1. Using those data plus the market wage rate, we have analyzed the firm's decision-making process of maximizing the profit by hiring the maximum number of labor input. Using this data, the demand and supply curve of labor input is derived and illustrated in Figure 16.1 to determine the equilibrium wage and labor input as the optimum of labor market efficiency. The distinction between a firm's demand curve for labor and market demand curve for labor is also explained at the end of this section.

Section 16.2.2 explained the other factors inside and outside the model that constantly change the derived demand and thus shift the demand curve either right or left depending on the nature of changes. The key factors discussed in this section are changes in the marginal productivity of labor, product price, wage elasticity of labor curve, other input prices, and technology.

Section 16.2.3 introduced the supply-side model of the labor market and explained the degree of responses by labor's willingness to changes in wages. The response behavior is discussed in the context of income effect and substitution effect as wage rates increases. This behavioral aspect of the labor supply function is shown as a backward-bending supply curve. This typical supply curve of a typical labor curve was explained and illustrated in Figure 16.2. In the same figure, a comparison was made between the shape of the backward-bending supply curve individual labor supply and the shape of upward-sloping market supply curve. Students are encouraged to read that part of the section effectively and acquire the knowledge of the realistic market supply behavior of labor input.

Section 16.2.4 explained the key factors other than wage rates that cause the change in labor supply function and thus labor supply curve to shift the supply curve to the right or left depending on the nature of changes. The key factors explained in this section are the labor force growth rate (with special reference to the US labor force growth), population growth rate and immigration policy, and labor participation rate. Students are encouraged to review those factors to relate to the process by which equilibrium wage rates do change over time.

Section 16.3 combined the derived labor demand and labor supply functions discussed in Sections 16.2.2 and 16.2.4 to determine the market equilibrium wage and quantity of labor. The equilibrium process is illustrated in Figure 16.3. Further explanation is made regarding the shifting of demand and supply caused by the factors explained in Sections 16.2.2 and 16.2.4. Students are encouraged to identify some of those factors and practice analyzing the process of change in equilibrium wage and labor quantity when demand and/or supply shift.

Microeconomics Principles, Applications, and Policy Implications

The analysis of labor market equilibrium wage and quantity explained in Section 16.4 was based on assumptions of perfect competition in both labor market and goods market introduced in Sections 16.1 and 16.2. In this section, those assumptions were relaxed to provide more realistic scenario of imperfect competition than competitive market. The examples of the existence of monopoly, monopolistic competition, and oligopoly market structures were discussed to determine the equilibrium wage and quantity of labor. The difference in model structure of labor market under imperfect competition is explained in detail by making comparison with that of under competitive market. The sources of imperfect competition of labor market were also discussed in detail and explained how those sources of imperfection distort the labor market behavior on both demand and supply side and thus causing inefficient wage structure and wage differentials. The key sources of imperfect factor market, especially the labor marker, explained in this section are discriminatory practices of hiring managers, labor union pressure, entrepreneurship and human capital, and labor market segmentation. Students may also explore some other factors that potentially impact the efficiency of wage determination.

In the last subsection of Section 16.4 (Section 16.4.3), the importance of gig economy and its profound impact on labor market transformation was explained. This rapid transformation of labor market structure from traditional labor market to fit the digital economy market is explained in detail. The students are strongly encouraged to read this section and thus foresee the major changes coming in the near future, not only in the existing labor market behavior but also in other factor markets, as well as the way we will work in the future. At the end, the potential impact of gig economy activities on the future workforce was discussed as a game changer, especially the pros and cons of telecommuting as we have seen during the unprecedented crisis of the COVID-19 pandemic in spring of 2020.

Application Activities

1. Using the general form of production function equation introduced in this chapter, briefly explain the input and output relationship to explain the difference between labor-intensive production function and capital-intensive production function. Give a comparative example of labor-intensive industry and capital-intensive industry in the context of US economy.

2. Based on your answer in Q1, explain why the labor-intensive industry in the United States seems to have a comparative disadvantage in producing goods and services that are labor intensive as compared to that of capital-intensive goods and services. Give an example as part of your answers to substantiate.

3. Compare and contrast MP_L and MVP_L. Using hypothetical data, give a numerical example by using the production function given in the chapter. How do you compare between marginal productivity of labor and average productivity of labor? Give a numerical example from the same data you will have used for the first part of this question.

4. Use the hypothetical data in Table 16.2 to answer the following questions.

Table 16.2: Production and MVPL of BKC*

Labor Input (1)	Total Output* q = F (K, L) (2)	Marginal Product MPL = $\frac{\delta q}{\delta L}$ (3)	Price Kayak in $s (4)	Marginal Value Product MVPL=MPL*P (5)	Wages In $s monthly (6)	Marginal Profit MVPL-W (7)
0	0	0	500	0	0	?
1	2	?	500	?	2,000	?
2	6	?	500	?	2,000	?
3	15	?	5,00	?	2,000	?
4	21	?	500	?	2,000	?
5	25	?	500	?	2,000	?
6	25	?	500	?	2,000	?

*Total output is the quantity of kayak production per month, given fixed capital input

a. Fill out the spaces with question marks in Columns (3), (5), and (7).

b. How many labor inputs should the firm hire at how many units of output?

c. What is the optimum level of output the firm should produce to maximize profit given the competitive wage rate of $2,000 per month?

d. Illustrate the equilibrium wage and quantity of labor from your answer in Q4.c.

e. 4.5. What assumptions do you need to make for both the output market and labor market to determine the equilibrium wage and labor quantity you have solved in Q4.d?

5. Explain why the supply curve of individual labor is backward bending but the market supply of labor is upward sloping.

6. Explain why the market and individual firm demand curve for labor is downward sloping.

7. What are the sources of imperfect input market, especially the labor market? In the imperfect market conditions, how do you determine the equilibrium wage differentials as compared to the competitive market conditions? Use a hypothetical diagram to illustrate and explain in your own words the conditions of the following three cases of imperfect competition:

a. The output market is competitive, and the labor market is a monopsony (Buyer's monopoly).

b. The output market is a monopoly, and the labor market is competitive.

c. The output market is a monopoly, and the labor market is a monopsony.

8. Briefly explain the role of entrepreneurship and human capital in the process of economic growth and prosperity. From your explanation, do you think they should be rewarded much more compensation than they receive currently? Why or why not?

9. What are the sources of wage discrimination that create significant wage gaps across the entire labor market? While explaining those sources, provide concrete examples to justify your logic.

10. Critically explain why college professors with the highest terminal PhD degrees with a total of more than 20 years of total schooling earn much less compensation than the compensations earned by sports superstars, top film stars, or celebrity TV talk show host Judge Judy?

Chapter 17

Income Distribution and Poverty in the US Economy

Learning Objectives

As they read the chapter, students will learn:

▶ The Structure of the Wealth Gap and Income Inequality in the United States

▶ Measures of Income Inequality and Their Sources

▶ Income Inequality and Its Effects on the Economy and Society

▶ Policy Implications for Reducing Income Inequality

▶ Poverty Structure and Measures of Poverty

▶ Sources of Poverty and Their Effects on Economy and Society

▶ Policy Implications to Reduce Poverty: Scope and Limitations

Introduction

This last chapter of the textbook focuses on the economics of income distribution and poverty in the context of the US economy. In Chapter 16, we discussed basic theories and applications of factors of production, with special focus on labor market structure to determine the wages and quantity of labor under conditions of a perfectly competitive labor market vis-à-vis imperfect labor market conditions. In analyzing the wage determination in both conditions of market behavior, we also discussed the sources of wage differential and their policy implications to improve the conditions of wage gaps. This chapter is an extended analysis of the current structure of income distribution and poverty in the US economy. The chapter starts with a theoretical understanding of income distribution and poverty and their different dimensions. The issues regarding increasing income inequality and poverty in the United States over the last four decades have been prominent in the political and economic mainstream agendas. Almost every adult American is aware that despite the almost continuously positive economic growth rate and low unemployment rate, the rate of poverty and the income gap between rich and poor has been skyrocketing during the same period. The 99% versus the 1% (referring to the income and wealth gap in America) has been the talk of every American adult since September 17, 2011, when the Occupy Wall Street movement emerged in New York City. This 99% versus 1% rhetoric has come from the fact that the top 1% of wealthy Americans occupy over 90% of total wealth while the same 1% earn over 25% of income per year as evidenced from the most recent statistics. It is also common knowledge that more than 15% of all households are living below the poverty line defined by the US Census Bureau in 2014 (which has not improved much since then). The purpose of this chapter is to provide a basic theoretical understanding of these two important topics in economics. Readers are expected to acquire in-depth knowledge on how to look at the pattern of income distribution and poverty and thus analyze the data related to these two aspects of economics with particular focus on sources of income inequality, poverty, and their effect on society. Policy implications of mitigating these two major economic and social issues are also presented at the end of the chapter.

17.1. The Structure of the Wealth Gap and Income Inequality in the United States

As mentioned in the introduction, the top 1% of wealthy Americans occupy over 90% of total wealth, and the same group earn over 25% of total income; however, more than 15% of all households live below the poverty line. This section focuses on understanding the difference between wealth and income, the current structure of wealth, the income gap, sources of income inequality, the data analysis of rising income inequality, and policy implications.

17.1.1. Wealth Versus Income and Rich Versus Poor: Conceptual Differences

At the outset, it is imperative for students to understand the conceptual difference between **wealth** and **income. Wealth** is a stock of assets in the form of common stocks, bonds, real estate, precious metals, retirement funds in various forms, and similar other assets that individuals and households invested in the past and/or inherited from their families or trust funds. This stock of capital assets has different rates of return every year and the asset owners receive a routine stream of investment returns. On the other hand, **income** is cash flow coming from the daily routine of work schedule by individuals in all walks of life with a continuous flow of earnings during the entire work–life cycle. For example, if an individual or household owns a handful of assets such as stocks, bonds, and real estate with the luxury of not working while maintaining their current living standard and lifestyle, we consider that individual or household to be wealthy. On the other hand, if the same individual or household members also work like other working people regardless of their level of wealth, they receive a continuous flow of cash at a regular interval from working in the form of wages and salaries. Of course, the difference in wages by different individuals will be discussed in detail in later sections of this chapter.

The terms **rich** and **poor** can be explained through the concept of income mentioned in the previous paragraph—a rich person may not necessarily be a wealthy individual since a wealthy person does not have to depend on cash flow coming from a daily routine of work. Therefore, the difference between **rich** and **poor** comes from the amount of earnings per pay period or per calendar year provided to an individual or household to make ends meet. Being **rich** means the individual or household lives comfortably with their cash flow of earnings and has surplus cash to invest in other assets and/or spend on goods and services beyond their basic necessities and the maintenance of a comfortable living standard. On the other hand, the term **poor** means that an individual or household cannot make enough income to meet their basic necessities for living (i.e., food and nutrition, clothing, shelter, access to healthcare, utilities, transportation, access to education and social safety). The statistical threshold of earnings described as the poverty line that distinguishes among rich, poor, middle-income, and low-income (but not poor) will be discussed in detail in later sections of this chapter.

17.1.2. Income and Wealth Gap Structure in the United States

From our understanding of the conceptual difference between wealth and income described above, this section provides the current structure of the **wealth and income gap** for the US economy for the period between 1989 and 2016. As we mentioned earlier in this chapter, over 90% of total wealth is occupied by the top 1% of wealthy Americans, and the same group earns over 25% total gross income and wealth (before taxes). Table 17.1 indicates how the income and wealth gap has widened since 1989.

Table 17.1: Income and Wealth Gap Between 1989 and 2016

Household Income Shares (Pre-Tax):	1989 ($7.12 Trillion in 2016 Prices)	2016 ($12.88 Trillion in 2016 Prices)	Income Range In 2016 only
Top 10%	42%	50%	$176,000 and above
Middle 50%–90%	43%	37%	$53,000 to $176,000
Bottom 10%	15%	13%	$0 to $53,000
Total %	100%	100%	
Household Wealth Shares (Pre-Tax)	**1989 ($32.87 Trillion in 2016 Prices)**	**2016 ($87.87 Trillion in 2016 Prices)**	
Top 10%	67%	77%	
Next 40%	30%	22%	
Bottom 10%	3%	1%	

Source: Federal Reserve Bank of St. Louis (https://www.stlouisfed.org/open-vault/2019/august/wealth-inequality-in-america-facts-figures)

From the data in Table 17.1, it is evident that both the income gap and the wealth gap have widened significantly between 1989 and 2016 (adjusted for 2016 prices). The wealth share of the top 10% of households has increased from 42% to 50% in just 27 years. On the other hand, the next 40% of household earnings actually declined from 43% to 37%; the bottom 10% lost earnings by 2% from 15% to 13% for the same period.

The wealth gap data shows even more strikingly that the top 10% of wealthy Americans increased their wealth share from 67% (already two-thirds of total household wealth) in 1989 to 77% in 2016. The next 40% of households lost their share of wealth, declining from 30% to 22%; the bottom 10% declined to 1% from 3% during the same period. It is striking to see how significantly the wealth of top 10% increased at the expense of a sharp decline in the wealth of 90% of households, despite the growth of wealth between 1989 and 2016 increasing by more than 167%.

17.2. Measures of Income Inequality and Their Sources

The income and wealth gap structure shown in Table 17.1 is just a snapshot of US economic inequality. A more in-depth understanding can be gained by introducing a basic theory of income distribution and observing its application in real-world data expressed in percentage distribution. Students may have already learned about the measures of GDP (gross domestic product) growth rate in percentage from year to year for every country in the world. We also know that the higher the GDP growth rate, the higher the living standard for citizens. However, it is also important to keep in mind that an increase in GDP growth rate alone, even if adjusted for inflation, does not give any information about whether the living standard has increased for everyone in the country or just for a few. In order to determine which percentage of households receive which percentage of the economic pie, this section focuses on understanding the concept of income distribution and how to measure income inequality for any country, with specific data analysis for the US economy. This section also explores the sources of the growing income inequality in the United States over the last four decades.

17.2.1. Measures of Income Distribution

The national income or total gross domestic product (GDP) for the US economy can be divided into five sources: wages, proprietor's income, rents, corporate profits, and net interest income. According to the data compiled by the US Bureau of Economic Analysis (bea.gov), the functional distributions of these five categories towards 2019 GDP of $21,429 billion are 69% from wages and salaries, 10% from proprietor's income, 4% from rental income, 14% from corporate profit, and 3% from interest income. From these sources of income, it is possible to measure the income distributional pattern of household incomes for any chosen year. Table 17.2 is the current distributional pattern of US households compiled by the US Department of Commerce economic analysis unit (bea.gov).

Distribution by Quintile of Households	2018 % of GDP	1967 % of GDP
Lowest quintile	3.1	4.0
Second quintile	8.3	10.8
Third quintile	14.1	17.3
Fourth quintile	22.6	24.2
Highest quintile	52.0	43.6
Top 5%	23.1	17.2
Summary Measures		
Gini index of income inequality	0.486	0.397
Mean logarithmic deviation of income index	0.616	0.380
Theil index:	0.436	0.287
Atkinson index: e = 0.25	0.105	0.071
e = 0.50	0.205	0.143
e = 0.75	0.311	0.220

Source: Bureau of Economic Research of the US Department of Commerce (www.bea.gov)

Table 17.2 above shows the actual estimated data of income distribution for the US economy for 1967 and 2018 distributed in quintiles (every 20% of households) against the percent of total GDP earned by each successive quintile. We can observe that in 2018 the lowest 20% of household earners made only 3.1% of total GDP and the highest 20% of household earners made 52% of total GDP, almost 18 times that of the lowest quintiles. It is also interesting to see that adding the first, second, and third quintiles shows 60% of households made a total of about 25% of the GDP, which is almost the same as income share earned by the top 5% (23.1% of GDP). Comparing the data of 2018 with that of 1967 in the same table, we can see the distribution pattern of each quintile was more equitable in 1967 than in 2018. For example, the lowest quintiles earned 4% of GDP and the highest quintiles earned 43.6% of GDP in 1967 as compared to 3.1% and 52% respectively in 2018. The first 60% of households earned about 32% of GDP in 1967 as compared to only 25% in 2018. The top 5% earned 17.2% in 1967 as compared to 23.1% in 2018. The data comparison between 1967 and 2018 clearly indicates that income inequality got worse in the 50 years despite the continuous rise of GDP at an estimated annual growth rate of 3% over the same time period. The distributional pattern also indicates that the share of the economic pie earned by the lowest 20% and the fourth quintile (the middle-income households) did not change much. Digging deeper into this data analysis, the next sub-section focuses on a graphical presentation of the income inequality in terms of the Lorenz curve and Gini coefficient index.

17.2.2. Lorenz Curve and Gini Coefficient Index

In Table 17.2, we see other information under summary measures of the Gini index of income inequality, mean logarithm deviation (MLD) of income index, and the Atkinson index. The Gini coefficient index is the graphical representation of the data in Table 17.2 derived from the Lorenz curve of income distribution. The other indices listed in the table are alternative measures of income inequality estimated by the researchers at the Bureau of Economic Research. For the sake of simplicity, we focus on only the Lorenz curve and the Gini coefficient index, illustrated in Figures 17.1 and 17.2 for 2018 and 1967, respectively.

The Lorenz Curve: Figure 17.1 illustrates the income distribution shown from Table 17.2 for 2018 in the box ABCD, where the diagonal line BD is the perfectly equal distribution of income among all households (i.e., every quintile of households would have earned the same % of GDP by sharing equally; the slope of the line BD is equal to one as a 45-degree line). But from a realistic perspective of income inequality, the **Lorenz curve** is derived from the % share of GDP earned by each of the five quintiles as plotted far below the equality line of BD. The horizontal axis displays the % of households in quintiles and the vertical axis shows the % share of GDP earned by each of the quintiles of households. The lowest quintiles starting at point 2 on the horizontal axis showing 3.1% GDP share earned found on the vertical axis because point 1 to the left starts at zero income and zero households. Similarly, point 6 on horizontal axis is the highest quintile of households earning 52% of GDP marked from the vertical axis. The other shares of income distribution among the second, third, and fourth quintiles are marked by the dots along the Lorenz curve. To interpret the distributional pattern more clearly, please note that the closer the Lorenz curve is to the diagonal line BD, the more equality of income distribution. Conversely, the further away the Lorenz curve is from below the diagonal line BD, the more inequality of income distribution. The numerical value estimated from the area between the line BD and the actual Lorenz curve is called the Gini coefficient index, as explained below.

Figure 17.1   Lorenz Curve: Income Distribution 2018

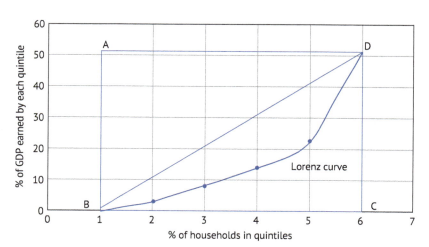

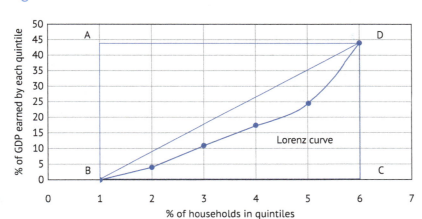

Figure 17.2   Lorenz Curve: Income Distribution 1967

Gini Coefficient Index: Gini coefficient index is the estimated parameter from the Lorenz curve illustrated in Figure 17.1 for 2018 and the same parameter in Figure 17.2 for 1967. Gini index is the ratio of the area between the diagonal line BD and the Lorenz curve divided by the area of the entire triangle. The closer the Lorenz curve is to the equality line BD, the lower the value of the Gini coefficient and thus the more equal the distribution of income. Therefore, the range of values of the Gini coefficient must be between zero and 1.

The values of the Gini coefficient index vary widely across the countries, with industrialized countries showing less than 0.50 in recent decades—the United States is the highest among all industrial countries. The list of Gini coefficients by countries can be found at the World Bank database[1] with detailed reports. The estimate of the Gini coefficients from the Lorenz curve is useful for visualizing the actual distributional pattern of a country's income and thus comparing it with the rest of the world. This comparison helps policymakers and researchers analyze the economic well-being of the society and take the necessary policy actions to improve the living standard for everyone rather than only a limited group of households on the top. Since the lower values of Gini coefficients indicate more equal distribution and higher values indicate more unequal distribution, the US data comparison between 1967 and 2018, with 0.397 in 1967 and 0.486 in 2018 (see Table 17.2 above), clearly indicates more unequal distribution of income in the last 50 years. This increase in the Gini index from 0.397 to 0.486 can also be seen from the Lorenz curve in Figure 17.2 when compared to the same curve illustrated in Figure 17.1. The Lorenz curve in Figure 17.1 is further away from the diagonal line BD with a coefficient of 0.486 compared to the Lorenz curve illustrated in Figure 17.2 with a coefficient of 0.397, which is much closer to the equality line BD.

17.2.3. Sources of Income and Wealth Inequality in the United States
In the previous sections, we have seen the increasing income inequality in the US economy since the late 1960s. It is not practical to expect perfect equality of income distribution

1   https://data.worldbank.org/indicator/SI.POV.GINI?view=map

because this would require unrealistic assumptions of identical skill and productivity of all workers, perfect mobility, equal preference, and equal ability across the entire labor force. Therefore, there are several economic and non-economic factors and/or sources of wealth and income inequality discussed in this sub-section.

Ability of Factors of Production: The ability to work in different types of jobs is based on the capability of individuals and varies widely from job to job and industry to industry. With a diverse form of specialization of labor force participation in different types of industries, workers have different skill sets to specialize. This specialization creates a highly segmented labor market with higher demand for specific skills such as software and network engineers, doctors, lawyers, software programmers, construction, and similar highly skilled work. Less supply for these specialized skills raises the wages for these workers compared to less skilled work required in other jobs. So wage differentials across industries and the labor market are primarily based on differences in the ability of workers.

Productivity Difference: Similar and somewhat related to the difference in ability explained above, the productivity difference among workers is also a significant factor in income inequality. Since workers are generally paid on the basis of their values of marginal productivity of labor hours, the higher the value of marginal productivity the higher the wages and salaries they receive. The efficiency wage rate is an example we discussed in Chapter 16.

Entrepreneurial Skills and Risk-Taking Skills: Entrepreneurial motivation and risk-taking ventures are common sources of wealth in a free market capitalist system. But there are only a handful of entrepreneurial ventures in each generation. The most recent entrepreneurs who became very successful and wealthy are the founders of Microsoft (Bill Gates and his co-founders); Apple (Steve Jobs); Facebook (Mark Zuckerberg); Google (Sergey Brin and Larry Page); Amazon (Jeff Bezos); and Alibaba (Jack Ma). These entrepreneurs, along with many others, became wealthy in high-tech industries because of their clear vision and willingness to take enormous risks while using venture skills.

Job Preference and Compensating Variation: There are certain jobs, such as construction, highway work, railway repairs, cleaning, plumbing, and work in energy industries that many individuals would prefer to avoid. Therefore, wages that are higher than the standard have to be offered to attract workers to those jobs.

Wealth by Inheritance: Some household members are born with wealth from their family that will grow further in their own generation and after. This stock of inherited wealth could take many forms—for example, financial assets, real estate, stocks, bonds, and education or skills.

Wealth in Life Cycle of Experience: In most economies, older workers with their long experience, specialization, and skills earn much more than the younger generation of workers. They not only make higher income but also build other assets as sources of wealth in the form of financial assets and real estate.

Education and Human Capital: The level of education and quality of training in specialized jobs is one of the most significant factors contributing to the income and wealth gap in recent decades. In a high-tech society like the United States, the economy has transformed from a factory-based economy to a knowledge-based economy, which requires higher education in all fields. Aside from the need for the physical capital, human capital with higher education and training is in demand for those jobs. A more educated workforce can bargain for higher wages and salaries because of the limited supply of human capital. Therefore, investing in human capital generates more income when compared to low-skill workers. As students may recall in the beginning of this textbook, we discussed that the wage difference between workers with a high school diploma and college-educated workers over a lifetime could be as much as ten times larger. Table 17.3 shows the income difference between workers with higher education and workers with a high school diploma compiled by the US Census Bureau and Bureau of Labor Statistics.

Table 17.3: Income/Wealth Differential by Education and Human Capital

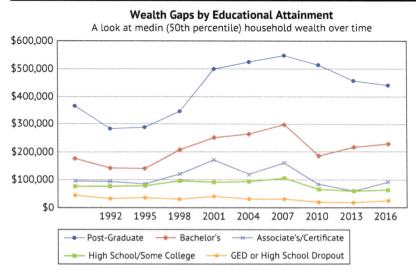

Source: Federal Reserve Bank of St. Louis

The above data clearly indicates that workers with college degrees and post-graduate degrees have greater wealth/earnings than their counterparts with high school degrees. For example, household members with college degrees or post graduate degrees have wealth/ earning in 1989 between $150,000 and $375,000 per year compared to individuals with a high school degree or a non-high school degree earning between $45,000 and $94,000 in the same year. In 2016, we actually see a much wider difference in wealth/earnings between higher educated workers and high school degree holders, with a range of values between $230,000 and $450,000 for post-graduates and graduate degree holders and a range between $24,000 and $93,000 per year for high school and non-high school degree holders. This implies that real wages actually declined for workers without a college degree in 2016.

Racial and Gender Discrimination: Wage discrimination is defined as the pay difference between employees with the same education and experience when there is a bias based on characteristics such as gender, race, ethnicity, religion, or sexual orientation. Discrimination in the United States has been the subject of continuous debate in all spheres of life and has economic, political, legal, and social implications. Despite the landmark legislation of the Equal Pay Act of 1963 aimed at ending wage discrimination in the workplace, statistical evidence shows that discrimination by gender, race, ethnic background, and age still exists (although it has improved significantly in recent years since the 2009 Lilly Ledbetter Fair Pay Act signed by President Obama). Table 17.4 shows the most recent average wage structure in the United States based on gender, race, ethnicity, and age.

Table 17.4: Earnings by Worker Characteristics, 2018

Worker Characteristics	Weekly Average Earnings	% Difference in Earnings
Men	$1,007	–
Women	825	−19% less than men
White	935	–
Black	737	−23% less than white
Asian	1,157	+24% more than white
Hispanic	696	−26% less than white
Workers age 25–34	872	−20% less than age 35–54
Workers age 35–54	1,090	25% more than age 25–34
Workers age 55–64	1,082	Almost same as age 35–54

Source: https://www.bls.gov/news.release/pdf/wkyeng.pdf

The data in Table 17.4 clearly shows that a female worker, on average, earns 79 cents for every dollar earned by her male counterpart with an equal level of education, job position, and experience. However, this wage gap has improved—20 years ago a female worker earned 65 cents for every dollar earned by her male counterpart. The racial bias still shows significant discrimination; a black worker, on average, makes 77 cents for each dollar earned by a white worker and Hispanic workers make, on average, 74 cents for each dollar earned by a white counterpart. But for Asian workers average earnings show a significant increase—24% higher than their white counterparts. This significant difference may be attributed to the educational level of Asian immigrants in recent decades who are mostly highly skilled workers. Several independent studies also show the increasing role of human capital in income inequality in recent years.

Overpricing of Essential Products: The skyrocketing price of many essential consumer products caused by monopolies and oligopolies brings enormous profits to the companies at the expense of consumers. As a result, middle-income and low-income households live at a subsistence or below subsistence level while the increasing corporate profit margin raises the wealth of the top 5%. Overpricing in these circumstances doesn't seem to have any economic basis besides increasing the shareholder's equity.

Tax System: The current supply-side tax system implemented by the Trump administration in 2017 has been regressive in nature and disproportionately favors corporations and the wealthy classes of society at the expense of the middle class. It also created more tax loopholes for giant corporations. As a result, the base providing tax revenue to finance the rising government budget outlays has become narrower. This has negative effects: First, the wealthy class has become wealthier while the middle class pays more taxes with less disposable income. Second, the budget deficit increased significantly since 2017, which means the US Treasury has been borrowing more money than ever before by issuing treasury securities. This massive volume of borrowing via selling treasury securities is expected to create more uncertainty about the future and a possible rise in interest rates and inflation.

17.3. Income Inequality and Its Effects on the Economy and Society

Although conventional economic theories argue about the trade-off between efficiency and equity on the grounds that income inequality provides incentives for innovation, invention, and entrepreneurship, growing income inequality has many negative consequences in society not only from the point of view social justice and fairness but also from the viewpoints of sustainable economic prosperity and social stability. Increasing income inequality has the potential to cause social unrest if not checked in the long run. Unfair wages and discriminatory practices at the workplace based on gender and race have the potential to create an environment of low morale. The decline in morale among low-wage workers can have a serious consequence: loss of worker productivity and loyalty. The basic economic theories suggest that income inequality based on human capital and value of marginal productivity can be justified as a fair level of income inequality. But when the top executives of large corporations make tens of millions of dollars per year, plus more millions in other perks, one must consider whether the productivity of CEOs and other executives is worth that much compensation at the expense of the lowest paid majority workforce in the same company. This question of how much a CEO is worth compared to what he or she is paid by the board of directors seems worthy of further research.

In another note, rising poverty and income inequality could cause social unrest, political chaos, and psychological disturbance in many hardworking low-income households. The social and economic burden of rising poverty and income inequality has the consequence of increasing crimes rates, drug and substance abuse, and family breakups. In order to maintain a balance between income and efficiency, appropriate policy actions must be undertaken by the government. It is also a moral and economic responsibility. It is hoped that by adapting corporate social responsibility (CSR) into the corporate culture, a fair and equitable wage structure based on the actual value of the productivity of each employee can be established.

17.4. Policy Implications for Reducing Income Inequality

The policy implications of reducing income inequality have been in the forefront of American politics and academia since the beginning of the 1980s, after the implementation of supply-side economics (called Reaganomics) executed by President Ronald Reagan. The issue of income inequality has become one of the hottest political topics in recent years, dividing party lines into far left (the liberal Democrats) and far right (the conservative Republicans).

The left argues in favor of a progressive income tax rate and wealth tax and the reduction of income taxes for the middle class. The left also recommends expanding existing social welfare programs such as Medicare, Medicaid, housing support, universal health insurance, education subsidies, and free higher education for the poor. On the contrary, the right argues that higher taxes for corporations and the wealthy would create disincentives for private investment and would thus reduce jobs and economic growth leading to even less tax revenue. They further argue that policy should be focused on faster economic growth that would benefit low-income households across the board by raising their earnings and building wealth. At the end of the day, neither side crosses the aisle to compromise and formulate a viable policy. This issue will be discussed further in the last section of this chapter; however, we will first discuss the **economics of poverty** in the next section.

17.5. Poverty Structure and Measures of Poverty

This section focuses on an economic analysis of poverty in the context of the US economy. As we have discussed in the section concerning income inequality, over 15% of 330 million Americans live in poverty, officially defined as a household of four earning $26,000 or less annually. There are 49.5 million Americans living in poverty in a country which is perceived as wealthy and developed. In the previous section we discussed the wide disparity of income and wealth in the United States. In this section, we will discuss the idea that, given the depth of poverty in America, this country is not really rich in any true sense.

The basic question to ask at the outset is how to live as poor in America, where the living standard and cost of living is one of the highest in all industrialized countries. One thing to keep in mind is that the poverty threshold in the context of the American living standard and cost of living is not comparable with the poverty threshold in very low-income countries where the average wage is less than $2 a day. On the other hand, the working poor in the United States earn $26,000 per year—at least $12.50 per hour or $100 dollars per day at the minimum wage rate mandated by law. Therefore, being poor in America is quite different than being poor in most countries in the world. In addition, poor households with annual earnings of $26,000 or less in America are supported by other means such as healthcare subsidies, food stamps, housing subsidies, educational support, and other forms of social welfare programs. Poor households earning less than $2 a day in less developed countries do not have that social safety net from their governments. Therefore, the concept of poverty and its structure widely vary across countries. In this section, we will introduce the current structure of poverty followed by measures of poverty and sources of poverty. We will also conclude the section with a discussion of the policy implications.

17.5.1. Structure of Poverty

Table 17.5 illustrates the 2018 structure of poverty in the United States compared to the previous two years estimated by the US Census Bureau. The table shows the official definition of poverty for a four-member household (two adults and two children under 18).

Table 17.5: Poverty Structure in US Economy (US$)

Measure	2016	2017	2018
Official poverty measure	24,339	24,858	25,465
Owners with mortgages	26,336	27,085	28,342
Owners without mortgages	22,298	23,261	24,173
Renters	26,104	27,005	28,166

Source: US Census Bureau (https://www.bls.gov/pir/spm/spm_thresholds_2018.htm)

If we consider $26,000 earning per family as an approximation in 2018 for the poverty threshold, then the per-week income comes out to $500 per household. With this income level it is quite impossible to meet basic needs such as housing, healthcare, food, transportation, clothing, utility bills, and children's education expenses. That is why the social safety net in the form of food stamps, housing subsidies, and other social security benefits are provided by both state and federal programs. To see the poverty structure in greater detail, the poverty threshold for households larger than four members is shown in Table 17.6. In that table, we can see the poverty structure of households with up to eight family members along with their respective poverty threshold. We can see that in an eight-member household, the threshold goes up to $50,681.

Table 17.6: Poverty Structure with Larger Household Size, 2017

Size of family unit	Weighted average thresholds
One person (unrelated individual):	12,488
Under age 65	12,752
Aged 65 and older	11,756
Two people:	15,877
Householder under age 65	16,493
Householder aged 65 and older	14,828
Three people	19,515
Four people	25,094
Five people	29,714
Six people	33,618
Seven people	38,173
Eight people	42,684
Nine people or more	50,681

Source: US Census Bureau.

Although the poverty line in terms of absolute poverty (income below the poverty threshold) versus relative poverty (income above poverty threshold but still poor) is much more complex than the information in the table, we will discuss our measures of poverty based on the official poverty threshold estimated by the US Census Bureau.

17.5.2. Measures of Poverty

There are several ways to measure poverty for every country in the world. The common practice by economists is to start from the definition of the poverty line and identify the poverty gap below and above the poverty line. Economists define the poverty line as the minimum income level below which an individual is considered to be poor. In the context of the United States, students will be able find several articles and books related to the "two tales" of America, where poor Americans have been living distinctly different lives than the non-poor since the 1960s. Despite being one of the wealthiest countries in the world with the largest economy and the highest per capita healthcare cost, America has been plagued by extreme poverty and obesity since the declaration of the "War on Poverty" by President Lyndon Johnson in 1964. Unfortunately, the War on Poverty did not improve living conditions, rather they have become worse since 1980s. In 2018, the US Census Bureau estimated over 15% of the population lived at or below poverty level based on the official poverty lines presented in Tables 17.5 and 17.6. The increasing rate of poverty in America over the last four decades, combined with rising income inequality, has become a hotly debated public policy and economic policy issue in recent years. Poverty in many cases causes obesity, mental anxiety and other illness, substance abuse, crime, and social unrest along with growing homelessness. Given the complexity of measuring the poverty level depending on the size of households, economists have struggled to define poverty and the poverty line threshold. In an effort to answer these fundamental questions, two types of poverty measures are commonly taken into consideration: the **absolute poverty line** and the **relative poverty line.**

The **absolute poverty line** is the minimum income level below which a household or individual cannot meet their basic necessities of life. This measure is complicated because the living standard for Americans living below the absolute poverty line is very different than that of poor people in India or Bangladesh in South Asia. The poor in America enjoy a much better standard of living compared to the poor in South Asian countries. That brings us to the next type of poverty measure: the relative poverty line.

The **relative poverty line** defines poor households who fall far behind the median income of the country. For example, if the per capita income of America in 2018 is $62,000, the people who are above the absolute poverty line but far below the median value of $62,000 are considered relatively poor. So depending on the severity of the income inequality, it is fair to say that the higher the income inequality, the more difficult it becomes to distinguish between the absolute and relative poverty lines. The poverty line measurements help categorize the entire population into poor, lower-middle class, middle class, upper-middle class and the rich and wealthy class. Table 17.7 allows us to visualize this income classification along with income distribution among all American households.

Table 17.7: Median Income Distribution by % of Households in 2018

Year	Lowest 5th	Second 5th	Third 5th	Fourth 5th	Highest 5th	Top 5%
2018	13,775	37,293	63,572	101,570	233,895	416,520
2000	10,157	25,361	42,233	65,653	142,269	252,400
1989	6994	17,401	28,925	43,753	85,529	138,185

Source: US Census Bureau (www.uscensus.gov; Table H-3 2018)

Table 17.7 shows the data of median income for American households by quintile for years 2018, 2000, and 1989. Students may observe a number of interesting facts relating to both income inequality and poverty levels since 1989. The first observation is the change in poverty line for the third 5th of households was $28,925 per household in 1989, increased to $42,233 in 2000, and increased further to $63,572 in 2018. The second observation is that the highest 5th income group shows median income approximately equal to the combined median incomes of all four quintile groups below it. This pattern of income has not changed much since 1989. The other disparity of income is seen from the median income groups between the top 5% and the highest 5th, as the median income of the former is almost twice the median income of the latter group.

In terms of poverty indicators, it is easy to see that the lowest 40% of households (the lowest 5th and second 5th) do fall under the category of absolute poverty and the third 5th of households seems to fall in the relative poverty category. In other words, we can conclude that 40% of American households lived in absolute poverty in 2018. The third quintile of households are between the relative poverty level and the low-middle class income group. Households earning median income over $200,000 make up only the top 20% of households. Looking at the data comparison of income distribution and poverty measures since 1989, it seems clear that 60% of American households are not really rich in terms of cost of living and living standard for the country. It is also interesting to see that a household with a median income of $101,560 in 2018 is above 60% of households who have median income lower than $100,000. In other words, 60% of households earn way less than $100,000 per year, and only the top 20% earn median income of $200,000 or more. That information also implies that not all households in the top 20% make more than $200,000 because that is just the median income. As a matter of fact, all households earning over $200,000 constitute only the top 5% of households in 2018.

As the poverty rate has increased in the United States over the last four decades, so has the rate of crime and social unrest—this is of great concern to social scientists, economists, and politicians. The US Census Bureau estimates that 13.4% of people in the United States were living below the poverty level during 2017 and 13.1% in 2018. More specifically, there were 42,583,651 Americans living below the poverty level in 2017 and there are about 41,852,315 people living below the poverty level in 2018.[2] The poverty distribution by age, sex, and ethnicity for 2018 is also listed in Table 17.8. This data illustrating poverty distribution based on population characteristics helps us take a closer look at how poverty level disproportionately affects minorities, especially African Americans.

---

2   https://www.census.gov/content/dam/Census/library/publications/2019/acs/acsbr18-02.pdf

Table 17.8: Poverty Distribution by Demographic Characteristics

Race/Origin	% of population	% change from 2017
White	10.1	−0.5
White, not Hispanic	8.1	−0.4
Black	20.8	−0.9
Asian	10.1	+0.4
Hispanic (any race)	17.6	−0.8
Gender		
Male	10.6	−0.4
Female	12.9	−0.6
Age		
Below 18	16.2	−1.2
18 to 64	10.7	−0.4
65+	9.7	+0.2

Source: US Census Bureau (https://www.census.gov/content/dam/Census/library/visualizations/2019/demo/p60-266/Figure8.pdf)

Table 17.8 indicates that African Americans living below the poverty level in 2018 make up 20.8% of the total population living below the poverty line. On the other hand, whites and Asians living below poverty level are both at 10.1%. The distribution of Hispanics living below the poverty line is also very high at 17.6% in 2018. The percent change of this distributional pattern among different demographics between the years of 2017 and 2018 made a very little progress, with a range between 0.4% and 0.5%, respectively. The poverty rate for the female population is also much higher at 12.9% as compared to the male counterpart at 10.6%. In terms of poverty distribution by age group, between the ages of 18 and 64 10.7% live in poverty, while among those over 65 years of age, 9.7% live at or below the poverty line. The data on poverty across all demographic groups shown in Table 17.8 clearly indicates that, despite the legislative initiatives by the US government in 1964 to eliminate poverty, the poverty rate has actually increased over the last 50 years. The next section demonstrates key sources of poverty and reasons for the failure of government policy in its efforts to alleviate poverty.

17.6. Sources of Poverty and Their Effects on Economy and Society

The factors contributing to the poverty rate of over 15% in America are not limited to traditional explanations such as lack of skill, low education, and government failure. The sources of poverty are a combination of several factors that include the rising income disparity since the implementation of supply-side economic policies in the 1980s. The complexity of the labor market and a discriminatory wage structure are other major factors contributing to rising poverty in the last several decades. Although detailed data analysis of the poverty trend and its sources is beyond the scope of this textbook, a list of the key sources of poverty is provided here with a brief explanation.

Wage Structure: Various economic analyses on wage data show that the rate of increase in wages for low-income workers has been far below the rate of increase of inflation, measured by the rise of cost-of-living expenses such as the CPI index. For example, the minimum wage law of the United States has failed to keep up with the rising cost of living. This situation has worsened with the increasing income inequality discussed in Section 17.2 of this chapter.

Globalization and the New Economy: Rapid globalization and the emergence of the new economy since the Internet Revolution in late 1990s has transformed the US economic structure from a traditional factory-based economy into a new economy based on information and knowledge. As a consequence of this transformation, labor intensive manufacturing sectors have disappeared from the United States and gone to highly populated countries such as China, India, and dozens of similar countries in Asia and South America. This transformation has put the US labor market in an unfavorable position, especially for the factory workers. The factory workers lost their jobs over the last three decades and many of them ended up working for minimum wage or were forced to retire early.

Technological Shift: The growth of advanced technology in software, hardware, and network- and Internet-based industries has created a significant gap between skilled workers and unskilled workers across many industries. The workers with less technological expertise and education/training are not able to bargain for higher wages.

Education and Training: The rising cost of higher education and training for jobs in the new economy has trapped millions of Americans in low-wage jobs living below the poverty level. The supply of skilled labor could not match the rising demand for human capital in advanced technology industries. This crisis is further aggravated by social unrest, physical and mental disabilities, substance abuse, and drug addiction. Government programs did not effectively address these issues and failed to make significant progress.

Geographical Disparity: One of the striking features of American poverty is the locational disparity related to the disappearing traditional manufacturing factories. The labor force employed in traditional factories did not relocate to other areas of the country to find new jobs in new industries. As a result, the lack of higher paid jobs in those distressed areas kept them in poverty for a long time. These areas are mostly located in Pennsylvania, Ohio, Michigan, Wisconsin, Louisiana, Alabama, Illinois, Indiana, and a few other states in the Midwest.

Rising Cost of Healthcare and Utilities: As mentioned in Chapter 4 in this textbook, skyrocketing healthcare costs and other utility expenses such as gas and electricity bills, heating oil expenses, and Internet and telephone expenses have put many low-income families in severe financial distress in recent decades.

Change in Social and Family Composition: The rising trend of divorce and single parenthood have split the family compositions in half for over 60% of American households in recent decades. More than 60% of Americans living alone and/or as single parents has been one of the key factors contributing to rising poverty and social unrest. Government policy intervention in this area of concern has become more important than ever before. Some of the policy implications are provided in the last section of this chapter.

17.7. Policy Implications for Poverty Elimination and Income Inequality

From the analysis of poverty structure and sources of poverty in America discussed in the previous section, we have seen that poverty and income inequality have gotten worse over the last four decades. Although legislation to eliminate poverty was enacted in 1964, it has failed to achieve its objective. Based on the comparison between absolute poverty and relative poverty explained in the previous section, it is unambiguously true that over 20% of American households live in either absolute or relative poverty. However, people living below the absolute poverty level are receiving social welfare benefits to maintain their basic needs. As their position is supported by the social safety net, it is much better than the absolute poverty of some developing countries where the impoverished are earning less than $2 per day. The social safety net in the United States provides a number of social welfare programs such as free public education, housing subsidies for low income families, Medicare and Medicaid, unemployment insurance, food stamps, and nutritional support for children. However, funding these programs has been a challenge for the government because of chronic increases in the budget deficit and public debt. Social and political thinkers have quite different ideological and philosophical views regarding the best way to address poverty and income inequality. Some recommend increasing the budget for welfare programs and funding through higher rates of progressive taxes on wealthy. Others have different views of supporting and encouraging policy reforms for economic self-sufficiency by dependent poor households. But the reality is much more complex than the continuous political and social debates that have been going on for decades. The areas of complexity and the policy implications are presented below.

Policy on Changes in Wage Rate Structure: Scope and Limitation

Since the current wage structure and existing minimum wage laws have been found to be ineffective for reducing poverty and income inequality, economists recommend implementation of a policy reform on existing wage structure to redistribute the economic growth more equitably. In doing so, minimum wage law should be developed that it is consistent with balancing market efficiency and eliminating the unfair wage structures practiced by most employers. Anti-discrimination policies for employment and wage determination also require effective implementation with dedicated effort by the government. However, political bickering along party lines has hindered the legislative branch of the federal government in its efforts to reform the current wage structure. And corporate lobbying against any policy change is also a major obstacle to reform. Elected officials will need to be united with a common goal for the greater interest of the people who live under the shadow of poverty and growing income disparity.

Policy Reform on Tax Structure

The current supply-side tax policy, with generous tax breaks to wealthy households and corporations, is highly regressive and causes a continuous rise in income inequality and the poverty rate. In order to reduce both income inequality and poverty, more progressive tax rates not only on household incomes but also on corporate profits and capital gains are necessary. The ongoing political divide on this issue has been another obstacle to any changes for the better.

Policy on Education Funding

We have emphasized the role of higher education in career advancement, higher wage jobs, and increased productivity. Education funding that provides equal opportunity to all members of society has never been more vital than it has become since the beginning of this century. Generous funding of school and college education as a higher percentage of GDP is the best investment to overcome the problems of poverty and income inequality. The statistics clearly indicate a positive cause-and-effect relationship between higher education and higher income. The more opportunity for an education is provided to the citizens the more educated people become, thus increasing their access to higher paid work. This positive spillover not only increases the national income but also helps reduce poverty, income inequality, and discriminatory practices. Government policy at both the federal and state level needs to increase education funding for all at a much higher percentage of GDP than the current allocation. In 2018, federal spending on education funding was about 8% of total GDP. History and statistics suggest that investing in human capital is the best (if not only) way to reduce poverty and the wealth gap.

Policy Incentives for Relocation of Labor Force

It is important for policymakers to provide enough financial incentives, including tax breaks and housing subsidies, to relocate unemployed labor force from economically distressed regions to regions of economic boom. These incentives are expected to have significant positive effects in reducing poverty caused by regional economic disparity.

Alternative Policy Implications and Their Effectiveness

Aside from the controversial debate on efficiency versus equity in a free market system, the majority of economists and social justice experts do agree that policy reform in the existing welfare system, tax rate policy, and education funding policy will be important steps toward transforming the existing poverty rate into a more equitable and egalitarian society. To achieve that goal, investment in human capital and equitable wage structures based on worker productivity should be the focus of policy reform. However, the effectiveness of such policy reform needs a sincere political will and unity among party lines, which has not been seen in the American political system since the 1960s. Elimination of political bickering is a necessary condition for effective policy reform to reduce poverty. In that perspective, private and government sectors both play an important role in mitigating poverty and reducing income inequality and discrimination.

Chapter Summary

Chapter 17 introduced the concepts and structure of income equality and poverty along with data analysis in the context of the US economy and policy implications. The chapter starts with a basic foundation for a theoretical understanding of income distribution and poverty and their different dimensions. The focus is on an in-depth understanding of the basic concepts and patterns of income distribution and poverty, their relevance in analyzing the actual data on poverty and income distribution, and their effects on society. At the end of the chapter, some policy implications are recommended to mitigate these two major economic and social issues. The summary of the key sections of our discussion is presented below.

17.1. The Structure of the Wealth Gap and Income Inequality in the United States

According to the US Census Bureau, the top 1% of wealthy Americans occupy over 90% of total wealth and earn over 25% of total income, while more than 15% of all households live below the poverty line. With this basic information at the outset, the sub-sections focus on understanding the difference between wealth and income and the current structure of the wealth and income gap, sources of income inequality, the data analysis of rising income inequality, and policy implications.

17.1.1. Wealth Versus Income and Rich Versus Poor: Conceptual Differences

At the outset in this section, students were encouraged to understand the conceptual differences between **wealth** and **income. Wealth** is a stock of assets in the form of common stocks, bonds, real estate, precious metals, retirement funds in various forms, and similar other assets that individuals and households invested in and/or inherited from their families or trust funds. On the other hand, **income** is cash flow coming from the daily routine of work performed by individuals in all walks of life with a continuous flow of earnings during the entire work–life cycle. Examples are given in that section to differentiate between them.

The terms **rich** and **poor** are also explained from the concept of income. The difference between **rich** and **poor** comes from the amount of earnings per pay period or per calendar year by an individual or household to make their ends meet. Being **rich** means an individual or household lives comfortably with their cash flow providing a surplus for saving or to invest in other assets to build equity. On the other hand, the term **poor** means an individual or household cannot earn enough income to meet their basic necessities for living such as food and nutrition, clothing, shelter, access to healthcare, utilities, transportation, access to education, and social safety.

17.1.2. Income and Wealth Gap Structure in the United States

This section provided the current structure of the **wealth and income gap** for the US economy during the period between 1989 and 2016. It is evident from Table 17.1 that both the income gap and the wealth gap have widened significantly between 1989 and 2016, adjusted in 2016 prices. The top 10% of households has increased from 42% of total household income to 50% in just 27 years. On the other hand, earnings for the next 40% of households actually declined from 43% to 37%, and the bottom 10% lost their earnings share by 2% from 15% to 13% for the same period.

The wealth gap data is even more striking: the top 10% of wealthy Americans increased their wealth share from 67% (already two-thirds of total household wealth) in 1989 to 77% in 2016. The next 40% of households lost their share of wealth, declining from 30% to 22%; the wealth share of the bottom 10% declined to 1% from 3% during the same period. It is also striking to see how significantly the wealth share of the top 10% increased at the expense of the next 90% of household wealth, despite the growth of wealth between 1989 and 2016 at more than 167%.

17.2. Measures of Income Inequality and Their Sources

From the data on income and wealth gap explained from Table 17.1, more in-depth analysis is provided by measuring the pattern of income inequality in this section that is not indicated in the data for GDP growth rate alone. This section also explores the sources of income inequality for the United States over the last four decades.

17.2.1. Measures of Income Distribution

The national income or total gross domestic product (GDP) for the US economy comes from five different sources: wages, proprietor's income, rents, corporate profits, and net interest income. The functional distributions of these five categories towards 2019 GDP of $21,429 billion are 69% from wages and salaries, 10% from proprietor's income, 4% from rental income, 14% from corporate profit, and 3% from interest income. Table 17.2 demonstrated the current distributional pattern of US households compiled by the US Department of Commerce economic analysis unit at bea.gov.

Table 17.2 shows actual estimated data for income distribution in the US economy for 1967 and 2018 as distributed in quintiles (every 20% of households) against % of total GDP earned by each successive quintile. We can observe in the table that in 2018 the lowest 20% of earners made only 3.1% of total GDP and the highest 20% of earners made 52% of total GDP, almost 18 times that of the lowest quintiles. It is also interesting to see that by adding the first, second, and third quintiles 60% of households made a total of about 25% of GDP, which is almost the same as the income share earned by the top 5% (23.1% of GDP). Comparing the data from 2018 with that of 1967 in the same table, we can see the distributional pattern for each quintile was much better in 1967 than in 2018. Details with examples are provided in that section.

17.2.2. Lorenz Curve and Gini Coefficient Index

In Table 17.2, we have also seen other information under summary measures of Gini index of income inequality. The Gini coefficient index is the graphical representation of the data in Table 17.2 derived from the Lorenz curve of income distribution. The other indices listed in the table are alternative measures of income inequality estimated by the researchers at the Bureau of Economic Research. But the focus here is only on the Lorenz curve and Gini coefficient index as illustrated in Figures 17.1 and 17.2 for 2018 and 1967, respectively.

17.2.3. Sources of Income and Wealth Inequality in the United States

Several economic and non-economic sources of wealth and income inequality are discussed in this sub-section. They are summarized briefly below.

Ability of Factors of Production: The ability to work in different types of jobs is based on capability of individuals and varies widely from job to job and industry to industry. With a diverse form of specialization of labor force participation in different types of industries, workers have different skill sets to specialize.

Productivity Difference: Similar and somewhat related to the difference in ability explained above, the productivity difference among workers is also a significant factor in income inequality.

Entrepreneurial Skill and Risk-Taking Skills: Entrepreneurial motivation and risk-taking ventures are common sources of wealth in a free market capitalist system. But there are only a handful of entrepreneurial ventures in each generation. Examples of the most recent successful entrepreneurships are provided in this section.

Job Preference and Compensating Variation: There are certain jobs, such as construction, highway work, railway repairs, cleaning, plumbing, and energy industries, that many individuals would prefer to avoid. Therefore, wages that are higher than the standard have to be offered to attract workers to those jobs.

Wealth by Inheritance: Some household members are born with wealth from the family that will grow further in their own generation and after. This stock of wealth inherited could take many forms—for example, financial assets, real estate, stocks, bonds, and education or skills.

Wealth in Life Cycle of Experience: In most of the economies, older workers with their long experience, specialization, and skills earn much more than the younger generation of workers. They not only make higher income but also build other assets as sources of wealth in the form of financial assets and real estate.

Education and Human Capital: The level of education and quality of training in specialized jobs is one of the most significant factors contributing to the income and wealth gap in recent decades. In a high-tech society like the United States, the economy has transformed from a factory-based economy to a knowledge-based economy, which requires higher education in all fields. Table 17.3 shows the income difference between workers with higher education and workers with a high school diploma compiled by the US Census Bureau and Bureau of Labor Statistics. Students are strongly encouraged to review the data analysis of this table and note the enormous value added from investing in education and technology.

Racial and Gender Discrimination: Wage discrimination is defined as the pay difference between employees with same education and experience when there is a bias based on characteristics such as gender, race, ethnicity, religion, or sexual orientation. Table 17.4 shows the most recent average wage structure in the United States based on gender, race, ethnicity, and age.

Overpricing of Essential Products: The skyrocketing price of many essential consumer products caused by monopolies and oligopolies brings enormous profits to the companies at the expense of consumers. As a result, the middle-income and low-income households live at a subsistence or below subsistence level while the increasing corporate profit margin raises the wealth of the top 5%.

Tax System: The current supply-side tax system implemented by the Trump administration in 2017 has been regressive in nature and disproportionately favors corporations and wealthy classes of society at the expense of the middle class. It also created more tax loopholes for giant corporations.

17.3. Income Inequality and Its Effects on the Economy and Society

Growing income inequality has many negative consequences in society, not only from the point of view of social justice and fairness, but also from the viewpoints of sustainable economic prosperity and social stability in the long run. Growing income inequality has the potential to increase poverty and social unrest if not checked in the long run. Unfair wages and discriminatory practices at the workplace based on gender and race have the potential to create an environment of low morale. The decline in morale among low-wage workers can have a serious consequence: loss of productivity and loyalty. More explanations regarding CEO compensation are given in this sub-section.

17.4. Policy Implications for Reducing Income Inequality

The policy implications of reducing income inequality have been in the forefront of American politics and academia since the beginning of the 1980s, after implementation of supply-side economics (called Reaganomics) executed by President Reagan. The ongoing political and academic debates have been discussed in this section, highlighting the political bickering between left wing and right wing political parties with no sign of resolution anytime in the near future. This issue is further discussed in the last section of this chapter after discussing the economics of poverty.

17.5. Poverty Structure and Measures of Poverty

This section focuses on an economic analysis of poverty in the context of the US economy. As we have discussed in the section concerning income inequality, over 15% of 330 million Americans live in poverty, officially defined as a household of four earning $26,000 or less annually. There are 49.5 million Americans living in poverty in a country which is perceived as wealthy and developed. A detailed data analysis is provided in this section about the current structure of poverty and its sources in the US economy.

17.5.1. Structure of Poverty

Table 17.5 illustrates the 2018 structure of poverty in the United States compared to the previous two years estimated by the US Census Bureau. Considering an annual earning of $26,000 or below per family as the poverty threshold in 2018, the per-week income comes out to $500 per household. With this income level it is quite impossible to meet basic needs such as housing, healthcare, food, transportation, clothing, utility bills, and children's education expenses. That is why the social safety net in the form of food stamps, housing subsidies, and other social security benefits are provided by both state and federal programs. To see the poverty structure in greater detail, the poverty threshold for households larger than four members is shown in Table 17.6. In that table we can see that in an eight-member household the threshold goes up to $50,681.

17.5.2. Measures of Poverty

The poverty line is defined as the minimum income level below which an individual is considered to be poor. Interested students will be able find several articles and books related to the "two tales" of America, where poor Americans have been living distinctly different lives than the non-poor since the 1960s. The US data on poverty in 2018 estimated by the US Census Bureau indicates over 15% of population based on the official poverty lines presented in Tables 17.5 and 17.6. Given the complexity of measuring the poverty level depending on the size of households, economists have struggled to define poverty and the poverty line threshold. In an effort to answer these fundamental questions, two types of poverty measures are commonly taken into consideration: the **absolute poverty line** and the **relative poverty line.**

The **absolute poverty line** is the minimum income level below which a household or individual cannot meet their basic necessities of life.

The **relative poverty line** defines poor households who fall far behind the median income of the country. Examples are provided in more detail in the sub-sections, and Tables 17.7 and 17.8 display the income distribution among all American households across the demographic characteristics.

17.6. Sources of Poverty and Their Effects on Economy and Society

The factors contributing to the poverty rate of over 15% of households in America are not limited to traditional explanations such as lack of skill, low education, and government failure. The sources of poverty are a combination of several factors that include the rising income disparity since the implementation of supply-side economic policies implemented in 1980s. The key sources listed below are explained in detail in Section 17.6.

Wage Structure

Globalization and the New Economy

Technological Shift

Education and Training

Geographical Disparity

Rising Cost of Healthcare and Utilities

Change in Social and Family Composition

17.7. Policy Implications for Poverty Elimination and Income Inequality

Based on the analysis of poverty structure and sources of poverty in America discussed in Section 17.6, a list of policy implications and recommendations are provided in this last section of Chapter 17.

Policy on Changes in Wage Rate Structure: Scope and Limitation

Policy Reform on Tax Structure

Policy on Education Funding

Policy Incentives for Relocation of Labor Force

Alternative Policy Implications and Their Effectiveness

Application Activities

1. Annual economic growth is usually measured in percentage by the equation $(Y_t - Y_t - 1) / Y_t - 1 \times 100$, where Y_t = current year GDP and $Y_t - 1$ = previous year GDP. It is expected that a positive annual GDP growth rate would increase the standard of living and thus improve the economic and social well-being of all citizens of a nation. Briefly explain, with examples, why the positive GDP growth rate alone doesn't necessarily indicate the economic well-being of all residents of a country. What is the alternative piece of information we need to measure the true living standard for everyone?

2. How do you distinguish between the terms rich and poor? How about wealthy versus rich? Give examples.

3. How do you distinguish between the terms wealth and income? Give examples for both cases.

4. To measure income distribution, we have demonstrated the two types of measures: the Lorenz curve and the Gini coefficient index. Briefly explain the difference between them and give examples with the help of a hypothetical diagram. No specific data is required for this question.

5. How do you distinguish between efficiency and equity? Are they compatible with re-distributing the wealth and income to eliminate poverty and income inequality? In other words, is there any trade-off between efficiency and equity in undertaking public policy actions to redistribute wealth and income by adapting a progressive income tax for the wealthy and rich?

6. Provide some key factors for rising income inequality and poverty in the United States since the 1980s. Evidence-based numerical examples are required for completing your answer to this question.

7. Distinguish between the term absolute poverty and relative poverty and use the most recent year data on the US economy for income distribution and poverty to determine what percent of households or population live in absolute poverty as well as relative poverty.

8. Assume that the poverty threshold for a four-member household (two adults and two children under age 18) in America is defined by the government as $27,000 a year. Use the table below to rank the position of absolute poverty and relative poverty for each group of households against their income levels. Filling out the last two columns would be fine.

Households	Annual Income per Household in $	Absolute Poverty Yes?	Relative Poverty Yes?
Family 1	40,000		
Family 2	30,000		
Family 3	20,000		
Family 4	15,000		
Family 5	12,500		

9. Use the income distributional pattern of two countries listed in the table below in quintiles to answer the following questions. The income distribution in each of the two countries is expressed in percentage of total national income.

Income of Each Quintile	Country X in %	Country Y in %
The lowest 5th	9%	3%
The second lowest 5th	13%	8%
The middle 5th	22%	15%
The fourth 5th	26%	25%
The highest 5th	30%	49%

a. Illustrate the above income distribution in two separate Lorenz curves for two countries.

b. Estimate the Gini coefficients for both countries by showing your numerical estimations.

c. What country has a better income distribution as estimated in 9.a and 9.b? Why so?

d. Using the income distribution for the US economy in 2019, which of these two countries closely matches the United States?

10. Suppose you are a member of a presidential commission tasked with recommending fiscal and legislative policy actions to significantly reduce current income disparity and poverty in the US economy within 10 years. List a plausible list of policy recommendations that would be effective to achieve the goal along with their pros and cons. Hint: It will be easier to make a chart or table for your list of recommendations with pros and cons.

Microeconomics Principles, Applications, and Policy Implications

Index

About the Author

Nurul Samiul Aman was born in Patuakhali District, a southern part of Bangladesh, and received his BA with honors in economics from Dhaka University, Bangladesh, and his master's in economics and MBA in finance from Northeastern University, Boston, USA. He also received his PhD from Capella University in Minneapolis, Minnesota, USA, with a concentration in information economics with applications in information technology and organizational management.

Nurul Aman is a published author of **Macroeconomics Principles, Applications and Policy Implications**. As a financial economist, Aman has been effectively teaching in Boston area colleges since 1988 in various courses in economics and business. He is currently a senior lecturer at the University of Massachusetts Boston (UMB) in Boston, Massachusetts, USA. He has been teaching at UMB since 2001, including the following courses: Principles of Micro and Macroeconomics, Micro and Macroeconomics Theories and Applications, Economic Development, Money and Financial Institution, and

Comparative Economic Systems. He also taught graduate-level applied economics courses at Northeastern University, including Sustainable Economic Development, Economics of E-Commerce, Economics of Human Capital, and Financial Management. Since 2006, Aman has served as a member of the editorial board of the *Asian Journal of Inclusive Education*, a peer-reviewed journal for inclusive education and development. He also teaches overseas as a visiting professor at various universities in China. As an international speaker, Dr. Aman is also affiliated with Allied Academies of Food and Nutrition Science and travels in North America, Europe, and Asia delivering keynote speeches on food sustainability and poverty elimination in developing nations. He also organizes and hosts the annual International Conference on Sustainable Development Goals at Harvard University in collaboration with the International Sustainable Development Institute (www.ISDIWorld.com) and the government of Bangladesh. In the 1990s and early 2000s, Aman worked as a business analyst and business control manager of information technology departments at PictureTel Corporation (now PolyCom), Rational Software, and IBM in Lexington, Massachusetts, USA.

CPSIA information can be obtained
at www.ICGtesting.com
Printed in the USA
LVHW021113260820
664218LV00001B/9

9 781516 595167